John Locke's Politics of Moral Consensus

The aim of this highly original book is twofold: to explain the reconciliation of religion and politics in the work of John Locke and to
explore the relevance of that reconciliation for politics in our own
time.

Confronted with deep social divisions over ultimate beliefs, Locke
sought to unite society in a single liberal community. Reason could
identify divine moral laws that would be acceptable to members of all
cultural groups, thereby justifying the authority of government. Greg
Forster demonstrates that Locke's theory is liberal and rational but
also moral and religious, providing an alternative to the two extremes
of religious fanaticism and moral relativism.

This fresh new account of Locke's thought will appeal to specialists and advanced students across philosophy, political science, and
religious studies.

Greg Forster is a senior research associate at the Manhattan Institute
for Policy Research.

John Locke's Politics of Moral Consensus

GREG FORSTER
The Manhattan Institute for Policy Research

CAMBRIDGE
UNIVERSITY PRESS

CAMBRIDGE UNIVERSITY PRESS
Cambridge, New York, Melbourne, Madrid, Cape Town, Singapore, São Paulo

Cambridge University Press
40 West 20th Street, New York NY 10011-4211, USA

www.cambridge.org
Information on this title: www.cambridge.org/9780521842181

© Greg Forster 2005

First published 2005

Printed in the United States of America

A catalog record for this book is available from the British Library.

Library of Congress Cataloging in Publication Data

Forster, Greg, 1973–
John Locke's politics of moral consensus / Greg Forster.
p. cm.
Includes bibliographical references and index.
ISBN 0-521-84218-2 (alk. paper)
1. Locke, John, 1632–1704 – Contributions in political science.   2. Locke,
John, 1632–1704 – Religion.   3. Political science – Philosophy.   4. Politics and
religion.   I. Title.
JC153.L87F67   2005
170′.92–dc22   2004054766

ISBN-13   978-0-521-84218-1 hardback
ISBN-10   0-521-84218-2 hardback

This book is dedicated with love and admiration to
Elizabeth Ann Forster

Plato has no hesitation in asserting that
to be a philosopher is to love God.

It immediately follows that the seeker after wisdom
(which is the meaning of "philosopher")
will only attain to happiness
when he has begun to enjoy God.

Augustine of Hippo
The City of God, Book VIII, Chapter 10

I want to know God's thoughts.
The rest are details.

Albert Einstein

Contents

Acknowledgments

I wish to thank the many people who helped make this book a reality. As with any book, there are far too many people to thank them all, but I will do my best not to leave any truly heinous omissions.

The guidance of Professor Steven Smith of the Yale Political Science Department, Professor Norma Thompson of the Yale Whitney Humanities Center, and Professor Nicholas Wolterstorff of the Yale Divinity School was invaluable as I was writing the doctoral dissertation that produced this book. They read drafts, provided advice, and gave generously of their time. They corrected innumerable errors and flaws, for which I am grateful; no doubt errors and flaws remain, for which I take sole responsibility. My dissertation committee – Professor Smith, Professor Thompson, and Professor Jennifer Pitts of the Yale Political Science Department – also made a large investment of time and labor for which I am grateful.

Brett Marston, John Gould, and Patricia Nordeen provided help, advice, and mutual support to a fellow graduate student, for which I owe them a good portion of my sanity.

The faculty, graduate students, and staff of the Yale Political Science Department provided invaluable academic and administrative support as I was working on this book.

Yale University provided significant funding for the completion of this book.

The editors and staff of Cambridge University Press worked diligently to successfully bring this book to completion.

I am not in the least ashamed to thank my mother, Susan Forster, for her love and support over the years, as well as my brother Brian Forster.

The unfailing friendship of Caroline Stack, Mandy Bissell, Mike Carter, and Jennifer Rackow has sustained me through more hardships than I care to recall. I can never hope to repay their many kindnesses.

I am indebted beyond expression to my wife, Elizabeth Ann Forster. "Many waters cannot quench love, neither can floods drown it; if a man offered for love all the wealth of his house, it would be utterly scorned" (Song of Solomon 8:7). This book is dedicated to her.

Above all I am grateful to God. "Wisdom is supreme; therefore get wisdom. Though it cost you all you have, get understanding. . . . If you call out for insight and cry aloud for understanding, and if you look for it as for silver and search for it as for hidden treasure, then you will understand the fear of the Lord and find the knowledge of God" (Proverbs 4:7 and 2:3–5).

List of Abbreviations

The following abbreviations are used in this book to refer to Locke's major works. Spelling and capitalization have been updated to the current standard, but punctuation has been left undisturbed. Italics have been removed except where they are necessary to convey the meaning of a passage.

E   Followed by Book.Chapter.Section, Page (e.g., E IV.10.1, 619)
An Essay Concerning Human Understanding
Edited by Peter H. Nidditch
New York: Oxford University Press, 1979.

R   Followed by Paragraph, Page (e.g., R 242, 172–3)
The Reasonableness Of Christianity as Delivered in the Scriptures
Edited by George W. Ewing
Washington, DC: Regnery, 1965.

L   Followed by Paragraph, Page (e.g., L 37, 31)
A Letter Concerning Toleration
Edited by Patrick Romanell
Englewood Cliffs, NJ: Prentice–Hall, 1950.

T   Followed by Treatise.Section, Page (e.g., T I.88, 63)
Two Treatises of Government
Edited by Mark Goldie
London: Everyman, 1993.

John Locke's Politics of Moral Consensus

"Reason Teaches All Mankind, Who Will But Consult It"

John Locke and Moral Consensus

Western liberalism has come full circle. It was born when members of western societies gradually learned, over the course of the sixteenth and seventeenth centuries, to tame their violent religious fanaticisms and co-exist as members of shared political communities. This accomplishment was so successful that fundamental moral disagreement and religious violence became steadily less threatening to society, and various other types of problems moved to the top of the theoretical agenda. Liberal political theory became less and less involved with what was, historically, its foundational concern: getting members of different religions to live together in peace. The subject gradually receded into the far corners of liberal consciousness, and as the study of liberalism's founders came to reflect this change, the portions of their works dealing with religion and religious violence were increasingly either ignored or skimmed over even by most scholarly specialists.

Now the circle has closed, and in a very real sense we are back where we started. Violent religious fanaticism and fundamental moral discord threaten the legitimacy and even the very existence of liberal societies. Liberal theorists are failing to cope with these challenges adequately because their longstanding neglect of moral and religious problems has left them unfamiliar with the basic philosophical concepts that once helped them better understand religious belief and moral law, and hence the intricate relationship between religion, morality, and politics. Liberalism will not remain the governing philosophy of western nations if it cannot give a moral account of itself that will satisfy the overwhelming majority of people who believe, through various religions, that the universe is divinely ordered. And there is no hope for providing such an account if liberal theorists do not begin by learning from the wisdom of the great thinkers who designed liberalism in the first place.

Ironically, the liberal thinker who has suffered the most neglect is the one who can lay the most plausible claim to be the founder of liberalism as we know it: John Locke. He towers over the history of liberalism precisely because virtually everything he wrote was directed at coping with the problems that gave birth to liberalism – religious violence and moral discord. When these problems no longer seemed to pose a mortal threat to liberal societies, Locke came to be read and studied less, and respected and admired less, by scholars and laymen alike. To those living in societies where religious factions hadn't actually gone around killing one another for centuries, it just didn't seem like such a big accomplishment that Locke had provided the definitive, foundational guide for how liberal societies of that kind could be built in the first place. Now that religious factions are once again actively killing, and western societies are increasingly characterized by large and growing conflicts over moral and cultural differences, the study of Locke can no longer be safely neglected.

RELIGION AND POLITICS: RECOVERING LOCKE

We are living through a fascinating and in many ways frustrating period in Locke scholarship. In the past thirty years, scholars have made revolutionary advances in understanding Locke, both in uncovering more about his role as a political actor and in restoring a historically accurate reading of his philosophic works. In particular, the deep and pervasive influence of religion on Locke's beliefs has been a continual source of new discoveries, reshaping our understanding of how Locke used the concepts of property, authority, rights, natural law, toleration, and virtually everything else in his politics. More and more scholars have come to the conclusion that, as Eldon Eisenach writes, "Locke's political theory and epistemology cannot be understood apart from his writings on religion."[1]

But accounting for Locke's religion is no small adjustment because Locke's Christianity is an extraordinary accomplishment unto itself. Locke blends elements drawn from diverse theological traditions – ranging from theologically conservative Calvinism to what we might now call the "liberal" movement of Anglican Latitudinarianism – into an alloy that stands apart from standard theological classifications. This is why Locke scholars have never agreed on what religious label Locke should wear.[2] Incorporating this unique theology into our understanding of Locke will require a complete reconstruction of that understanding.

Unfortunately, the opposite is occurring – by and large, Locke scholarship's recent advances in taking account of Locke's religion have either failed to penetrate the discourse of political theorists or have done so with unfortunate results. Too many political theorists in the profession at large, along with what seems to be a large majority of people in the general intellectual population, still understand Locke more or less the same way he was understood thirty years ago. This naturally encompasses a wide range of views. Locke is variously seen as a libertarian defender of absolute individual rights; a secularist who sought to remove religion from politics; an apologist for capitalism; a rationalist who sought to found natural law doctrine on pure reason, unassisted by revelation; a theorist of tolerance whose theory is marred by bigotry against atheists, Muslims, and Catholics; and so on. Some, following Leo Strauss, believe that Locke was a closet atheist and/or Hobbesian.

Moreover, those political theorists who do acknowledge the importance of Locke's religious beliefs have all too often followed this acknowledgement to the wrong conclusions. Some theorists have deliberately set aside Locke's religion and sought to apply his political doctrines without reference to their religious context. This ensures that the doctrines collapse into absurdity, unless they are rescued by intellectual contortions that alter them beyond recognition. Even in the best cases, this approach drains Locke's theory of its animating moral concerns. Locke's readers are left deaf and blind to the great confrontation that takes place in his works: one of the most brilliant minds that ever lived taking on the greatest and most troublesome of all political problems. Other scholars, understanding that extracting Locke's politics from his religion is impossible, cite Locke's religious beliefs as a reason for disregarding Locke altogether as irrelevant to modern political discourse, as if Christianity had gone out with the feudal system and Ptolemaic astronomy.[3]

Both of these responses occur primarily because the modern world looks with distrust, and sometimes open hostility, on any prospective role for religion in political life. Theorists today view the presence of religion in a political theory as something that must be either removed or delicately worked around if the theory is to speak to us. Our distrust of religion in politics takes many forms, such as the ongoing quest for a "public reason" that can solve our moral problems without reference to religion, but its root cause seems to be a fear that religion is inseparable from passionate, primordial forces in the human psyche that are potentially dangerous, especially in politics.

It is understandable that we should have developed this fear of religion in politics. It is the outcome of historical trends, including the legacy of the religious wars of Locke's own time. We are naturally apprehensive at any prospect that such horrors, having finally been banished from our politics, might somehow be let back in. These apprehensions are particularly strengthened when we consider that we have before us, in some other parts of the world, cautionary examples of societies in which violent religious fanaticism has not yet been successfully tamed.

But however understandable our modern distrust of religion in politics might be in light of historical developments, it is one of the arguments of this book that the ideal of a separation between religion and politics simply cannot be sustained. Over the past half century, liberal theorists have experimented with various forms of "neutralism" to serve as replacements for political theories that are grounded in moral (and therefore, necessarily, religious) reasoning. But their attempt to remove morality from politics has never quite been able to overcome the contradiction upon which it is based. That government ought to be neutral with regard to morality is itself an "ought" statement – a moral proposition. All action, including political action, is guided by some scheme of normative commitments, and so politics is constantly brought back to moral problems.

Some have sought to build a more morally aware liberalism by appealing to the empirical fact of popular agreement on certain moral topics, such as support for a broad sphere of individual liberty. However, this does not alleviate the basic problem, because it does not provide a moral theory to justify the views on which it builds. If there is no moral theory to sustain public adherence to liberal principles, the popular consensus in favor of such principles will inevitably erode over time. People will generally do what they believe is morally right rather than what is approved by the political order, unless the political order is itself invested with moral legitimacy. Eventually, a political order unsupported by a moral theory will collapse under the weight of this problem.

What's more, a political community built upon merely coincidental overlap in the preferences of its members can never claim more than a mercenary sort of allegiance from those members. If I support the political community because it follows policies I prefer, but my reasons for preferring those policies are not admissible in public discourse, my solidarity with the political community will be tenuous at best. I will always be on the lookout for political movements catering to my specific moral and religious beliefs, and those movements may or may not be liberal.[4]

To overcome this problem, the liberal political community must unite its members behind a common moral vision. This is not to say that government should impose proper beliefs coercively. One of greatest achievements in the history of western political theory is Locke's demonstration that any such project is both cruel and futile. But if liberal political institutions cannot shape people's beliefs using the tools of coercion, it is all the more urgent for liberal political theorists to shape those beliefs using the tools of persuasion. As Locke himself shows, toleration is not the last thing that needs to be said about religious belief in a liberal society. It is, in fact, barely the first thing.

Uniting the liberal community behind a common moral vision also doesn't mean that there must be social agreement on all religious questions, or even on the greatest question of all: which religion is the true one? Locke's political theory, contrary to what some have written about it, does not seek to justify a distinctively Christian political community. It envisions a multireligious political community, justified by arguments that are not particular to any one religion, with fully equal citizenship for members of all religions. But, as Locke frequently insists, this multireligious society can only hold together if it has the moral courage of its liberal convictions. That is, it must be willing to put forward the liberal ideal as a moral ideal, and require all members to abide by the moral rules of peaceful coexistence and mutual toleration derived from that ideal. An unabashedly moral theory is needed to justify the coercive rules that are the only hope of keeping a multireligious society from falling apart at the seams.

The aim of this book is to reintroduce the historically accurate Locke into the discourse of political theory, with his religious views intact, in a way that shows his continuing relevance to politics in our own time. Locke is uniquely qualified to allay our distrust of religion in politics because he shares our fear of the primordial forces religion can unleash, and bends over backwards in every part of his philosophic system to tame and suppress those forces. He argues that a proper faith does not burst forth from "enthusiastic" feelings (as they were called in his time); it must grow naturally from a rational weighing of evidence and argument. In fact, he goes so far as to say that enthusiastic religious feelings are not only dangerous to politics and other secular concerns; they are dangerous even – and perhaps primarily – to religion itself, because enthusiasm encourages false religious beliefs. Thus, religion and politics have a mutual interest in taming religious enthusiasm. Locke utterly rejects the primordial and the passionate as a basis for politics.

There is no denying, of course, that our time and place is significantly different from Locke's. Seventeenth-century arguments cannot just be picked up out of old books and set down unchanged in the present. Our situation is different both in terms of social facts, including the rise of multiracial and multireligious societies such as have not been seen since the ancient empires, and in terms of knowledge, including the advance of science and technology. It would be foolish to think that the *Two Treatises of Government* could be published today as a political tract and hope to gain much support.

But in every great book there is a stock of wisdom that can be drawn on in any era and applied even to radically different situations. Otherwise, there would be little point in reading old books. Applying this wisdom to our time is a process of adjustment, of figuring out which of its aspects would change when applied to our environment, and how. The basic problems of human life change remarkably little over time. These problems are manifested in a variety of different ways, as different societies situated in different circumstances each come to grips with these problems in their own ways. However, one lesson we learn from reading the great works of philosophy in history is that the underlying problems – such as the problematic relationship between reason and revelation, or between the community and the individual – are woven into the fabric of human nature.

This book argues that Locke's main political project was to unite members of different religious groups into a single political community, and that his political, religious, and philosophical works construct a moral theory that can accomplish this goal. Locke never explicitly acknowledged any single intellectual project uniting his major works, but each of them is primarily addressed to one or another aspect of this same overall goal. As we will see, when the arguments of Locke's works are taken together they form a unified philosophic system. Locke himself did not describe his works as forming such a system, and as he was writing them he may not even have intended that they would ultimately fit together in this way. Nonetheless, they are all addressed to coping with the same problem – the political works to the political aspect of the problem, the religious works to the religious aspect of the problem, and the philosophical works to the philosophical aspect of the problem – and there are no significant conflicts between the positions taken in the various works. Thus, there is a natural intellectual confluence among Locke's works. This book argues that a unified system of thought arises from this confluence; we will refer to this system of thought as Locke's theory of "moral consensus."

The goal of Locke's theory of moral consensus was not simply to make society into a merely political coalition, by showing groups that they had a mutual interest in peaceful relations. Such a society would fall apart into civil war every time some religious prophet came along to lead the faithful of his group in a struggle against the heathens and blasphemers of the other groups. The goal was to forge a unified political community among the faithful of different religions. In support of this goal, Locke's works provide a moral theory proving, in arguments that would be acceptable to all groups, that peaceful relations and a shared political community are divine moral imperatives. The essential foundation of a shared, multireligious political community is not the belief that such a community serves everyone's interests; it is the belief that such a community is the command of a supreme divine power, whose word is the ultimate standard of moral authority. In a community built on moral consensus, social and political solidarity has a moral rather than merely mercenary foundation.

Building this vision of moral consensus, and in particular finding moral arguments that members of different religions will all accept, is obviously a complex task. It requires us to confront difficult questions dealing with such issues as the nature of faith, the limits of certainty in human knowledge, and the visibility of a moral design in our universe. However, the relevance of such a body of thought to the political and social situation of our own time ought to be just as obvious. We, like Locke, are confronted with the challenge of building a common political community for an increasingly fragmented culture. It will be well worth the effort if we can recover the body of wisdom Locke has left for us on this topic. As this book will show, Locke created an integrated philosophic system, consisting of epistemology, theology, and political theory. This system, taken as a whole, provides a road map for building moral consensus.

METHOD AND STRUCTURE OF THIS BOOK

The best method for reintroducing Locke into liberal discourse is a step-by-step reconstruction of Locke's politics from the ground up, starting where Locke thought a philosopher should start, with epistemology, and following his logic from there until we have a view of his comprehensive system of theology and politics.[5] Such a reconstruction of Locke is necessary because there are so many different understandings of his

philosophy to be addressed – held variously by libertarians, communitarians, Marxists, Straussians, and others – that only a complete review
of Locke's system can efficiently answer them all. The alternative would
entail a separate critique of each alternative reading of Locke, which
would make this book much longer, much more redundant with other
Locke scholarship, and of much less interest to readers who are not Locke
scholars. In a few places, where the point is important enough, this book
digresses to briefly discuss alternative readings of Locke, particularly the
Straussian reading. For the most part, however, its specific responses to
other interpretations have been placed in the notes.

Another purpose for adopting this method is to show that Locke did
in fact have a "system," that is, a set of mutually consistent arguments that
fit together to form a unified philosophic structure. Locke's works have
often been portrayed as sloppy, inconsistent, and conflicting, and one of
the major purposes of this book is to refute that portrayal. We will argue
that the perception of deep conflicts in and among Locke's works dis-
appears when we properly understand his views, especially regarding his
distinction between knowledge and belief and his account of reason and
faith. This book will show the coherent architecture of Locke's philosophy. With some oversimplification we can say that his political principles
are based on his natural law doctrine, his natural law doctrine presumes a
particular kind of theology, and his theology arises from his epistemology.
Of course, the lines from one book to the next are not actually that clearly
drawn, but in broad outline the books do follow each other in this way.
As Raymond Polin observes, Locke's "metaphysics, morals, and politics
are tightly interwoven . . . the meaning of his political liberalism, a truly
moral doctrine, can be understood only in the light of his philosophy
considered as a really coherent totality."[6]

In order to carry out this method it has been necessary to select a few
key works from the enormous number of writings Locke produced. To
begin with, it seems sensible to stick with Locke's published works rather
than including any of his unpublished papers, so that we can be sure
we are dealing with the arguments he wanted us to consider. His private
letters and notes may contain arguments he was unsure of, or did not
consider at length, or even arguments that he did not personally agree
with but wanted to record for some other reason. A separate but related
concern is the consideration of works written early in Locke's career,
which have recently received enormous scholarly attention.[7] Some of
these are complete, well-crafted essays that clearly do reflect Locke's well-
considered opinions at the time he wrote them, but there is good reason

not to include them here. With all the attention recently given to Locke's intellectual development, scholars risk losing sight of the gap of over twenty years between the writing of Locke's early works in 1662–7 and the publication of his more famous works in 1689. Locke changed his mind on many issues during that time, and tracing the development of Locke's thought is a separate scholarly concern from analyzing the final form of that thought.

This book concerns Locke's mature thought, defined as his thought after 1689, the year that saw the publication of the *Essay Concerning Human Understanding*, the *Two Treatises*, and the *Letter Concerning Toleration*. The philosophic merit and historical influence of these works demand their inclusion. We also have room for one other major work, and here the choice is dictated equally by the work's inherent merit and by the need to fill a particular gap in the 1689 works. Those works do not provide a theology, and (as this book will argue) their arguments rely so heavily on religion that they cannot be understood apart from theology. *The Reasonableness of Christianity*, published in 1695, provides the necessary theology and is a distinguished enough intellectual achievement in its own right to stand unabashedly next to the 1689 works. Unfortunately, there is no space to give the many other works Locke published after 1689 the treatment they deserve, but we will sometimes refer to them when they illuminate the four works we have chosen.

Chapter 2 will begin where Locke thought we ought to begin, with epistemology, looking at Books One through Three of the *Essay*. Locke's emphasis on separating reliable beliefs from unreliable beliefs through rational inquiry is his most distinctly and uncompromisingly modern quality. Before Locke can build his case for moral consensus around a set of beliefs that are very certain, he must show the uncertainty of other beliefs, with particular emphasis on the beliefs that were causing social conflict in his time. He constructs an epistemology of limits, in that he emphasizes understanding the limits of the human mind, and therefore the topics on which our beliefs are unavoidably tainted with a degree of uncertainty. Moral consensus cannot be maintained unless members of the community acknowledge that they do not know everything – that due to the limits of the human mind, they cannot possibly know everything – and so cannot legitimately write all their beliefs into law, to be coercively enforced upon others.

Chapter 3 completes the account of Locke's epistemology by showing how Locke thought reliable beliefs could be formed. This covers Book Four of the *Essay*. Locke's epistemology begins with the supreme importance of God in human life. Religious knowledge is understood to be every person's most important concern. Locke wants reason to regulate beliefs about God because that is the best way to ensure that our beliefs about God are true ones, and because it ensures we will distinguish between more and less reliable beliefs. Locke's rational epistemology, which is sometimes accused of encouraging deism and the compartmentalization of religion and politics, actually encourages theistic religious belief because its general premises for rational belief strongly point toward that conclusion. Locke's account of the unity of reason and faith is a necessary prerequisite for a politics of moral consensus, because it shows that reason need not be set aside – indeed, must not be set aside – in religious matters. This makes it possible for reason to build the common ground both within and among religions upon which moral consensus will rest.

Chapter 4 presents Locke's arguments on the basic content of Christianity. This covers approximately the first two-thirds of the *Reasonableness* and most of the *Letter*. It also looks to parts of the *Essay* and *Two Treatises* to illustrate Locke's method for reading scripture. Following the epistemological rules of the *Essay*, Locke constructs a biblical exegesis that places religious faith on rationally solid ground, and shows that while there is much in the Bible that is above human reason, the fundamental content of Christianity (human beings are sinners who need salvation; salvation is available through repentance and faith in Christ) is simple, clearly conveyed in scripture, and rationally certain. In the *Reasonableness*, Locke shows that Jesus teaches that the rational evidence of miracles, rather than enthusiastic religious feelings, is the legitimate basis of belief. Locke also shows that only faith in Jesus' Messiahship and repentance for sin is necessary to salvation in Christ, from which he concludes that Christians can disagree on all other doctrinal matters and still accept one another as Christians. This makes it both possible and desirable that Christians should stop killing each other over doctrinal disputes.

Chapter 5 shows Locke's account of how moral law works, and why Locke thinks it is necessary to incorporate religious beliefs into the moral basis of politics. This includes sections of the *Essay* and *Letter*, but is mostly drawn from the last section of the *Reasonableness*. Locke argues that because God is all-powerful, beliefs about God will – and should – trump other beliefs, in the political sphere and everywhere else. He writes in an analysis of the ancient world that where religion and philosophy have gone to war with each other, religion has always won because people are rightly afraid of the supernatural. But for Locke such a conflict between religion and philosophy is a sign of intellectual degeneracy. Locke wants us to understand faith and reason as necessary helpmates to one another – faith provides the moral authority necessary for legitimate politics, and reason regulates the beliefs provided by faith, to guard against enthusiasm and arbitrary interpretations of texts. The moral supremacy of religion implies that government can never be built on a foundation that excludes religious beliefs, because people would disobey the dictates of such a government whenever their religious beliefs required it.

To sustain moral consensus, we must find an account of moral law that is rationally sound and clear to all, and not devoted to one particular revealed religion. Chapter 6 examines how Locke uses his rational religious epistemology to justify a method for analyzing human nature and drawing conclusions about God's intentions for human life. Because human nature was made by God, it can show us God's moral plan for humanity. The *Essay*'s account of human psychology provides the intellectual foundations for this method, the *Reasonableness* provides support for it in scripture, and the *Two Treatises* uses it to examine human nature and discern God's law. Locke analyzes human customs and behaviors to show that there are moral laws implicit in the design of human nature. This is a key component of moral consensus, because it provides a moral basis for politics that is independent of revelation, avoiding the epistemological pitfalls of scriptural interpretation and making possible a political community based on moral laws that are shared between members of different faiths.

Chapter 7 shows how Locke's treatment of authority, which he considers the fundamental problem of politics, fulfills his goal of building moral consensus. In the *First Treatise*, Locke shows Christians that the Bible does not contain a grant of political authority to any specific person. If government is to be based on moral consensus among different religious groups, the grounds on which rulers are authorized must not arise from the revelation of any one religion. But if Christians believe that the teachings of the Bible give one or another particular person the authority to rule, they will not agree to be ruled by any other person. In both the *First Treatise* and the *Second Treatise*, Locke builds a political community by appealing to moral rules derived from the natural law under which human life is sacred – murder is against divine law, parents have a special duty to nurture their offspring, private property is sacred because it is necessary to preserve life, and so on. He justifies these rules with his rational method for analyzing human nature, and he discounts almost all other rules from politics either because they are epistemologically uncertain or because they are outside government's capacity for enforcement.

LOCKE SCHOLARSHIP AND MORAL CONSENSUS

The proposition that Locke's main political goal was to establish moral consensus among disparate political groups requires us to look at Locke in a very different light, because it forces a reevaluation of Locke's concerns and priorities. In particular, it requires a step back from some of the premises of the more historically oriented Locke scholarship of the past few decades. Most analysis of political thought belongs to one of two methodological schools, the historical school and the theoretical school. Scholars taking the historical approach have interpreted Locke's thought by comparing it to the content of other natural law theorists whom Locke had read, and to the historical exigencies that prompted him to write his political works.[8] Scholars in the theoretical school have sought to rationally reconstruct the content of Locke's politics from textual evidence, often by connecting the arguments of his political works with arguments from the *Essay* and other works.[9] Both these approaches have produced valuable insights that help us better understand the content of Locke's theory, particularly where they draw on one another rather than standing in isolation.[10]

Historically oriented scholarship on Locke has dominated the scene for several decades, and its contributions to our understanding of Locke have been enormous. This book relies heavily on many of those contributions. There has been, however, too much confidence in the premise that we can understand Locke's purposes by looking at the purposes of other authors in or before his time. Locke's vision of a society built on moral consensus is not without philosophical precedents in preexisting intellectual traditions, and we will point out the most important of these sources in the course of this book. But Locke combines elements of many different intellectual sources into a philosophic whole that bears little resemblance to any one of the individual sources from which it draws. Interpreting Locke through the lens of only one tradition, from which he is alleged to have grown, will blind us to his broader accomplishment. Locke drew from a wide variety of traditions and made from them something astonishingly new and different.

John Dunn came on the scene at a time when Locke's politics were almost always studied without reference to religion. His 1969 book, *The Political Thought of John Locke*, shook the foundations of Locke scholarship by reminding scholars that Locke was immersed in religion his entire life, that all political questions in his time were ultimately religious questions, and that every aspect of Locke's thought is explicitly and thoroughly grounded on his religious beliefs. This much of Dunn's argument is true, and we owe him a great debt for forcing Locke scholarship to confront Locke's religion.

However, Dunn is much too quick to seize on certain conceptual similarities between Locke's thought and the demonstrative rationalism of Descartes, Hobbes, and seventeenth-century deism on the one hand, and the fideism of seventeenth-century Calvinists on the other. Dunn reads Locke only in terms of these two totally incompatible traditions, setting up a view of the world in which there are only two possibilities: rigid logical deduction from self-evident theological first principles, or fideism, which abandons rational foundations of thought in favor of beginning from an arational leap of faith. Dunn, following a mistaken reading of the *Essay* common to many Locke scholars, argues that Locke aspired to build a purely logical moral and political theory, and that the *Two Treatises* was meant to accomplish this task.[11] Since the *Two Treatises* utterly fails at this, Dunn describes it as an absurdity, a hopeless tangle of contradictions that glosses over all the questions it is supposed to be addressing. Dunn also thinks Locke later abandoned reason and turned to religious faith to supply the necessary theological foundations that reason had failed to establish. Quoting statements in the *Reasonableness* about the inadequacy of unassisted human reason, he argues that at some point between 1689 (when the *Essay* and the *Two Treatises* were published) and 1695 (when the *Reasonableness* was published), Locke despaired that rationalism could work, and turned to fideism.[12]

Such a wild swing from one intellectual extreme to the other would be a remarkable event in any life, and an extraordinary one in a figure of such towering philosophic importance as John Locke. Perhaps not surprisingly, though, the story is vulnerable on both ends. As we will argue in Chapters 2 and 3, a careful reading of the *Essay* shows that Locke was never devoted to anything like the vision of purely logical morality that Dunn ascribes to him. The *Essay* is primarily concerned not with the realm of absolute deduction but with the realm of judgment and probability. Locke's rationalism is most importantly an attempt to show how reasonable beliefs can be separated from unreasonable beliefs through a process of sound judgment. And in particular, the *Essay*'s epistemology encourages the rational embrace of religious faith. Similarly, as we will show in Chapter 4, Locke's statements about the weakness of reason in the *Reasonableness* were meant to contrast the weakness of unassisted natural reason with the strength of reason that is open to, and therefore assisted by, faith.

The fundamental problem in Dunn's reading of Locke is that he looks only at seventeenth-century Calvinist thought when seeking to place Locke in the context of the religious thought of his day. Locke does owe some important debts to Calvinism, as Dunn shows. In particular, Locke's heavy emphasis in the *Two Treatises* on the moral dimension of labor as a fulfillment of humanity's duty to God is recognizably Calvinist.[13] However, much of Locke's theological thought arises from other intellectual sources that Dunn neglects. Even his voluntarism – his absolute reliance on God's will as the basis of morality – bears more resemblance to the voluntarism of certain strands of medieval natural law philosophy, and particularly to his contemporary Samuel Pufendorf, than to seventeenth-century Calvinist voluntarism.[14] Most importantly, Locke utterly rejected throughout his life all claims that any belief, religious or otherwise, was not subject to the regulation of reason; he lumps all such claims together under the derogatory label of "enthusiasm." For Locke, rational faith was superior to either unassisted reason or enthusiastic faith. The deep dichotomy that Dunn draws between reason and faith obscures this point.

If Dunn fails to take account of Locke's debt to the late medieval natural law tradition, James Tully takes into account only that debt. His 1980 *A Discourse on Property* depicts Locke's *Second Treatise* as the culmination of intellectual trends over the course of the sixteenth and seventeenth centuries in natural law property right theory. This narrows the scope of Locke's political concern considerably. Tully acknowledges the general political context of the *Two Treatises*, but Locke's larger political theory gets reinterpreted through his property right theory in a way that distorts its actual content. For Tully, Locke's theory of how property is created becomes the general moral theory of the *Second Treatise*, such that property and only property is the basis of all moral claims.

Tully proposes what he calls the "workmanship model," under which a person has a property right in a thing if that person made that thing – that is, if the thing is his workmanship.[15] The workmanship model is essentially an intellectual extension of God's creation of the universe. God has the moral right to rule the universe because the universe is his workmanship. People are God's property because they, too, are his workmanship, and from this it follows that they may not destroy each other without God's permission. People, in turn, make other things, in a process analogous to God's creation of the world, and thereby acquire rights to these things.

There can be no doubt that Locke's analysis of labor and workmanship is important to the *Second Treatise*, and Tully's emphasis on it helps bring out some subtle points that are not often noticed by other Locke scholars. Tully also does an outstanding job of showing the large points of continuity between Locke's political theory and those of previous religious natural law thinkers. One of the more important of these is Locke's conception of social virtue primarily in terms of the negative duty not to harm others, in which he is similar to both Grotius and Pufendorf.[16]

But Tully misses the deeper foundations of Locke's moral thought. He stretches the workmanship model to encompass the entirety of Locke's moral and political thought, when in fact workmanship is only a small, subordinate part of the moral whole. Workmanship as such conveys no moral justification; the mere act of making something is not what conveys moral authority over it. As we will see in some detail in Chapter 5, God is the rightful ruler of the universe not because he made it but because of his infinite power and knowledge. While there is obviously a connection between God's omnipotence and his creation of the world, it is important to distinguish which of these is the foundation of his authority. If God has authority because of his power rather than because of his workmanship, then human beings gain moral rights not through their workmanship but through God's will. Human labor creates a property right in the thing created because God says that it does, not because labor is analogous to God's creation. Or, to be more precise, labor creates property rights because God commands that human life is to be preserved, and labor-based property rights are the only way for human beings to carry out this command. All moral concerns, including those of workmanship, are ultimately derived from God's command.

Tully's overemphasis on the workmanship model obscures Locke's rationalism. Tully depicts Locke's property rights as being essentially based not on rationally justified rules, but on a great metaphor, the workmanship model, whose validity is allegedly "self-evident."[17] In his brief account of the *Essay*, Tully rejects the idea that Locke sought a purely logical morality, but Tully goes too far in the other direction, watering down Locke's concepts of "demonstration" and "self-evident" truth in order to show that Locke's epistemology is consistent with the metaphorical reasoning he ascribes to the *Two Treatises*.[18] In fact, the use of metaphors in religious reasoning – a common practice among the medieval scholastics – is specifically and pointedly rejected in the *Essay*, on grounds that a metaphor is not a rationally certain argument.[19] Locke, in a great cosmic irony, was gifted with a particular genius for the effective rhetorical use of metaphor. But he uses metaphor only for illustrative purposes, to give rhetorical power to arguments that are not, in their definitive formulations, dependent upon metaphor.

Locke builds his case on rational arguments, rather than on metaphors and other such devices, because their epistemological certainty is crucial to political universalism. A metaphor cannot unite members of different belief groups because it does not demonstrate its point with sufficient certainty. By depicting Locke's theory as founded on a religious metaphor rather than on rational argument, Tully transforms Locke into a parochial figure, the last and greatest of a long line of medieval theorists who struggled to find an adequate metaphor to explain private property in the framework of Christian belief. Locke was, in fact, a transcultural figure, a thinker who drew on concepts from a variety of cultural sources, and built a set of rational arguments that is not dependent on the parochialisms of any one culture or religion.

Richard Ashcraft's otherwise excellent exegesis of the *Two Treatises* in his 1987 *Locke's Two Treatises of Government* also goes astray because it overlooks Locke's purpose of building moral consensus. Ashcraft, whose concerns are more historical than theoretical, keeps asking Locke for more details and specifics. Who will be allowed to vote – every adult male, as some of Locke's egalitarian moral and legal concepts suggest, or only landowners, which was the prevailing practice at the time?[20] What specific acts constitute the explicit granting of political consent?[21] Is a constitutional legislature, institutionally separate from the executive, a moral requirement for all societies, or only for advanced societies, or only for societies where the people demand such a separation of powers?[22] Although Ashcraft defends Locke against the accusation that his work is riddled with contradictions and incoherencies, he is dissatisfied with the lack of supporting detail in Locke's account of natural law, concluding that Locke presents much that is "necessary" to a natural law theory, but not all that is "sufficient" for such a theory.[23]

It was never Locke's purpose to present the specific kind of detailed exposition of natural law that Ashcraft simply assumes Locke must have intended to provide. Discussing Locke's statement in the *Two Treatises* that "it would be besides my present purpose, to enter here into the particulars of the law of nature," Ashcraft expresses tentative agreement with critics who find this statement to be "evidence of a rather loose or disingenuous attitude towards the importance of natural law to Locke's argument."[24] But it is just possible that Locke understands better than Ashcraft does the importance of natural law to Locke's argument. Its purpose is not to settle all important political questions, such as who will vote and under what circumstances it might be acceptable to unite the legislative and executive. The medieval natural law theorists wanted natural law doctrine to answer all important questions, but not Locke. The purpose of Locke's natural law theory is to rationally demonstrate some, but not all, of the provisions of the moral law, in order to lay the moral foundations of a common political authority. All the rest, the "particulars" of moral law, need not be thus demonstrated, and can safely be left to the good judgment of individuals, communities, and rulers.

What Locke provides is not a constitutional theory, such as we find in, say, *The Federalist Papers*, but a moral theory. There were, of course, constitutional issues at stake in the English political crisis of the 1680s. But Locke simply wasn't very interested in settling this kind of question in the *Two Treatises*, as is evident from the absence of constitutional details that Ashcraft bemoans. The fundamental reason that English society was coming apart at the seams was not because of disputes over constitutional law but because it could not agree on what moral theory should be the basis of, and therefore constrain, government action. The *Two Treatises* addresses this deeper moral problem.

Ashcraft's expectation that Locke will provide a detailed constitutional theory leads him to attribute one to Locke that Locke himself does not provide. Ashcraft argues that the *Two Treatises* bears a resemblance to the political theories published by the Levelers, a radical movement devoted to universal suffrage and economic egalitarianism.[25] Ashcraft's Locke is a radical Whig with ambitions for large-scale political reform. It is true that Locke presents an account of democratic government that does not mention any limits on who should have the right to vote, and strongly endorses jural equality and government by consent of the governed, but Ashcraft has missed a step in the argument. Locke's account of democratic government is conditional; he describes how a government works if it is democratic. As John Marshall points out, Locke does not require that governments be democratic, only that they be founded on the consent of the governed in some form.[26] Locke always speaks of "subjects," or "members" of the community; he never speaks of "citizens."[27] Certainly we can reasonably infer from Locke's commitment to jural equality that if a government is democratic it must have universal suffrage, but Locke shows no overt sign of any interest in major political or constitutional reform in the *Two Treatises*. His main purpose is not to change laws and institutions but to change hearts and minds. No doubt his theory has ramifications for constitutional design, but Locke does not pursue them.

OUR LOCKEAN WORLD: RIGHTS, CONSENT, FREEDOM, AND PROPERTY

It is a premise of this book that Locke's time is not so radically different from ours that Locke has nothing to teach us, or not much to teach us, or can teach us only at the level of method rather than at the level of practical content. Dunn is the great skeptic on this score. He wrote in his major work on Locke: "I simply cannot conceive of constructing an analysis of any issue in contemporary political theory around the affirmation or negation of anything which Locke says about political matters."[28] In an unfortunately neglected article, Dunn later formally retracted that sentence, calling it an "expression of stupidity" reflecting "intellectual myopia."[29] That it certainly was, but for reasons far deeper than Dunn goes on to admit.

Dunn is now willing to acknowledge some aspects of Locke's theory as "living" – that is, useful for today's political problems – but only at the level of pure method. Locke does not take social trust and civil order for granted, as many current political theorists do; Locke portrays social order as a contract, which is a method many still find plausible; Locke treats political institutions as the result of messy historical accidents and compromises rather than as divinely or naturally ordained; and a few other similar observations.[30] He writes that Locke's substantive political positions have been "killed off," primarily by "the extinction of Locke's Christian conception of the nature of the human habitat and the role of the human species, at least as an animating frame of current theoretical understanding." He admits that "there are of course still a great many Christians," but argues that this "overlap in strictly theological conventions" cannot sustain the "intellectual currency" of Locke's political thinking. Too much else has changed in the world of philosophy for Locke to speak to us politically even if we are willing to accept his thought on its own religious terms.[31]

Dunn's four examples of topics on which he thinks we are radically separated from Locke – the fact/value distinction, elections and consent, freedom of expression, and the proper origin and use of property – do not stand up to scrutiny. Some fail because Dunn is wrong about the state of philosophy and political thought in the world today, and others fail because Dunn is wrong about what Locke's positions are. In each case the differences between how we see these topics and how Locke sees them are not nearly radical enough to justify Dunn's conclusions. Indeed, there is more continuity than difference between our views of these topics and Locke's views. In many ways, we are living in the world Locke envisioned.

Dunn points out that for Locke prepolitical rights are "a legal fact, a fact of value," and that the idea of legal facts "has been regarded with considerable contempt by many modern philosophers."[32] Certainly we must reject an absolute distinction between facts and values if Locke is to speak to us, but why should this be impossible merely because "many modern philosophers" have said it is? Many modern philosophers also said that the historical triumph of Marxism was inevitable. Among academics the absolute fact/value distinction has long since lost its aura of scientific inevitability, and among the population at large its retreat has been even more dramatic. The fact/value distinction never held much power with the population at large to begin with; very few people outside of academe ever believed that there was a radical division between facts and values. In the United States, this widespread public rejection of the fact/value distinction has become even more evident since the 2001 terrorist attacks – there do not seem to be more than a handful of Americans willing to seriously entertain the opinion that the difference between Osama bin Laden and Todd Beamer is merely a matter of which values one prefers. Dunn defends the fact/value distinction by arguing that "it is the political history of a culture, not the nature of the universe or the properties of the human species as such," that makes people believe in prepolitical rights.[33] But, by Dunn's own admission, that is not the opinion of the general population. Cultural relativism may be fashionable in the academy, but most of the general population still believes in what are now called "human rights" – rights that people have as humans, prior to politics.

Dunn also mischaracterizes our current situation regarding consent theory. He argues that no one believes any more that elections convey genuine consent, because "it is apparent enough that these ceremonies play an exceedingly tangential role in determining the direction in which political power is exercised."[34] This drastically overstates the theoretical demands on consent theory. Locke, like the American founders, did not argue that government policy should be guided by the fickle winds of public opinion. His position is that a government is legitimate if and only if its people freely agree to be governed by it. Locke's theory requires no political participation as such by the people, only their consent in some form. In this sense, elections are still very much understood as morally important events rather than merely as ceremonies. This was forcefully demonstrated after the November 2000 U.S. election – each side in that rancorous dispute accused the other of violating not simply the law or the Constitution, but the very moral fabric and foundation of the American political system. We do differ from Locke in that many today believe that elections should do more than just convey bare consent, but that is beside the point so long as people still believe, as the 2000 election dispute shows they do, that authentic elections bestow the consent of the governed. Locke's careful treatment of the authenticity of election results, occasioned by the king's attempts to jerry-rig parliamentary election procedures, is perhaps the topic on which his philosophic framework and ours are most similar (see T II.155–8, 194–7; 167, 201; and 212–16, 223–4).

Dunn asserts, mistakenly, that Locke believes people do not have human rights as such to freedom of conscience and expression. Locke denies atheists the right to express their atheism, so Dunn concludes that for Locke rights belong not to human beings as such but to religious believers as such.[35] Dunn simply misunderstands Locke. Locke does not think that atheists have no rights at all; quite the contrary, he thinks that all people, atheists included, have the same human rights because they are all, atheists included, created by God. But these rights do not include the right to say things that are inherently dangerous to civil order, of which atheism is, for Locke, only one example among many. We may now believe that society can tolerate atheism and still survive, but that does not call into question Locke's general theory of toleration so long as we still believe, as Locke did, that toleration does not extend to speech that undermines civil order at its roots. We do still believe this, as is evident from the widespread support for laws against hate speech, for the suppression of dangerous religious cults and radical groups, and (in the United States) laws against flag desecration. These policies are controversial, of course, but the controversy is almost always over whether such things as hate speech are in fact dangerous to civil order, rather than whether in principle speech dangerous to civil order can be banned. We are not as sensitive as Locke was to the danger of speech that threatens civil order, but this is only because we can take civil order much more for granted than Locke could, living as he did in the firestorm of seventeenth-century England.

Finally, Dunn is also mistaken in arguing that because Locke understood property in the context of God's having given the world to humanity for his (God's) own purposes, it must follow that for Locke there is "one and only one way at any time that natural goods ought to be appropriated to human use and at best a pretty restricted range of ways in which the goods themselves ought to be enjoyed."[36] Since no one believes that anymore, he writes, Locke's views on property are politically dead. This mischaracterization of Locke is even more serious than his misreading of

Locke's views on atheism. Locke did believe that property was only to be appropriated and used in accordance with the purpose of God's donation of the world to humanity, but his understanding of God's purpose is expansively broad: the sustenance and comfort of human beings.[37] Far from imposing narrow constraints, this view endorses a remarkably wide variety of modes of appropriation and use of property. Use of property is limited only by God's moral law, which is mostly negative (do not steal, do not deprive others of the opportunity to earn a living, do not destroy goods wastefully, and so on). And for that matter Dunn is simply wrong in his blithe assertion that since the rise of capitalism there is no room anymore for morally restrictive views of private property – surely one need not look far these days to find people interested in placing moral restraints on capitalism!

People today still believe, as Locke did, in prepolitical rights as legal facts. They still believe, as Locke did, that government derives its just powers from the consent of the governed. They still believe, as Locke did, that all people have rights to freedom of speech and conscience but that those rights are limited by the need to preserve civil order. And they still believe, as Locke did, that property rights are very broad but still constrained by moral law. Despite our differences, we are philosophically close enough to Locke for his politics to speak to us.

Indeed, it is largely due to Locke's influence that these beliefs are so widespread today. In Locke's time they were controversial, even radical arguments, where today they are the settled political consensus, in some cases verging on platitudinous. Our world is very much a Lockean world, at least in its deepest intellectual premises if not in all of its day-to-day political issues and controversies. By Dunn's standard, then, Locke's politics are more "alive" in our time than they were in 1689! It's a good thing nobody ever told Locke that political arguments are "dead" when they diverge radically from prevailing opinion, or he might never have published them.

OUR LOCKEAN MOMENT: RELIGION, FOUNDATIONS,
AND VIOLENCE

A more important problem confronting our reading of Locke is one that Dunn, perhaps inadvertently, pushes into the background: the role of religion in public life. The most important difference between Locke's world and ours is the return of multireligious societies. Locke wrote in seventeenth-century England, a Christian nation in a part of the world where all the great powers were Christian. He did not have to work very hard to defend the idea that religious belief would play a role in political philosophy. Indeed, his main problem was that the public philosophies of his time were too religious, in the sense that religious matters on which reasonable people could disagree were settled by law, with not enough toleration for dissent. This is not to say that Locke offers no justification for a religious public philosophy; it is only to say that Locke disposes of that problem quickly on his way to dealing with other problems that were more urgent in his time. We will have to articulate Locke's argument for a religious public philosophy at greater length than he did himself, without distorting what Locke actually said or attributing to him things that he didn't say. This is tricky, but it can be done, and this book attempts to do it.

That having been said, the return of multireligious societies has not fundamentally altered the basic problem of religion and politics that Locke confronted. Indeed, Locke's historical situation and our own, for all their important differences, also share some remarkably deep similarities when it comes to the politics of religion. We have reached a point in our history when our society has lost much of the religious and cultural homogeneity it once had, presenting a great challenge to our political foundations. Our politics is built on premises – individual liberty, moral and legal egalitarianism, rationality, and so on – that were once widely accepted as truths but are now accused of being no more than the parochial preferences of one cultural group. If our political institutions are to endure in an age of greater and deeper cultural divisions, these foundational premises must be shown to be universally preferable moral principles rather than merely the ethnocentric, socially constructed "norms" of one culture.

Our moment in history is also similar to Locke's on a much more specific, short-term level, as the specter of mass violence motivated by religious conflict has recently become the most prominent item on the world agenda. If religious belief is not leavened with the guidance of reason, enthusiastic believers can justify – to themselves, if not to anyone else – almost any horrendous conclusion. Such ideas have consequences, as world events are forcefully reminding us. Religion, and in particular the relationship between reason and faith, is not a matter of purely private concern. The formation of beliefs is the most basic political topic, because politics requires regulating human action, and actions are governed most directly and most powerfully by the beliefs of the actor. As Locke points out, moral and religious beliefs "influence men's lives, and give a bias to all their actions," and are hence the beliefs whose regulation is most important (E IV.12.4, 642). If political theorists and liberals generally do not have something to say about the content of people's religious beliefs and the moral vision of the cosmos to which the political community should be devoted, violent fanatics in every religion around the world stand ready to fill that void.

Of all the great philosophers in history, Locke is the one whose historical situation is closest to ours, both because of the long-term problem of cultural fragmentation and the short-term problem of religious violence. He is therefore the philosopher from whom we stand to gain the most useful insight. Faced with similar circumstances, Locke did not abandon in despair the possibility of a moral theory that could unite fragmented cultural groups into a single political community. He believed that human reason, which is shared by all, could overcome even the chasm that stood between members of hostile faiths who had only recently been quite literally at one another's throats. How he thought this could be achieved, and what we can learn from it, is the subject of this book.

To understand what was at stake for him, we must begin by reviewing the circumstances to which he was reacting. John Locke was born into a nation at war with itself. In 1642, when Locke was ten years old, the long-festering hatred between Anglicans and Puritans gave birth to one of the nastiest episodes in English history – the Civil War. Locke's father served as a captain in a cavalry regiment in that war.[38] And the Anglicans and Puritans maintained their underlying contempt for one another long after the restoration of the monarchy under Charles II in 1660 put an end to the particular period of conflict characterized by the Civil War and its aftermath. This cultural hostility continued to fracture and disfigure English society for decades to come.

Locke was entangled in this conflict for his entire life. Historians disagree over the extent of Locke's personal participation in some of the key political events of the time, but the conflict between Anglicans and Puritans was omnipresent and of fundamental importance in the world he lived in. It played out constantly in the internal politics of Oxford, where the young Locke served as a lecturer and, eventually, as moral censor. When Locke left Oxford in 1667 to join the household of Lord Ashley (later Earl of Shaftsbury), he became drawn into its political dimension. Though he joined the household as a medical doctor – saving his patron's life in 1668 by overseeing a daring surgical operation – he was soon writing political tracts for Shaftsbury and his circle of Puritan operatives. As Charles II grew more and more willful and heavy handed, Shaftsbury's political circle gradually evolved into a cell of political resistance, and ultimately became a violent revolutionary cabal. Locke, who as a young Oxford don had written tracts in favor of absolute government authority, spent his middle age working for a man who lived in the dark world of secret identities, coded messages, underground meetings, and assassination plots. Locke may have been one of the conspirators himself.

This conflict between Anglicans and Puritans must be understood in the context of the much older and deeper – and equally violent – conflict between Protestants and Catholics. For 150 years, much blood had been shed over the Catholic Church's claim to ecclesiastical supremacy, within England as well as in the rest of Europe. Every time a new monarch with a different religious allegiance came to the throne, the whole nation was required to either convert or accept the outcast status of oppressed "dissenters." This provided an enormous incentive for Protestants and Catholics alike to ensure by any means necessary that the throne passed to a person of the correct religious allegiance. Even after the supremacy of the Anglican Church, and hence the Protestant affiliation of England, seemed finally settled, the ongoing struggle between Protestants and Catholics continued to be a source of discord. The ruling Anglicans viewed Puritans and Catholics alike as threats to national sovereignty, given that both groups had conducted violence against the crown within living memory. But they were decidedly more sympathetic toward Catholics, whose religious forms were recognizably similar to theirs. They expressed this preference in greater legal toleration and better social treatment for Catholics than for Puritans. This, in turn, intensified Puritan resentment toward the Anglican Church, which they viewed as a corrupt imitator of what was, for them, the great fountainhead of corruption, the Catholic Church.

It was against this background that the political crisis of the 1680s occurred. Charles II, whose father Charles I had been executed by the Puritans in the Civil War, had long sought to draw more power to the crown as a result of his constant fights with the Puritan-controlled Parliament. Shaftsbury was a leading opponent of Charles's efforts to expand the crown's power, not least because at some point – probably in 1673 – he had learned, from someone in his network of contacts and spies, a shocking secret. In order to gain French assistance against the Dutch in a war over trade in 1670, Charles had secretly signed a treaty with France promising that he would eventually, when the time was right, openly convert to Catholicism and return England to the ecclesiastical control of the Catholic Church.[39] Of course, the supposed right time for this conversion never came, given that England was overwhelmingly Protestant and very jealous of its independence from Rome. Charles does not appear ever to have made any move toward fulfilling his promise. But Shaftsbury and his allies did not have the benefit of hindsight, and for them the mere existence of such a promise was sufficient evidence that England's independence from Rome – and potentially the very existence of Protestantism itself, since England was the predominant Protestant power – was in jeopardy.[40]

The political waters began to boil in 1679–81. Charles had no legitimate son, and a protracted struggle ensued over who would succeed him. The next in line to the throne was his brother James, who was Catholic. Parliamentary forces, afraid that James might attempt to convert England back to Catholicism, sought to exclude James from succession to the throne on grounds of his religion. It was during this crisis, known as the Exclusion Crisis, that the political labels "Whig" and "Tory" first appeared.[41] Matters came to a head in 1681 when Parliament tried to meet to vote for the exclusion of James from the throne. Charles prevented it from meeting by exercising his constitutional authority to dissolve Parliament for new elections, and then refraining from actually holding new elections. This had the effect of abolishing Parliament entirely, essentially ending any hope of lawful political resistance to the crown. The king became, in fact if not in law, the whole of the English political system. For Shaftsbury and his circle this was the final proof that Charles was a threat to England's freedom, independence, and Protestantism. They quickly resolved upon a course of action they had previously refused to even contemplate: violent resistance. The following year Shaftsbury plotted to assassinate Charles and was arrested and charged as a traitor. A Whig-dominated jury threw out the charges.[42] Shaftsbury fled into exile in the Netherlands, and died not long thereafter. In 1683, following another failed assassination plot by Shaftsbury's cabal, Locke went into hiding under an assumed name in Amsterdam.[43]

We have recounted this story here partly to provide some historical reference for understanding the content of Locke's works, but also, and more importantly, to establish the deep similarity between Locke's historical situation and ours. Our moment in history is very much a Lockean moment. We do not, of course, have civil wars or assassination plots among cultural groups within the political community. We do, however, have the breakdown of a cultural unity that was once taken for granted. Like Locke, we face a crisis of legitimacy that is, at bottom, a religious crisis caused by the fragmentation of society into cultural groups with different beliefs.

Surely we need not wait until fragmented cultural groups start actually killing one another before we can say that the political unification of such groups is increasingly uncertain and in dire need of attention. And we face, in a much more immediate way, the same problem of religious violence. Our problem is not religious violence from within the political community, as in seventeenth-century England, but it is religious violence nonetheless.

The relationship between faith and reason, long neglected by contemporary theorists, stands in urgent need of theoretical attention. If faith and reason inherently conflict, then the choice between them is simply a radical, existential choice, and there can be no argument as such over which way one ought to choose – argument itself being a function of reason. We could have no serious reply to the violent fanatics of the world other than just killing them. A political community devoted to rational argument could share no common moral beliefs, and would therefore remain nothing more than a mercenary agreement among groups who share nothing in common but a coincidental overlap of interests. If, however, it is possible for a person to be both fully rational and a religious believer at the same time, then there is hope that religious people can be persuaded that fanaticism and violence are against God's wishes, and that people of different faiths can share a common rational community.

LOCKE'S POLITICS OF MORAL CONSENSUS

In seeking to apply Locke's political wisdom to the problems of our own time, another problem we need to consider is that Locke professes to believe not in "religion" but specifically in Christianity. In a multireligious society we cannot embrace a public philosophy that is convincing only to Christians. This point needs to be clear from the outset: this book is not a brief for Christianity, nor does it argue that Christianity is inherently more liberal than other religions. Locke shows us, however, that we are not limited to a choice between the two extreme paths of an ecclesiastical political community or an irreligious one.

This is a lesson Locke himself learned in 1665 as a young scholar attached to a diplomatic mission to the town of Cleves. There, he saw a way of life that had previously been unimaginable to him: members of different faiths living together in a common political community. Most (though not all) people enjoyed equal legal rights regardless of religion. In a letter, Locke expressed astonishment that members of radically different Protestant denominations, and even Protestants and Catholics, could worship in separate churches on Sunday morning and then, upon stepping out of their church doorways, mix freely and easily together as fellow citizens and neighbors. "They quietly permit one another to choose their way to heaven; for I cannot observe any quarrels or animosities amongst them upon account of religion."[44]

In his works, Locke suggests the possibility of an ecumenical religious philosophy of liberalism. This approach builds politics on the premise that the political freedom and equality of mankind is divinely ordained – that it is the will of a divine power that all human beings be treated politically as free and equal. This is a religious premise but it does not entail any necessary commitment to a particular religion. There are elements that are at least suggestive of this premise in all the major religions. Persons of different religions who agree on the divine imperative of political freedom and equality could all subscribe to a liberalism built on that premise, though their reasons for believing in the premise would be different. In spite of their different faiths they would share what we will call a "moral consensus." This book will show that building such a moral consensus was the political and philosophical goal to which all of Locke's major works were addressed.

Moral consensus is decidedly not the same as the "overlapping consensus" that neutralist liberal theorists have sometimes invoked to justify liberal moral principles.[45] The "overlap" Locke seeks to build, and build upon, is at the level of metaphysics, theology, and moral theory. This gives Locke's political theory the moral depth necessary to create a robust liberal order that can hold together members of conflicting religions. When neutralist liberal theorists ground their theories on an appeal to preexisting consensus on liberal principles, they rule out any attempt to provide moral justification for those principles. A liberalism of moral consensus, by contrast, lays the moral foundations of politics in a shared moral philosophy. Religious divisions are ineradicable, and liberals can either despair of ever building common moral ground across those divides or build a moral consensus around the moral principles over which the different religions are not deeply divided.

Building moral consensus has epistemological, theological, and political aspects. In its epistemological aspect, Locke's philosophy shows each denomination that because its beliefs are not straightforwardly obvious in the same way that $2 + 2 = 4$ is straightforwardly obvious, it has a responsibility not to act as if its beliefs were so clearly true that questioning them would be irrational. The purpose of the *Essay* is to show how it is possible, through rational regulation of belief, to simultaneously believe in a revelatory religion and yet not treat all one's revelatory beliefs as absolutely certain. It accomplishes this by applying a concept of "degrees of assent," which Locke uses to craft a distinction between beliefs with different levels of certainty. The *Essay* also addresses a number of specific beliefs that were preventing the mutual toleration of different religions in Locke's time, showing that those beliefs are unavoidably contaminated with uncertainty.

In its theological aspect, Locke's philosophy argues that morality must be based on divine command, and that some divine commands are more certain than others. From this it follows that we ought to differentiate between what might be called core moral beliefs, based on divine commands of which we can be certain (such as the prohibition of murder), and ancillary moral beliefs, based on divine commands of which we cannot be as certain (such as those regarding forms of worship). Following the epistemological rules of the *Essay*, the *Reasonableness* constructs a Christian theology that reflects an appreciation for the limits of human certainty. Locke demonstrates to Christians that while the beliefs that are necessary to the religion of Christianity – such as Christ's Messiahship – are conveyed clearly and with great certainty by scripture, on most theological subjects – such as the complexities of metaphysics and Christology – the teachings of scripture do not justify so great a level of certainty that we can say a person is not a Christian unless he agrees with one particular understanding of those doctrines. In other words, Christians can disagree with one another about the metaphysics of the soul or the Trinity and still all be members of the same Christian faith. This goes a long way toward pulling the fangs of religious persecutors and violent fanatics. It also reinforces the religious argument for the politically crucial prohibition against murder, since it demonstrates that this belief is, compared to other religious moral beliefs, extremely certain.

In its political aspect, Locke's philosophy argues that politics ought to be based on moral beliefs that are both very certain and very clearly within government's sphere of competence. The moral law that most easily passes these tests is the requirement that human life is to be preserved. Locke's *Two Treatises* demonstrates that this law is very certain even without the assistance of revelation, because it is visible in God's design of human nature. Because this law can be made out with natural reason, it is common to all religious groups, and hence it can be the basis of a shared public moral philosophy. However, revelatory religion is also necessary to the political community, because without revelation we cannot know that this "natural law" is in fact a law – that is, an obligatory

rule laid down by an authoritative lawgiver. Only the moral authority conveyed by the divine can establish that preserving life is morally mandatory
rather than simply a praiseworthy thing to do. The *Letter* demonstrates
that other moral laws besides the law that human life is to be preserved
are not amenable to coercive enforcement, thus setting the boundaries
of government competence in matters of morality and religion. Because
of this natural limit on government's abilities, the *Letter* rules out any
possibility that the Bible can be the exclusive revelation admitted by the
community. The *Two Treatises* relies on the Bible because Christianity was
overwhelmingly dominant in Locke's time and place, but anyone who
believes in some revelation that affirms the preservation of human life as
a divine law can be a member of the political community.

For Locke the all-important political problem is the establishment of
authority. There are only two possible ways to govern a society: by authority or by brute force. This dichotomy dominates the *Two Treatises*. If we
do not wish to govern people by simply beating them into submission,
we must govern them by showing them a reason why they should voluntarily submit to government. Only moral reasons are sufficient for this,
because moral beliefs overrule other beliefs. If people do not have moral
reasons to obey government, they will disobey government whenever they
think moral reasons require it. Moral theory is what separates a politics
of authority from a politics of brute force, so any political theory must
show moral reasons why people should submit to government. But establishing a common moral authority is tremendously difficult in a society
characterized by deep disagreement over religion, which is the ultimate
arbitrator of morality. Locke's account of natural law is an attempt to
ground political action in a source of divine moral authority – the law
that human life is to be preserved – that can be recognized by members
of conflicting religious denominations.

Locke's careful attention to the problem of moral authority in the
absence of a shared community religion speaks directly to the problem of
moral authority in liberal political theory today. Because liberal political
theory is now almost totally isolated from moral thought, it does not
establish moral authority for liberal government. If political theorists are
required to remain neutral between different "conceptions of the good,"
as they often put it, they cannot construct an argument that obedience
to government is a necessary component of the good life – that is, the life
that is best for human beings. And a government that claims to be neutral
in all questions of morality by definition cannot also claim to act with
moral authority. Locke's works contain a forceful argument that moral

authority grounded in the divine is the indispensable difference between government by consent and government by brute force; his theory of moral consensus shows how it is possible to build such moral authority in a multireligious society.

LOCKE'S METHOD OF MORAL CONSENSUS

There have been many arguments over the content of Locke's political theory – the conditions under which he allows property to be privately appropriated, how much authority he allows government to exercise over private property, which people he envisions as having the right to vote, and so on. Scholars have found different ways to make sense of the theory's content. But there has been remarkably little scholarly attention to the method of Locke's political argument, as opposed to its content. The method by which Locke presents his political theory, while it has been the subject of some scholarly work, has not generally been considered to be of nearly as much importance as its content.[46] With the major exception of Strauss and his followers, whose interpretation will receive particular attention throughout this book, Locke scholarship has generally proceeded on the premise that Locke's presentation of his political theory is not methodologically complex.

This is an important oversight. Locke's most important political concerns can be discovered by examining the method of his works as well as their doctrinal content. Locke seldom comments on methodology in his works. The arguments justifying both his method of reading scripture and his method of analyzing human nature are present in his works, but they are brief. To a large extent we are in the realm of unspoken inferences rather than explicit doctrine when examining Locke's political method. To explain Locke's method, we must draw some conclusions from Locke's text that Locke does not make explicit. In our analysis, every effort has been made to remain faithful to Locke's text, and to show that the method we ascribe to Locke is really the one that he uses.

Locke's political method is far more subtle than it at first appears to be. Locke has a longstanding reputation for reasonableness and moderation, and to understand why one need only read his political works. For the reader who is not predisposed to be hostile toward him, Locke's meticulous philosophic assault on absolutism, religious persecution, and patriarchy generate an almost irresistible sympathy. Locke appears as the noble voice of reason against all forms of bigotry and passion, and particularly against the lust for power. How straightforward and obvious he makes it all seem, as though no one in his right mind could disagree. It is quite easy, when reading the *Two Treatises*, to forget that the purpose of that work is to convince the reader to support the violent overthrow of the king by a cabal of radical revolutionaries. Indeed, by the time one has finished the last chapter of the *Two Treatises*, rebelling against Charles II or James II not only seems like a reasonable alternative, it seems like the only reasonable alternative.

This sympathy is made possible by Locke's ingenious philosophic method, which allows him to build a political theory on a small set of almost universally held moral beliefs, while avoiding any direct conflict with other, more controversial beliefs his readers might hold. In this, the contrast between Locke and Hobbes is instructive. Hobbes's political theory in *Leviathan* requires an extensive account of psychology, ethics, metaphysics, theology, and semiotics, such that *Leviathan* ends up attacking the fundamental beliefs of almost any person who reads it. Some respond by abandoning the beliefs they held previously in favor of Hobbes's worldview, but more respond by rejecting Hobbes on the grounds that his theory is inconsistent with beliefs that they are not willing to abandon. Locke, by stark contrast, deliberately crafts a political theory that will generate, as Steven Forde puts it, "minimum controversy and maximum appeal."[47] Rather than attempt to persuade you to abandon your fundamental account of the universe in favor of a different one, Locke attempts to persuade you that your fundamental account of the universe, whatever it is, is based on premises that will, if you understand them correctly, lead you to endorse his political theory.

To do this, Locke builds his theory on elements that are common to virtually all fundamental accounts of the universe. These elements are laid out explicitly in the *Essay*, and only implied in Locke's political works. His bedrock premise is that a divine power exists in the universe. Onto this he piles a number of other crucial premises, most importantly that this divine power has a will regarding our actions, that it has communicated this will to us through some means, and that it enforces its will with rewards and punishments after death. All of these premises are common not only to every religious group in Locke's England, but to virtually all religious groups everywhere. By appealing to these premises, Locke builds moral consensus by making moral arguments with appeal to members of vastly different religious and cultural groups, laying the foundation for a shared political community among such readers.

The problem, of course, is to figure out exactly what the divine power's will for us is. Since Locke and his audience all agree that the Bible is an authentic revelation of divine will, Locke uses a scriptural method to investigate that will as revealed in the Bible. However, if the divine will is known only through revelation, there can be no common moral law among persons who adhere to different religions. Furthermore, because there are inherent epistemological problems in interpreting any text, it is inevitable that disagreements will arise in the interpretation of the Bible. Therefore, Locke also needs a natural method for discerning the divine will, or at least part of it, in a nonrevelatory source. Because it is nonrevelatory, all will acknowledge it as a genuine account of divine will, and it is not subject to the epistemological problems of scriptural interpretation. Locke finds the solution to this problem in the design of human nature. If human beings were created by a divine power, that power's will for humanity must be reflected in its construction of human nature.

This two-track method of moral consensus makes it possible to bring feuding groups together both within and among religions. The scriptural method demonstrates that the Bible clearly endorses a moral law of human preservation, and demonstrates this in a way all Christians must accept, because it relies solely on the Bible itself for points of interpretive reference rather than on the traditions of a particular denomination or sect. The natural method shows this same law of human preservation visible in the design of human nature, thus proving to anyone who believes that humanity was created by a divine power, regardless of his religion, that human preservation is a divine imperative. This moral law of human preservation in turn supports a political order, as Locke shows by working out its implications for a variety of political topics. This is the fruition of Locke's theory of moral consensus – government built upon a moral law that is justified with arguments all groups must accept.

LOCKE'S RATIONALITY AND MORAL CONSENSUS

Locke's theory of moral consensus should be understood as a form of rationalism. Unfortunately, the word "rationalism" has acquired a great deal of unnecessary baggage among both political theorists and theologians. Locke did not wish to totally reorganize human life according to some all-encompassing system of rules, nor did he favor purely abstract theory over empirically informed analysis.[48] Locke did argue against religious fanatics who refused to allow rational examination of their doctrines. "I find every sect, as far as reason will help them, make use of it gladly: and where it fails them, they cry out, *'Tis a matter of faith, and above reason*"

(E IV.18.2, 689). But he was equally against those, like the Cartesians and the medieval scholastics, who refused to recognize the inherent limits of reason itself. We put ourselves in great danger of believing falsehoods and falling prey to fanaticism if we do not learn to "sit down in quiet ignorance of those things, which, upon examination, are found to be beyond the reach of our capacities" (E I.1.4, 45).

Neither would Locke have us reject any belief unless we can prove it by natural reason without the assistance of revelation, which is what some mean by the term "rationalism." Obviously this idea of rationalism is fundamentally opposed to any kind of belief in a revealed religion, since the whole idea of revelation is that we accept something as true because God says it is true rather than because we figured it out for ourselves. So, for example, if the Bible says that the Holy Spirit gives spiritual strength to Christians but we cannot prove this independent of the Bible, a "rationalist" on this account would say that we should reject that belief. By contrast, for Locke it is perfectly rational to believe that God has revealed things to us. He declares that "reason must be our last judge and guide in every thing," but then he goes on to say: "I do not mean, that we must consult reason, and examine whether a proposition revealed from God can be made out by natural principles, and if it cannot, that then we may reject it" (E IV.19.14, 704). Rationalism in Locke's case means only that reason must always be the judge of which alleged revelations are genuine, and what is the most accurate interpretation of a given revelatory text. Once those issues are settled, we must believe whatever God reveals.

The nature of the rationalism embraced by Locke is perhaps best clarified by what it is opposed to: traditionalism and enthusiasm. The purpose of reason is to provide reliable knowledge and belief that does not depend on people's particular situations or predispositions, as traditionalism and enthusiasm do. Locke thought that these forces were the main causes of disharmony in his time because their epistemological dependence on particularity – one does not appeal to "tradition" as such or "enthusiasm" as such but to particular traditions and enthusiasms – was divisive rather than unifying.[49] Locke prefers reason because its epistemology is universal; rational arguments are the same no matter who makes them, and stand or fall on their own merits. The pivotal moral premise of the *Two Treatises* is that the "law of nature . . . obliges everyone," and this is so because "reason, which is that law, teaches all mankind, who will but consult it" (T II.6, 117). As Hans Aarsleff puts it, Locke "rejected the possibility that truth could be private. It must be public, for all to see and assent to, and it is public because reason is the measure. . . . Reason alone is universal, public, and the guarantor of peace and order."[50] Rational arguments can demonstrate a doctrine equally well to members of different groups, and thus hold out the hope of social unity.

To say that Locke sought to use reason to build on areas of agreement is not to deny the radicalism of some of his conclusions. The idea of a natural right to rebellion, for example, was a radical departure from the prevailing beliefs of his day and certainly not an area of "agreement" in any sense. But Locke saw it as an area of potential agreement, because he thought it arose from moral principles with potentially wide appeal, such as the idea that legitimate political power is based on consent. If the right to rebellion was not widely accepted, Locke thought that with the right rational arguments it could be widely accepted, as indeed it eventually was, particularly in a certain backwater English colony on the other side of the Atlantic.

Locke's alleged optimism on a variety of subjects, such as the goodness of human nature, has often been overestimated, but regarding reason's potential to build moral consensus around even radical ideas Locke was a firm optimist. By basing his case solely on rational arguments that were very strong and clear, he believed he could persuade the adherents of different religious systems to agree on a set of core moral principles. There is considerably less optimism today about building moral consensus through reason,[51] but there shouldn't be. Lest we forget, the popularity of Locke's ideas in his own time and the success of liberalism in the centuries that followed largely vindicated Locke's optimism. The prospects for peace and mutual toleration among conflicting social groups were far more dismal in seventeenth-century England than they are anywhere in the developed world today, and yet Locke's attempt to make peace and promote toleration can only be judged a spectacular success.

If political theory that trusts reason to build a common political foundation has declined in the years between Locke's time and ours, and "rationalism" has come to be a dirty word in some quarters, it is only because people were so impressed with reason's success that they began to demand too much of it. Reason was expected to dispel all conflicts with irrefutable arguments, or repair the moral failings that are inherent in human nature, or replace religion as a way of explaining the universe. Given such expectations, rationalism could hardly help but "fail," and given this "failure" a backlash against reason was almost inevitable.

This is an outcome that Locke foresaw as a possibility and explicitly warned against. He writes in the *Essay* that "we should not . . . be so forward, out of an affectation of a universal knowledge, to raise questions, and perplex our selves and others with disputes about things, to which our understandings are not suited" (E I.1.4, 45). Inquiry that purports to be rational but fails to respect the natural limits of reason leads philosophers to hold "various, different, and wholly contradictory" opinions with "such assurance, and confidence," each holding his own unjustified opinion with such "fondness, and devotion," that observers will conclude that "there is no such thing as truth at all; or that mankind hath no sufficient means to attain a certain knowledge of it" (E I.1.2, 44). Much of the subsequent intellectual history of the West – though by no means all of it – has sadly borne out this prediction.

Locke devoted much of his epistemology to preventing this outcome. We will see in the next chapter how he distinguishes genuine, humble rationalism from the false pretensions of arrogant, overweening rationalism. If some liberals today are discouraged about the possibility of moral consensus produced by rational argument, a good stiff dose of Lockean philosophy may be just the thing to replenish their spirits.

LOCKE'S CHRISTIANITY AND MORAL CONSENSUS

To properly understand Locke's theory of moral consensus, we must understand the role played in that theory by his work in the field of Christian theology. Unfortunately, despite the many important insights that have been developed in the last thirty years, current Locke scholarship has not adequately grasped the relationship between his religious thought and his political thought. We must clarify the nature of this misunderstanding in order to provide a more accurate picture of how Locke's religious thought does (and also how it does not) shape his vision of moral consensus.

Locke scholars in our time have been of two minds about the role of religion in Locke's politics. Fifty years ago, Locke's political theory was almost universally understood as an essentially nonreligious theory with a big heap of Bible quotations thrown in for window dressing. Locke was depicted, in Ashcraft's words, as "the defender of atomistic individualism, competitive self-interest, authoritarian liberalism, and capitalistic property owners."[52] This approach culminated in two major schools of thought, one upholding Leo Strauss's thesis that Locke was secretly an enemy of Christianity who sought to replace Christian politics with a neo-Hobbesian political theory, and the other upholding the Marxist thesis, put forward most prominently by C. B. Macpherson, that Locke was an apologist for bourgeois capitalism.[53] What these schools shared was a belief that Locke's political concerns are thoroughly materialistic and thus irrelevant or even hostile to religion.

Both these schools faded into the background, however, after the introduction of a new approach to Locke. First championed by Dunn, this approach understood Locke's political purposes to be centrally characterized by religion.[54] Rather than a materialistic political theorist who was interested in religion only insofar as it affected truly important matters like property and civil order, this new school presented Locke as a Christian political theorist who was interested in property and civil order only insofar as they affected the one truly important human concern, the free and sincere worship of God. On this reading, the main purpose of the *Letter* is not to preserve civil order by removing religion from politics but to preserve Christian humility and virtue by removing politics from religion.[55] And the *Two Treatises*, according to this interpretation, is concerned with the application of the same religious principles on a larger intellectual scale. This approach emphasizes the historical exigency from which the *Two Treatises* arose, and the way in which that exigency was understood by those who participated in it. Seen in this light, the *Two Treatises* was written to defend the liberty of a Protestant nation against tyrannical schemes emanating from Catholic and quasi-Catholic political actors motivated by Catholic ideology, and thus should be understood as defining "liberty" in terms of a distinctively Protestant understanding of natural law.[56] In the past thirty years, this religious interpretation of Locke's politics has grown to become by far the dominant mode of Locke scholarship.

Unfortunately, both the old and new approaches tend to oversimplify the role of religion in Locke's argument, though in different directions. The previous generation of scholars often leaves us with the impression that there is no place for religion in Locke's central concerns. On the other hand, the new generation often leaves us with the impression that those concerns are dominated by Locke's commitment to Protestant Christianity, such that Locke's political theory must be understood as a theory applicable only to a distinctively Protestant political community. Neither of these pictures sufficiently captures the complexity of the relationship between Christianity and Locke's political theory. While Locke's politics are unambiguously founded on God and God's law, the specific religion of Christianity plays a more nuanced role.

Locke's primary concern is to persuade an overwhelmingly Christian audience, so throughout his political works when he presents arguments drawn from human nature he seeks to confirm them with arguments drawn from scripture. However, the foundational assumption on which his political theory rests is not the truth of Christianity as such, but the existence of a divine power that enforces the natural law that human life is to be preserved. This does not mean that revealed religion plays no role at all; while natural reason can help us figure out the content of the natural law, only revelation can conclusively show that this law is enforced by a divine power and is thus morally obligatory. The Bible plays this role in the *Two Treatises* because Locke was a Christian writing to other Christians, but in the *Letter* Locke explicitly extends participation in civil society to anyone, of any religion, who believes that the natural law is divinely enforced, so long as he does not also hold other beliefs inconsistent with the maintenance of civil order. The political community he envisions is not specifically Christian – he writes that "there is absolutely no such thing under the gospel as a Christian commonwealth" – and is open to participation by members of any religion that upholds moral obligation to the natural law (L 56, 43).

This point has been lost in some analyses of the *Two Treatises* that emphasize its religious content. Dunn errs in asserting that for Locke governments are illegitimate if their laws are "formally incompatible" with subjects' "discharge of their Christian duties."[57] Such a rule would make political law dependent upon the question of exactly what a person's "Christian duties" are. This can end in only two possible results: either the community provides a definition of "Christian duties," in which case toleration is impossible and the state is theocratic, or each individual decides for himself what his "Christian duties" are, implying that the individual also decides where the boundary of legitimate government will be drawn for him, in which case government is impossible. What governments must not trespass upon for Locke is not "Christian duty" – any government will necessarily trespass upon somebody's idea of "Christian duty" – but the natural law as clearly discernable in God's construction of human nature. The duty that must not be interfered with is the duty to preserve all human life, and this duty is not a Christian duty, it is a natural duty of all human beings regardless of faith.

A far more serious charge, also leveled by Dunn, is that Locke's ecumenism is in fact a sham. Dunn writes that even when Locke intends to present a moral theory that members of different religions can agree on, he is really just sneaking Christianity in through the back door: "Locke claims to be considering the human condition at large in terms of reason but what he perceives in it is what he already knows (from Christian revelation) to be there."[58] As we have already remarked, Dunn believes that Locke set out to demonstrate a purely logical morality in the *Two Treatises* and failed in this task. According to Dunn, Locke's Christian faith made him so sure of the clear truth of the natural law that he didn't even realize he had failed to make it out through natural reason. The problem here is that Dunn has missed a third possibility – that Locke's political argument rests on neither absolute logical demonstration nor an intellectually crippling dependence upon the Bible, but on empirical observation of human behavior according to rational rules of evidence gathering and hypothesis confirmation. In Dunn's account of Locke's thought, whatever is not demonstrated through ironclad logic is by definition a matter of faith that has nothing to do with reason. But the ground Locke actually stakes out is a rational middle ground belonging neither to absolute logic nor to faith as such, but to well-regulated empirical observation. On this ground it is possible for Locke to build a moral argument that is not exclusively dependent on any one revelation.

Before leaving the topic of the relationship between Christianity and Locke's political thought, one more subject needs to be addressed: the Straussian reading of Locke, by which Locke is secretly an atheistic (or at least deistic or agnostic) enemy of Christianity, and of political theory based on religious premises. This reading has lost much ground in the last three decades among Locke scholars, but that development is more a result of methodological differences than of direct confrontation between the arguments of Straussians and other Locke scholars. New biographical evidence about Locke and his times has energized Locke scholars whose approach to political theory is more historical than analytical. These scholars, because they interpret Locke through the belief systems and intellectual traditions of his time, are methodologically inclined to read his works as sincerely religious. The result has been that Straussian and non-Straussian Locke scholars often talk past one another rather than to one another.[59]

This book, though it strives to present an analysis that is historically informed, is generally analytical in method. This makes it possible for us to provide a more direct confrontation with the Straussian reading than has heretofore been achieved in most Locke scholarship. It is not our purpose here to challenge the Straussian method in general; that is far too large a question for this book. Rather, this book argues that even by the standards of the Straussian method there are no grounds for attributing to Locke a secret or esoteric doctrine. That is, we will not rule out *a priori* the possibility that Locke had a secret teaching, but we will show that this hypothesis is not supported by Locke's texts.

We take the view of Ruth Grant, who writes in response to Strauss:

> In following out Locke's reasoning... there seemed to be no inconsistencies of the sort that would require the conclusion that apparently contradictory statements are meant to indicate some deeper unifying thought. Most apparent inconsistencies evaporated on further consideration of the context of conflicting statements, their place in the argument, or Locke's word usage. Most often, when I thought I had met with an inconsistency, I had merely misunderstood some portion of the text because I had assumed too readily that I already knew what it meant.[60]

This book will attempt to show that the appearance of significant contradictions in Locke's works is, in virtually every case, dispelled by careful and attentive study of the works.

Strauss and those who follow his reading make arguments along a number of broad interpretive lines, so no one argument can refute the Straussian reading as such. However, the most important single mistake behind the Straussian reading is a failure to appreciate the profound teaching on reason and faith in Book Four of the *Essay*. Straussians typically draw a bright, shining line between rational argument and religious belief, but it was one of Locke's most persistent ambitions – bordering on an obsession – to erase that line and to unify reason and faith as interdependent helpmates. Throughout this book we will stop to take up the Straussian reading wherever we touch on one of its important interpretive lines of argument. Furthermore, the notes of this book will provide point-by-point responses to the Straussian reading of Locke, with the intention of directly refuting as many particular Straussian interpretive arguments as is possible in the limited space available.

In our time, religion and liberal political theory have diverged widely, because the latter's commitment to rationalism and to the political unification of disparate cultural groups has been seen as inconsistent with admitting any account of the divine. Locke's theory of moral consensus in epistemology, theology, and political theory demonstrates that this is not the case. The purpose of this book is to show, with guidance from Locke, how liberalism can be built on a moral foundation that includes an account of the divine without becoming illiberal, irrational, or exclusionary. Liberalism must reconnect with the divine in order to sustain itself, and Locke's thought is surely the most appealing place to begin examining how that can be done.

"Sit Down in Quiet Ignorance"

Locke's Epistemology of Limits

Locke's *Essay Concerning Human Understanding* must be the starting point for any proper understanding of the rest of his works. The *Essay* is logically first – its principles are the basis of everything else in Locke's philosophic system. The *Essay* settles the epistemological questions that must be settled before other questions, such as those in the fields of theology and political theory, can be raised. Locke did not explicitly draw this connection between the *Essay* and his other works, but he did hold that one's view of epistemology defines one's view of everything else, and his other works presuppose epistemological commitments that are defended in the *Essay*.

This is not to say that Locke's other works spring forth from the arguments of the *Essay* as a matter of logical necessity. Locke's theological and political positions are not simply deduced from his epistemology as one might deduce a geometric proof. Another way of putting this is that Locke's theology and politics are not the only theology and politics that one could conceivably hold within the ambit of his epistemological system. Accepting Locke's epistemology does not necessarily entail accepting his theology and politics. However, rejecting Locke's epistemology does necessarily entail rejecting (or modifying beyond recognition) the bulk of his theology and politics.

Until recently, the most common view among Locke scholars was that the lack of an ironclad deductive connection between the *Essay* and Locke's other works implied that there was really no connection between them at all, or at least no important connection. A widespread misunderstanding of some of Locke's comments in the *Essay* on demonstrative morality, discussed in some detail in the next chapter, had led many scholars to conclude that if the *Two Treatises of Government* and the *Letter Concerning Toleration* did not provide an ironclad logical demonstration of moral rules, they could not be considered as bearing any relationship to the vision of moral reasoning that was allegedly elaborated in the *Essay*.[1] This led Locke scholarship down something of a blind alley, as scholars who all shared the same mistaken belief in the *Essay*'s alleged desire to build a purely demonstrative morality debated whether and how the political works might be understood in relation to this aspiration.[2]

Recent Locke scholarship has begun to investigate other ways in which the *Essay* might be understood in relation to Locke's other works, showing that some of the principles laid down in the *Essay* are taken for granted in the other works as implicit premises. The two-track system of argument used Locke's political works, which confirms Locke's positions with both scriptural and natural arguments, presumes the *Essay*'s argument that faith and reason are compatible and will reach perfectly consistent conclusions.[3] In particular, the indispensable premise that people can know of God's existence through reason alone is defended in the *Essay*.[4] Furthermore, the *Essay*'s epistemology imparts more certainty to moral reasoning, understood as reasoning about human beings' relationships with God and one another, than it does to natural science.[5] Its analysis of human behavior and God's providence provides philosophical underpinnings for a theory explaining how God governs humans by means of a natural law.[6] Finally, the *Essay*'s argument against adopting traditional religious opinions without examination justifies the bold scriptural exegesis found in *The Reasonableness of Christianity*.[7]

Despite these contributions, the connection between the *Essay* and Locke's other works is much deeper than it has been made to appear in Locke scholarship. The *Essay* serves as the foundation of Locke's overall philosophical ambition of building moral consensus. Locke did not describe the *Essay* in this way, and it may not even have been his intention when he was writing it that it would end up playing this role. Nonetheless, Locke's other major works use the epistemological conclusions of the *Essay* as premises upon which they build their moral, religious, and political arguments. In the philosophic system that emerges from Locke's body of works taken as a whole, the *Essay* is the starting point from which all else proceeds.

As Nicholas Wolterstorff has recently shown, the *Essay* is primarily a response to the fragmentation of the religious and cultural tradition in Europe after the Reformation.[8] This interpretation of the *Essay* has received great attention within the world of epistemological theory, because it requires a revision of our understanding of Locke's place in the history of epistemology.[9] But this new way of looking at the *Essay* also implies the need for a serious revision of our understanding of the connection between the *Essay* and Locke's religious and political works, insofar as the motivating problem of the *Essay* is now understood to be religious and political. Wolterstorff, whose concern is to critique the content of Locke's epistemology, does not address how his understanding of the *Essay* affects our understanding of Locke's other works and the connections between them. This chapter and the next will take up this task.

If the *Essay* is not a detached, purely academic text but a culturally engaged response to urgent social problems, and these problems were the very same ones that motivated the *Reasonableness*, the *Two Treatises*, and the *Letter*, this suggests that these four works might be understood as four aspects of a unified whole. That whole is Locke's comprehensive response to Europe's cultural fragmentation. Although the works often take up narrower issues and debates, some of which are related only tangentially to their main subject, the system as a whole pursues a single purpose – to build moral consensus among the many hostile religious and cultural groups left in the wake of the Reformation.

HOW NOT TO READ THE *ESSAY*: KNOWLEDGE AND BELIEF

The *Essay* is by far the largest and most ambitious work Locke ever produced, as befits its foundational place in his philosophic system. Unfortunately, its size and ambition have contributed to, and magnified the importance of, a number of common mistakes about its purpose and method. To appropriate Locke's famous metaphor, there is much rubbish lying in the path to a proper understanding of the *Essay*, and we will begin here by clearing the ground a little (E Epistle, 10).

For a very long time the *Essay* was read as an early work in the "empiricist" tradition. The practice of describing Locke as a foil to the rationalist Descartes and a forerunner to empiricists like Berkeley and Hume has too often biased readers of the *Essay*. Even those who have argued against such an understanding of the *Essay* often read it through the prism of the "rationalist" and "empiricist" epistemological categories. Locke has been made to look like a participant in academic debates that did not yet exist in 1689. Applying these foreign categories to the *Essay* can only obscure the author's meaning and intent, not least because it distracts attention from Locke's primary concern for belief regulation. If we read the *Essay* looking for Locke's answer to our question of whether knowledge is formed by pure reason or by experience, it will probably escape our notice that Locke is much more concerned about what he calls "belief" than he is about what he calls "knowledge."

The characterization of the *Essay* as "empiricist" has been increasingly challenged in the scholarly literature, and with good reason.[10] Locke does say that knowledge is perception, but this is not empiricism. In fact, Locke's understanding of that proposition comes much closer to what we would categorize as epistemological rationalism rather than empiricism.

To understand the *Essay*, we must understand Locke's particular meaning of the word "knowledge." Locke's concept of what counts as knowledge in the strict definition of that word is deeply influenced by the medieval concept of knowledge as logically rigorous *scientia*. Although Locke's epistemology breaks radically with medieval epistemology, he retains the fundamental medieval distinction between "knowledge" and "belief."[11] Something is not knowledge in the strict sense unless it is either intuitively self-evident or a conclusion that follows from self-evident premises by ironclad steps of logical deduction, each step being self-evidently true to anyone who understands it. Locke writes that "sometimes the mind perceives the agreement or disagreement of two ideas immediately." He calls this "intuitive knowledge" (E IV.2.1, 530–1). For example, 2 + 2 = 4 is self-evidently true, once we understand the definitions of the terms, because the idea represented by "2 + 2" is self-evidently identical to the idea represented by "4." In other cases "the mind perceives the agreement or disagreement of ... ideas, but not immediately." Rather, it relies on "the intervention of other ideas ... to discover the agreement or disagreement, which it searches" (E IV.2.2, 531–2). Locke calls this "knowledge by intervening proofs," or "demonstration" (E IV.2.4, 532). For example, if we take as granted that the angles of a triangle always add up to 180 degrees, the proposition that when two angles of a triangle are each 60 degrees the third angle must also be 60 degrees is demonstrative knowledge. By contrast, anything that arises from real-world observations rather than from intuition alone or from purely abstract logical necessity is belief, not knowledge.

This distinction between knowledge and belief is only taxonomic and does not imply that belief is in any way unreliable. Some beliefs are unreliable, but others are highly reliable, and some are so reliable that they are effectively indistinguishable from knowledge. Locke writes of beliefs that "sometimes ... the probability is so clear and strong, that assent as necessarily follows it, as knowledge does demonstration" (E IV.17.16, 685). For example, Locke writes that "though it be highly probable, that millions of men do now exist, yet whilst I am alone writing this, I have not that certainty of it, which we strictly call knowledge," and yet "the great likelihood of it puts me past doubt" (E IV.11.9, 635–6). Or, for an even more clear example, take the old syllogism that all humans are mortal, and Socrates is a human, therefore Socrates is mortal. "All humans are mortal" is not technically knowledge, since we cannot prove it logically. We believe it based on our observation that every human who has ever been observed has died. Similarly, "Socrates is a human" cannot be proven. With a little imagination, we can conceive of other possibilities – he could be an android from the future or an alien visitor in disguise. But we can be sufficiently certain of the beliefs "all humans are mortal" and "Socrates is a human" that they operate just as if they were knowledge.

It was not long after Locke's time that the strict use of the terms "knowledge" and "belief" to reflect this sharp epistemological distinction began to disappear. It has now been gone for so long that it is difficult to recover an understanding of Locke's vocabulary, but it is essential to do so if we are to understand his epistemology. There is knowledge, which includes only those things that are either self-evident or are proven by incontrovertible logic from self-evident premises, and there is belief, which includes everything else.

The vast majority of our epistemological dilemmas, then, are about belief rather than knowledge. Locke believes that in most cases, as in the example of Socrates being human and mortal, knowledge of a subject is impossible but belief is more than good enough for all intents and purposes. Locke would not call into doubt as an operating premise the proposition that all humans are mortal. He just wants us to understand the labels properly – that we are dealing with belief, not knowledge – and therefore understand that in almost all human affairs we are concerned with belief regulation, not the production and organization of knowledge. Proper governance of beliefs will substitute for knowledge in cases where knowledge is impossible. And in those cases where knowledge truly is possible, we must still determine where knowledge ends and belief begins.

A lack of sufficient appreciation for Locke's distinction between knowledge and belief, and particularly for his view that belief can be just as certain as knowledge, has distorted the view of Locke's epistemology in much Locke scholarship. If we are not mindful of the real basis of Locke's distinction between "knowledge" and "belief," this distinction may seem like a separation between reliable and unreliable ways of understanding, such that belief is taken to be inherently less reliable and hence less important than knowledge. It is true that to justify a belief we face a number of epistemological problems that we do not face in the case of knowledge. However, these problems are not insurmountable and are very frequently overcome.

The most important manifestation of this problem in Locke scholarship has been the mistaken belief that the *Essay* seeks to justify building a system of moral laws entirely through logical demonstration, an issue we will discuss in some detail in the next chapter. Also, much of the Straussian reading of Locke is based on a similar misunderstanding. Strauss and those who follow his reading think that Locke did not recognize religious belief as rational.[12] Strauss quotes one of Locke's discussions of the epistemological problems inherent in matters of religious belief, in which Locke declares that our assurance that a particular revelation "came at first from God, can never be so sure as the knowledge we have from the clear and distinct perception of the agreement or disagreement of our own ideas."[13] Strauss declares that this statement constitutes a wholesale separation of "the province of reason" from "the province of faith," with the former consisting exclusively of "knowledge we have from the clear and distinct perception of the agreement or disagreement of our own ideas."[14] The epistemological superiority of what Strauss calls "reason" leads Strauss to think that Locke secretly rejected all else as a basis of politics and morality.

However, the separation Locke actually makes here is not between "reason" and "faith" but between knowledge and belief, and the content of the former is so small that it could never support anything like a comprehensive moral or political theory. "Knowledge we have from the clear and distinct perception of the agreement or disagreement of our own ideas" is limited to statements in the nature of "$2 + 2 = 4$," as well as statements that can be logically derived from such statements. "Reason" includes both knowledge and belief for Locke, so saying that faith is a form of belief rather than knowledge does not separate it from reason. In fact, Locke's purpose in the passage quoted by Strauss is to refute the very position that Strauss is attributing to Locke – that is, the argument that reason must be laid aside in matters of faith. If it were possible for "clear intuitive knowledge," such as $2 + 2 = 4$, to be contradicted by God's word, then this would "subvert the principles, and foundations of all knowledge, evidence, and assent whatsoever: and there would be left no difference between truth and falsehood" (E IV.18.5, 692). Locke is not casting doubt on revelation, he is only arguing that no genuine revelation, properly understood, could ever contradict the truths of rational demonstration; if this could happen, it would be impossible to maintain any knowledge or belief of any kind whatsoever.

Appreciating that Locke's most urgent concern in the *Essay* was belief regulation rather than knowledge production is crucial to understanding his theory of moral consensus. The first step in building common ground among hostile religious groups is to get them to appreciate the nature of what they are arguing about. If each group understands its religious doctrine as knowledge, epistemologically equivalent to $2 + 2 = 4$, then it will look on any groups that oppose its doctrine as fundamentally irrational and deranged. "Nothing is so dangerous, as principles . . . taken up without questioning or examination; especially if they be such as concern morality, which influence men's lives, and give a bias to all their actions" (E IV.12.4, 642). If, however, groups can be made to see that their doctrines are beliefs rather than knowledge, the door will be opened for rational investigation of the difference between very certain, less certain, and uncertain beliefs. "We should do well to commiserate our mutual ignorance, and endeavor to remove it in all the gentle and fair ways of information; and not instantly treat others ill, as obstinate and perverse, because they will not renounce their own, and receive our opinions" (E IV.16.4, 660). In particular, Locke will spend a great deal of time and energy at the end of the *Essay* on religious belief, showing how the epistemological nature of religion, because it consists of beliefs, forces us to work carefully to separate true religious beliefs from false ones if we don't want to fall prey to fanaticism.

MORALITY, RELIGION, AND RATIONAL INQUIRY: THE ORIGIN OF THE *ESSAY*

The *Essay* is a strikingly personal document, in that it relates the story of Locke's intellectual development. He tells us the problems that brought him to write the book, explains his starting point (an analysis of the ideas a mind can form and the properties of those ideas), and lays out his reasoning through intermediate steps to the conclusion (a prescription for rational religious faith). Throughout the book he presents his ideas in the first person, as in: this seems wrong to me for the following reasons, I can think of no other explanation for this, and so on. We get not only Locke's ideas but the *story* of Locke's ideas; how he follows them from a starting point to an endpoint. Like Plato's *Apology*, Locke's *Essay* seeks to capture the reader's imagination by telling the story of the philosopher, although Locke's story is different from Plato's.

Locke appears to have begun work on the *Essay* in 1671. This foray into the world of technical philosophy – epistemology, metaphysics, semiotics, and so on – seems to have been remarkably abrupt. Before 1671, there is no evidence of his having had any interest in these areas of inquiry. While earning his bachelor's and master's degrees, he studied the minimum amount of this type of material that was necessary to meet school requirements, which were not very exacting. Oxford was still teaching the same rigid scholastic curriculum that had struck Hobbes, when he was subjected to it half a century earlier, as no more than a mountain of obscurely worded nonsense. Locke's reaction to it was about the same.[15] Between obtaining his master's degree in 1658 and beginning work on the *Essay* in 1671, Locke was an avid reader of books on medicine, natural science, travel, and theology, but if he read any more than a trivial amount of technical philosophy, no record of it survives.[16]

Then, in 1671 at the age of 39, Locke produced a short draft of the *Essay*. Later that same year he produced a longer and more sophisticated draft. He would continue to revise and refine the *Essay* for the rest of his life, through its first publication in 1689 and the publication of new editions – including some very significant changes and additions – up until his death in 1704 at age 72. The *Essay* was, in a very real sense, his life's work.

Why the sudden turn in 1671 to subject matter that he had rejected for so long as dreadfully boring and hopelessly confused? In the *Essay*'s introductory "Epistle to the Reader," Locke relates that he first became interested in the nature of human understanding after a discussion with some friends failed to produce any results; they found themselves "at a stand," unable to proceed (E Epistle, 7). Though Locke only hints at it in the *Essay*, a manuscript notation made later by another participant in that fateful conversation indicates that the subject being discussed was morality and revealed religion.[17] The discussion appears to have arisen because of a pamphlet war over religious toleration that was first touched off by the publication of Samuel Parker's *Discourse of Ecclesiastical Polity* in 1670. By then, Locke had been actively engaged with political controversies for several years as a member of Lord Ashley's household, and toleration was very much the issue of the moment. A discussion of toleration among members of his intellectual circle would have been of more than academic interest to him; arguing over toleration was becoming more and more a part of his professional duties.

Locke, who had opposed toleration as late as 1662, had written an essay in favor of it in 1667. That essay, however, did not delve into the philosophic foundations that implicitly supported its political stand. Its case stood primarily on the prudential advantages of toleration and the impracticability of coercion in religious matters.[18] Parker's case against toleration denied the premises upon which Locke's 1667 toleration theory was built, claiming that all government arose from the patriarchal authority of fathers and therefore should be viewed as an essentially paternal enterprise. This forced Locke to confront deeper philosophic questions in order to justify toleration. The notes he took on Parker's *Discourse* indicate that Locke realized he would have to turn to epistemology in order to refute Parker.[19]

According to Locke's telling of the story, the great discussion in his chamber went on for some time without coming any closer to a clear resolution of the issues at hand. He eventually realized that the discussion had failed because they had approached the subject in the wrong way. It dawned on him that they could only proceed if they first determined the scope of what it was possible to understand – what human minds "were, or were not, fitted to deal with." He therefore felt the group had a duty to investigate the nature of the understanding before continuing to discuss its original topic. He proposed this to the group, and the group, he recalls, readily agreed. Locke proceeded to "set down against our next meeting" his "hasty and undigested thoughts, on a subject I had never before considered" (E Epistle, 7). It was this project that eventually, after much revision and expansion of his original "undigested" ideas, produced the first 1671 draft of the *Essay*.

So if we take Locke's own word for it, Locke turned to epistemology and other technical areas of philosophy in 1671 because he had discovered, inadvertently, the reason scholars before him had devoted so much time and energy to these fields: namely, that moral, religious, and political thought depends upon them. We cannot understand what is right, or just, or holy, until we understand what "understanding" itself consists of. We cannot use language to express ideas about these things until we understand what language is and how it relates to the ideas we seek to express with it. And we cannot think about our relationship to the divine without implicating ourselves in debates over just what the divine is and just what we ourselves are. In short, rational inquiry into the most urgent areas of human life cannot go forward until rational inquiry has first understood rational inquiry itself, and settled the terms of its conduct. Thus, Locke fled from the complex obscurities of scholastic philosophy toward the practical social questions of morality, religion, and politics, only to discover that the intellectual road he was fleeing on led him right back to where he had started – the fields of epistemology, semiotics, and metaphysics. For all their abstractions, confusions, and mistakes, it turned out that those medieval scholars weren't quite so dumb after all.

The *Essay*'s analysis of the understanding, which appears so abstract and apolitical to twenty-first century eyes, is motivated by the desire to understand moral, religious, and political questions. Locke affirms repeatedly in the *Essay* that he feels a moral duty to undertake his study of the understanding in order to understand God and religious truth. The "main end of these enquiries" is "the knowledge and veneration of him, being the chief end of all our thoughts, and the proper business of all understandings" (E II.7.6, 131).[20] This does not mean that Locke takes a particular account of God as a prerequisite for rational inquiry; that would violate the very mission and purpose of the inquiry. Locke requires all moral, religious, and political knowledge and belief to pass the test of philosophic scrutiny. But Locke's desire to engage in such inquiry is motivated by a desire to discover the truth about God, whatever that is, so that Locke can properly know and venerate him.

As we will see in this chapter and the next, this settling of epistemological and other technical questions in order to prepare the ground for rational inquiry into religious, moral, and political questions serves as the foundation of Locke's theory of moral consensus in two ways. First, by showing the natural limits of rational inquiry on such questions, it proves that on some questions it is simply impossible to achieve a high level of certainty. Locke's two great opponents here are Cartesian innatism, which holds that God placed certain ideas directly into the mind, and scholastic essentialism, which holds that we can know and study the essences of physical and metaphysical things. Both of these doctrines seek to conduct rational inquiry beyond the natural boundaries within which such inquiry is possible. Second, by showing how rational inquiry, despite its limits, can confirm some questions with a high degree of certainty, it refutes religious enthusiasts who reject reason altogether, and lays the foundation for beliefs that all rational people – including members of different religions – can agree on. This chapter explains the first aspect of the *Essay*'s contribution to moral consensus; we will examine the second aspect in the next chapter.

What emerges from the *Essay* is a portrait of philosophy as a sacred calling, driven by urgent moral problems and devoted to a demanding standard of evidence. The *Essay* is about humanity's search for truth, especially its search for religious truth. At its heart is an argument, often left implicit but always present, in favor of a life devoted to that search.[21]

Locke does not use the word "philosophy" very often, but his distinction in Book Three between "civil" and "philosophical" language shows us what he meant by the term: careful and precise investigation of truth (E III.9.3, 476).[22] This is "philosophy" in the broadest sense, as the rational search for truth in any field, from politics and religion to biology and physics; its practitioners include far more than those we call "philosophers" in the current meaning of that term. A minister practices philosophy when he contemplates the meaning of a Bible passage, provided he is genuinely seeking its meaning with an open mind and not simply justifying a preordained interpretation. A naturalist practices philosophy when he dissects an animal, an economist practices philosophy when he analyzes interest rates, an explorer practices philosophy when he charts an uncharted region, a doctor practices philosophy when he develops a new treatment. Any life devoted to uncovering truths is in this sense a life of philosophy.

THE BEGINNING OF MORAL CONSENSUS: LIMITED SKEPTICISM

Careful attention to epistemology as the foundation of inquiry into other concerns was especially important for Locke because the political problems of his time were overwhelmingly epistemological. The old canon of knowledge in European society had disintegrated. Before the Reformation this canon had presented itself as a unified whole. There were no deep fissures in the European tradition; any appearance of contradiction or disagreement among its great texts was illusory. It was understood that such appearances of conflict were caused by our insufficient understanding, and would eventually be dispelled by the scholars who labored to reconcile the great works with one another.[23] The Reformation blasted this great vision of a philosophically unified tradition to smithereens. The ensuing disagreements over beliefs fueled two centuries of warfare across Europe, within and among fragmented religious orders.

In particular, historians have recovered an appreciation of the role religious belief played in causing the English Civil War. At one time the Civil War was typically viewed either through the Marxist lens, as a war between the aristocratic regime and the rising bourgeoisie, or through the lens of Whig history, as a war between the old monarchic order and the new parliamentary order. There are, of course, elements of truth in both these explanations, but the dominant causal factor in the war is now understood to be the struggle between Anglicans and Puritans for ecclesiastical legitimacy, and the political power that went with it.[24] The rise of the English bourgeoisie and the establishment of parliamentary supremacy were byproducts of what was, for the participants themselves, primarily a war over which church was the one and only authentic Christian church in England.

Wars over beliefs are, at bottom, wars over how and why people believe what they believe, and how and why they should believe what they ought to believe. In short, they are wars over epistemology. Locke thinks that such religious conflicts can be defused by careful examination of the nature and reliability of beliefs. Change the way people go about deciding what's true and what's false, and you can change religion, morality, and politics.

To some extent, Locke's purpose is to refute certain beliefs that cause conflict, such as Cartesian innatism, scholastic essentialism, and religious enthusiasm. These beliefs, as we will see, must be directly refuted because they distort the very nature of rational inquiry. However, beyond this, Locke is not primarily interested in disproving the particular claims made by competing groups, and still less in disproving the claims of one side in order to vindicate the other. The more important mission of the *Essay* is to show that large areas of human belief are unavoidably tainted with uncertainty. Once these boundaries are shown, "we should not then perhaps be so forward . . . to raise questions, and perplex our selves and others with disputes about things, to which our understandings are not suited" (E I.1.4, 45). Beliefs in areas that are beyond our natural capacities, such as those concerning the more obscure areas of metaphysics and theology, are not necessarily wrong, but they are necessarily uncertain.

The point is not so much to refute particular beliefs as it is to discount all beliefs on certain topics. Some especially dangerous beliefs must be directly refuted in order to clear the path for epistemological reform, but other than that, Locke steers clear of actually affirming or denying the particular beliefs of particular groups. To vindicate one side at the expense of another is merely to participate in cultural warfare. To show that no one has, or could possibly have, the one set of beliefs on a given topic that is definitely and beyond question correct is to defuse cultural warfare on that topic entirely.

This project of discounting uncertain beliefs is the first step in building moral consensus. If the motivating problem is to get hostile belief groups to join in a common political community, the first obstacle to overcome is each group's total certainty that on the controversial beliefs that divide the groups from one another, it has the one clearly right set of beliefs, which all the other groups deny only because they are fundamentally irrational. So long as each group is very certain that it has the obviously right answers on all the myriad topics addressed by its religious beliefs, each group will reject political union with the others. "Men presuming themselves to be the only masters of right reason, cast by the votes and opinions of the rest of mankind, as not worthy the reckoning" (E I.3.20, 80). Each group measures political legitimacy solely on the basis of its own particular beliefs. Moreover, most groups holding such beliefs will continually seek to gain exclusive control of the political community, in order to ensure that the false beliefs of the other groups are not imposed on them, and to impose their own true beliefs on those other groups.

Locke's path out of this impasse is to show, with an exhaustive analysis of the capacities of the human mind, that on some topics certainty is impossible. Locke tells us, as we have already recounted, that he began writing the *Essay* in the hope of solving certain disputes by showing what human minds "were, or were not, fitted to deal with." The content of controversial beliefs would matter less if people can be convinced to treat those beliefs as less than absolutely certain, on the grounds that the natural limits of the human mind make certainty on some questions impossible. People would be willing to accept the legitimacy of disagreement on those topics. "It would, methinks, become all men to maintain peace, and the common offices of humanity, and friendship, in the diversity of opinions" which is an inevitable consequence of our natural mental limits (E IV.16.4, 659). People would continue to hold controversial beliefs, of course, but these controversies would not cause political conflict if each group could be convinced not to behave as if its beliefs were so obviously correct that no one could legitimately question them. They could instead "commiserate" their "mutual ignorance" of the mysteries of the universe (E IV.16.4, 660). Once this discounting of controversial beliefs was achieved, the political community could then build moral consensus on the areas of belief that are capable of great certainty.

This last point is important. Locke is not a skeptic as such; he rejects skepticism as we understand that term, meaning the rejection of all attempts to find certain knowledge. To abandon altogether the hope of gaining any knowledge is a character flaw, a sign of intellectual laziness. "If we will disbelieve every thing, because we cannot certainly know all things; we shall do much-what as wisely as he, who would not use his legs, but sit still and perish, because he had no wings to fly" (E I.1.5, 46). Total skepticism is also impious, since it implies that God made us and our faculties in vain. We "have cause enough to magnify the bountiful author of our being, for that portion and degree of knowledge, he has bestowed on us, so far above all the rest of the inhabitants of this our mansion" (E I.1.5, 45).

Locke wrote that total skepticism was primarily a response to cultural fragmentation. People hold opinions "so various, different, and wholly contradictory; and yet asserted . . . with such assurance, and confidence," that anyone observing them "may perhaps have reason to suspect, that either there is no such thing as truth at all; or that mankind hath no sufficient means to attain a certain knowledge of it" (E I.1.2, 44). As groups competed for social dominance, they made wilder and wilder arguments to justify their own claims to divine authority. Those with excessive faith in their own capacity for knowledge claimed to understand mysteries of the universe that are beyond the reach of the human mind. "Thus men, extending their enquiries beyond their capacities . . . raise questions, and multiply disputes, which never coming to any clear resolution, are proper only to continue and increase their doubts, and confirm them at last in perfect skepticism" (E I.1.7, 47). Each group's arguments inevitably fail to persuade those who do not already share their beliefs, and they raise so many doubts and irresolvable disputes that the prospect of any knowledge begins to appear impossible.

Locke wraps up his critique of total skepticism by declaring that "our business here is not to know all things, but those which concern our conduct," that is, to "find out those measures" by which a person "ought to govern his opinions, and actions." A sailor need not have a line deep enough to "fathom all the depths of the ocean"; he only needs a line "long enough to reach the bottom, at such places, as are necessary to direct his voyage" (E I.1.6, 46). And the "first step" in uncovering measures to govern our conduct, Locke writes, is "to take a survey of our own understandings, examine our own powers, and see to what things they were adapted" (E I.1.7, 47).

What's more, even within this broad category of things that "concern our conduct," there are certain particular concerns in which Locke is especially interested: knowledge and belief on moral and religious matters. While Locke quotes II Peter 1:3 to the effect that God has provided "whatsoever is necessary for the conveniences of life, and information of virtue," he is clearly more interested in the latter than he is in the former. He writes of humanity that "how short soever their knowledge may come of an universal, or perfect comprehension of whatsoever is, it yet secures their great concernments, that they have light enough to lead them to the knowledge of their Maker, and the sight of their own duties" (E I.1.5, 45). Knowledge of God and of moral duty are our "great concernments."

Thus the *Essay* begins by laying out the fundamental connection between religion and morality – which are the most important and controversial measures by which we govern our conduct – and epistemology. People must learn to "be more cautious in meddling with things exceeding" the mind's "comprehension; to stop, when it is at the utmost end of its tether; and to sit down in quiet ignorance of those things, which, upon examination, are found to be beyond the reach of our capacities" (E I.1.4, 45). Starting with the fourth edition of the *Essay*, the title page quotes Ecclesiastes 11:5, a declaration of human ignorance: "As thou knowest not what is the way of the Spirit, nor how the bones do grow in the womb of her that is with child, even so thou knowest not the works of God, who maketh all things." We must understand which things we cannot possibly know or justifiably believe, so that we can restrain ourselves from trying to know or believe them.

The proper approach is to seek knowledge only of those things we actually need to know about. We must carry out a carefully limited search for truth. Locke's project of discounting beliefs is intended to prepare the reader for his next project, which is to show how beliefs can be formed with great certainty on some subjects despite the mind's natural limitations.[25] In particular, Locke believes that by carefully canvassing the powers of the human mind, we can have sufficient certainty of the boundaries of certainty itself. That is, we can effectively separate the areas where certain belief is possible from the areas where it isn't. Locke writes that his purpose is to "discover the powers" of the understanding, "how far they reach; to what things they are in any degree proportionate; and where they fail us," in order to persuade "the busy mind of man" to stay within its proper boundaries (E I.1.4, 44). For example, Locke wants us to be very certain that Cartesian innatism, scholastic essentialism, and religious enthusiasm are wrong. He also wants us to be very certain that it is possible for us to have very certain beliefs on moral and religious subjects despite the failures of the Cartesian, scholastic, and enthusiastic epistemologies. For this reason, Locke's project of discounting beliefs would be best described as one of "limited skepticism."

That Locke's skepticism was limited rather than total is an important reason that it had revolutionary political consequences. If no beliefs were certain enough to serve as a guide for political action, then there would be no grounds for demanding social change. In such a case, there would be no reason for challenging the beliefs and traditions already governing society, since it cannot be established that any other beliefs are any more reliable. This is why skepticism usually produces a conservative political agenda. Locke's innovation is to present a limited skepticism that rejects most claims to knowledge or justifiable belief, but also claims that some knowledge and justifiable belief is possible, including, crucially, that we can be sufficiently certain in our beliefs about where the limits of our certainty lie. If we can be sure, or sure enough, of which things we can justifiably believe and which we cannot, then we can justify a program of political reform: we can demonstrate the illegitimacy of existing knowledge and belief claims and demand political changes to reflect our ignorance of things we cannot know or justifiably believe. And if we can also be sure that we have the right to use violence to protect ourselves from those who do not respect the limits of human knowledge, we can even justify a revolution. Paradoxically, if people are authorized to use violence for far fewer purposes than had previously been believed, for Locke this justified violence – a revolution – to establish that doctrine as government policy.

INNATE IDEAS AND TRADITIONALISM: THE PROBLEM OF BLIND BELIEF

The opening chapter of the *Essay* lays out Locke's fundamental concern, which is the problem of conducting rational inquiry in an environment of religious conflict, dominated by groups whose only interest is to promote their respective doctrines.[26] He writes that he knew he needed to write the *Essay* when he realized that until we "take a survey of our own understandings . . . and see to what things they were adapted," rational inquiry "began at the wrong end, and in vain sought for satisfaction." Locke is impressed from the very beginning of these philosophic explorations with the chaotic fragmentation of the West's received wisdom in his age. So many competing religious schools and creeds are vying for authority that it has become impossible for an intelligent bystander to believe that any of them has the certain possession of truth that it claims to have. As we have seen, for Locke these factions "raise questions, and multiply disputes" to such a degree that they "are proper only to continue and increase their doubts, and to confirm them at last in perfect skepticism" (E I.1.7, 47). This fragmentation of religion into competing denominations had given rise to a seemingly endless succession of wars and persecutions over the previous two centuries.

For Locke, religion is *the* political problem. Where Socrates encountered conflicts between the Homeric religious tradition and the emerging new class of politicians, poets, and sophists in classical Athens, Locke encounters conflicts of different religious authorities with one another. There were poets and sophists in Locke's time, to be sure, but except insofar as they influence religion he rarely bothers with them, in the *Essay* or elsewhere. To him they are a minor annoyance compared to the major problem of religious communities that will not live in peace with one another. There is also the enormous upheaval of Enlightenment natural science, but for Locke any discord arising from this upheaval would have to be considered essentially a religious dispute between theological doctrines that accept natural science and those that reject it (see E IV.12.11–12, 646–7).

Religion presents a complex political challenge because religious doctrine, while unobjectionable in itself, is susceptible to blind and irrational devotion. The real problem, at least as far as social problems are concerned, is not that people have different religious beliefs but that they tend to hold some beliefs blindly, refusing to allow unrestricted rational examination of them. Locke writes of the "artificial ignorance, and learned gibberish" that prevail "in these last ages, by the interest and artifice of those, who found no easier way to that pitch of authority and dominion they have attained" (E III.10.9, 495). The impenetrably obscure discourse of each religious denomination serves as a barrier against rational inquiry by outsiders. "What have the greatest part of the comments and disputes, upon the laws of God and man served for, but to make the meaning more doubtful, and perplex the sense?" (E III.10.12, 496)

Of course, Locke has no illusions that people have either the ability or the inclination to constantly reexamine even their most important beliefs. Most beliefs most of the time are held unreflectively, and in itself this does not create a problem. "It is unavoidable to the greatest part of men, if not all, to have several opinions, without certain and indubitable proofs of their truths" (E IV.16.4, 659). The important thing is not that every belief be constantly examined, but that every belief be potentially subject to examination whenever such examination becomes necessary. And this examination must be genuine, unrestricted examination, not the false examination of blind believers who seek only to vindicate what they already believe. A person might not often engage in such rigorous examination, but he should be prepared to do it in crisis moments, such as when a belief causes a violent conflict. A person cannot "for every opinion that he embraces, every day... examine the proofs" (E IV.16.2, 658). However, it is enough if people "have once with care and fairness, sifted the matter as far as they could," and "after as full and exact an enquiry as they can make, they lay up the conclusion in their memories, as a truth" (E IV.16.1, 658). Blind belief, by contrast, is left unexamined even in crisis moments – indeed, it tends to be left unexamined especially in crisis moments. This is why it causes so much violent conflict.

For Locke the problem of conflict between blindly held religious beliefs is not simply a problem of his own time, it is a universal problem. People have a natural impulse to set up institutions whose goal is to preserve and perpetuate their beliefs, especially by imparting them to the young at an impressionable age (see E I.3.22, 81 and E IV.7.11, 598–603). People also tend not to question the beliefs they are taught as children, especially religious beliefs (see E I.3.23, 82 and E IV.20.9, 712). Thus, in all places and times, there is an enormous institutional bias for blind belief over open inquiry.

But, although Locke does not point this out in the *Essay*, this problem was especially acute in his own place and time. For over a thousand years the Catholic Church had stood as the supreme ecclesiastical authority in Europe. Its claim to be the authentic voice of the Holy Spirit, and thus the sole legitimate church, was recognized throughout the continent. But England in the seventeenth century no longer recognized that claim, and naturally each religious group tried to insert itself into the social and political void where Rome's authority had once stood. England was long accustomed to recognizing only one church as the exclusively true and authentic church, so the great political question seemed to be which church would play this role in post-Reformation England.

To buttress their claims to exclusive legitimacy, each group put forward arguments in favor of its particular theology and practices. These arguments purported to show the truth of each church's doctrine in its entirety. One of Locke's major purposes in the *Essay* is to show that the arguments of all these groups were based on epistemological principles that stymied true rational inquiry. Each group, knowingly or unknowingly, used bad epistemology to insulate its doctrine from effective rational examination. The product of this insulation was that each group's members believed in its doctrines blindly. Only by conducting genuinely unrestricted rational inquiry can we hope to distinguish truth from falsehood, knowledge from belief, and more certain belief from less certain belief.

Book One of the *Essay* argues against the doctrine of innate ideas, one of the most important epistemological devices by which blindly held beliefs were being shielded from rational examination. "Innatism" held that God had implanted certain ideas and principles in the human mind.[27] For example, two of the principles that were held by some in Locke's time to be innate were the principle that the same thing cannot both exist and not exist, and the principle that one should do unto others as one would have others do onto oneself.

Above we have characterized innatism as "Cartesian" because Descartes is by far the most well-known and influential advocate of innatism. Locke had a keen understanding of Descartes's works, and followed some of the controversies among Cartesian philosophers.[28] In taking up the argument against innate ideas, Locke joins a small number of intellectuals who opposed Cartesian innatism, such as Samuel Pufendorf and, ironically, Samuel Parker, whose attack on toleration in his *Discourse of Ecclesiastical Polity* appears to have been the proximate cause of Locke's original foray into epistemology.[29]

However, to understand the full import of Locke's assault on innatism we must appreciate how widespread the doctrine was in Locke's time. Far from being confined to Descartes and the circle of professional theorists who followed him, innatism was a widespread doctrine. Virtually everyone in England at that time, ruling Anglicans and dissenters alike, held that vital religious knowledge of some kind (of God's existence, or our duty of charity to others, or of some other kind) came to us through ideas or predispositions that were placed directly into the mind by God.[30] Locke's opposition to innatism was therefore held by many to be dangerous – so much so that the *Essay* was being publicly attacked even before it was published, because it was known (from an abridgement of the *Essay* published the previous year) that the *Essay* would contain an argument against innate ideas. Critics argued that denying innate ideas was tantamount to denying the existence of God and other immaterial spirits. This reaction was so immediate and so strong that Locke felt it necessary to respond to it in the Epistle to the Reader, pointing out that anyone who actually reads the *Essay* will see that it supports the existence of God and other spirits, and in a manner more philosophically sound than that provided by innate ideas (see E Epistle, 10).

Since the doctrine of innate ideas has long since passed out of favor, most Locke scholars (other than those who specialize in epistemology, and including even many of them) give Locke's attack on innatism little attention. This contrasts sharply with the obvious importance Locke himself placed on the issue. Locke devoted an entire book of the *Essay* to innate ideas, even in the face of what he must have known would be fierce opposition from both dominant and dissenting theological schools. No other single epistemological issue is singled out for such explicit and sustained attention in the *Essay*. And the attack on innatism is placed at the very front of the book, where the reader will encounter it before anything else. Given the intense opposition this was sure to invite, why did he do it?

We can get an idea of why Locke placed such a high priority on refuting innatism from one of the arguments he makes against it. He raises a variety of objections to innate ideas: for example, that if these ideas were truly innate we would be aware of them from birth, and we would also be incapable of doubting them. Of these objections, one stands out as offering some explanation of why innatism matters so much to Locke: that the doctrine of innate ideas, when it extends to moral principles, blocks rational examination of beliefs. "There cannot any one moral rule be proposed," he writes, "whereof a man may not justly demand a reason" (E I.3.4, 68).[31] For Locke the debating of reasons for moral principles is the essence of moral life, because "nothing can be so dangerous, as principles . . . taken up without questioning or examination; especially if they be such as concern morality, which influence men's lives, and give a bias to all their actions" (E I.4.24, 101). But those who believe in innate moral principles "worship the idols that have been set up in their minds," and "stamp the characters of divinity, upon absurdities and errors" (E I.3.26, 83). This idolatry metaphor suggests that innatism is impious, since it attributes to God principles that may be false. At the very least, innatism is dangerous to rational inquiry into moral and religious questions, because it places certain principles beyond the scope of argument. Innatism cripples the mind's ability to find truth.

It is this moral obstructionism, Locke believes, that makes the doctrine of innate moral principles attractive to the keepers of doctrine in each religious group. Locke's explanation for the popularity of innatism is that it had long been useful to "those who affected to be masters and teachers," who wish "to make this the principle of principles, that principles must not be questioned" (E I.4.24, 101). Locke puts such emphasis on refuting innatism because it is an effective tool for those who would control the beliefs of others for their own purposes. Locke draws a connection between his opposition to innatism and his overall project in the *Essay*, which is to expose and destroy the intellectual influence of those who use the authority of one or another tradition to block rational inquiry. "I have not made it my business, either to quit, or to follow any authority in the ensuing discourse: truth has been my only aim," he writes. "For, I think, we may as rationally hope to see with other men's eyes, as to know by other men's understandings. So much as we ourselves consider and comprehend of truth and reason, so much we possess of real and true knowledge" (E I.4.23, 100–1). To accept a principle on authority from another rather than on the basis of rational argument does not advance a person's understanding, even if the principle in question is a true one. "Such borrowed wealth, like fairy-money, though it were gold in the hand from which he received it, will be but leaves and dust when it comes to use" (E I.4.23, 101).

Thus, at the conclusion of his case against innatism, Locke also declares his opposition to traditionalism, the taking of opinions on the authority of a tradition. Locke returns to this theme at the end of the *Essay*, where he presents an argument that tradition is not an accurate indicator of truth. A credible eyewitness's report is "a good proof," but a credible witness's report of what another credible witness reported to him "is weaker," and so on, such that "in traditional truths, each remove weakens the force of the proof: and the more hands the tradition has successively passed through, the less strength and evidence does it receive from them" (E IV.16.10, 664).[32] This does not mean we should stop studying history. Locke writes, "I think nothing more valuable than the records of antiquity: I wish we had more of them, and more uncorrupted" (E IV.16.11, 664). Rather, Locke is warning us to always examine the moral and theological claims of a tradition on their own merits. Locke writes of traditionalists who urge that "propositions, evidently false or doubtful enough in their first beginning, come by an inverted rule of probability, to pass for authentic truths; and those which found or deserved little credit from the mouths of their first authors, are thought to grow venerable by age, and are urged undeniable" (E IV.16.10, 664). If we accept moral and religious truth on the authority of others, "men have reason to be heathens in Japan, Mahumetans in Turkey, Papists in Spain, Protestants in England, and Lutherans in Sweden" (E IV.15.6, 657). In short, religion would have nothing to do with truth.

Innate ideas, and traditionalism more generally, stand in the way of moral consensus. In a society divided between competing traditions – Anglican, Puritan, Catholic, and others – appeals to the authority of tradition had dangerous social consequences. "If we could see the secret motives, that influenced the men of name and learning in the world, and the leaders of parties," Locke writes, "we should not always find, that it was the embracing of truth for its own sake, that made them espouse the doctrines, they owned and maintained" (E IV.20.17, 719). Indeed, "the parties of men, cram their tenets down all men's throats, whom they can get into their power, without permitting them to examine their truth or falsehood" (E IV.3.20, 552). Persons whose beliefs are under the sway of traditionalist authorities are essentially enslaved, because "he is certainly the most subjected, who is so in his understanding" (E IV.20.6, 711). It is not hard to see what the results of this mental enslavement would be in a society where multiple traditions were competing for dominance; each group would seek to tighten its epistemological hold on its followers, in order to consolidate its political base in hopes of defeating other groups.

Only the power of reason can break such slaves loose from the belief-domination practiced by the gatekeepers of traditions. Reason is present in every human being – indeed, for Locke rationality is an essential part of the definition of what makes a being a human being (see E III.11.16, 516; see also T I.30, 24 and T II.8, 118). Reason can therefore liberate any person who chooses to exercise it from the shackles of traditionalism. "The subject part of mankind, in most places, might... with Egyptian bondage, expect Egyptian darkness, were not the candle of the Lord set up by himself in Men's minds, which it is impossible for the breath or power of man wholly to extinguish" (E IV.3.20, 552). Rational argument can demonstrate the bankruptcy of innatism and other epistemological doctrines by which traditions are shielded from rational inquiry. Once these barriers are down, rational inquiry can show which beliefs are very certain, which are less certain, and which are uncertain or demonstrably false.

All this is a necessary prerequisite for moral consensus. In refuting innatism, Locke seeks to replace an old way of thinking about moral discourse with a new, more epistemologically sophisticated way. Under the old way, moral discourse was presumed to take place within the confines of certain moral assumptions – the supposedly innate ideas – that were not themselves open do debate. These assumptions formed a foundation of preexisting moral knowledge that all persons would share. Locke's way also relies on assumptions in the foundations of discourse, of course. As we will see in the next chapter, he assumes that logic and immediate intuition produce accurate knowledge. But in Locke's case the assumptions are all epistemological rather than moral. Locke takes nothing for granted about God or moral law; this is the meaning of his statement that "there cannot any one moral rule be proposed, whereof a man may not justly demand a reason." There is no preexisting moral knowledge – that is, no moral knowledge is shared in common until we make it so by discussing, debating, and persuading. By demanding and debating moral reasons, rather than appealing to divisive cultural and religious traditions, we can find common moral ground in beliefs justified to all through reason.

Furthermore, as we will see in more detail in the next section, Locke strives to rely only upon assumptions that are absolutely necessary to the building of any theory of epistemology. If we are to avoid total skepticism, we must construct some kind of account of how we can legitimately know and believe certain things. Any assumption that is genuinely necessary to constructing such an account is therefore justified. All else is fair game for rational inquiry; it seems to be Locke's goal to take nothing for granted except that which must be taken for granted before inquiry can proceed.

FINDING EPISTEMOLOGICAL LIMITS, PART I: IDEAS

Once he has disposed of the epistemological roadblock posed by belief in innate ideas, Locke begins in earnest the project of exploring the capacities and limitations of the human mind. Book Two describes in detail the one thing of which we have direct, unmediated awareness – our ideas. By showing the limits of our ideas, Locke shows some of the limits of our understanding; we cannot reason adequately about things if we cannot form adequate ideas of them. For example, God is infinite and our minds are finite, so we cannot form an idea of God that adequately conveys the nature of his being, and thus there is much about God that is forever beyond our understanding.

To understand how Locke's account of human ideas performs this function of discounting controversial doctrine, we must begin with just what an "idea" is to Locke. All other awareness is mediated through ideas, because ideas are, on Locke's definition, the only thing of which we can be aware. "Idea," Locke writes, is "that term, which I think, serves best to stand for whatsoever is the object of the understanding when a man thinks" (E I.1.8, 47). For example, technically I am not aware that there is a computer in front of me right now, I am aware of the idea of a computer being in front of me. Objects have the power to create ideas of themselves in our minds, and these are what we perceive. Later, in Book Four, Locke will argue that we can be sure the ideas in our minds reflect an objective reality and are not just dreams or hallucinations (see E IV.4.4, 563–4; and IV.11.4–7, 632–4). But the distinction between our ideas and the objects that create them is far from a mere technicality. It plays an important role in Locke's analysis of theological knowledge, because the limits of our mental powers prevent us from forming adequate ideas of metaphysical objects such as God and other spirits.

Locke's epistemology of ideas was novel, and this novelty has caused confusion in both his time and ours. Descartes had used the word "ideas" in a manner similar to Locke's use of the term, but had not done so consistently.[33] Locke's consistent pursuit of the large philosophic consequences of this concept of "ideas" was unprecedented, and many of Locke's readers fail to see just what Locke is doing with this concept.

Locke's critics, from that day to this, have complained that Locke does not adequately specify what "ideas" are.[34] These demands for a more specific definition miss the whole point of Locke's epistemology. Anything the mind is capable of being aware of is an idea. In defining the term, Locke writes that he has "used it to express whatever is meant by phantasm, notion, species, or whatever it is, which the mind can be employed about in thinking" (E I.1.8, 47). A more specific definition would not be possible without assuming some knowledge of how the mind works, and discovering such knowledge is the purpose of the *Essay*. If the *Essay* began by implanting an epistemological theory into its definition of "ideas," the ensuing epistemology would be built upon unjustified assumptions, just like innatism. The definition of "ideas" at the beginning of the *Essay* is extremely broad because the rest of the *Essay* consists, in a sense, of filling in what this definition doesn't tell us.

To be sure, by the end of the *Essay* there is much we still don't understand about ideas. But then, as we have already seen, that is part of Locke's point: "our business here is not to know all things, but those which concern our conduct." That Locke does not strive to tell us everything that could possibly be said about ideas is a virtue, not a failing; Locke commits himself only to positions he can justify with arguments.

What was truly new about Locke's epistemology, and required a new language of "ideas," was that Locke systematically and consistently separated the objects of our thoughts (that is, ideas) from the act of thinking itself.[35] It was necessary for Locke to make such a separation in order to show the limits of the human mind. For example, we can think about God but we cannot do so with perfect accuracy because God is infinite and our minds are finite, and we can discuss this problem more easily by comparing God as he actually exists to our mental idea of God. The former is infinite but the latter is finite, and is therefore an inadequate representation of the former. Locke's novel vocabulary of "ideas" is nothing but a verbal shortcut for talking about this distinction between objects as they exist in reality and objects as they appear in our minds, with emphasis on how frequently the latter is inadequate to the former.

FINDING EPISTEMOLOGICAL LIMITS, PART II: THE SOUL

Book Two outlines the limits of our knowledge, especially knowledge of moral and metaphysical subjects, by examining our ideas and demonstrating their limits. On Locke's account there are only two sources of ideas. Ideas arising from the senses Locke calls "sensation"; these are distinguished from "reflection," the mind's ideas concerning its own operations (thinking, willing, believing, and so on), which arise from introspection rather than the senses (E II.1.1–5, 104–6). In Book Two, Locke provides a lengthy exposition of the various types of ideas in each of these categories and the ways in which they combine to form more complex mental constructs. We need not be detained here by every part of that system; in the interests of space, we will look only at the arguments that most directly support Locke's theory of moral consensus.

Book Two pays particular attention to our idea of the human soul, which is not as far beyond our capacities as God, but is still subject to significant epistemological problems. Locke's analysis of what we can know about the soul is an important example of his project of discounting beliefs that cause political and social conflict. Locke takes on the complex and controversial systems of metaphysical philosophy built up to allegedly prove the soul's immortality, showing that they cannot stand up to scrutiny. This is not a merely academic problem. Because each religious group was putting itself forward as the sole legitimate church, doctrinal disputes of this type were deeply divisive and contributed to violent conflict. Instead of fighting over such questions as who has the correct metaphysical account of the soul, Locke would have us accept that we cannot prove exactly how eternal life occurs, and simply rely on the Bible's revelatory promise of eternal life. The mere fact that eternal life has been promised to us is the only thing that concerns our conduct. The metaphysics of eternal life are irrelevant to actually achieving it.

For Locke the soul is a unique theological problem. Many aspects of its nature are unfathomable to us; Locke refers to "this ignorance we are in of the nature of that thinking thing, that is in us, and which we look on as our selves" (E II.27.27, 347). But our ignorance of the soul is not total, nor even as great as our ignorance of most metaphysical objects. There is much more that we don't know about God, for example, than about our own souls. In our very self-awareness and capacity for physical action, we have direct experience of the soul, which is not the case for any other metaphysical object. "Whilst I know, by seeing and hearing, etc. that there is some corporeal being without me . . . I do more certainly know, that there is some spiritual being within me, that sees and hears" (E II.23.15, 306). As we will see, because our experience of the soul is direct and immediate, for Locke the soul is our strongest epistemological connection to the metaphysical.

At the outset of Book Two, after defining what "ideas" are, Locke detours into a lengthy argument against the Cartesian doctrine that the soul always thinks. Descartes had argued that because the essence of the soul is thought and the soul must continually exist, the soul must continually think. He made this argument in order to show that his account of the soul was consistent with the soul being immortal, which in his view required that it continually exist. He explained periods of time during which we are not aware of ourselves thinking, such as dreamless sleep, by hypothesizing that we actually do think at those times but don't remember it later.

Of course, Locke cannot prove that this does not happen. Nonetheless, Locke takes a full ten sections (long paragraphs) to show, with a variety of arguments, the absurdity of Descartes's hypothesis. For example, he argues that Descartes's position implies that each body actually contains two different people unaware of one another, the one who thinks while the body is awake and the one who thinks while the body is asleep. He also points out that if Descartes is right, our thoughts during sleep ought to be more rational than the thoughts we have while awake, freed as they are from the irrational influence of bodily passions. Obviously this is not the case.

However, Locke's most important argument against Descartes, which he makes at some length at the outset and repeats near the end, is simply to point out that it is merely a hypothesis. " 'Tis doubted whether I thought all last night, or no; the question being about a matter of fact, 'tis begging it, to bring, as a proof for it, a hypothesis, which is the very thing in dispute." If we were allowed to follow this question-begging method, "one may prove anything," such as "that all watches, whilst the balance beats, think, and 'tis sufficiently proved, and past doubt, that my watch thought all last night." If a hypothesis is "not a self-evident proposition," we must "prove it by reason." Since this hypothesis is clearly not self-evident and cannot be proven by logical deduction from self-evident principles, "we can be no farther assured, than experience informs us" (E II.1.10, 109). But experience is precisely what we lack, since the hypothesis concerns things we don't remember. The hypothesis therefore not only cannot be proved true, it cannot even be shown to be probably true, as there are no arguments of any kind to be made for it.

Locke's dissection of the hypothesis that the soul always thinks is an excellent model of how his epistemology lays the foundation of moral consensus by discounting beliefs without disproving them. The first way in which this passage serves as a model is in its demand for proof. No moral or religious propositions may legitimately be taken for granted. A hypothesis must be proven with a rational argument consisting of some combination of self-evident principles, deduction from such principles, and the evidence of human experience. If it cannot be proven in this manner, it remains a hypothesis and cannot be accepted as truth. "The most that can be said" for this hypothesis, Locke writes, is that it is "possible that the soul may always think," to which Locke responds that "it is possible, that the soul may not always think; and much more probable" (E II.1.18, 114–15).

The second way in which this passage is a model for the *Essay's* epistemology is in its separation of questions that "concern our conduct," as Locke put it in the *Essay's* opening chapter, from questions that are unnecessary and beyond our concern. It is enough that "there is something in us, that has a power to think" (E II.1.10, 109). This tells us what we need to know, which is that "the perception of ideas" is to the soul "what motion is to the body, not its essence, but one of its operations," and there is no point in asking useless questions like whether this operation is performed at all times (E II.1.10, 108).

This is not to say that all questions concerning the soul are unimportant; the question of whether the soul exists is of great importance. In a passage added in the second edition of the *Essay*, Locke pointedly responds to what appears, from his phrasing, to have been an accusation against him that he found particularly offensive: "Men in love with their own opinions, may not only suppose what is in question, but allege wrong matter of fact. How else could any one make it an inference of mine, that a thing is not, because we are not sensible of it in our sleep? I do not say there is no soul in a man" (E II.1.10, 109). Whether human beings have souls is a question of supreme importance, but to deny extravagant and useless hypotheses about the soul, such as Descartes's, is not to deny the soul's existence.

Locke epistemologically separates proven hypotheses from unproven ones, highly probable hypotheses from improbable ones, and important epistemological issues from unimportant ones. By doing this, he makes it possible to build upon our agreement on the questions that are both important and subject to investigation with great certainty without trying to force one another into agreement on the unimportant, uncertain questions. People who agree that human beings have souls need not fight to the death over what the "essence" of the soul is, or other such matters. Such questions may seem to be of momentous import to a person who is keen to justify the whole doctrinal structure of a particular religious group or philosophy, but in the light of Locke's epistemology such questions appear as no more than intellectual ephemera. Once a person knows that he has a soul, the important matter for him is what he must do to get it into heaven. Why should he care whether it thinks while he's asleep, when that question is beyond all possible investigation and nothing of importance hangs upon it?

Book Two returns to the subject of the soul on two other occasions, in Chapter 23, "Of the Complex Ideas of Substances," and again at more length in Chapter 27, "Of Identity and Diversity." Chapter 27 was added in the second edition of the *Essay*, the same edition that saw the addition of Locke's heatedly defensive comment, noted previously, that he does not deny the soul's existence. It appears to have been a serious concern of Locke's in the second edition to prove that his epistemology of limits, while it might discount beliefs about the soul that many people hold dear, does not threaten or discount belief in the soul's existence or the promise of eternal life after death.

To understand the account of the soul in the later chapters of Book Two, we must first quickly review some of what Locke says about metaphysical ideas. Because we can add finite units together without limit $(1 + 1 + 1 + 1 + 1 + 1 \ldots)$ we can form an idea of infinity, but only as a negative – as the absence of a beginning or ending. We do not really understand the nature of infinity because our minds are finite and cannot contain an infinite idea. This obviously has implications for thinking about God. "When we apply to that first and supreme being, our idea of infinite, in our weak and narrow thoughts, we do it primarily in respect of his duration and ubiquity; and, I think, more figuratively to his power, wisdom, and goodness, and other attributes" (E II.17.1, 210). That is, we are capable of knowing that there is an eternal and infinitely large God, but our understanding of what that means is sharply limited, and our understanding of what it means that God is infinitely powerful, wise, good, and so on is even more limited. We cannot know "how these attributes are in God," although we can know that he does in fact possess them (E II. 17.1, 210; see also E II.17.17, 219–20 and II.17.20, 221–2.). Similar limitations apply to "finite spirits," immaterial beings other than God, such as angels. We can only think about them in terms of the limited ideas we receive from sensation and reflection (see E IV.3.17, 548; and IV.11.12, 637).

Some of these limits on metaphysical knowledge do not apply, however, to the human soul, which is a distinct kind of finite spirit. We are fully capable of perceiving our own faculties of thinking and motivity, which Locke identifies as the most direct source of our knowledge of the soul. "By putting together the ideas of thinking, perceiving, liberty, and power of moving themselves and other things, we have as clear a perception, and notion of immaterial substances, as we have of material" (E II.23.15, 305). The insensibility of the soul is no impediment to our having knowledge of it. We may not be able to sense it, but we perceive it by reflection when we perceive that we can think and move.

The soul is, for Locke, our most immediate proof that the metaphysical world exists. Locke holds that consciousness would be impossible without some metaphysical intervention, so consciousness proves the existence of metaphysical objects. "It is for want of reflection, that we are apt to think, that our senses show us nothing but material things. Every act of sensation, when duly considered, gives us an equal view of both parts of nature, the corporeal and spiritual" (E II.23.15, 305–6). Our knowledge of the soul, gained by reflecting on our power of sensation, is no less legitimate simply because we cannot sense the soul directly. Locke spends eleven sections of Chapter 23 showing that many of the epistemological problems we face regarding knowledge of the soul are equally present when we think about the body (see E II.23.22–32, 305–14). For example, we don't understand the soul's power of "exciting of motion by thought," but then "we are equally in the dark" regarding physical bodies' power of "communication of motion by impulse" (E II.23.28, 311). Locke wraps up by observing that it is "no more a contradiction, that thinking should exist, separate, and independent from solidity; than it is a contradiction, that solidity should exist, separate, and independent from thinking" (E II.23.32, 314).

Unlike most philosophers of his time, Locke is willing to entertain the possibility that the soul is material, that is, that our material brain thinks without a metaphysical aspect. As he explains in Book Four, when he returns to this subject in a chapter titled "Of the Extent of Human Knowledge," he allows this possibility in keeping with his larger goal of setting epistemological limits. "It becomes the modesty of philosophy, not to pronounce magisterially, where we want that evidence that can produce knowledge," and besides, "all the great ends of morality and religion, are

well enough secured, without philosophical proofs of the soul's immateriality" (E IV.3.6, 541–2). He says that it seemed very probable to him
that it is immaterial, and occasionally he writes as if the immateriality of
the soul were certain, but ultimately he takes the position that it falls just
short of true certainty (see E IV.3.6, 539–43; II.23.32, 314; and II.27.27,
347).

However, he holds firmly that matter could never gain consciousness
on its own; "cogitation" is "not within the natural powers of matter"
(E IV.3.6, 542).[36] Therefore, only God could make matter think. So one
way or the other, consciousness proves that something metaphysical exists. The soul tells us, first and most clearly, that something immaterial
exists in the universe, whether it is the soul itself or a higher power that
made matter think. The soul is our most immediate epistemological connection to the realm of the divine.

In the *Essay* Locke's main concern regarding the soul is its immortality. This is a consequence of Locke's refusal to foreclose the possibility
that the soul is material; he must show that this position does not call
into doubt the continued existence of the soul after death. The major
logical argument for the immortality of the soul in the history of western
philosophy, going as far back as Plato's *Phaedo*, is that the soul must be immortal because mortality is a consequence of the breakdown of material
structure, and immaterial objects like souls (so goes the argument) do
not break down.[37] This is why so many people in Locke's time thought
that we must hold that the soul is immaterial in order to believe that
it is immortal. But in Locke's epistemology we cannot absolutely know
from reflection alone whether the soul is material or immaterial. Thus,
the Platonic argument for the soul's immortality is foreclosed, and Locke
must show us an alternative way in which we can be satisfied that life after
death does occur.

Life after death is an issue of crucial importance, because it "concerns
our conduct" deeply. Locke argues repeatedly in the *Essay* and the *Reasonableness* that the afterlife is the only possible basis for morality, because
rewards and punishments after death are the only thing great enough to
give people a convincing reason to act morally in cases when immorality
would promote their earthly interests. Only "the rewards and punishments of another life, which the almighty has established, as the enforcements of his law, are of weight enough to determine the choice, against
whatever pleasure or pain this life can show" (E II.21.70, 281; see also
I.3.5–6, 68–9; II.21.55, 270; II.28.8, 352; II.28.12, 356–7; IV.12.4, 642;
and R 245, 182–5).[38] In an allusion to Paul's epistle to the Corinthians,

Locke declares that "if there be no prospect beyond the grave, the inference is surely right, *Let us eat and drink*, let us enjoy what we delight in, *for tomorrow we shall die*" (E II.21.55, 270).[39]

So, for morality to succeed, belief in the rewards and punishments of the afterlife must be strong enough to overcome our natural inclination to seek out worldly happiness, which is a hefty job. The arguments of unassisted human reason on this point, such as Plato's and Descartes's, are just too uncertain (see R 245, 182–5).[40] Instead of indulging in extravagant metaphysical speculations such as Descartes did, we ought to simply rely on the firm promise of an afterlife conveyed in divine revelation. "The state we are at present in, not being that of vision, we must, in many things, content our selves with faith and probability." Belief in an afterlife doesn't require extravagant metaphysical systems, so "'tis not of such mighty necessity to determine one way or the other" the metaphysical nature of the soul. Locke declares that "it is evident, that he who made us at first begin to subsist here, sensible intelligent beings . . . can and will restore us to the like state of sensibility in another world," but it appears that this is only "evident" through revelation (E IV.3.6, 542).

Locke's critics – in both his time and ours – have often done violence to his position on the materiality of the soul in order to use it against him.[41] Locke has been accused of denying the afterlife because he denies that the soul is necessarily immaterial. On one level, these depictions are unfair because Locke holds that the immateriality of the soul is almost certain. He just isn't willing to pronounce magisterially that it absolutely must be so. But the larger point is that Locke shows us that we can believe in the soul and the afterlife without even addressing this question. That renders the existence of the soul and the afterlife more certain, not less, because it cuts them loose from their traditional dependence on a body of metaphysical thought.

One of the greatest achievements of the *Essay*, which had a profound effect on philosophy and theology in the emerging modern world, is precisely its separation of the concept of an afterlife, and hence of morally responsible personhood, from the need for any particular account of the metaphysics of the soul. The chapter Locke added in the second edition on "Identity and Diversity" argues that life after death does not depend on the immortality of a metaphysical object ("the soul"), but on the preservation of our identity, specifically our consciousness (see E II.27.9, 335 and E II.27.18, 341). So long as we believe that God will maintain our consciousness of ourselves after death in some way, we need not inquire any further into how this will be done. This allowed moral reasoning to proceed on the premise that people will live on after death and be held responsible for their actions without moral theorists having to get bogged down in bickering over speculative metaphysics.

Locke's treatment of the soul demonstrates how his epistemology supports moral consensus. Locke's doctrine of eternal life through our conscious identity rather than through the soul as such renders the metaphysics of the soul moot, allowing Locke to sidestep a morass of doctrinal problems. This relieves social conflict because it drastically reduces the scope of philosophical agreement necessary to maintain society. We need not achieve consensus, for example, on the merits of Descartes's argument that the soul always thinks, or on a hundred other arguments that might be made about the metaphysics of the soul. For Locke, the important thing is that we know, because revelation tells us, that we will live on after this life and be rewarded or punished for our actions here. This is the only question about life after death that will "concern our conduct." Further questions, such as those about the metaphysics of the soul, need not be raised. If people learn not to ask questions that need not be asked and cannot be answered, they will have less cause for dispute over beliefs.

FINDING EPISTEMOLOGICAL LIMITS, PART III: ESSENCES

The *Essay* devotes a great deal of attention to a critique of the scholastics – theologians, based in the universities, who traced their intellectual lineage back to Aquinas in the thirteenth century. The scholastics saw themselves as engaged in an ongoing project to construct a comprehensive body of Christian knowledge. For Locke, the scholastics represented a serious obstacle to moral consensus because of their conviction that they possessed a special, privileged access to knowledge, in that they were the only ones who understood the enormous and extremely complex body of thought they had built up over the previous four centuries. Locke had to refute this claim in order to build moral consensus, which is based on the premise that no one has special access to knowledge.

Locke proved that the scholastic body of thought was not the achievement the scholastics held it to be, using the same method he applied to Descartes's account of the soul: he showed that, because of the limits of the human mind, no one could possibly achieve the knowledge that the scholastics claimed to have achieved. The scholastics claimed to be able to explain things in terms of their essences. As Roger Woolhouse puts it, according to the scholastics "one would have 'scientific understanding'

of something, say gold's being malleable, if one had demonstrated the
necessity of its being so by deriving it, from first principles, as the conclusion of certain syllogistic arguments that had to be constructed according
to strict canons of form." Crucial to this process was "a definition ... of the
'form' or 'nature' or 'real essence' of the kind of thing whose properties
were under investigation."⁴² Locke shows that no one can possibly have
the kind of knowledge about essences that the scholastics claimed to have.
This defuses social controversies arising from claims about essences.

Today Locke's confrontation with the scholastics – with its technical
arguments over "essences" and "substances" and "forms" and the "cor-
puscularian hypothesis" and so on – may seem hopelessly abstract and
obscure. Since the metaphysical essentialism of the scholastics has long
since been slung into the dustbin of history, it may be difficult for us to
see why these arguments were of such pressing importance. But Locke
scholars have identified a number of ways in which scholastic essentialism
had important social and moral consequences.

Perhaps the most obvious of these was how essentialism denied legitimacy to the Enlightenment's pursuit of natural science. Locke writes
that scholastic essentialism had "very much perplexed the knowledge of
natural things" (E III.3.17, 418). The advancement of natural science was
a moral and political issue at the time; Edwin McCann reminds us that
"the nature of body was one of the most hotly contested issues in the
seventeenth century. Its treatment not only defined who was a partisan
of the scientific revolution and who was not, but served to distinguish different factions among the revolutionaries."⁴³ McCann's choice of terms
like "partisan" and "revolutionaries" is appropriate, because Enlightenment science was as much a political movement as an intellectual one.
This was in part because scholasticism had "retained its stranglehold
on the curricula of the universities."⁴⁴ Advancing natural science required the creation of new institutions, such as the Royal Society, to support the necessary scientific work; this, in turn, required political support
for Enlightenment science.

Nicholas Jolley has shown that Locke had another, more directly moral
reason for taking on essentialism. Locke describes the tendency of essentialist thinkers to treat powers or faculties (for example, the stomach's
ability to digest) as though they were real, existing objects ("the digestive
faculty"). He writes that he is particularly concerned with the intrusion of
this tendency "into discourses concerning the mind," producing discussions of "the intellectual faculty, or the understanding ... and the elec-
tive faculty, or the will" (E II.21.20, 243–4). According to Locke, treating

the will in this way leaves us unable to adequately answer the question of whether human beings have what is usually called "free will." Locke wants us to realize that "the will is nothing but one power or ability" of human beings, and the real question is not "whether the will has freedom," but rather whether human beings have freedom (E II.21.16, 241). Unfortunately, we have no room for a full treatment of Locke's arguments concerning human will and freedom.[45] The important point is that Locke thought essentialism's tendency to treat powers as real objects prevented a clear understanding of human will and freedom, because it replaced the crucial question of whether human beings are free with the nonsensical question of whether their wills are free. As Jolley writes, Locke believed that "moral responsibility and divine justice require a robust conception of human freedom."[46] Essentialism as applied to the human mind makes a hash of our understanding of human freedom, and is hence a danger to moral responsibility and divine justice.

Jolley also shows how Locke's confrontation with essentialism is necessary to his larger philosophical mission of discounting controversial beliefs by laying out the limits of certainty in human ideas. Essentialism recognized no hard and fast distinctions between different areas of inquiry in terms of the level of certainty that was possible in each one. Thus, essentialists would claim that their conclusions in the field of metaphysics were as certain as their conclusions in the field of mathematics. Given the socially controversial nature of metaphysical issues, such as the nature of the soul, the implications for moral consensus are apparent: people must be shown that their metaphysical systems of thought are not so obviously true that anyone who disagrees with them is simply irrational or dishonest. One of Locke's goals in refuting essentialism was to show why some areas of thought (such as mathematics and ethics) were capable of greater levels of certainty than others (such as metaphysics and natural science) because of the greater role played by probabilistic reasoning in the latter areas.[47] Jolley sums this up concisely when he observes that while Book III of the *Essay* is presented as a treatment of language, much of it is "occupied with metaphysical and epistemological issues concerning classification [of essences] which can be treated independently of the role of language."[48]

However, the most important way in which Locke's refutation of essentialism serves his goal of promoting moral consensus is in its implications for natural law. As Francis Oakley documents, essentialism was the philosophical basis of the "intellectualist" tradition of natural law thought, which grew out of Aquinas' thought and was upheld by the scholastics.

This tradition sought "to understand the order of the created world . . . as a participation in a divine reason that is in some measure transparent to the human intellect." Oakley writes that intellectualism was "embedded" in "the whole metaphysics of essences" because it held an "understanding of the universe as an intelligible organism penetrable by a priori reasoning precisely because it was itself ordered and sustained by an indwelling and immanent reason."[49] All of which is to say that the predominant view among the scholastics was that the natural law could be figured out simply through rational analysis of the natural world, and this was so precisely because the scholastics believed in essentialism. Locke rejects the intellectualist school of natural law in favor of the "voluntarist" tradition, which grew out of William of Ockham's thought. This approach stresses God's will as the basis of moral obligation, rather than divine intelligence immanent in the physical world.

In Chapter 5 we will see at greater length why essentialism gives rise to natural law doctrines that exacerbate social conflict. The essentialists believed that their body of thought provided insight into the nature of the physical world. This, in turn, put them in communion with the divine reason that was immanent in that world. They therefore believed themselves to know better than others did what was good, right, just, and so on, on the basis of their essentialist metaphysics. On this view, true moral insight was restricted to those few who had mastered the large and complex body of essentialist thought. This claim to have a special, privileged access to moral knowledge is inconsistent with moral consensus. We will explore more implications of this doctrine in Chapter 5, when we look at the moral and political consequences of Locke's voluntarism.

Locke's critique of scholastic essentialism is based on an analysis of how knowledge and beliefs are formed. Book Two concludes with a chapter on the association of ideas. This chapter was not added until the fourth edition of the *Essay*, but it provides an excellent summary of how the epistemology of ideas laid out in Book Two works in practice. The mind forms knowledge and beliefs by perceiving the "natural correspondence and connection" between ideas (E II.33.5, 395). To learn is to mentally associate two or more ideas that are naturally connected. In some cases the connection between ideas is self-evident. We perceive that the ideas of "two," "four," addition, and equality are self-evidently connected in such a manner that two plus two equals four, so we learn to associate them in that way. In other cases we require the use of judgment to perceive the connection between ideas. For example, I learn how to turn on the computer by perceiving that the idea of pressing the power button is connected with the idea of the computer turning on. The connection between the ideas of pressing the power button and the computer turning on is not self-evident. I perceive it by repeated observation, and I must exercise judgment to determine whether I have observed accurately, and whether I have observed a sufficient number of instances to make a correct association between the ideas.

As Locke himself says at the end of Book Two, now that he has laid out what our ideas are we would expect him to move on to the question of how the mind uses them. Though Locke does not say as much, this is just what the *Essay* has been building toward; a proper understanding of how the mind uses ideas would give us a basis for discerning reliable knowledge and beliefs. But Locke does not provide this yet. Instead, he explains, there is another source of misunderstanding in addition to our failure to appreciate the limits of human ideas that must be dealt with first.

This other source of misunderstanding is the tendency to associate ideas without realizing that one is doing so, or without realizing the real reasons one is doing so. Through "chance" or "custom," it happens that "ideas that in themselves are not at all of kin, come to be so united in some men's minds, that 'tis very hard to separate them" (E II.33.5, 395). These unexamined assumptions can lead a person to hold absurd ideas even when the evidence against them is obvious, and "when this connection is settled and while it lasts, it is not in the power of reason to help us" (E II.33.13, 398).

The culprit behind these unconscious associations of ideas is faulty use of language; hence, Book Three, "Of Words." Failure to understand language is as much an impediment to moral consensus as failure to understand ideas. Locke sees "wrong and unnatural" associations of ideas as the major source of "the irreconcilable opposition between different sects of philosophy and religion." People have a tendency to allow their leaders to build fantastic doctrines upon false associations of ideas, and will swallow those doctrines blindly so long as the underlying false associations are not exposed. Fanatic devotion to false opinions is often blamed on self-love, miseducation, and prejudice, all of which often do play important roles, but "that reaches not the bottom of the disease, nor shows distinctly enough whence it rises, or wherein it lies" (E II.33.3, 395; see also II.33.1–3, 394–5). The underlying cause of religious and philosophic conflict is unconscious association of ideas that ought not to be associated, made possible by mistakes in our use of language. All of which leads Locke to the conclusion that "were the imperfections of language . . . more thoroughly weighed . . . the way to knowledge, and, perhaps, peace too," would "lie a great deal opener than it does" (E III.9.21, 489).

Words, properly understood, signify only ideas in the mind of the speaker, but we normally take for granted two additional correspondences. The first is a correspondence between the idea associated with each word in the speaker's mind and the idea associated with that word in the listener's mind, "for else they should talk in vain, and could not be understood" (E III.2.4, 406). The second is the correspondence of this shared idea to something in reality, "because men would not be thought to talk barely of their own imaginations, but of things as really they are" (E III.2.5, 407). If a person speaks to another person about dogs, they both assume that they have the same idea of what a "dog" is, and that this idea accurately reflects a real type of animal.

These two premises are necessary conditions for any kind of communication, and Locke does not seek to eliminate them. Rather, he wants us to examine them so that they will be sound premises rather than unexamined assumptions. Because words can "almost as readily excite certain ideas, as if the objects themselves . . . did actually affect the senses," and because "by familiar use from our cradles, we come to learn" words "very perfectly, and have them readily on our tongues," we often speak without paying attention to whether our words really do correspond to what others take them to mean and to reality. In such cases, we speak not thoughtfully, but rather "as parrots do," without really understanding what we say (E III.2.6–7, 407–8).

This view of language – that words signify ideas in the mind of the speaker that correspond (or ought to correspond) to reality, and that the purpose of language is to convey those ideas from speaker to listener – is characteristic of Enlightenment epistemology. It takes for granted that each text, spoken or written, has one genuine or authentic meaning, namely the meaning the author intended to convey. The common root in the word "authentic" and "author" embodies this view; the authentic meaning of a text is the meaning it has in the mind of the author. This stands in stark contrast to the theory, dominant among professional linguists today, that language is a sort of public-domain game in which everyone participates in the creation of meaning, everyone is therefore an author, and there is no such thing as an inauthentic meaning.

For Locke the author-oriented view of language is not problematic. He does not seem to see any need to defend it. This is probably explained by his critique of total skepticism, which we discussed previously. Our inability to have perfect knowledge of everything doesn't justify giving up on having any knowledge at all. Just as we don't give up on walking with our legs because we cannot fly with them, the presence of some uncertainty in any effort to figure out the authentic meaning of a text doesn't justify the conclusion that it does not in fact have an authentic meaning. Indeed, our daily experience of successful communication (defined as the successful conveyance of ideas from author to audience) refutes this. How can we justify the belief that talking and writing don't convey our intended meaning to others, given that every day the people we speak and write to respond in ways that indicate otherwise? And if we do believe that language doesn't convey meaning from speaker to listener, why bother to speak at all?

The two assumptions on which language relies – that the idea associated with a word in the speaker's mind corresponds to the idea associated with that word in the listener's mind, and that this idea also corresponds to reality – imply two ways in which language can fail. Language is badly used when it is used in such a way that one or both of these assumptions does not hold. This is most likely to happen, Locke argues, when we discuss ideas that are especially complex, when our ideas do not refer to a real object, when our ideas refer to a real object that is difficult to perceive, or when we try to discuss things whose essences we cannot know. "In all these cases, we shall find an imperfection in words," in their relationship to our ideas (E III.9.5, 477). Moral ideas, which we will discuss in the next chapter, are particularly susceptible to the first two of these problems. Natural and metaphysical ideas are particularly susceptible to the last two.

Applying this analysis, Locke presents an extended critique of scholastic philosophy on the grounds that it takes as real distinctions that are matters of arbitrary definition. Scholastic philosophy tried to justify knowledge of essences based on a taxonomic system of genera and species. The theory was that if we deduce what qualities are essential to each genus (such as "mammal") and species (such as "dog"), and we know which genus and species each object belongs to, we can know the essence of every object.

These "essences" were taken to have theological – and hence political – implications. The system of genera and species was not intended merely to serve as a helpful guide to prevent people from mistaking their dogs for rocking chairs. It was understood as providing accurate insight into metaphysical reality. Each species of thing is metaphysically different from each other species of thing, in that it partakes of a different essence.

Once we understand the essence of each species – from inanimate objects and animals to human beings, angels, and God – we can construct a doctrine of how to understand each species and treat it according to its essential nature. Thus, the question of what genus and species a given thing belongs to will affect our moral and theological understanding of that object's place in the world and our proper treatment of it. Obviously this has political implications, insofar as the rules that people follow for how to treat certain kinds of things are determined politically.

Locke argues that, due to the limited power of human sensation, we can never actually have any knowledge of the so-called "essence" of any real object. Locke introduces the term "real essence" to refer to the essence of a real object.[50] An object's real essence is the substance that causes the object to have the properties that make it what it is. "By this real essence, I mean, that real constitution of any thing, which is the foundation of all those properties, that are combined in, and are constantly found to co-exist" in every object of a given type (E III.6.6, 442; see also III.6.2, 439). Unfortunately, we cannot sense the process by which the "real constitution" of an object, which Locke also calls its "substance," gives rise to its particular "properties" or qualities, because the only thing we sense about an object is its qualities. "Our faculties carry us no farther towards the knowledge and distinction of substances, than a collection of those sensible ideas, which we observe in them," which is "remote . . . from the true internal constitution, from which those qualities flow" (E III.6.9, 444). For that reason, whenever we group objects by type we do so according to their sensible qualities, not their real essences. Our ideas of types or species of things do not correspond to real essences. This problem applies to all real objects, even our own bodies.

Return to the example of the computer in front of me, which we used to illustrate Locke's definition of "ideas." As we noted, I don't sense the computer itself, I sense the idea of the computer. I have this idea of it because of my senses of sight, touch, and hearing, so I can only sense the computer's appearance, solidity, texture, sound, and so on. I cannot sense the substance that creates those sensations. Therefore I cannot know what essence or essences constitute it. Is the monitor made from one kind of essence, the keyboard another, and the CPU another? Is the monitor all one essence, or does the screen have one kind of essence and the casing another? Or is each of these itself made up of multiple essences? If I declare "screen" to be one type of thing and "casing" to be another type, this is only because they have different sensible qualities; I have no idea whether they have different essences, or whether there is really only one essence that is particular to each of them. Indeed, for all I know, each individual particle of matter in the computer might have a completely different kind of essence. Or it might be that physical matter has no distinct kinds of essences at all; the universe might be made up of an unfathomably large number of identical particles of matter that all have the same essence but can join together in a variety of different ways. None of these questions can be answered, because the process by which substances create sensible qualities is not itself sensible.

Locke held that the genera and species examined and theorized about by the medieval scholastics are not real categories existing in nature. They are only labels – labor-saving mental devices created by human beings to make communication easier. When we think about "genera and species, and their essences," we are not thinking about "things regularly and consistently made by nature" with "real existence in things"; our ideas of genera and species are "an artifice of the understanding" (E III.5.9, 433–4). We cannot sense what substance makes a dog have the sensible qualities that it has. We can only invent a word, "dog," to designate all objects with that particular set of qualities. This makes it easier to talk about dogs, but it doesn't change our ignorance of what makes a dog have those particular qualities. "There is not so contemptible a plant or animal, that does not confound the most enlarged understanding" (E III.6.9, 444). The study of genera and species is therefore not the study of the essences of things but merely the study of the definitions of words. "The species of things to us, are nothing but the ranking [of] them under distinct names" (E III.6.8, 443). What makes an animal a dog is not that it possesses an essential dogness but that it conforms to a widely accepted definition of the word "dog."

It is tempting to think of Locke's theory of insensible "essence" and "substance" as roughly equivalent to Kant's theory of the unknowable "thing-in-itself," but in fact Locke's theory does not go that far. By "substance" Locke had in mind the microstructure of objects, what we now call the atomic structure, that gave them their observable properties. For Locke, this microstructure was unknowable not because it was inherently impossible for sensation to perceive it but because human sensation was just not powerful enough to do so. He writes that the "minuteness" of the "insensible corpuscles" that make up matter "keeps us in an incurable ignorance of what we desire to know about them" (E IV.3.25, 555–6). It seems likely that if Locke had lived in a time when powerful microscopes could make the atom visible, he would have said we can have some knowledge of substances after all. But that would probably not damage his theory in any meaningful way, because it has turned out that seeing the atom is not enough – we have discovered subatomic structures, and sub-subatomic structures, and so on. Our power to perceive microstructure, though it will no doubt continue to grow, will always be finite, so no one can ever be sure where this sequence ends. Thus, even the ability to perceive the atom does not give us complete knowledge of substances. Also, we now know that knowledge of microstructure cannot tell us everything Locke thought it would tell us if we could know it. The physical universe is more complicated than it appeared to be in 1689, and knowing the atomic structure of an object does not necessarily tell us everything there is to know about its observable properties.

Unfortunately, we come to mistakenly think that our ideas of genera and species are ideas of real essences. And since real particular objects do not always conform to our systems of classification, such systems run into countless difficulties when applied to the real world. "Because we cannot be certain of the truth of any general proposition, unless we know the precise bounds and extent of the species its terms stand for, it is necessary we should know the essence of each species, which is that which constitutes and bounds it" (E IV.6.4, 580; see also E IV.6.4–6, 580–2). General propositions relying on knowledge of real essences are therefore mired in uncertainty.

To take one example that has momentous political implications, Locke asks which creatures are "men" and which are not – "men" referring not to males but to human beings. At various points he brings up fetuses (E III.10.22, 503; and IV.7.17, 607), blacks (E IV.7.16, 606–7), and "changelings" (that is, children born with severe defects; E IV.7.17, 607; and IV.4.14–16, 569–73), as well as reports, which he appears to have taken perfectly seriously, of the existence of mermaids (E III.4.12, 447), people who look and act like humans but have hairy tails, and people among whom the men do not have facial hair and the women do (E III.6.22, 450). Locke notes that there are some who would deny the status of "men" to each of these. There are, of course, clear and distinct differences between people who are or are not black, fetuses, changelings, mermaids, hairy-tailed, or born with inverted sex characteristics. But Locke argues that the classification of some of these as "men" and others as "not men" cannot be guided by any knowledge of the real essences of these things, or of the real essence of humanity. For all practical purposes, the essence of humanity is whatever we define the word "humanity" to mean, since the abstract idea of the species "human" does not refer to any particular real object but is rather, like all abstract ideas, a mental construct.

This is not to say that we cannot have any reliable beliefs about human beings and the proper way to treat them, or that we can justify any belief about human beings by manipulating the definitions of words. We will see in the next chapter how reliable beliefs, including moral beliefs such as those governing how human beings are to be treated, are properly justified in Locke's account. The point here is that we cannot appeal to the "essence" of human beings in order to adjudicate which particular creatures are human rather than something else.

The rejection of scholastic essentialism is a necessary part of Locke's theory of moral consensus. Theories of genera and species result in the building of moral and political doctrines based on what is taken to be knowledge of the real essences of various things, especially human nature. But those real essences are unknowable, and thus the moral and political doctrines built on these theories go astray. This, Locke writes, is why "the whole mystery of genera and species, which make such a noise in the schools . . . are, with justice, so little regarded out of them" (E III.3.9, 412). The scholastics were perhaps the ultimate insulated belief group, protecting its doctrines from rational inquiry with an enormous wall of complex and erudite theory, all of it based on the false assumption that we can know real essences. "By amusing the men of business, and ignorant, with hard words, or employing the ingenious and idle in intricate disputes, about unintelligible terms, and holding them perpetually entangled in that endless labyrinth," the scholastics seek to maintain "authority and dominion" (E III.10.9, 495).

The scholastics still dominated the university curriculum, as Locke himself knew quite well from having had to trudge through the study of scholastic theory in his Oxford days. Like Hobbes before him, Locke knew there was no hope for social peace so long as the universities maintained an educated class that thought of itself as the keepers of a theory that explained the mysteries of the universe. Such people could not help but also see themselves as the guardians of the human race itself. Clearly this belief would have dangerous political ramifications. To build moral consensus, Locke had to convince the scholastics that they did not have privileged knowledge, that they were subject to the same epistemological barriers as everyone else.

EPISTEMOLOGICAL LIMITS AND MORAL CONSENSUS

Locke was drawn to epistemology because he realized that epistemological questions had to be settled first before theological and political questions could be settled. His epistemology of limits begins the task of building moral consensus in two ways. First, it refutes belief in innate ideas, traditionalism, and other obstacles to open rational examination of beliefs. This is a necessary precondition of moral consensus because when groups think that their beliefs have descended directly from the finger of God into their minds, or treat their cultural tradition as if adherence to it were obligatory, they treat people with beliefs different from their own as willfully irrational rather than as potentially reasonable people who have reached different conclusions than they have. This contribution to moral consensus is summed up in Locke's statement that "there cannot any one moral rule be proposed, whereof a man may not justly demand a reason" (E I.3.4, 68). The point here is not that every rule by which we live must be justified by rational argument – such a task could never be completed. The point is that when people come to disagree about moral rules, rational argument is the only legitimate method by which to settle such disagreements. Cultural groups must recognize reasonable differences as being reasonable, and allow them to continue to exist, if all are to live together in peace.

The second way Locke's epistemology of limits supports his theory of moral consensus is by showing that we cannot establish highly certain beliefs on some topics, and that we need not reach agreement on those topics in order to establish sufficient agreement on the matters that are of greatest concernment. "Our business here is not to know all things, but those which concern our conduct" (E I.1.6, 46). For example, we cannot know with great certainty, and we need not reach agreement upon, the intricacies of the metaphysics of the human soul. The important thing for our conduct is that human beings will live on after death and be rewarded or punished for their actions, and all cultural groups already agree on this. Similarly, we cannot know what the essence of a thing is, but we need not know its essence in order to know how to treat it. The important question about each thing is what God's law says about it, not its essential nature. Locke sought to establish this so that controversial philosophies of essentialism would no longer cause social unrest by providing a flawed basis for moral theory, and so that those who had mastered its arcane details would not be able to claim a special access to knowledge, and thus an entitlement to a superior social status.

Locke's epistemology of limits does not serve as the foundation of his political theory. Refuting innatism and traditionalism, and showing the limits of our knowledge in such matters as the soul and essences, are all important projects for moral consensus, but they are not specifically political projects. This is why Locke did not incorporate them into his political theory, a point to which we will return in Chapter 7. Rather, the purpose of Locke's epistemology is to persuade people to distinguish between questions on which we can or cannot reach highly certain conclusions, and to be willing to brook reasonable disagreement on questions that are not of fundamental importance. Modesty about knowledge claims is essential to shaping the kind of society in which moral consensus can take place.

But while encouraging this epistemological modesty is not a political endeavor, it is just as important for moral consensus as properly laying the foundations of the political order. Overly ambitious knowledge claims fueled much of the political and social conflict of Locke's time, both by creating disagreements over beliefs and by artificially inflating the perceived importance of those disagreements. A society of people who believe that God and morality are at stake in every trivial quibble over the nature of the soul or the essences of natural objects will be beset by social discord and constantly in danger of civil war. By forcefully and systematically drawing the distinction between topics on which we can or cannot have certainty, and also the distinction between topics on which we do or do not need social agreement, Locke defuses the primary sources of social conflict.

3

"The Candle of the Lord"

Locke's Rational Faith

The *Essay Concerning Human Understanding* provides the epistemological basis of moral consensus in two discernable steps. We have seen how Locke uses his epistemology of limits to discount controversial beliefs in order to clear the ground for more reliable beliefs. Having done this, Locke must now show how reliable beliefs can be justified even within the natural limits of the human mind. These beliefs must be made out with clear and convincing arguments that are not undermined by the epistemological problems Locke has described in the *Essay*.

Only beliefs made out in this manner can serve as a basis for moral consensus, because only such beliefs will be convincing to members of all religious groups. The stronger the epistemological ground on which an argument is built, the wider a potential audience it will have. An argument made out with the most highly certain rational arguments will appeal to virtually all people, and can thus serve to unite fragmented religious factions. By adhering to very high epistemological standards, Locke shows how to build arguments that have the power to unite a divided society.

The *Essay* is an almost perfect bridge between the medieval and the modern. Like the medievals, it is relentlessly concerned with the problems of theology and religious belief, treating them as the defining problems of human life. But its foundational emphasis on epistemology, particularly its rationalistic separation of highly reliable beliefs from less reliable or unreliable beliefs, places it squarely within the modern world. To some this might suggest that the *Essay* is bound to its time, speaking only to those who lived during the transition period between the medieval and modern eras. Part of our purpose here is to show that the *Essay*'s reconciliation

of the medieval concern for theology and the modern concern for epistemology is precisely what makes the *Essay* – and the rest of Locke's works,
insofar as they are built upon the *Essay*'s epistemology – so uniquely time-
less. It incorporates the dominant concerns of both eras, tempering the
excesses of each one by subjecting it to the critique of the other. In the
Essay, Locke seeks to reconcile reason and faith rather than simply sub-
ordinating one to the other, an ambitious aspiration that will speak to
people in all historical situations.

For Locke there is simply no disjunction between reason and faith. At
all times, he writes, "reason must be our last judge and guide in every
thing," because if reason does not examine the truth of our persuasions
"by something extrinsical to the persuasions themselves; inspirations and
delusions, truth and falsehood will have the same measure, and will not
be possible to be distinguished" (E IV.19.14, 704). We must use reason
if we hope to accurately perceive not only "truth" in general but also
"inspirations" in particular; this is the ultimate foundation of Locke's
attempt to reconcile reason and faith. Human beings "have light enough
to lead them to the knowledge of their maker, and the sight of their
own duties," because God has given them reason, which allows them to
think for themselves (E I.1.5, 45). Reason is "the candle of the Lord,"
the instrument God has given us to illuminate his truth (for example,
E IV.3.20, 552 and R 231, 162).[1] We must not believe anything without
allowing reason to examine it; to do otherwise is to impiously neglect the
one reliable tool God has given us to distinguish true teachings, including
true religious teachings, from false ones.

This is a profound teaching that has been widely misunderstood. It
has been taken as an embrace of, or at least an invitation to, deism –
the rejection of belief in revelations from God in favor of investigation of
God exclusively through natural reason (that is, reason unassisted by
revelation). It has also been taken as leading inevitably to the rejection, or at least serious discounting, of all religious beliefs, and consequently to the compartmentalization of politics and religion – the re-
moval of religious beliefs from political discourse on the grounds that
they are too doubtful on Locke's own terms to be part of shared political
discourse.

When Locke says that "reason must be our last judge and guide in every
thing," he goes on to say: "I do not mean, that we must consult reason,
and examine whether a proposition revealed from God can be made out
by natural principles, and if it cannot, that then we may reject it." That
epistemological rule would amount to deism. Instead, Locke writes that

reason must be our last judge and guide in that "consult it we must, and by it examine, whether" the proposition in question "be a revelation from God or no" (E IV.19.14, 704).

The difference between those two epistemological approaches – demanding that the content of revelation be confirmed by reason, and demanding only that the authenticity of revelation be confirmed by reason – is crucial. The former rule wipes out revelation entirely, by rendering it redundant with natural reason. Any revelation that might be accepted under this rule would, by definition, be unnecessary since it would only show what natural reason had already established. The latter rule, by contrast, allows us to accept things on God's authority without confirming them by natural reason, but maintains natural reason as the gatekeeper of revelation. Natural reason examines each alleged instance of revelation to determine whether or not it is a genuine revelation from God.

It is true that deism and compartmentalization are historically connected to Locke's philosophy. Locke's philosophic career was followed by the flourishing of deism and, eventually, by the rise of compartmentalization, as a goal if not as a fact. Some of Locke's contemporary critics predicted this outcome as a result of his philosophy.[2] But this connection between Locke and deism was not inevitable. It was caused by the later misappropriation of Locke's ideas by deists with an agenda very different from Locke's. Deist epistemologists reproduced most of Locke's epistemological system, but with a crucial (and unacknowledged) change: Locke's theistic rule that reason must judge the authenticity of revelation but not its content was replaced by the deistic rule that reason must judge both the authenticity and the content of revelation. The distinction between Locke's epistemology and that of the deists who followed him was quickly lost, with two unfortunate consequences – Locke was saddled with a false reputation for promoting deism, and Locke's argument that faith and reason should coexist as helpmates, rather than faith being simply subordinated to reason or vice versa, faded from view in the intellectual world.

In reviewing Locke's religious epistemology, this chapter will show not only that Locke rejected both deism and the casting of epistemological doubt upon religion, but also that these outcomes are fundamentally incompatible with Locke's philosophic system. They ought to be understood not as natural outgrowths of that system but as corruptions or distortions of it. The historical details of the deists' misappropriation of Locke for their own ends have been laid out elsewhere, and it is beyond the scope of this book to recount that story.[3] Our purpose here is to show that Locke's works themselves not only do not lend themselves to deism, but in fact tend strongly against it.

We must understand that deism is not invited by Locke's epistemology in order to see how that epistemology supports his political theory of moral consensus. Locke seeks to regulate faith with reason not in order to discount faith, but precisely because faith is so indispensably important to all aspects of human life. It has to be properly regulated because it is the matter of greatest concern to us. By having reason regulate faith, Locke seeks to encourage true beliefs about God and discourage false ones, and to distinguish between more and less reliable beliefs. A faith regulated by reason can provide highly reliable beliefs upon which the community can build moral consensus, while allowing for legitimate disagreement in matters of faith that are less reliable. This vision of a rationally regulated faith is the *Essay*'s greatest achievement. But if Locke's epistemology had the effect of discounting faith, that achievement would be worthless, and the *Essay* would have produced almost nothing of practical value. Moral consensus would be impossible, as the distinction between reliable and unreliable beliefs on which it is built would result in an insufficient amount of reliable belief for the community to build upon.

REASON AGAINST TRADITIONALISM AND ENTHUSIASM

Locke appeals to reason as "our last judge and guide in every thing" in order to counter the dangerous and divisive influence of two other sources of belief: traditionalism and religious enthusiasm. Both of these had been the source of much social conflict and outright bloodshed over the previous two centuries. Locke hopes that reason, which is shared in common among all human beings, might serve as a unifying agent against the highly particularizing forces of traditionalism and enthusiasm.

Appeals to the authority of tradition became more and more dangerous as the western tradition, which had been understood as a coherent entity up through the Middle Ages, fragmented after the Reformation into many competing religious orders. Tradition had become a point of social conflict rather than a point of social consensus. English society did share a certain amount of common cultural heritage, not least a common language, and such bonds are not to be dismissed as insignificant. But it was universally understood in that society that religion was more important than any other concern – this, too, was a cultural heritage common to all. And in matters of religion, English society in the seventeenth century simply did not share a common culture or tradition. There was no one "Christian tradition" in that time and place; there were multiple Christian traditions. Any appeal to "Christian tradition" had to start by clarifying just which one was being appealed to, and would inevitably divide rather than unite the political community.

The problem here is not tradition as such. Locke does not think reason can replace tradition. In the *Essay* he points out that it would be impossible to organize all of human life according to rational rules. A person seeking to do this would be so busy setting out rules for himself that he would have no time to do anything else! Locke certainly does not expect lives of philosophy from "the greatest part of mankind, who are given up to labor, and enslaved to the necessity of their mean condition; whose lives are worn out, only in the provisions for living. These men's opportunity of knowledge and enquiry, are commonly as narrow as their fortunes; and their understandings are but little instructed, when all their whole time and pains is laid out, to still the croaking of their own bellies, or the cries of their children" (IV.20.2, 707). Even those whose situations allow for more philosophizing will have to accept some things from others. "Indeed there are millions of truths, that a man is not, or may not think himself concerned to know"; in such cases, where no urgent concerns are at stake, "there 'tis not strange, that the mind should give it self up to the common opinion" (IV.20.16, 717).

What is necessary, in Locke's view, is to rationally regulate our beliefs on those particular matters that are most important. Locke calls these the matters of greatest "concernment," and the distinction between matters of great or little concernment runs throughout the *Essay*.[4] Presumably, tradition will be the overwhelming influence in areas of life that are of less than utmost concernment and thus need not be rationalized.

The paramount matter of "concernment" for Locke is religious belief, with politics running a close second. As we saw in the last chapter, he calls knowledge of God and of moral duty the "great concernments" of all humanity (I.1.5, 45). Anyone familiar with his political writings will be aware that he also thought politics to be a matter of much concernment. These areas of life must be rationalized because they are too important for us to blindly trust in the tradition that we happen, by random chance, to have been born into. Even in religious and political matters, Locke subjects only the most fundamental or constitutional questions to rational analysis and leaves people to their own devices with regard to the less important matters. But in the most important concerns in the areas of religion and politics, rational analysis is indispensable. Each person must reflect on his own morality rather than just passively adopting moral opinions from others. Otherwise, "men have reason to be heathens in Japan, Mahumetans in Turkey, Papists in Spain, Protestants in England, and Lutherans in Sweden" (E IV.16.6, 657). To adopt opinions because others hold them is to adopt them without regard to the truth of their content, which Locke regards as immoral (see esp. E II.21.70, 281).

Locke stresses that reflection upon religion and morality could be and must be engaged in even by those laborers whose lives are mostly dedicated simply to earning a living. In the passage quoted previously he described these same laborers as "enslaved to the necessity of their mean condition" and whose "opportunity of knowledge and enquiry, are commonly as narrow as their fortunes." But he goes on to insist "that God has furnished men with faculties sufficient to direct them in the way they should take, if they will but seriously employ them that way, when their ordinary vocations allow them the leisure. No man is so wholly taken up with the attendance on the means of living, as to have no spare time at all to think on his soul, and inform himself in matters of religion" (IV.20.3, 708).

What Locke opposes is not the existence of traditions, but what is sometimes called "traditionalism" – the treating of tradition as though it were capable of authoritative pronouncements, such that even in matters of great concernment we must obey tradition over our own reason because of its authority. Tradition is not a legitimate basis of authority for Locke because the mere fact that something is traditional does not show a moral justification for it. This is both a positive and normative limitation on tradition: if an individual concludes that a tradition is immoral, not only will he not follow it, he will in fact have a moral duty not follow it. If tradition is treated as authoritative, then adherents of different traditions can have no common political community, as they will be beholden to different authorities.

Reason, by contrast, can serve as a common source of authority, because reason is the same for all. What is traditional for one person need not be traditional for another, but what is known to be true for one person cannot be known to be false for another. People have different opinions about truth, of course, because reason does not always provide one clear answer. However, where reason does provide one clear answer, such as on the question of whether murder is morally permissible, common moral authority is possible. If a tradition is rationally examined and found to be morally sound, then that tradition can become a common authority, but it is the moral soundness of the tradition, not its status as a tradition, that makes this possible.

Reason also serves to oppose the divisive influence of irrational religious fanaticism, which in Locke's time bore the derogatory label "enthusiasm." After the fragmentation of Christian churches in the sixteenth and seventeenth centuries, as religious tradition ceased to be an effective restraint on many people's beliefs, dangerous religious enthusiasms began to emerge. People claimed that God spoke to them, or inspired their actions, and used these claims to justify continuing religious conflict. After all, if God is guiding my actions, my actions must be right, while anyone who stands against me must be wrong, and my divine mandate gives me all the authority I need to do whatever it takes to accomplish my mission, whatever it may be. An enthusiast not only "does violence to his own faculties" and "tyrannizes over his own mind," he also "usurps the prerogative that belongs to truth alone, which is to command assent by only its own authority" (E IV.19.2, 698).

Enthusiasm is far more dangerous to politics than traditionalism. Where traditionalism simply causes different people to apply different standards to restrain their behavior, enthusiasm removes all restraints on behavior, since anything an enthusiast believes is, in his mind, justified by the mere fact that he believes it. "This is the way of talking of these men: they are sure, because they are sure: and their persuasions are right, only because they are strong in them" (E IV.19.9, 700). Because of the greater danger posed by enthusiasm, Locke attacks it more directly and more emphatically than he does traditionalism.

Enthusiasm, like traditionalism, prevents adherents of different faiths from sharing a common community, and for the same reason. If I obey the divine voice I hear in my mind, and you obey the divine voice in your mind, we cannot be members of a common political community because we adhere to different authorities. It is inevitable, if we each fail to regulate our own beliefs with reason, that we will seek to impose our beliefs upon one another. "For how almost can it be otherwise, but that he should be ready to impose on others belief, who has already imposed on his own? Who can reasonably expect arguments and conviction from him, in dealing with others, whose understanding is not accustomed to them in his dealing with himself?" (E IV.19.2, 698).

Locke's epistemology of rational belief is intended to replace traditionalism and enthusiasm with a unifying source of belief. People can never be brought into full agreement on all things, of course, and Locke does not even aspire to bring them into agreement on most things. Rather, he seeks to bring them into agreement on the relatively small number of things that are of greatest concernment and are subject to the least epistemological uncertainty. This is the foundation on which moral consensus is built.

MORAL IDEAS: THE BUILDING BLOCKS OF MORAL REASONING

Book Two of the *Essay*, in canvassing the various types of ideas, gives an account of moral ideas, such as "justice" and "cruelty." A moral idea does not refer to any real object – that is, to any objective existence. It is solely a product of thought; it is made by the mind. They are "not to be looked upon to be the characteristical marks of any real beings that have a steady existence, but scattered and independent ideas, put together by the mind" (E II.22.1, 288).

This is not to say that moral ideas are a matter of pure abstraction, untainted by empirical experience. We construct moral ideas based on our experience of the world in which we live, and in turn these moral ideas have practical applications and consequences (see E II.22.2, 288–9). For example, when we form an idea of "murder," we do not simply pluck it fully formed out of the ether. We draw on our memories of various instances in which people have killed one another, in order to draw distinctions between murder and other types of homicide. However, the process of drawing those distinctions – deciding just what kind of homicide counts as murder – is a purely mental process, a process of reasoning. Experience can tell us the various ways and circumstances in which people kill, but not where to draw the lines that differentiate one kind of killing from another.

Because moral ideas are made by the mind, there are no inherently right or wrong moral ideas. Locke writes that an idea can only be "true" or "false" relative to something outside itself (see E II.32.1–5, 384–5). However, since moral ideas refer to no real object, they can never be inherently true or false. A moral idea contains "no reference to any pattern existing, and made by nature: it is not supposed to contain in it any other ideas, than what it hath; nor to represent any thing, but such a complication of ideas, as it does" (E II.32.17, 390). For example, our idea of a particular murder represents a real event, but our idea of murder in the abstract does not. If we think the butler did it when in fact it was the jealous husband, we have a false idea of who committed the murder. But our idea of murder in the abstract does not represent a real event, or any real thing, and therefore cannot be false. A moral idea cannot falsely represent something, since it represents only itself.

This denial that there is a causal epistemological connection between our empirical experience and our abstract moral ideas furthers Locke's goal of moral consensus. It is a consequence of, and a continuation of, his denial of scholastic essentialism. Observing human beings does not tell us what the essence of a human being is, and therefore does not give us any moral knowledge regarding how to treat human beings in a manner appropriate to their essence. Moral ideas about human beings are constructs of thought. This supports moral consensus because it denies that there is one empirically true vocabulary of morality. The enormous and complex jargon of moral discourse employed by the scholastics is no more or less "true" than any other. Indeed, because so many of its terms are poorly defined and inconsistently used, it is an actual hindrance to clear moral discourse (see E III.11.4, 509–10). Before different groups can establish moral consensus, they have to speak to each other clearly, which they will not do so long each group clings to its own predetermined body of jargon. By denying that moral ideas can be inherently right or wrong, Locke removes any grounds for insisting any one particular set of definitions over any other.

Locke's position that moral ideas cannot be inherently right or wrong does not make him a relativist.[5] Quite to the contrary, Locke believes that once we set clear definitions of our moral terms and understand them, self-evident moral truths emerge. "If we but separate the idea under consideration from the sign that stands for it, our knowledge goes equally on in the discovery of real truth and certainty, whatever sounds we make use of." The basis of these truths is the permanent and unchangeable relationships between the ideas that make them up. Locke writes that the properties of a given geometric figure do not change, whether we call it an "*equilaterum* or *trapezium*, or any thing else . . . as soon as the figure is drawn, the consequences and demonstration are plain and clear." Similarly, "let a man have the idea of taking from others, without their consent, what their honest industry has possessed them of, and call this *justice*, if he please . . . but strip the idea of that name . . . and the same things will agree to it, as if you called it *injustice*" (E IV.4.9, 567). We can change our moral ideas, for example by changing our definition of "justice," but we cannot change the naturally occurring relationship between any given idea and any other given idea. These relationships, which form the basis for knowledge and belief, are fixed and immutable.

We can see how this works by comparing moral ideas with mathematical ones. The ideas of two, four, addition, and equality are perceived purely by reasoning and refer to no real object, and therefore cannot be right or wrong in themselves. But once we define those terms and understand them, we can express the self-evident truth that $2 + 2 = 4$. We could decide to redefine our idea of addition such that it would not produce the result $2 + 2 = 4$, but the underlying relationship between the ideas of two and four would not change; the only thing that would change is how we express that relationship. Similarly, to take one of Locke's examples, our ideas of murder, desert, and death are neither right nor wrong, but once we define and understand them we can express the self-evident truth that "murder deserves death." Locke presents this as an example of a universal moral principle, and despite some ambiguity in the wording he seems to put it forward as being a self-evident truth. In discussing the difference between abstract moral rules and real actions, he writes that "if it be true in speculation . . . that murder deserves death, it will also be true in reality of any action that exists conformable to that idea of murder" (E IV.4.8, 566). It appears that for Locke, "murder deserves death" is simply a natural implication of the ideas of murder, desert, and death, just as $2 + 2 = 4$ is implied by the ideas of two, addition, equality, and four. And if we define "deserves" such that each person deserves to have done to him what he does to others, then Locke is right. By that definition, "murder deserves death" is as self-evident as $2 + 2 = 4$.

Of course, the suggestion that murder self-evidently deserves death will be controversial to readers today, but it will be less so if we understand it properly. "Murder deserves death" is not the same as "murderers should be put to death," nor does it imply that we have absolute knowledge of who has committed any particular murder, or whether any particular killing was a murder rather than a justifiable homicide. "Murder deserves death," therefore, does not imply any necessary position on the death penalty. Locke did firmly support having the state put murderers to death, of course, but that position is not a self-evident truth for him – it is a contingent belief. What is a self-evident truth for Locke is that murderers *deserve* to die – that it would be perfectly fair if, say, God were to kill them for their crimes. Whether human beings have the right to execute murderers, and whether it would be prudent to do so, are questions of another order.

This example also illustrates the presence of a general limit on self-evident moral truths that Locke does not explicitly acknowledge, but which becomes clear after just a little thought: self-evident moral truths cannot be applied in the form of moral laws unless we also justify certain beliefs about the divine. "Murder deserves death" depends on an idea of desert that is only one possible standard for treating people. Locke's definition of desert seems to be something like, "people deserve to be treated in the same way they treat others." How do we know whether we ought to treat people as they "deserve" to be treated on this definition of desert, rather than in some other way? It does not appear to be a self-evident truth. One can easily imagine, say, Nietzsche denying it. His definition of desert would no doubt be quite different. Locke asserts that "murder deserves death" is self-evidently true, but Nietzsche would probably dismiss that sentence as utter nonsense. This would not be because of some misunderstanding over what is meant by the words "murder" or "death," but because he disagrees with Locke over the meaning of the word "deserves." For Nietzsche there are many murderers who not only don't deserve death but actually deserve admiration and praise. Thus "murder deserves death" is only self-evidently true if we accept a certain definition of what "deserves" means.

We must establish belief in some source of moral authority as a basis for moral action before self-evident moral truths can be applied to the world. If we do not know that we ought to treat people as they "deserve" to be treated, according to some specific definition of desert, then the statement "murder deserves death" has no practical implications. If, on the other hand, we believe that God commands us to treat people as they "deserve" to be treated according to a particular definition of desert, then "murder deserves death" becomes the basis of an enforceable moral law.

This shows the essential role that religious belief must play in any attempt to build moral consensus. If we accept Locke's epistemology, only religious belief can make it possible for us to leap from abstract moral truth to practical moral law. If we don't appeal to a moral authority, all our reasoning about moral ideas consists of no more than defining terms and showing their relationship to one another. Moral ideas are made by the human mind, so without a divine moral authority who is to say which ideas are the ones that ought to be embodied in an enforced law? To show that premeditated, unjustified homicide is murder is only to give the definition of a word; to show that this or that particular act amounts to murder is only to show the relationship between our idea of murder and our idea of that act. To justify forbidding murder by law and punishing murderers, we must do something more than this – we must show that murder is wrong. We will discuss this in more detail in Chapter 5 when we take up Locke's analysis of moral law.

Moral ideas are also limited in their practical application by our igno-rance of the real essences of physical objects, another point that Locke does not make explicit. Locke argues that we can know moral truths in the abstract despite our inability to know the real essences of physical objects. He writes that "the names of substances ... can no more disturb moral, than they do mathematical discourses: where, if the mathemati-cians speak of a cube or globe of gold, or any other body, he has his clear settled idea, which varies not, thought it may, by mistake, be applied to a particular body, to which it belongs not." Just as a mathematician can deduce in the abstract the properties of a cube of gold of a given size, such as its weight, without knowing whether any particular cube of yellow metal is in fact made out of gold, so we can deduce the moral proper-ties of human beings without knowing whether some particular creature is in fact human. The properties of human beings in the abstract – of what Locke calls "moral man" – are the same regardless of which actual beings are or are not human (E III.11.16, 516). This makes moral knowl-edge and discourse possible despite our ignorance of the real essences of substances like gold or human beings.

However, because of this ignorance, applying those truths to real objects cannot be a matter of mathematical certainty and will require the intervention of judgment. This leaves us with areas of uncertainty in the application of moral rules. Even if we knew with perfect certainty in the abstract what our duties were in various kinds of situations, we would still always need to use judgment to figure out which kind of situ-ation we were in at any given time, and thus which moral rules applied to our actions. Moral life is overwhelmingly a matter of exercising sound practical judgment rather than just abstract reasoning.

Sometimes these uncertainties of application are very large. For ex-ample, Locke takes up the problem of the moral status of changelings, children born with severe defects. Recall from the previous chapter that because we cannot know the real essences of physical objects, we cannot settle the question of whether changelings are or are not human beings, with the moral rights pertaining to humans, by appealing to their real essences. Moral reasoning can tell us our duties toward other human beings in general, but what moral duties do we have toward a particular child born with severe defects?

Audaciously, Locke leaves this problem explicitly unsolved. He is keenly aware of the frustration this will cause, since it forecloses areas of inquiry that we naturally take an interest in. If we do not settle the ques-tion of whether changelings are human, Locke writes, "without doubt it

will be asked . . . what will become of them in the other world? To which
I answer . . . it concerns me not to know or enquire." Changelings "are in
the hands of a faithful creator and a bountiful father, who disposes not of
his creatures according to our narrow thoughts and opinions" (E IV.4.14,
570).

This is indeed a frustrating conclusion, because we must have some way
to determine what our moral duties are when faced with ethical dilemmas
involving children with severe defects. In some cases, Locke's definition
of "man" as a "corporeal rational being" is helpful – a baby born without
a brain, for example, could not be a rational being and therefore (on
Locke's definition) cannot have the moral rights of a human (E III.11.16,
516; see also IV.4.15–16, 570–3; and T II.16, 122–3, where Locke explains
why only rational beings have moral rights). But in other cases, such as
where the brain is present but damaged, no absolutely definitive solution
can be reached. Because we cannot know their real essences, we cannot
always know which creatures are rational and which are not. In such cases
we will have to leave people to rely on probabilities and opinions rather
than knowledge.

This places an important epistemological limit on moral ideas, a limit
that promotes moral consensus as part of Locke's larger epistemology of
limits. Because of our ignorance of the real essences of physical objects,
there are certain questions moral theory simply cannot answer. Moral theory can often show our abstract duties with great precision, but applying
these duties to particular cases is a matter of judgment. By showing this,
Locke can reign in the ambition of moral theorists who seek to answer
every question.

For example, the question of the moral status of children with birth
defects is one that different religious groups fight over, and did in Locke's
time. Locke even frames his consideration of the status of changelings as
a response to scholastic essentialists. Asserting that a changeling without
reason is "something between a man and a beast," he writes that he is
rejecting the "prejudice" of those who hold the "false supposition, that
these two names, man and beast, stand for distinct species so set out by
real essences" (E III.4.13, 569). And Locke expects the essentialists to
interpret his challenge as nothing less than an attack upon religion. If
we were wise, he writes, we would not ask whether changelings without
reason were human beings or beasts, "but I am not so unacquainted with
the zeal of some men, which enables them to spin consequences, and
see religion threatened, whenever any one ventures to quit their forms of
speaking, as not to foresee, what names such a proposition as this is like

to be charged with" (E III.4.14, 570). Against these zealous guardians of special moral knowledge, Locke shows that moral theory cannot always tell us which particular babies are or are not human beings, and thus the moral status of each child must be determined in each case by the judgment of some authoritative decisionmaker rather than by theorists. Moral theory can provide a clear guide to the abstract categories necessary for moral discourse, for example by defining what a "human being" is, but applying those categories to particular beings is beyond its reach.

THE LIMITS OF DEMONSTRATION AS A TOOL OF MORAL REASONING

In the previous chapter, we discussed the distinction Locke draws in the *Essay* between knowledge and belief. For Locke "knowledge" in the strict sense of that term occurs in two forms: intuitive and demonstrative. An intuitive truth is immediately visible in the relationship between two given ideas (see E IV.2.1, 531). For example, the idea represented by "2 + 2" and the idea represented by "4" are self-evidently the same idea, which we express by writing "2 + 2 = 4." A demonstrative truth is one that takes certain premises for granted and derives logically necessary conclusions from them (see E IV.2.2, 532). For example, if all men are mortal and Socrates is a man, it follows self-evidently that Socrates is mortal.

Locke proposes that, if we define our terms clearly and use them consistently, "morality is capable of demonstration, as well as mathematics" (E III.11.16, 516). This is because "certainty being but the perception of the agreement, or disagreement of our ideas," and "demonstration nothing but the perception of such agreement, by the intervention of other ideas" in a chain of logical steps, "all the agreement, or disagreement which we shall find" in moral ideas "will produce real knowledge, as well as in mathematical figures" (E IV.4.7, 565). That is, moral ideas are naturally related to one another like all other kinds of ideas, and so logical demonstration will work as well for them as for any other kind of idea. Locke suggests that the only reason demonstration is so easily accepted in mathematics but remains controversial in morality is that "vices, passions, and domineering interest" color our thinking on moral topics, and "oppose, or menace such endeavors" (E IV.3.18, 549).

However, Locke's argument that there are moral demonstrations that qualify as knowledge in the strict sense, just like mathematical demonstrations, is not as large a claim as it might seem. This is clear from Locke's two examples of moral demonstration: that "where there is no property, there is no injustice," and "no government allows absolute liberty." In both cases, the demonstrations follow directly from the definitions Locke provides for the terms involved. He defines "property" as "a right to any thing," and "injustice" as "the invasion or violation of a right," from which it is easy to see that "where there is no property there is no injustice." Similarly, Locke writes that by definition something is not a "government" if it is not "the establishment of society upon certain rules or laws," so "no government allows absolute liberty" is an easy deduction (E IV.3.18, 549–50). Moral demonstration, like all forms of demonstration, does no more than show the necessary consequences of certain premises.

The heavy lifting in Locke's moral theory, as presented in the *Two Treatises of Government* and the *Reasonableness*, is done not by demonstration but by methods that have some empirical element and therefore require the intervention of judgment and belief. For example, by itself the statement "where there is no property, there is no injustice" answers no really important moral or political questions. It does not tell us in what things, or under what conditions, people have property rights; nor does it tell us what to do about injustice when it occurs; nor does it tell us whether there are any other forms of moral wrong besides "injustice" as such, or what to do about them. Moral demonstrations produce absolute knowledge, but they are only a part (although a necessary part) of a larger framework of moral reasoning.

For this reason, we ought to think of moral demonstration not as constituting an independent body of inquiry, analogous to mathematics, but as a tool of moral reasoning – one tool among many. Locke makes declarations like, "morality is capable of demonstration, as well as mathematics," and "moral knowledge is as capable of real certainty, as mathematics," but this is not the same as saying that morality ought to rely exclusively upon demonstration, as mathematics does (E III.11.16, 516; and IV.4.7, 565). In all his works, Locke never sought to provide a moral system derived entirely from self-evident principles in a manner analogous to mathematics.

There is only one passage in the *Essay* that tends against this reading. Strikingly, at one point Locke writes that it is theoretically possible to build a moral theory on logic alone, proceeding from the existence of an omnipotent God and our dependence on him. A moral theory requires "foundations of our duty and rules of action," which are supplied by "the idea of a supreme being, infinite in power, goodness, and wisdom, whose workmanship we are, and on whom we depend; and the idea of ourselves, as understanding, rational beings." These ideas, Locke writes, "are clear in us" (E IV.3.18, 549). Locke thinks it is possible, if only in theory, to logically demonstrate moral rules arising from these foundations. Such a system would be tantamount to deism, or at the very least would be a clear invitation to deism, because it would construct a moral theory without the assistance of revelations from God. No doubt this passage accounts in large part for the praise heaped on the *Essay* by deists upon its publication, and their subsequent appropriation of it for their own purposes.

But in fact the passage gives the deists nothing more than an acknowledgement that the moral ideas necessary for a purely demonstrative morality are present in the human mind, and thus such a system is theoretically possible. Ideas, however, are only the building blocks of moral reasoning. Saying that we have the necessary materials to build something is not the same as saying that we can actually build it. One immediate problem is that the passage attributes to God, as a necessary basis of the theory, not only infinite power but infinite "goodness." As we will see, Locke demonstrated God's existence, his omnipotence, and his omniscience, but he left all of God's other qualities in the sphere of belief rather than demonstration. Another problem is the need to show rewards and punishments in the afterlife. On Locke's account, as we will see at some length in Chapter 5, rewards and punishments are what give a law is distinctive character as law. A demonstrative moral theory arising from our obligation to God would somehow have to logically demonstrate that God rewards virtue and punishes sin in the afterlife.

Locke makes no attempt to perform the feat of building a purely demonstrative morality in any of his published works. A draft chapter for the *Essay* on ethics, which Locke never published, is sometimes described as an abandoned attempt at such a demonstration but was actually nothing of the sort.[6] When friends wrote him to urge him to publish a treatise on purely logical morality, at first he wrote back that he would attempt it when he had the spare time, but eventually he abandoned the idea, saying that it was far beyond his capacities, and it was not necessary in any event since God's law was already so clearly apparent in both revelation and human nature. "Did the world want a rule, I confess there could be no work so necessary, nor so commendable," he wrote to a particularly insistent friend. But "the gospel contains so perfect a body of ethics, that reason may be excused from that enquiry."[7] In the *Reasonableness*, Locke declares that since natural reason alone, without revelation, has never succeeded in constructing a moral theory, it is reasonable to conclude that the task is impossible (see R 241, 170; 242, 174; and 243,

177). The *Reasonableness* is even more clear on the need for revelation to show rewards and punishments in the afterlife as the basis of moral law (see R 245, 183–5). Purely demonstrative morality is nothing more than a hypothetical idea in Locke's philosophy, a sidebar mentioned once, in passing, in the *Essay.*

Many scholars' accounts of Locke have been badly damaged by misunderstandings of this point. In an introductory essay to a 1960 edition of the *Two Treatises,* Peter Laslett wrote that there was no important connection between the *Essay* and the *Two Treatises* because the former allegedly demands a purely demonstrative moral theory and the latter does not provide it.[8] This account was widely accepted, and Locke scholarship was led down a blind alley as scholars wrestled with its implications. Some of those following Leo Strauss's reading argued that Locke's alleged promise to provide a demonstrative morality and subsequent failure to provide one is a sign of his insincerity.[9] Others agreed with Dunn's argument that Locke was just sloppy and incoherent when it came to the role of reason in his theory – when reason failed to accomplish what he wanted it to, Locke fell back on religion as an intellectual crutch.[10] A widely cited article by David Wootton argues that Locke is not really a natural law theorist because he thought that natural law theory required a demonstrative morality.[11] James Tully bravely attempted to rescue Locke from himself by arguing that we should not understand Locke's concept of "demonstration" as implying absolute logical certainty.[12] But this just doesn't fly; throughout the *Essay* Locke explicitly affirms that demonstration produces absolutely certain knowledge (see for example E III.11.16, 516 and E IV.3.18, 549). Until recently, John Yolton was the scholar who came closest to correcting this problem; in a 1985 book he accurately perceived the limits of moral demonstration in Locke's account, but did not conclude from this that Locke's main concerns lay elsewhere.[13] It was left to Nicholas Wolterstorff, in his 1996 book on the *Essay,* to reach the conclusion that Locke's epistemology is primarily aimed at belief regulation and not demonstrative knowledge.[14]

The recent upheaval among scholars of Locke's epistemology brought on by Wolterstorff's book hopefully signals the beginning of a major reorientation in scholarship on the *Essay* and the *Two Treatises.* The connection between these works ought to be understood in terms of Locke's larger undertaking of building moral consensus. That undertaking requires belief regulation – Locke seeks to show that some beliefs are epistemologically very clear and thus shared by all religious groups, while other beliefs, which are particular to different groups, are epistemologically problematic. Once this is shown, the community can build politics on the highly certain beliefs that are shared, and groups can be persuaded not to attempt to force one another into agreement on the difficult beliefs that divide them. To see this unifying theme in the *Essay*, the *Two Treatises*, and Locke's other works, and particularly to see how Locke relies crucially on revelatory religion to provide some of the necessary beliefs on which moral consensus is built, we must set aside the idea that Locke sought political union in a demonstrative moral theory.

THE FOUNDATION OF LOCKE'S PHILOSOPHY: GOD'S EXISTENCE

In Book Four, Locke sets out to fulfill the *Essay*'s promise: to establish knowledge and beliefs in a manner consistent with philosophic inquiry. Since religious knowledge had already been found to be most important, Locke first seeks to prove that God exists, and that he is all-powerful and all-knowing. Locke wishes to "prove" this in the strictest sense of that term, with no room for uncertainty, because the existence of God must be certain before Locke can construct the rest of his philosophic vision. This is a matter too important to be trusted to anything less. Locke declares that with "thought and attention," we will come to see that God's existence is "the most obvious truth that reason discovers," whose evidence is "equal to mathematical certainty" (E IV.10.1, 619).

The dependence of Locke's philosophy on God's existence can hardly be overstated. In this chapter, we will see how God's existence is an indispensable premise of Locke's justification for belief in miracles. In Chapter 6 we will see how it is equally indispensable for Locke's rational method of discerning the natural law. While Locke's system of moral theory does not aspire to show every point of moral law through demonstration, the system's ultimate foundation in God's existence does draw its epistemological strength from demonstration. Indeed, the reason it is plausible in Locke's system to accept beliefs about God on grounds less absolute than those of demonstration is precisely that we are absolutely sure God exists; this strongly implies that some communication from him must be available. A person who knows that God exists is going to be far more open to belief in miracles, or to an argument that divine law can be perceived in the design of nature, than an atheist or agnostic. It is not for nothing that Locke so frequently asserts that the existence of God is beyond dispute – if that existence were subject to any serious doubt, Locke's philosophy could not function.

What is all the more remarkable, given the importance of this point, is the disarming simplicity with which Locke disposes of it in the *Essay*. His proof is simple in both a positive and negative sense of the term. It is simple in a positive sense because it is straightforward, is accessible to any moderately intelligent reader, and claims no more than what is necessary for the argument; it is simple in a negative sense because it has an axiomatic character that some find easy to dismiss.[15]

Locke presents a version of what theologians call "the cosmological proof." He begins with the familiar Cartesian position that every person knows that he himself exists. All are compelled to believe this – "if any one pretends to be so skeptical, as to deny his own existence ... let him for me enjoy his beloved happiness of being nothing, until hunger, or some other pain convince him of the contrary" (E IV.10.2, 619–20). For Locke, this knowledge of our own existence is the only knowledge we need to deduce that there is an eternal God, if we also accept the axiom that nothing can come into existence out of nothing – "bare nothing" cannot "produce any real being." If anything has ever existed, something must have always existed, eternally, from which that thing was created. If "we know there is some real being, it is an evident demonstration, that from eternity there has been something; since what was not from eternity, had a beginning; and what had a beginning, must be produced by something else" (E IV.10.3, 620). Only an eternal being could ever create or destroy things; temporal forces can change the form of matter, but cannot create or destroy it. So if I exist, God must exist to have created me. Some of God's properties are proven by the same reasoning: power and knowledge, like matter, cannot come into existence out of nothing, so all power and knowledge must exist in an eternal being before they can exist in the created universe. God is therefore all-powerful and all-knowing.

The axiom that something cannot come into existence out of nothing is perfectly sensible and has an ancient pedigree but cannot be logically proven. Locke is less than fully explicit on the basis of this axiom, but it is not too hard to make sense of his argument.[16] He declares the axiom to be an "intuitive certainty" and that anyone who would deny it would also have to deny "any demonstration of Euclid" (E IV.10.3, 620). If by "intuitive certainty" Locke means the same thing as when he defines "intuitive" knowledge earlier in Book Four, which seems to be the case, we can infer that the basis of the axiom is an immediate mental observation of the properties of certain ideas. When we compare the idea of something coming into existence with the idea of nothing existing, we observe that they are self-evidently inconsistent, much as we can observe that 2 + 2 is self-evidently consistent with four but inconsistent with three or five. God's existence, then, is a deductive certainty that is deduced from two intuitive certainties – that something exists and that something cannot come into existence out of nothing.

Thus, the ultimate foundation of religion for Locke, as for Aquinas, is logical proof that God exists. By founding itself in reason, ultimately resting upon rational proof of God's existence, religion can unify reason and faith, eliminating the danger of irrational religious enthusiasm. This rational approach to religion serves the cause of moral consensus in several ways. The refutation of enthusiasm is obviously one major way, and we will deal with it at much greater length later. More broadly, demonstration of God's existence provides an epistemological basis for moral consensus by strengthening the beliefs that depend on God. Rational belief in miracles is justified primarily because once we know that God exists, it stands to reason that he would want to communicate with us. Demonstration of God's existence also sets the stage for a method of investigating God's will that does not rely on revelation. If we know that the universe was created by an omnipotent being, we can examine its structure to discern that being's design. As we will see in Chapter 6, this is just as important for moral consensus.

THE BASIS OF MORAL LAW: GOD'S TOTAL AUTHORITY

In examining Locke's proofs of the existence and qualities of God, it is important to notice what qualities Locke does not establish. Locke makes no attempt to demonstrate, independent of scriptural revelation, that God is just, benevolent, or loving – in short, that God is good.[17] Locke's proofs that God is all-powerful and all-knowing are potentially consistent with a God who is indifferent or even hostile to humanity. God's authority to make rules for human beings, which Locke repeatedly affirms, is derived from his completely superior knowledge and power, not his goodness. "The rewards and punishments of another life, which the almighty has established, as the enforcements of his law, are of weight enough to determine the choice, against whatever pleasure or pain this life can show" (E II.21.70, 281). In many passages Locke attributes God's authority to his general superiority, and mentions God's superiority of wisdom and goodness as well as his superiority of power and knowledge, which may seem to imply a moral dimension to God's authority (see E II.28.8, 352; IV.3.18, 549; and IV.13.3, 651). But in some passages Locke explains God's authority solely in terms of our "fear" of him (E IV.11.13, 638). Also, perhaps more importantly, throughout the *Essay* Locke treats God's authority as clearly established even though the *Essay* never proves God's goodness.

This is enough to justify the conclusion that for Locke God's authority is morally arbitrary. Locke's invocations of God's goodness would have served to bolster his argument for God's authority, but God's goodness is not the necessary basis of God's authority in the *Essay*. As Francis Oakley puts it, in Locke's works "natural law owes its obligatory force" to "the fact that it is, indeed, a disclosure of... divine will," and divine will conveys obligation not because it embodies a higher moral order but because it is "a superior will" and "the formal cause" of natural law.[18] Wootton, with much justice, compares Locke's picture of God to a Hobbesian sovereign.[19] In fact, this doesn't go quite far enough; the Hobbesian sovereign is bound by the natural law and ultimately accountable to God, whereas Locke's God is ultimately bound by no law but his own and ac-countable to no one but himself. God is the ultimate arbitrary ruler – to take the most extreme example, it would arguably be consistent with Locke's proofs if God were a sadistic tyrant who created us so that he could torture us for his own amusement. Of course, Locke does not ac-tually believe God is indifferent or hostile to humanity; in the *Essay* and throughout his other writings, private and public, Locke consistently de-scribes God as completely wise, just, and benevolent. But that position is not justified until later in Locke's epistemological journey, through the revealed truths of scripture, and then as a matter of belief rather than knowledge. In the foundations of our knowledge we can know that we were created by a supreme being but not that our creator is just or loving.

By the standards of Locke's epistemology, which emphasizes the limits of the human mind, this makes sense. To demand logical demonstration of God's goodness is to demand that we put ourselves in a position to pass moral judgment on God, a position that we are decidedly unqualified to occupy given that our minds operate within narrow and immovable limits. If God is all-knowing and we are not, who are we to question his wisdom?

The theological term for this unconditional acceptance of God's au-thority to make moral law is "voluntarism." As Oakley shows, Locke fol-lows in a line of voluntarist theologians stretching back three centuries to William of Ockham.[20] In voluntarist theology, we must accept our place in the universe with complete humility; we are utterly in God's power. If God rules us arbitrarily, who are we to complain? If discovering God's will is difficult and we have no prior assurance it will be benevolent for us, what alternative do we have? We know we cannot escape God's vigilance, and if we displease God we know that God has the power to make us infinitely and eternally sorry for it. Locke appears to have taken for granted that a person who believes in an all-powerful, all-knowing God would have no problem acknowledging God's total authority. "Having the idea of God and myself, of fear and obedience, I cannot but be sure that God is to be feared and obeyed by me" (E IV.11.13, 638; see also II.21.70, 281; II.28.8, 352; and IV.13.3, 651).[21] To take the extreme case suggested above, if God really is a sadistic tyrant who created the world to torture us, we would still be well advised to seek out his will and try to follow it rather than risk his wrath.

Voluntarism is a necessary consequence of Locke's epistemology of moral consensus, and in turn it helps support the moral and political aspects of moral consensus. His epistemology of limits shows that we are not qualified to judge God's goodness; God inhabits a plane of existence of which we can have only the scantiest understanding, and even for much of that scanty understanding we are dependent on God's revelation. We are certainly in no position to make judgments about God's moral worthiness. Within the narrow limits of human understanding, voluntarism is the only sound approach to explaining God's authority. And voluntarism has the effect of promoting moral consensus in moral theory and politics, because it takes off the table all question of justifying God's pronouncements. If we all agree that God commands a certain thing – for example, that we are not to murder one another – we need not argue over God's reasons for doing so. Voluntarism requires us to simply accept God's command; the potentially controversial question of why God commands what he commands is rendered moot, giving us one less religious topic to argue about.

SEARCHING FOR GOD'S WILL IN THE WORLD AROUND US

So far, Locke has produced knowledge of the existence of only two things – a person knows that he himself exists and that an all-knowing, all-powerful God exists. To learn the rest of what he must know, a person must struggle. His daily experience of his own "short-sightedness and liableness to error" is a "constant admonition" to him that he must seek "with industry and care" to improve his understanding (E IV.14.2, 652).

But of course he cannot devote all his energies to this effort; that would waste all the other faculties God has given him. Since he knows he was created by an intelligent being, he can surmise that he was not given his life or his faculties to be wasted. "The understanding faculties" were "given to man, not barely for speculation, but also for the conduct of his life" (E IV.14.1, 652). A large portion of most people's labor is required simply to sustain life, so the labor of seeking knowledge should be reserved for those matters of greatest concernment – those of which correct knowledge is most important. We will have to trust in appearances and conventional opinions for the rest, since this is the only way we can live life usefully rather than waste it by analyzing every point, however trivial, that comes to our attention.

The matter of greatest importance, of course, is God's will. The most urgent task, once a person knows that both he and God exist, is to establish communication with God and learn God's will. "Our proper employment lies in those enquiries, and in that sort of knowledge, which is most suited to our natural capacities, and carries in it our greatest interest; i.e. the condition of our eternal estate. Hence I think I may conclude, that morality is the proper science, and business of mankind in general" (E IV.12.11, 646). Locke takes it for granted that once we know there is a God, it is not plausible to believe that he would leave his creation in a state of comprehensive ignorance.[22] The idea that God might create humanity but have no will or preferences regarding humanity does not receive any consideration. Richard Ashcraft aptly describes this as an "Aristotelian philosophical maneuver," in that it takes existence to imply purpose.[23] However, for Locke this maneuver is distinctively religious in a way that it was not for Aristotle. If there is a God in the universe then he simply must have some kind of will, and seeking it simply must be our most important concern. Since God would want us to discover his will, he would have given us evidence by which to discover it.[24] And, presuming that such evidence exists, we would be obliged to seek it out, because God has the authority to govern us.

Unfortunately, as Locke established in his critique of innate ideas, the mind does not contain any ideas placed there directly by God. We must therefore search for communication from God in the world around us. This requires us to abandon the realm of perfect knowledge in favor of the realm of belief and judgment. "In the greatest part of our concernment," God "has afforded us only the twilight, as I may say, of probability, suitable, I presume, to that state of mediocrity and probationership, he has been pleased to place us in here" (E IV.14.2, 652).

The conduct of this search is the greatest concern of the *Essay*. The first three books of the *Essay* clear away unreliable beliefs and epistemologies to prepare us for Book Four, while the first half of Book Four explains "knowledge" in the strict sense and makes clear its limited scope in order to prepare us for the second half of Book Four. Here the *Essay* culminates in Locke's account of beliefs, and this account is in turn primarily concerned with religious belief. This is the apex of epistemology for Locke. Absolute, epistemologically perfect knowledge may be the most unassailable thing in the human understanding, but what really fascinates Locke is the epistemologically messy process of investigating the world in which we live, because that is where we learn the most about God.

Like Descartes, Locke feels the need to show that the world we perceive outside ourselves is real and not simply an illusion. But Locke's several arguments for this – for example, that it hurts to look directly at the sun or be exposed to heat or cold, but it does not hurt to remember these experiences later, and therefore the actual experience must be more than merely sensations inside our minds – fall short of deductive certainty. Locke acknowledges this explicitly: "How vain, I say, it is to expect demonstration and certainty in things not capable of it; and refuse assent to very rational propositions, and act contrary to very plain and clear truths, because they cannot be made out so evident, as to surmount the least (I will not say reason, but) pretence of doubting" (E IV.11.10, 636). All experience of the physical world is belief, not knowledge, but those who attribute any real importance to this distinction are asking for more than the world can give them.

In sharp contrast to Descartes, Locke argues that it does not matter in the slightest if we lack perfect logical assurance that the world exists. As Nicholas Jolley puts it, "Locke's worry is not the Cartesian one . . . that the human intellect is systematically unreliable; he is not haunted by the fear of a malicious demon who endows us with only false beliefs."[25] Locke writes that "the certainty of things existing *in rerum Natura*, when we have the testimony of our senses for it, is not only as great as our frame can attain to, but as our condition needs." That is to say, our certainty of the world around us is already as great as it can possibly be, given that we cannot perceive the world except through sensation, and it is as great as we need it to be, because it provides the stimuli that God has constructed our minds to respond to. Our "assurance of the existence of things without us, is sufficient to direct us in the attaining the good and avoiding the evil, which is caused by them, which is the important concernment we have of being made acquainted with them" (E IV.11.8, 634–5). As we will see again in Chapter 6, for Locke the existence of God implies that human psychology is part of a divine plan. If God constructed us to perceive the world through sensation, then we should be content to perceive it that way. The desire for absolute assurances about the world around us is a desire for knowledge that we cannot have and do not require, and Locke therefore resists it as dangerous to genuine philosophy. "He that in the ordinary affairs of life, would admit of nothing but direct plain demonstration, would be sure of nothing, in this world, but of perishing quickly" (E IV.11.10, 636).

This would probably be Locke's reply to the objection, raised by Hume and echoed by Wolterstorff, that Locke's epistemology cannot work because the associations between ideas that we form through experience – such as the association between pressing the power button and the computer turning on – are not natural connections, but are only the result of our mental habits. Wolterstorff argues that such associations ought to be accepted because we need them to live in the world, but this "is not a manifestation of reason but of that very different dynamic of belief-formation which Locke called *custom* and which he warned us so firmly against."[26] The idea of pressing the power button and the idea of the computer turning on are, on this view, associated only by custom, not because there is a natural connection between them. We cannot get beyond custom to observe the world as it "really" is, independent of custom, because we can never logically justify a formal system of rules for determining how much empirical data about the world constitutes a representative sample. Thus, we can never have logical assurance that a particular empirical observation is legitimate. "We can confirm that one sample is representative of another sample. What we cannot do is confirm that our sample is representative of reality – without having sampled all the reality on the matter."[27]

Wolterstorff demands more epistemological certainty than the mind is capable of having. In short, his standards are too high. We may not be able to logically justify a formal system for declaring which empirical observations are legitimate and which are merely artifacts of habit, but this does not mean we can never hope to transcend habit with a reasonable degree of certainty. Locke trusts God not to leave us at the mercy of habit and custom; he trusts God to give us a connection to the world as it really is. "As to my self," he writes, "I think God has given me assurance enough of the existence of things without me," because his senses convey what he needs for the "great concernment of my present state" (E IV.11.3, 631). Sorting legitimate from illegitimate observations may be a messy process, consisting of belief rather than knowledge, but this does not mean that reason is helpless in the case. The decision to accept one or another amount of data as representative of reality is not systematic or logical, but neither is it wholly irrational guesswork. By trial and error in empirical experience, we learn what amounts of data provide sufficient certainty for our various purposes. Locke's epistemology is based on the assumption that we must, in the end, trust God to have put us in a world where this empirical process produces understanding of the world as it actually is.

This clash between Wolterstorff's Humean skepticism and Locke's willingness to accept rationally regulated beliefs about the world illustrates a foundational premise of Locke's theory of moral consensus. If Wolterstorff is right that we cannot form beliefs about the world that are independent of habit and custom, then there is no hope for an epistemology of reason independent of tradition. As he says, "examination of tradition can take place only in the context of unexamined tradition, and . . . in our examination, our convictions as to the facts are schooled by our traditions." All belief is, at bottom, belief within a cultural tradition. If this is the case, there can be no hope for a moral or political theory that transcends the boundaries of tradition to unite members of different cultural groups. Wolterstorff desires a "'liberal' politics" with an "animating vision of a society in which persons of diverse traditions live together in justice and friendship."[28] No doubt there are significant elements within each tradition that support, or might be developed to the point where they would support, liberal politics. But if we are each epistemologically confined to a mental world defined by a particular tradition, the best we can hope for on that score is not a single political community but the peaceful coexistence of separate communities, each defined by its own separate tradition.

Locke's theory of moral consensus seeks to provide a more solid foundation for liberal politics by uniting these disparate groups into a single political community. His goal was to use careful epistemological analysis to separate very certain beliefs from less certain ones, in order to show that the very certain beliefs reflect the world as it really is. If he could show this, members of different groups would be compelled to acknowledge the validity of those beliefs, and could be united behind a moral and political theory justified by them. For moral consensus to work, we must be willing to believe that our most certain beliefs are not just tradition-bound habits but reflections of the real world – that pressing the power button and the computer turning on really are linked by a natural connection that actually happens in the world rather than being simply two ideas that are conjoined in our minds by habitual association.

To find signs of God's will in the world around us, we must decide how to know revelation when we see it. There are many competing claims of revelation, most of them mutually exclusive to some degree. If we can accept one of them as a genuine revelation from God then we will be able to discern much more about his will, but to do that we need to be able to distinguish between true revelation and false. We must weigh the evidence for each claim of revelation and judge which are sufficiently attested by God to be accepted as genuine revelation.

Obviously this raises the question of what counts as "evidence" for or against any given proposition, and how we are to weigh it. Locke uses the word "assent" to describe the acceptance of a proposition. Mapping out how people ought to regulate their assent – that is, how we ought to distinguish truth from falsehood – is the principal task of the second half of Book Four. In the *Essay*, Locke identifies three grounds on which people give assent to propositions: reason, faith, and enthusiasm.

REASON AND "DEGREES OF ASSENT"

Reason is a faculty of perception, specifically the perception of agreement or disagreement between two or more ideas. Reason "so orders . . . ideas, as to discover what connection there is in each link of the chain" (E IV.17.2, 668). As we saw in Locke's proof of God, for example, reason perceives that the idea of something coming into existence is inconsistent with the idea of nothing existing. In some cases, such as the example of pressing the power button and the computer turning on, the agreement of propositions is not logically necessary but rather observed through the senses. Here reason requires the exercise of judgment. Judgment "is the putting ideas together, or separating them . . . when their . . . agreement or disagreement is not perceived" to be certain, "but presumed to be so" (E IV.14.4, 653). We make this presumption when the association between two ideas in our experience is "frequent and usual" (E IV.17.17, 685).

When reason operates only through intuition and logic, and does not rely on the senses, what it produces is knowledge in the strict sense of that term. On the other hand, when reason makes use of ideas that come from sensation, it must exercise judgment to evaluate whether the relationship between the ideas has been properly perceived. For example, I can observe an association between the rooster crowing and the sun rising, but good judgment tells me not to conclude that the former causes the latter. Such cases produce belief rather than knowledge, although sometimes the belief is so strong that it is just as certain as knowledge, and the distinction is irrelevant in practice. "This, though it never amounts to knowledge ... yet sometimes ... the probability is so clear and strong, that assent as necessarily follows it, as knowledge does demonstration" (E IV.17.16, 685).

When a proposition does not arise from absolute logical certainty – that is, when it is a belief rather than knowledge – we not only use judgment to determine whether we assent to it, we also use judgment to determine how we assent to it. We can believe it as something that is probably true, or almost certainly true, or for all intents and purposes equal to knowledge. When all indications are in favor of its truth, we accept it as an "*assurance*" or "*confidence*," but in other cases "arguments and proofs, *pro* and *con*, upon due examination," will "preponderate on either side," producing "*belief, conjecture, guess, doubt, wavering, distrust, disbelief*, etc." (E IV.16.6–9, 662–3) Locke calls these designations "degrees of assent" (see E IV.16, 657–68).

Degrees of assent distinguish between types of belief. To believe that something is probably true is quite different from believing that it is almost definitely true, which in turn is different from believing that for all intents and purposes it is as certain as $2 + 2 = 4$. This is Locke's mechanism for acknowledging the limited certainty of most human beliefs without rendering those beliefs epistemologically illegitimate. We may not have absolute knowledge that "there is such a city in Italy as Rome: that about 1,700 years ago, there lived in it a man, called Julius Caesar; that he was a general, and that he won a battle against another called Pompey," but we still give a very high degree of assent that these things are true (E IV.16.8, 662). A person who understands the significance of degrees of assent can cultivate a healthy appreciation for the distinction between knowledge and belief, and between more and less certain beliefs, without becoming a skeptic.

It is important to understand that Locke's emphasis on degrees of assent does not cast doubt on religion as such, but only on those parts of religion and theology that cannot be examined with a high degree of certainty due to the natural limits of the human mind. The existence of God is not called into the slightest degree of doubt here, since it is proven through pure logic. Indeed, by applying degrees of assent Locke casts some level of doubt on most empirical beliefs, thus emphasizing the comparative certainty of logic, and hence of God's existence. And, as we have already remarked, once the existence of God is established as a premise, the plausibility of belief in revelation is substantially improved. As Wolterstorff puts it, Locke and other religious reformers of that time were arguing that an "appropriately tempered firmness" of religious belief, rather than a zealous insistence on absolute certainty in every theological point, was "quite sufficient for the religious life."[29]

The idea of degrees of assent is the foundation of Locke's doctrine of toleration, a connection that Locke makes almost immediately in his chapter on degrees of assent. Certain beliefs, for example many beliefs about the nature of God, cannot rightly be held in a high degree of assent owing to the limits of the human mind. In such cases it is unavoidable that people will disagree, since no one can force another person to believe something that doesn't appear to him to be true. Therefore "it would . . . become all men to maintain peace, and the common offices of humanity, and friendship, in the diversity of opinions" that prevails in human life, since such diversity is inevitable. "We should do well to commiserate our mutual ignorance," Locke writes, "and endeavor to remove it in all the gentle and fair ways of information" (E IV.16.4, 659–60).

Toleration based on degrees of assent takes on a distinctive form that is appropriate for Locke's desire to build moral consensus. If the need for toleration arises from the inherent uncertainty of some kinds of beliefs, this suggests that toleration does not apply to all beliefs. Toleration is required because there are things we cannot be sure of, so toleration need not extend to subjects on which the truth is clear and very certain. Any theory of toleration must place limits on what is tolerated, of course, but this particular way of drawing the boundary, based on principles of epistemology, is a natural complement for moral consensus. Highly certain beliefs, for example that murder is against divine law, can unite the political community, and dissent from those beliefs need not be tolerated.

The Lockean doctrine that reason must regulate all important beliefs, with special attention to degrees of assent, was – inadvertently – one reason for the rise of the ideal of compartmentalization of religion and politics. This ideal holds that religious arguments are not legitimate bases of government action. Locke sought to reduce the degree of assent people gave to certain beliefs regarding creeds and forms of worship, so that such beliefs would be treated as conditional and therefore inappropriate bases for government action. But in our time, to a large extent at least, this conditional status has been ascribed to all religious belief, including belief in God's existence and belief that God's law for external actions can be discerned with sufficient certainty to be enforced. Among those who accept this epistemological change, all religious belief is considered insufficiently certain to be politically enforced. Meanwhile, nonreligious arguments purporting to provide justification for government action, particularly the arguments of neutralist liberalism, have gained in credibility among the political and intellectual classes, such that these classes are sure enough of these arguments to enforce them.

The possibility of this historical outcome was reasonably foreseeable, and, as we have already noted, some of Locke's contemporary critics did in fact foresee it. However, compartmentalization is not actually implied by Locke's philosophy. In fact, the two are mutually exclusive possibilities – we can adopt one or the other, but not both together. Locke holds, for reasons we will examine in Chapter 6, that moral laws derived from God can be sufficiently certain for political enforcement. He also holds, for reasons we will examine in Chapter 5, that only such laws can provide an adequate basis for political action. On the other hand, compartmentalization requires us to believe the opposite of both these positions: that religious beliefs are not sufficiently certain for enforcement, but that other beliefs can provide an adequate basis for politics. One position does not grow from the other as a logical necessity; rather, Locke's moral system and the system of compartmentalization are two different applications of the idea of degrees of assent.

Because of this fundamental difference between Locke's philosophy and the ideal of compartmentalization, it would not be fair to dismiss Locke on the grounds that his theory somehow inevitably gives rise to compartmentalization. The historical connection between Locke and compartmentalization was not inevitable. The misappropriation of Locke's epistemology by others who had a different political agenda was a contingent historical development arising from the particular conditions that prevailed in a certain time and place, and the decisions made by particular people who lived then and there. We are different people living in a different time and place, and we can make different decisions. There is no reason we could not adopt Locke's epistemology of degrees of assent without adopting the ideal of compartmentalization of religion and politics.

FAITH: REASON'S NECESSARY HELPMATE

Reason's great weakness is that it is limited in scope. "Reason, though it penetrates into the depths of the sea and earth, elevates our thoughts as high as the stars, and leads us through vast spaces, and large rooms of this mighty fabric, yet . . . there are many instances wherein it fails us" (E IV.17.9, 681). We have examined these limits on reason at length in this chapter and the previous one, so they do not require additional elaboration here. The most important consequence of these limits is that reason, alone and unassisted, cannot tell us enough about our most important concern, which is God. We can use natural reason to discover what is "according to reason" or "contrary to reason," but there is also much that is "above reason," and we must have some way of investigating it (E IV.17.23, 687). Hence, Locke's chapter on reason ends with an introduction to the second ground of assent, faith.

Locke identifies faith as the granting of assent on the evidence of miracles – disruptions in the physical world so extreme as to be attributable only to a supreme being. Faith accepts a proposition "upon the credit of the proposer, as coming from God, in some extraordinary way of communication" (E IV.18.2, 689). The miracles performed by a prophet are what give him "credit" as a "proposer," attesting that the prophet is genuinely an agent of God. This is because only God, "who has the power to change the course of nature," could cause a miracle (E IV.16.13, 667). And once the authenticity of the prophet is established, the prophet's teachings must also be accepted as revelatory. "Miracles . . . well attested, do not only find credit themselves; but give it also to other truths, which need such confirmation" (E IV.16.13, 667). The premise here is that God would only give the power to perform miracles to a prophet whose teachings he wanted us to believe.[30] Accepting a revelation as genuine is a matter of judgment, so it is a belief rather than knowledge. "Faith" refers to any belief of this type – that is, any belief ultimately grounded on the acceptance of a miracle, and hence a revelation, as genuine.

The position that faith is grounded on miracles is an alternative to the position that faith is simply a work of the Holy Spirit in our minds that bears no relationship to rational argument. Locke classifies religious beliefs of this type, which the believer attributes to direct inspiration without rational foundation, as "enthusiasm" rather than "faith." Locke's position does not preclude the Holy Spirit from playing a role in the origin of faith; for example, it may be that the rational evidence supports faith but our sinful natures cause us to irrationally reject that evidence unless the Holy Spirit works in our minds to make us more rational. But Locke's position does imply that any action by the Holy Spirit in our minds is carried out in support of reason rather than in opposition to it.

There is plenty of precedent in the history of Christianity for treating faith as arising from evidence rather than as a belief that has no rational basis. However, this approach has large consequences, particularly in the context of Locke's epistemology. As Wolterstorff puts it, treating faith as grounded in miracles is "traditional" but "bristles with problems."[31]

One of the problems we face in using miracles to justify faith is the crucial role that judgment must play in deciding what does and does not count as a miracle. We do not have knowledge, in the strict sense of that term, of the laws of nature (see E IV.12.10, 645). Therefore, we cannot pronounce with demonstrative precision which events are or are not disruptions in the laws of nature and therefore miraculous. Miracles can only be judged by comparison with our observations of normal physical events; we observe that normally the dead do not rise, seas do not part, and so on, so we can only attribute such occurrences to God's power. A certain degree of subjectivity and epistemological fuzziness is inextricable from this process.[32] There is a danger that we will mistake unusual natural phenomena for miracles. But as we have already seen time and again, for Locke practically all of life is subject to this kind of epistemological fuzziness. In most matters of human concern, knowledge is unattainable, and we must rely on belief, and hence on judgment.[33] Locke simply doesn't take it as problematic that when we see someone turn water into wine, heal the sick, feed multitudes with almost no food, and top it all off by rising from the dead, we will naturally take these events as miraculous.

Of course, most people today have never personally witnessed anything they take to be miraculous. Religious belief today relies by and large on accounts of miracles having taken place in the past. The issue of secondhand accounts of miracles is one we will take up in the next chapter when looking at Locke's biblical exegesis in the *Reasonableness*. Here we are concerned with Locke's epistemology of miracles when witnessed firsthand, because for Locke this is the direct origin of all subsequent religion. Locke made this point explicit in his posthumously published *A Discourse of Miracles*, in which he declares that "he that believes the history of the facts, puts himself in the place of a spectator."[34] Faith occurs because people witness miracles; later ages can have faith in those miracles only because the original witnesses recorded them.

Another epistemological problem with basing faith on miracles is the possibility that miracles might be performed by other powers besides God. In telling the story of Jesus' life in the *Reasonableness*, Locke notes that the Pharisees accused Jesus of performing miracles by demonic power. Locke refers to "the falsehood and vanity of their blasphemy" without explaining why, exactly, it was blasphemous (R 90, 57).[35] Obviously if we accept the Messiahship of Jesus for reasons other than his miracles, we can argue on those grounds that the Pharisees blasphemed in this accusation. But if our belief in Jesus is grounded on his miracles, we must first show that Jesus' miracles were not demonic before we can establish that the Pharisees were blaspheming. Locke alludes to Jesus' own statement, made in the same scriptural passage, that demons could not cast one another out, but this argument is not persuasive unless we believe that Jesus teaches truthfully, which is the very point we are seeking to establish.

Neither the *Essay* nor the *Reasonableness* even considers the possibility that evil spirits may be able to produce miracles. There was no pressing need for Locke to take up the issue, as not many people in seventeenth-century England argued that Jesus was an agent of Satan. But Locke did provide a way out of this dilemma in *A Discourse of Miracles*. There, although he did not take a stand on the question of whether evil miracles are possible, he argued that God would not allow anyone to perform miracles greater that those of his genuine revealers. That would leave humanity with no hope of distinguishing true prophets from false ones. "God's power is paramount to all, and no opposition can be made against him with an equal force to his," so he "can never be supposed to suffer his messenger and his truth to be born down by the appearance of a greater power on the side of an imposter."[36] When two apparent miracle workers make contradictory claims and we cannot establish that one or the other is faking, we should conclude that the prophet whose miracles are greater is the true one. Here, Locke relies again on the presumption that God must have communicated his will to us in some effective manner.

Locke insists that faith properly arises within the bounds of reason. Since the weighing of miraculous evidence is a matter of judgment, it is performed by reason. The truth or falsehood of statements like "Moses miraculously parted the Red Sea" or "the teachings of Moses are communications from God" is evaluated by reason; if reason concludes in the affirmative, the statement becomes an article of faith. Though faith "is ordinarily placed, in contradistinction to reason," it is actually "nothing else but an assent founded on the highest reason" (E IV.16.14, 668). Reason weighs miraculous evidence just as it would weigh evidence for any other proposition. Reason observes that pushing the power button is closely associated in numerous instances with the computer turning on, and judges that this is indicative of a causal connection: pushing the power button causes the computer to turn on. Similarly, reason observes that a person claiming to be a prophet is closely associated in numerous instances with miracles, and concludes that the prophet causes the miracles.

Thus, faith and reason are perfectly complementary for Locke. Reason is the foundation upon which faith is built, but faith can reach higher than unassisted reason because revelation can communicate truths to us that reason cannot deduce on its own. Nothing is so offensive to Locke as the suggestion that faith and reason are opposites. Reason does not stop where faith begins – wherever there is belief of any kind there must be reason to guide it.[37] Our beliefs, at least those on subjects of great importance, must "be regulated" by reason; this is "our duty" because God has given each person "discerning faculties...to keep him out of mistake and error." Locke concludes: "he that believes, without having any reason for believing, may be in love with his own fancies; but neither seeks truth as he ought, nor pays the obedience due to his maker" (E IV.17.24, 687–8).

The claim that reason does not regulate faith is most often used, in Locke's view, by clergy who want to stop discussion of particular subjects for fear that some of their doctrines will be revealed to be false: "I find every sect, as far as reason will help them, make use of it gladly: and where it fails them, they cry out, *'Tis a matter of faith, and above reason*" (E IV.18.2, 689). To not rationally regulate one's beliefs about God is to recklessly put oneself in danger of believing things about God that are false, which violates our most basic duty to God and, given that one's beliefs about God tend to determine one's beliefs about all other things, potentially disastrous. "Nothing is so dangerous, as principles...taken up without questioning or examination; especially if they be such as concern morality, which influence men's lives, and give a bias to all their actions" (E IV.12.4, 642). This partnership between reason and faith is so strong for Locke that at one point he insists that "reason is natural revelation" and "revelation is natural reason enlarged by a new set of discoveries" (E IV.19.4, 698; see also IV.7.11, 598).[38] That is to say: natural reason is, in a sense, revelatory, because it is an avenue by which God makes things known to us; revelation, in turn, is simply a new supply of raw material for our reason to work upon.

One of Strauss's major lines of argument supporting his reading of Locke relies crucially on the assumption that for Locke reason and faith follow radically separate epistemological paths. He argues that if Locke really believed, as he professed, that the New Testament was the highest sanction of the natural law, then for him "the complete and perfectly clear natural law teaching...would consist of properly arranged quotations from scripture and especially from the New Testament."[39] Locke did not follow this approach, according to Strauss, because for him revelatory natural law "belongs to the province of faith and not to that of reason."[40] Locke bases his real politics on human nature rather than the

Bible, Strauss asserts, because only a law derived from human nature can be known to reason.[41] On this view, rational moral law is a radically different concept from revelatory moral law, and since Locke's moral law is rational it can only be seen as fundamentally opposed to revelatory moral law.

Locke's epistemology shows that reason and faith do not follow radically separate epistemological rules; in fact, they follow the same rules. For Locke the provinces of faith and reason are not separate – they are indeed "distinct," as he puts it in a chapter title, but that is not the same as saying they are separate (see E IV.18, 688–96). Rather, the province of faith is a wholly contained subset of the province of reason. As we have noted, Locke writes that although faith "is ordinarily placed, in contradistinction to reason," it is actually "nothing else but an assent founded on the highest reason" (E IV.16.14, 668). Reason, and therefore the rational law of nature, can include beliefs derived from both revelatory and nonrevelatory sources.

Strauss treats reason and revelation as entirely separate sources of belief.[42] From this he concludes that Locke's arguments drawn from human nature represent a rejection of scripture as a basis for natural law. But Locke's epistemology shows that reason and natural law are inclusive of both scriptural and natural reasoning. Revelatory and nonrevelatory beliefs are all properly regulated by reason, and must work together to provide a unified account of the world. The New Testament is the highest sanction of the natural law for Locke because it shows the divine authority of that law, but in making out the particular requirements of that law we must often turn to nonrevelatory reasoning, because there are many questions about natural law that scripture does not answer. As we will see in detail in Chapters 5 and 6, for Locke revelatory and nonrevelatory reasoning are each epistemologically suited to investigating the natural law in a different way. Locke was completely confident that, so long as we make no errors, these two methods would never produce contradictory conclusions because they are both ways of discerning God's truth.

The unification of faith and reason is one of Locke's most important steps in building moral consensus. The rest of this chapter and the next chapter will work out the major consequences of this doctrine for Locke's epistemology and theology. We will begin with the most direct consequence – the regulatory role it gives to reason over faith. By giving an account of how reason can regulate faith without vitiating it altogether, Locke simultaneously disproves the dangerous claim of religious enthusiasts that reason is antithetical to faith, and prepares the way for religious belief that can support moral law in a community characterized by religious disagreement.

HOW REASON REGULATES FAITH

Locke's chapter on faith begins with a declaration that the chapter's purpose is "to lay down the measures and boundaries between faith and reason." Because his audience is almost exclusively composed of believers, his driving purpose is not so much to justify faith as it is to justify a particular kind of faith, characterized by a particular understanding of the relationship between faith and reason. Failure to address this relationship "may possibly have been the cause, if not of great disorders, yet at least of great disputes, and perhaps mistakes in the world. For till it be resolved, how far we are to be guided by reason, and how far by faith, we shall in vain dispute, and endeavor to convince one another in matters of religion" (E IV.18.1, 688–9). As in the rest of the *Essay*, the motivating problem is moral consensus. Disorders and disputes must continue so long as faith and reason are not reconciled. People can simply "cry out, *'Tis a matter of faith, and above reason*" to protect themselves from rational scrutiny, "and I do not see how they can argue with any one, or ever convince a gainsayer, who makes use of the same plea, without first setting down strict boundaries between faith and reason" (E IV.18.2, 689).

Reason does not pass judgment on the content of revelation. If God declares something to be true, or requires us to perform a certain action or adhere to a certain rule, we have no grounds for dissent. What we take on faith "as absolutely determines our minds, and as perfectly excludes all wavering as our knowledge itself; and we may as well doubt of our own being, as we can, whether any revelation from God be true" (E IV.16.14, 667). God is God, after all, and in principle his word supercedes all epistemological rules. "Revelation, where God has been pleased to give it, must carry it, against the probable conjectures of reason" (E IV.18.8, 694). What God declares, we must believe.

However, all that having been said, we must be sure that it is really God who speaks to us, and that God is really saying what we think he is saying, before we accept some pronouncement as revelatory. "Faith is a settled and sure principle of assent and assurance, and leaves no manner of room for doubt or hesitation. Only we must be sure, that it be a divine revelation, and that we understand it right" (E IV.16.14, 667). Reason regulates faith in these two ways: by judging "first, that we deceive not ourselves in ascribing it to God; secondly, that we understand it right" (E IV.18.5, 692). Even if God were to reveal a truth to us directly, not through the teachings of a prophet but immediately in our minds, "our assurance" of the thing revealed "can be no greater, than our knowledge is, that it is a revelation from God" and not just a delusion (E IV.18.5, 691). God's word may supercede all epistemological rules in principle, but those same epistemological rules are crucial for determining what really is God's word, so they are never actually transcended.

The authenticity of a revelation is judged by empirical rules of evidence – how great were the miracles performed by the prophet, how well attested is the account of the miracles, and so on. The accuracy of an interpretation, on the other hand, is judged by rules of logic. If we are being asked to believe something contrary to our "clear intuitive knowledge" of the "principles and foundations of knowledge," we must reject the interpretation (E IV.18.5, 692). "For the knowledge, we have, that this revelation came at first from God, can never be so sure, as the knowledge we have from the clear and distinct perception of the agreement, or disagreement of our own ideas." After all, Locke might ask, what is more likely: that all logic is illusory or that we have misinterpreted a particular scriptural passage?[43] He illustrates this with an example from geometry. A revelation that the angles of a triangle add up to 180 degrees can never convey as much assurance "as the knowledge of it, upon the comparing and measuring my own ideas" (E IV.18.4, 691). Similarly, an alleged revelation that the angles of a triangle do not add up to 180 degrees must be rejected as being either inauthentic or misinterpreted.

Locke goes even further, writing that it is incoherent to reject reason in order to adhere to an article of faith, because without reason there can be no faith. Reason is necessary for the construction and acceptance of any proposition, including revelatory propositions. Setting aside reason in matters of faith "would be to subvert all the principles, and foundations of all knowledge, evidence, and assent whatsoever." How can we conclude that any given revelation comes from God without using reason to weigh the evidence, and how can we understand the content of a revelation if reason does not interpret it? "We cannot tell how to conceive that to come from God... which if received for true, must overturn all the principles and foundations of knowledge he has given us; render all our faculties useless," and "wholly destroy the most excellent part of his workmanship, our understandings." God would not make us rational and then require us to believe things contrary to reason, which would "put a man in a condition, wherein he will have less light, less conduct than the beast that perisheth" (E IV.18.5, 692–3).

Because faith is a species of assent, degrees of assent apply to our judgments in regulating religious beliefs (see E IV.18.2, 689). A revelation can be accepted as almost certainly genuine or as only probably genuine. Likewise, an interpretation of a given revelation can be accepted as almost certainly accurate or as only probably accurate. In his chapter on religious enthusiasm, Locke writes that "one unerring mark" of persons who genuinely seek for truth is "the not entertaining any proposition with greater assurance than the proofs it is built upon will warrant." Of those who do not respect this epistemological rule, he says that "whatsoever degrees of assent he affords it beyond the degrees of that evidence, 'tis plain all that surplussage of assurance is owing to some other affection, and not to the love of truth" (E IV.19.1, 697). Attention to degrees of assent is the crucial distinction between proper faith – that is, faith within the bounds of reason – and religious enthusiasm.

Observing degrees of assent in religious belief is a crucial foundation of moral consensus. Without degrees of assent, religious belief becomes an all-or-nothing proposition; there is only blind, unregulated belief or blind, unregulated unbelief. Locke describes at the end of his chapter on faith how "if the provinces of faith and reason are not kept distinct by these boundaries, there will, in matter of religion, be no room for reason at all," leading to the unrestricted embrace of "extravagant opinions and ceremonies," "absurdities," "strange opinions, and extravagant practices" (E IV.18.11, 696). Without degrees of assent there can be no distinction between more and less certain beliefs within the bounds of religion. Every tenet, every point of doctrine, becomes equally certain once we have made the great irrational leap of faith and decided to believe. This is the cause of "disorders" and "disputes" Locke describes at the beginning of the chapter. To build moral consensus, we must be able to hold some beliefs with great certainty and other beliefs with less certainty, in order to facilitate social solidarity around the former while maintaining toleration regarding the latter.

The requirement that reason regulate faith, and religious beliefs be held with attention to degrees of assent, must not be read as dismissing scripture in favor of unassisted reason. Locke's point is that reason and faith should work together, that one should use reason in accepting and interpreting revelation rather than make a choice between reason and revelation. This is the key difference between Locke's epistemology and that of the deists who followed him. Locke insists that we apply reason when reading scripture, but scripture is still authoritative for him. Any claim from scripture must be backed up with a rational argument that the claim genuinely follows from scripture, but within the bounds of that requirement, "because scripture says so" is a legitimate argument in his system.[44] And once we are satisfied that scripture does in fact say so, that argument is dispositive; it forecloses all debate on the subject.

Both sides of this coin – the willingness to accept God's word on subjects reason cannot investigate on its own, and the willingness to use reason to strictly test our interpretations of God's word – are necessary for Locke's theory of moral consensus. Natural reason alone cannot supply sufficient beliefs for social cohesion. In particular, as we have already remarked, the existence of rewards and punishments in the afterlife for God's moral law are not adequately made out by natural reason and require the testimony of revelation. As we will see in Chapter 5, God's rewards and punishments are the basis of moral authority, which in turn is necessary for a cohesive political community. However, just as reason without faith is insufficient for moral consensus, faith unregulated by reason is dangerous to the maintenance of moral consensus, because it leads people to reject the distinction between very certain and less certain beliefs. Moral consensus can only be maintained if people are willing to enforce the very certain divine rules (such as that against murder) while not enforcing the less certain rules. Those who do not regulate their faith with reason come to believe that all their tenets of faith are very certain, and naturally seek to force others to conform to them. For this reason, Locke's chapter on faith is followed by a chapter on the *Essay*'s third and final ground of assent, enthusiasm.

THE DANGER OF ENTHUSIASM

Locke defines "enthusiasm" as "that which laying by reason would set up revelation without it" (E IV.19.2, 698). The enthusiast interprets his inner experience of belief as evidence that God wants him to believe, that God is directly inspiring his thoughts. Because regulating our opinions with reason is "tedious and not always successful," some people "pretend to revelation" and "persuade themselves, that they are under the peculiar guidance of heaven in their actions and opinions." They believe that they have "an immediate intercourse with the deity, and frequent communications from the divine spirit" (E IV.19.5, 699). It is true, Locke writes, that because God is omnipotent he must have the ability to directly inspire people. But if people do not look for external evidence such as miracles to confirm that this inspiration is genuine, for them "whatever groundless opinion comes to settle itself strongly upon their fancies, is an illumination from the spirit of God" (E IV.19.6, 699).

The word "enthusiasm" was a derogatory term in Locke's time, connoting images of fringe groups with weird beliefs and practices. Locke clearly wanted to maintain the negative image associated with enthusiasm, but he uses the term in an unusually broad sense. He seeks to expand the set of beliefs to which that negative image will be attached. Locke's formal definition of enthusiasm – "that which laying by reason would set up revelation without it" – does not convey this broader use of the term. Taken in a limited sense, it could be read to include only those denominations that afford no or almost no role for reason in religious belief. This would include Quakers and other enthusiastic groups that were marginalized and despised in seventeenth-century England. More significantly, it could also include the Puritans of that time, who generally placed faith above rational regulation. But it would not include either Anglicans or Catholics, insofar as both of these drew upon the medieval scholastic tradition, which had a large role for reason. However, when Locke writes that enthusiasm would set up revelation without reason, he means belief in any occurrence of revelation not subject to reason, however limited in scope. In short, anyone who ever believes on any occasion that God is directly inspiring his thoughts is dabbling in enthusiasm. In this sense, what Locke calls "enthusiasm" encompasses a wide range of beliefs, present to some extent in nearly every religious tradition.

This is not to say that everyone who holds any such belief is guilty of all the flaws Locke attributes to "enthusiasts." Locke seems to have in mind a certain ideal type – one is tempted to say a caricature – of the "enthusiast," which any individual person may resemble to a greater or lesser degree. This archetypal enthusiast, if we may call him that, is a full-fledged fideist, a person who believes that no religious belief, not even the very existence of God, is subject to independent examination by reason. Certainly the Puritans of Locke's time fit this description, and would have been the enthusiasts who were most worrisome to Locke, given their central role in the political conflicts of seventeenth-century England. Nonetheless, Locke's general definition of enthusiasm is quite broad, and presumably any belief falling into that category would be dangerous to some degree.

Locke's attack on enthusiasm is unrelenting. He describes enthusiasts as basing their beliefs on "the ungrounded fancies of a man's own brain," and that enthusiasts' arguments amount to saying that "they are sure, because they are sure: and their persuasions are right, only because they are strong in them" (E IV.19.3, 698 and IV.19.9, 700). Enthusiasm is circular: the more strongly an enthusiast believes, the more sure he is (on the evidence of the strength of his belief) that his beliefs are true; the more sure he is that his beliefs are true, the more strongly he believes. And because there is no independent standard of logic or evidence to limit enthusiasm, this circle continues to feed on itself indefinitely. "For strong conceit like a new principle carries all easily with it, when got above common sense, and freed from all restraint of reason, and check of reflection" (E IV.19.7, 699).

One of the immediate causes of enthusiasm, according to Locke, is that people allow their desire to know God and God's will to overwhelm their reason. The strength of this desire is understandable, given the importance of God for human life. However, this does not excuse those who are either too lazy or too vain to rationally examine their beliefs. Locke is especially eloquent on this point: "The love of something extraordinary, the ease and glory it is to be inspired and be above the common and natural ways of knowledge so flatters many men's laziness, ignorance, and vanity, that when once they are got into this way of immediate revelation; of illumination without search; and of certainty without proof, and without examination, 'tis a hard matter to get them out of it" (E IV. 19.8, 700).[45] The need to work and struggle to discover God's will is one of Locke's most emphatic points in the *Essay*, so it is no wonder he excoriates those who believe they know God so easily.

And there is another, even more sinister possibility in explaining enthusiasm. Locke points out that, if enthusiasts are right that good spirits can excite ideas in their minds, evil spirits may do so as well. Just because a belief is revealed by a spirit doesn't mean "it is a revelation from God. Because there be spirits, which, without being divinely commissioned, may excite those ideas" (E IV.19.10, 701). For all we know, the devil could be inspiring people's enthusiastic religious feelings for his own purposes. "To talk of any other light in the understanding" but that of reason "is to put ourselves in the dark, or in the power of the prince of darkness." That prince, "the son of the morning," can "transform himself into an angel of light," so "if strength of persuasion be the light, which must guide us; I ask how shall any one distinguish between the delusions of Satan, and the inspirations of the Holy Ghost?" (E IV.19.13, 703–4).

The underlying cause of enthusiasm is a philosophic failing. We may experience feelings of inspiration for various reasons, but we only embrace them as legitimate because we misunderstand the relationship between reason and faith. In short, enthusiasm is a result of understanding faith and reason as opposites rather than compliments. After all, if we believe that we must choose between faith and reason, once we choose faith we will see no need to regulate our beliefs by reason. Enthusiasts "feel the hand of God moving them within," and thus they "are sure reason hath nothing to do with what they see and feel in themselves" (E IV.19.8, 700). Because enthusiasm sets reason aside, it is completely incompatible with any genuine search for truth. Locke expresses this in a shocking but perfectly apt metaphor: "he that takes away reason, to make way for revelation, puts out the light of both, and does much what the same, as if he would persuade a man to put out his eyes the better to receive the remote light of an invisible star by a telescope" (E IV.19.4, 698).

Degrees of assent are meaningless to the enthusiast. The enthusiast's separation of reason and faith not only results in his accepting false beliefs, it also results in his accepting all his beliefs as extremely certain rather than paying attention to degrees of assent. When a person believes that his beliefs are directly inspired by God, every belief is a completely certain belief.

Locke does not say that we should never believe that we are receiving inspiration from God. "God I own cannot be denied to be able to enlighten the understanding by a ray darted into the mind immediately from the fountain of light" (E IV.19.5, 699). He only argues that in the absence of miraculous testimony we should only believe in such direct inspirations with a low degree of assent. The crucial consequence of this is that these beliefs should be tested against other, better-attested beliefs. "Where the truth embraced is consonant to the revelation in the written word of God; or the action conformable to the dictates of right reason or holy writ," we "run no risk in entertaining it" as a true revelation, because "we are sure it is warranted" by the better-attested revelation of scripture (E IV.19.16, 705–6).

The *Essay*'s chapter on enthusiasm was added in the fourth edition, published in 1700; the first three editions of the *Essay* analyzed only reason and faith at length, dismissing enthusiasm briefly. The timing of this addition is significant. After 1689, which saw the publication of the *Essay*, the *Letter Concerning Toleration*, and the *Two Treatises of Government*, Locke's attention had been devoted more and more to religion. His theological masterpiece *The Reasonableness of Christianity* was published in 1695, and from that year until his death in 1704 almost everything Locke wrote was about one or another aspect of religious philosophy. So Locke added the chapter on enthusiasm to the *Essay* after more than five years of immersion in religious matters. Something in that religious immersion seems to have brought Locke to the conclusion that enthusiasm was a more important threat than he had realized when writing the *Essay*. Locke was always against enthusiasm, of course, but he appears to have been much more worried about it in 1700 than he had been in 1689.

A likely source of this change in emphasis is the particular vulnerability of Locke's religious epistemology to the dangers of enthusiasm. Locke's religious ideal is direct communication between each person and God. A person begins in a position of ignorance and must discover God's will, and since no one is authorized to speak for God (as no genuine miracle workers are evident) each person must find God on his own. This system is very effective at separating religious belief from the potentially corrupting influences of institutional power, such as the "artificial ignorance, and learned gibberish" of the medieval scholastics (E III.10.9, 495). However, it provides little discouragement for enthusiasm. Locke's immersion in religious problems at the end of his life may have brought this weakness more clearly to his attention.

Locke's attack on enthusiasm is not, however, just an adjustment needed to make his epistemology work better. It is a central part of his theory of moral consensus. Enthusiasts ruin all hope of using reason to build common epistemological ground, because they reject reason altogether. Reason is shared by all, but enthusiastic inspiration is particular to the individual. The enthusiast "usurps the prerogative that belongs to truth alone, which is to command assent by only its own authority." Enthusiasts will not necessarily agree with principles demonstrated by reason, which are the foundation of moral consensus. Moreover, because enthusiasts do not limit themselves with reason, they frequently treat their private religious inspirations as public truths to which all must submit, "assuming an authority of dictating to others . . . For how almost can it be otherwise, but that he should be ready to impose on others' belief, who has already imposed on his own?" (E IV.19.2, 698). This is supremely dangerous not only to moral consensus but to civil order itself, as those upon whom the enthusiasts impose will certainly rebel against such treatment.

PHILOSOPHIC FAITH AND MORAL CONSENSUS

Locke's epistemology serves moral consensus in several important ways. By appealing to reason as "our last judge and guide in every thing,"

Locke creates an epistemological ground on which disputes can be settled without reliance on divisive and exclusionary appeals to particular cultural traditions. By constructing an epistemology of reason that separates demonstration from probable judgment, and that uses degrees of assent to treat beliefs differently according to their differing levels of certainty, Locke shows how we can treat some beliefs as highly reliable despite the epistemological limits laid out earlier in the *Essay*. And by reconciling faith with reason, Locke paves the way for religious beliefs that are properly regulated by reason and thus both more likely to be true and less likely to be dangerous to civil order.

This philosophic faith, devoted to rational investigation of God's truth, requires the believer to give up on, or at least seriously discount, enthusiastic religious experience, which he may believe to be a genuine connection with God. At best, Locke might allow him to believe in such inspiration with a low degree of assent; he can believe that God is guiding him so long as he treats this as a belief about which he is likely to be wrong. Obviously this approach removes the very thing that makes such beliefs attractive in the first place – the believer's liberation from the burdens of doubt and uncertainty. Locke demands that, at least in matters of great concernment, we never seek to put down these burdens except where we can legitimately dispel them with rational argument. The boundaries of certainty are inherent in the makeup of the human mind, as shown in the epistemology of limits earlier in the *Essay*. When we treat beliefs as certain because we wish them to be certain, rather than treating them with the level of certainty that is actually warranted by a rational weighing of the evidence, we violate our duty to God and forfeit our natural endowment as rational creatures.

By persuading us to accept beliefs, and to judge degrees of assent, on the basis of rational argument, Locke prepares us for his theology and political theory of moral consensus. Drawing us away from the kinds of beliefs that cause social conflict is the first step to such consensus, but only the first. To actually build such consensus, we must produce rational arguments to justify particular accounts of religion and politics. Locke's epistemology of reason shows how such highly certain arguments can be crafted. The epistemological rules outlined in this chapter shape Locke's arguments in his theological and political works, because arguments constructed according to those rules are epistemologically very sound and thus persuasive to a very broad audience. By building arguments in accordance with these rules, Locke can provide the highly certain beliefs on which moral consensus is based.

4

"The Only Foundation of Faith"

Reasonable Christianity

At the end of his life Locke became more intensely interested in religion. After the publication of the *Essay Concerning Human Understanding*, the *Two Treatises of Government*, and the *Letter Concerning Toleration* in 1689 – "Locke's *annus mirabilis*," as Peter Nidditch calls it – he returned to England with the triumphant Whig expatriates and took a job as Commissioner of Excise Appeals.[1] Later he was appointed to the Board of Trade. The political aspect of the great conflict between Anglicans and Puritans had largely been put to rest, and his public duties demanded only a small fraction of his prolific output, so Locke was able to concentrate his intellectual power on other matters. He made only minor revisions to the *Two Treatises* and published only one other major work in a related field, a tract on economics in 1691.

Religion came to dominate Locke's intellectual life. The only political issue outside of his professional duties in which he continued to take an active hand was the most distinctively religious political issue: toleration. In addition to publishing several more letters on the subject, he used his influence at court to assist the successful movement for greater toleration in the postrevolutionary government. And he published a series of major works about religion and related topics: a book on education stressing moral virtue in 1693, his theological masterpiece *The Reasonableness of Christianity* in 1695, a series of letters after 1695 defending both the *Essay* and the *Reasonableness* against religious critics, new editions of the *Essay* in 1694, 1695, and 1700 that considerably expanded sections on topics of religious interest, and – posthumously – a tract on the moral duty to examine one's beliefs, a short essay on miracles, and a lengthy exposition of the contents of Paul's epistles. The last of these, *A Paraphrase and Notes on the Epistles of St. Paul,* though not as intellectually ambitious as the *Reasonableness,* was by far the largest undertaking Locke took up after 1689. He didn't live to complete it, but he did manage to get through the first four epistles, which constitute the bulk of Paul's writings and include important treatments of a vast range of moral, theological, and ecclesiastical issues. Though incomplete, the *Paraphrase* is still almost as long as the considerably weighty *Essay.*

There is a particular reason why Locke's consuming interest in religious thought later in his life is important to understanding his philosophy. Doubtless this interest was in part personal; Locke was a lifelong asthmatic, and as his health failed sharply in his later years his thoughts would naturally have turned more urgently to his eternal fate. In fact, many of his religious works, and in particular the *Paraphrase,* are prefaced with notes from Locke that he undertook them at first for his own benefit. But Locke was also drawn to religion because of the role it plays in the larger scheme of his philosophic achievements. To promote moral consensus, it was not enough to build an epistemology and a political theory consistent with such consensus; it was not even enough to show that building moral consensus was consistent with Christianity, the religion professed by virtually all of his audience. He had to show that building moral consensus was not only permitted by the Bible but required by it. If moral consensus were merely consistent with Christianity, it would remain only one option among many for Christians. Since moral consensus requires Christians to give up having a political community specifically dedicated to their religion – something Christians had enjoyed for well over a millennium in Locke's time – Locke had to show not only that it was an acceptable option for Christians, but that it was the only acceptable option.

This chapter will show how the *Reasonableness* and the *Letter* construct a case that Christianity requires its adherents to support moral consensus. We will take the works out of their original chronological sequence, taking the *Reasonableness* first, in order to construct the case in the order that makes the most sense of the argument. Locke argues that the doctrinal content of Christianity – at least in regard to its paramount concern, the salvation of souls – is simple and clear in the Bible, and shared by Christians of all denominations. There are, therefore, no adequate grounds for attempts by any Christian denomination to force other Christians to conform to its particular beliefs, because such conformity is not necessary for salvation. Furthermore, it is the command of God, conveyed in the teachings of Jesus Christ and the apostles, that Christians seek to live in peace with people of different religious beliefs, whether they are fellow Christians of different denominations or members of other religions. This entails much more than simply refraining from killing or persecuting people over their beliefs. Christian revelation commands that Christians not use coercive power for any sectarian purpose, and join with those of other beliefs in a single political community, on equal terms, with charity and goodwill. For those who work for peace and toleration, heaven will provide a bountiful reward (provided, of course, they get into heaven, whose entrance requirements were naturally one of the major topics of Locke's religious thought). Meanwhile, those who persecute the weak and promote hatred, discord, and violence will one day face a heavy reckoning with the just judge of the universe.

This chapter addresses a subject that professional political theorists usually consider to be outside their field. Political theorists consider the abstract question of the relationship between religion and politics to be part of their intellectual turf, but they have long left the specific political questions arising from particular religions to the theologians of those religions. There is some sense in this division of labor; problems arising from religion generally are addressed by one group of scholars, while problems arising from particular religions are addressed by other scholars who specialize in those religions. The problem with this arrangement is that religion carries with it the supreme authority of the divine, and thus has the potential to overrule arguments from other disciplines. What Christians believe regarding whether the Bible requires them to accept or reject liberal politics must have ramifications for liberal political theory in societies that are predominantly Christian, at least in application if not at a deeper level. The question of whether the Bible commands, forbids, or is neutral toward liberal politics is therefore one in which professional political theorists ought to take some interest.

THE ORIGIN OF THE *LETTER* AND THE *REASONABLENESS*

The *Letter* was written in the winter of 1685–6 while Locke was in exile in the Netherlands. Its immediate catalyst was the revocation in October of 1685 of the Edict of Nantes, which had previously granted toleration for Protestants in France, and the ensuing crackdown on French Protestants. That crackdown, coupled with the failure of the Monmouth Rebellion in England in the same year, was cause for alarm among Protestants everywhere. With England once again under the rule of a Catholic monarch and France moving to stamp out Protestantism within its borders, the future of Protestantism itself was called into serious question. The right to worship Christ outside the ambit of the Catholic Church was in very real danger of disappearing entirely.

There was, of course, a larger history of social discord over religion both in Europe generally and in England specifically to which Locke was also responding. Ever since Luther published his ninety-five theses challenging the Catholic Church's ecclesiastical authority, all Europe, and particularly England, had been embroiled in a series of wars over the question of which church was the one true church, the only church whose members would be saved. Locke refers pointedly to this history in the second sentence of the *Letter*, which recounts how "some people boast of the antiquity of places and names, or of the pomp of their outward worship; others, of the reformation of their discipline; all, of the ortho-doxy of their faith – for everyone is orthodox to himself." When Locke concludes that these arguments "are much rather the marks of men striv-ing for power and empire over one another than of the church of Christ," he refers to a 170-year history of bloodshed, assassination, persecution, and misery with which his audience was all to intimately familiar (L 1, 13). The *Letter*'s argument for toleration is motivated by this history.

The *Reasonableness*, though it appeared only six years after the *Letter*, was written for a completely different world. Chaos and warfare had given way, at least in England, to a period of relative calm and stability after the Glorious Revolution. The continued existence of Protestantism had been secured. What's more, thanks in part to Locke's own influence in the postrevolutionary government, religious persecution and press restrictions on religious subjects had been dramatically relaxed. Locke, now out of hiding and secure in a civil service job, turned his attention to writing a book on the details of Christian theology, with more specific discussion of particular Bible passages and a more detailed account of basic theological concepts such as sin and salvation. To a large extent, then, the *Reasonableness* was written for less politically urgent reasons.

However, as we will see, the more detailed theology of the *Reasonableness* provides a religious foundation that the *Letter* takes for granted, but has no space to justify. The *Reasonableness* is therefore of great interest to the construction of moral consensus along the lines suggested in the *Letter*. Indeed, in some ways, such as in its argument that Christianity is in essence a simple faith, the *Reasonableness* carries moral consensus further than the *Letter*.

In his preface to the *Reasonableness*, Locke declares that he wrote the book because "the little satisfaction and consistency that is to be found

in most of the systems of divinity I have met with made me betake myself
to the sole reading of the scriptures (to which they all appeal) for the
understanding of the Christian religion" (R Preface, xxvii). Later we will
have occasion to discuss Locke's "sole reading" of the scriptures, setting
aside all extrascriptural "systems of divinity," at some length. What concerns us for the moment is Locke's reason for writing the *Reasonableness* –
the "little satisfaction and consistency" he found in those systems. The
Reasonableness addresses a set of interlocking theological disputes that all
came to a head in the 1690s. Though it does not present itself as a polem-
ical tract in the mode of the *First Treatise*, and does not even name the
participants in these disputes, it stakes out a position in each of them.

The most narrow of these disputes was a fierce pamphlet war between
strict and moderate Calvinists, which hit its peak between late 1694 and
the spring of 1695, on the relationship between faith and works. In his
preface to the *Second Vindication of the Reasonableness of Christianity*, Locke
tells us that in early 1695 "the controversy that made so much noise
and heat amongst some of the dissenters... drew me by degrees into a
stricter and more thorough inquiry into the question of justification."[2]
The strict Calvinists argued that works – a person's actions – played no role
in preserving his "justification," which is to say, the salvation of his soul.
If a person is saved in Jesus, argued the strict Calvinists, he can never
lose his salvation because all his sins have already been forgiven. This
position was widely associated with lawlessness and immorality because it
seemed too close to Antinomianism, the belief that saved Christians need
not even try to obey God's law. In fact, strict Calvinism does not entail
Antinomianism, but the association was still widely accepted. Anglicans
frequently used the label "Antinomian" as a smear against all dissenters,
so the moderate Calvinists were very anxious to loudly and publicly show
themselves to be against Antinomianism. In doing so, they staked out a
theological position very similar to the one being taken by many in the
dominant Anglican church on the same subject.[3]

Doubtless no one will be surprised to learn that the ever-reasonable
Locke was sympathetic to the moderate position in this argument. He had,
however, no interest in vindicating one side of the dispute over the other.
As John Higgins-Biddle points out, the "procedure and methods" of the
Reasonableness are "alien to the dissenters' debate."[4] Though, as Locke
says, that debate "drew" him "by degrees" to examine salvation, he ended
up far afield from the original concerns of the debate itself. As we will see,
in the *Reasonableness* Locke stresses elements of the moderate position
on salvation that support moral consensus. In particular, the Christian

argument for toleration in the *Letter* can be seen to rely on premises embodied in this view of salvation and emphasized in the *Reasonableness*.

A broader controversy was caused by the flourishing of deism in the 1690s. The general climate of greater toleration and reduced press censorship under the postrevolutionary government allowed this flourishing to occur, and it was encouraged by what Samuel Pearson, Jr. calls "a rather obvious shift in mood from religious enthusiasm to religious respectability" in the "dramatically altered society marked by a new political stability" after the Glorious Revolution. Where the death struggle (or so it had seemed at the time) between religious groups for control of the government in 1681–8 had produced "inordinate concern with revelation," now there was the risk of "indifference to the subject."[5]

In the preface to the *Second Vindication*, after stating that it was the dissenters' controversy over justification that first drew him to investigate more closely what scripture had to say on the subject, Locke informs us that he decided to publish the *Reasonableness* "especially" to change the minds of "those who thought either that there was no need of revelation at all, or that the revelation of our Savior required the belief of ... articles for salvation" that seemed "impossible to them." These two objections, Locke continues, were the principal arguments "made by deists against Christianity; but against Christianity misunderstood."[6] A correct account of the scriptures would prove the deists wrong.

It is important to understand that what was called "deism" in Locke's time was very different from deism as it developed in the eighteenth century and afterward. The deism that sprouted up in the 1690s did not understand itself as a movement opposed to Christianity, although its theist critics certainly saw it as such. These deists agreed with what they understood to be the teachings of Jesus Christ; what made them deists was their belief that those teachings were also fully discernable in nature, without the aid of revelation. In the deist view, Jesus did not bring any new teaching, he simply provided the most clear and complete exposition ever produced of the natural moral law. That these deists understood themselves as a movement within Christianity rather than against it is plain from the titles of the two of the most important deist books of the period: John Toland's *Christianity Not Mysterious* and Matthew Tindal's *Christianity as Old as the Creation: Or, the Gospel, a Republication of the Religion of Nature*.[7] Not until later did deism consciously separate from Christianity, reducing God to the status of cosmological watchmaker and replacing the teachings of Jesus with conscience and the "moral sense" as a guide to morality.

Locke's confrontation with the deists, therefore, did not address what would later become the major topic of debate between theistic Christians and deists: the accuracy of the scriptural account of Jesus.[8] The deists of Locke's time did not question the accuracy of scripture. Instead, Locke's case addresses the two deistic objections to theistic Christianity he identified in the preface to the *Second Vindication*: that revelation was unnecessary, and that the theistic view of Christian salvation entails irrational beliefs. The first of these subjects we will delay until the next chapter, where we will take it up at length as part of Locke's account of the relationship between religious belief and moral law. The second, however, we will take up when we look at what Locke says is necessary for Christian salvation. As we will see, Locke shows the doctrinal simplicity of Christianity in a way that will not only bring deists into the fold, but will also draw Christians into moral consensus with one another.

This argument for doctrinal simplicity brings us to a third theological controversy going on in 1690s England. This was perhaps the fiercest of the three controversies that we have taken notice of here, and yet – or perhaps one should say "hence" – the one in which Locke was least willing to acknowledge his participation. In 1687, an increasingly besieged Jamns II had relaxed religious censorship in a manner that allowed the printing of books sympathetic to unitarianism, the belief that God is separate from and superior to Jesus and the Holy Spirit. In fact, the label "unitarian" first became widespread at this time; previously, there had only been discussion of particular theological groups, like Arians and Socinians, that held this view. The debate came to be called the Unitarian Controversy.[9] According to Higgins-Biddle, the Unitarian Controversy "dominated the theological literature in England," and the outcry against it became so great that in 1696 William III issued an order restricting preaching and writing on unitarianism and instructing the church to prosecute unitarians in civil court.[10]

There has been a very interesting debate among Locke scholars over whether Locke himself actually embraced the unitarian view. There are reasonable arguments on both sides.[11] Locke was reluctant to discuss his beliefs regarding the Trinity – not only did he leave the subject unmentioned in the *Reasonableness*, he never publicly professed his beliefs on it, despite having been challenged by his critics to do so after the publication of the *Reasonableness*. He did write that he believed in the Trinity in a manuscript he composed at Oxford in 1661–2; the debate among Locke scholars is over whether he later withdrew from this position.[12] However, we are not here concerned with Locke's private beliefs but with the content of his published works. What interests us here is the consequences of Locke's silence on the Trinity in the *Reasonableness* for his theory of moral consensus.

Locke's silence on the Trinity has led to the general practice of describing Locke as a Socinian. This label is inaccurate and has caused serious distortion. The Socinians held a number of other heterodox beliefs with which Locke directly and specifically disagreed.[13] And, more importantly for our purposes, the Socinians explicitly denied the Trinity whereas Locke simply remained silent about it. This distinction is crucial because, as we will see, Locke seeks to build a religious community of all Christians in which disagreements over theological doctrine will be tolerated. To accomplish this, he has to show that trinitarians and unitarians who accept the gospel of salvation through Jesus Christ are all Christians and are all saved. His purpose in the *Reasonableness* is not to settle the argument over the Trinity but to show that salvation does not hinge on it.

We have recounted these three theological disputes to provide context for the *Reasonableness*, but we should also notice that Locke was not solely concerned with these disputes. As he comments in the *Second Vindication*, to fully answer the question of how we become justified through faith he had to investigate "what faith that was that justified."[14] So while he began with a narrow question concerning justification, his ultimate goal was to lay out the content of Christian faith. In a letter written about five months before the *Reasonableness* was published, Locke tells a friend that he wrote it "considering diligently wherein the Christian faith consists," and that "I am fully convinced that a sincere reader of the gospel cannot be in doubt as to what the Christian faith is."[15] For Locke, the *Reasonableness*'s account of salvation is not simply the answer to a set of doctrinal disputes in 1690s England, it is an exposition of "what the Christian faith is." The ambitiousness of this goal reflects Locke's agenda of building moral consensus – he is not out to settle a dispute, or even a set of disputes, but to alter the landscape of all Christian discourse by showing that all such disputes are secondary to what the scriptures declare to be the essential content of Christian faith.

THE REASONABLENESS OF AN EVIDENTIARY FAITH

Following the religious epistemology of the *Essay*, the *Reasonableness* seeks to persuade the reader that Jesus's miracles are the reason to believe that he is the Messiah. Locke argues that there is a "threefold declaration of the Messiah" (R 57, 35). The first declaration, performed by Jesus himself, is the miracles he performed to "evidence his mission" (R 58, 36). The second declaration is the "phrases and circumlocutions" in the Old Testament "that did signify or intimate his coming" (R 59, 37). This is only a proof of Jesus's Messiahship insofar as it takes Jesus's fulfillment of the prophesies and/or the prophesies themselves to be miraculous. The third declaration was performed by the apostles, to whom fell the task of "by plain and direct words, declaring the doctrine of the Messiah, speaking out that Jesus was he" (R 61, 38). This, too, is only a proof of Jesus's Messiahship insofar as we take the miracles performed by the apostles as evidence of their divine authority. Miracles are the sole source of belief in revelation in the *Reasonableness*; throughout the work, and especially in the story of Jesus's life, Locke recurs to Jesus's miracles as evidence of his Messiahship.[16]

The *Reasonableness* presents a different line of argument in favor of miracles over other reasons for belief than the one presented in the *Essay*. The *Essay* addresses itself to philosophic problems that are not particular to Christianity, and does not presume the truth of Christianity in any of its arguments, although it is clearly tailored for a Christian audience in matters of focus and presentation. Its argument for basing faith on miracles arises from the imperative for rational regulation of all beliefs, which is not a specifically Christian concern. By contrast, the *Reasonableness* addresses specific debates about Christianity, and avails itself of specifically Christian arguments. Here, Locke's argument is that Jesus and the gospel authors treat miracles as the correct basis of faith, collecting an impressive array of scriptural quotations to support this conclusion. For example, in recounting Jesus' first miracle, John declares, "this beginning of miracles Jesus made, and manifested his glory, and his disciples believed in him," and goes on to tell us that Jesus quickly gathered a following "because of his miracles" (R 76, 50 and 79, 51).[17] Jesus himself, asked by disciples of John the Baptist whether he was the Messiah, performed a series of miracles and then said: "Tell John what ye have seen and heard: the blind see, the lame walk, the lepers are cleansed, the deaf hear, the dead are raised, to the poor the gospel is preached, and blessed is he who is not offended in me" (R 90, 57).[18] Elsewhere, Jesus is even more direct: "the works that I do in my father's name, bear witness of me" (R 58, 36).[19]

Obviously a non-Christian will not take the word of Jesus or the gospel authors on whether we ought to believe in miracles; this argument is addressed to those who already believe in Christianity. Locke is showing us that believing in Christianity for reasons other than miracles is incoherent, since we have the word of Jesus himself, and of the gospel authors, that miracles are the reason to believe. Thus the *Essay*'s rationalist argument for faith based on examination of the evidence of miracles is supplemented by the *Reasonableness*' argument from Christian scripture for precisely the same kind of faith. One aspect of the "reasonableness" of Christianity is its basis in evidence and miracles – a faith based on evidence is a reasonable faith.

In making a Christian argument for evidentiary faith, the *Reasonableness* provides a crucial component of moral consensus that only theology can provide. The *Essay* provided an argument that faith must remain within the bounds of reason, but that argument was itself a rational argument. Its premise is that reason cannot be set aside in matters of belief because belief is incoherent without reason. But many devoted enthusiasts are prepared to stare down this kind of rationalism on its own terms. They are perfectly willing to abandon rational standards of coherence and logic to maintain fidelity to their faith. In order to effectively reach such people, Locke shows in the *Reasonableness* that not only does reason demand that faith stay within the bounds of reason, the Bible itself demands that faith stay within the bounds of reason, insofar as the teachings of Jesus attribute faith to miracles. This parallel argument leaves the enthusiast with no refuge – he cannot hide from the demands of reason even within his faith.

The *Reasonableness* follows the epistemology of the *Essay* in a broader way as well, because of the central place it gives to the problem of knowledge, ignorance, and belief in the story of human history. The three major topics of the *Reasonableness* are the story of Jesus's life, the covenant of grace he brought, and the need for revelation to communicate that covenant. In all three sections, Locke's primary concern is the struggle of human beings to remove their ignorance and achieve knowledge and justifiable beliefs about God, his law, and his plan for the universe. The *Reasonableness* is a natural extension of the *Essay*, following the *Essay*'s method in order to resolve the *Essay*'s motivating problem.

Locke's retelling of the life of Jesus, which takes just over a hundred long paragraphs, shows that the story of Jesus in the Bible is the story of God's messenger bringing to humanity rational reasons to believe in his revelation. On Locke's account, every important aspect of Jesus's life was calculated to maximize the evidence it would provide of his Messiahship, to his own time and future generations. Quoting John's remark about his own gospel, "these are written that you may believe that Jesus is the

Messiah, the son of God, and that believing you may have life in his name," Locke argues that we should "apply the same conclusion to the history of our savior written by the evangelists, and to the history of the apostles written in the Acts" (R 162, 122).[20] For Locke, the purpose of all four gospels and the book of Acts is to provide evidence of Jesus's Messiahship. This relentless concern for evidence shows the underlying rationalism of Christianity, insofar as it is rational to believe on the basis of evidence rather than enthusiastic feelings. Thus, the *Reasonableness* shows that Christianity teaches the need for rational faith not only by recounting Jesus's statements about miracles, but in its larger account of Jesus's life.

Locke stresses the complexity of Jesus's achievement in laying a rational groundwork for faith. Jesus faced a major obstacle, in that he had to make known his Messiahship without giving the political authorities any legitimate grievance against him. This was necessary so that Jesus could testify to his perfect meekness and humility by allowing himself to be put to a gruesome death despite being manifestly innocent of any wrongdoing. It was a "fuller manifestation and evidence of his being the Messiah" that he "should be led as a sheep to the slaughter, and with all quiet and submission be brought to the cross, though there were no guilt or fault found in him" (R 62, 40). To avoid giving any legitimate grievance to the authorities, however, required that he not openly declare himself to be the Messiah. Because the Jews were "expecting at this time their Messiah and deliverance by him from the subjection they were in to a foreign yoke, the body of the people would certainly, upon his declaring himself to be the Messiah and their king, have rose up in rebellion" (R 74, 47; see also 120, 82–3; 128–31, 88–94; 137, 96–7; 140, 98–9; and 144, 102–3).[21] Declaring himself the Messiah would have been seen as rebellion against the Roman government, and "drawn on him the reputation and death of a turbulent, seditious malefactor" (R 74, 48). As a result, Jesus had to make it known that he was the Messiah without explicitly saying so.

The task was further complicated by the need to avoid excessive disruptions in the natural course of events. Too many miracles on too great a scale would render the story of Jesus's life unbelievable to future generations who did not witness it. For example, Locke writes, God could have used "supernatural influence upon his mind" to cause Pilate to release Jesus and tolerate his ministry, but then "I ask whether posterity would not either have suspected the story, or that some art had been used to gain that testimony from Pilate?" (R 144, 103). The main plot of the story had to proceed according to a normal and natural course of events, with miracles reserved only for specific occasions on which Jesus demonstrated his Messiahship. "If it were not so, the course and evidence of things would be confounded; miracles would lose their name and force; and there could be no distinction between natural and supernatural" (R 143, 102). For miracles to maintain their evidentiary "force," they must be used sparingly.

So Jesus carried out a plan of "concealment" and "reservedness" by which he performed miracles and strongly *implied* that he was the Messiah, but did not explicitly declare it until after he had been condemned to death (R 62, 39–40; see also 119, 81; 141–2, 99–101; and 146, 104–5).[22] This is why it fell mainly to the apostles to perform the third part of the "threefold declaration" of Jesus's Messiahship, the part in which his Messiahship was declared "by plain and direct words" (R 61, 38). Most of Locke's account of the life of Jesus is devoted to showing how Jesus managed this difficult project of communicating his Messiahship to the people, and proving it with miracles, without actually declaring it in so many words. Jesus's message to the disciples of John the Baptist, recounted previously, is a perfect example; asked whether he was the Messiah, Jesus replied by performing miracles. Jesus also repeatedly encounters people possessed by evil spirits who attempt to reveal his Messiahship, and according to Luke, "he, rebuking them, suffered them not to speak that they knew him to be the Messiah" (R 61, 39).[23] When his own disciples figured out that he was the Messiah, according to Mark, "he charged them that they should tell no man of him" (R 61, 39).[24]

This extraordinary way of viewing Jesus's life supports moral consensus not only by proving that Jesus taught a religious epistemology based on the rational evidence of miracles but also by giving considerable support to Locke's agenda of toleration. Locke stresses that Jesus concealed his Messiahship because he wanted to make sure it was clear that he had no "design upon the government" in pursuing his ministry (R 131, 93). The story Locke tells in the *Reasonableness* emphasizes the stark contrast between Jesus, who eschewed political authority, and the Jews, who hoped to unify religious and political authority in their expected Messiah. The implication – which, as we will see later, Locke makes explicit in the *Letter* – is that later evangelists should follow Jesus's example. This sets the stage for moral consensus by making toleration an imperative of Christianity.

But this way of presenting Jesus's life also has a major drawback for Locke's political agenda: it puts a special emphasis on Jesus's refusal to rebel against Rome or to approve of such rebellion in others. Locke, the greatest theorist of the right to rebellion in the history of political philosophy, describes as "according to divine wisdom and suited to a fuller manifestation and evidence of his being the Messiah" the "quiet and submission" of Jesus in allowing himself to be horribly executed even after Pilate himself declared him innocent. Needless to say, there is at the very least a strong tension between this view of Jesus and Locke's endorsement of (and possible participation in) rebellion against his own king – no matter how bad King James was, Caesar was much worse, and for that matter William of Orange was no Jesus Christ. But this is not to say that there is a flat contradiction between Locke's view of Jesus and his support of political rebellion; it is only to say that Locke had to show how rebellion could sometimes be consistent with the example of Jesus, who did not rebel, and the teachings of the apostles, who counseled the early Christians to obey their governments. In Chapter 7, we will look at Locke's delicate handling of this problem in his analysis of the dissolution of governments.

A BRIEF DIGRESSION: LOCKE'S EPISTEMOLOGY AND THE ACCURACY OF SCRIPTURE

One subject that seems to be missing from Locke's account of Jesus is a consideration of the evidentiary merit of the scriptures from which the account is taken. Locke recounts miracle after miracle from scripture but never addresses the question of why we should believe that the scriptural account is accurate. In the *Essay* he wrote that miracles must be "well attested" to be believed (E IV.16.13, 667). The *Reasonableness* makes only an incomplete case that the miracles of Jesus are well attested. As we have seen, Locke writes that Jesus's life was arranged so that his Messiahship would be believable to succeeding generations, and that the scripture was written so we would know what to believe (see R 143–5, 101–4; 160, 119; and 162, 122). But this does not make the case for the accuracy of scripture as such. It only establishes that Locke believes scripture is accurate. Locke's account of Christianity as being evidentiary and hence reasonable in its foundations cannot stand unless it can be shown that it is rational to believe in Jesus's miracles on the basis of the scriptural account.

The closest Locke comes to a direct comment on the subject is when he proclaims, startlingly, that "the evidence of our Savior's mission from heaven is so great, in the multitudes of miracles he did before all sorts of people, that what he delivered cannot but be received as the oracles of

God and unquestionable verity. For the miracles he did were so ordered by the divine providence and wisdom that they never were, or could be, denied by any of the enemies or opposers of Christianity" (R 237, 164–5). And then, as if to make sure we do not dismiss this as a momentary indulgence in rhetorical overkill, three paragraphs later he repeats the assertion, saying that the apostles were "accompanied with miracles, which were done in all parts so frequently, and before so many witnesses of all sorts in broad daylight, that, as I have before observed, the enemies of Christianity have never dared to deny them" (R 240, 168–9).

This is a difficult passage to digest. Obviously it is not literally true that no person anywhere has ever denied that Jesus performed genuine miracles.[25] The difficulty here is particularly acute because the judgment call that decides whether a miracle is well attested is the crucial pivot of Locke's religious epistemology. However, we must bear in mind that the important claim being made in this passage is not that no one has ever denied Jesus's miracles, but that the grounds for accepting those miracles are very strong. The most plausible reading of this passage would be to take the former claim as a hyperbolic flourish meant to emotionally reinforce the more dispassionate latter claim. Despite his image as a writer of modest, reasonable prose, Locke was often given to flights of hyperbole, particularly when he saw himself as arguing for a moderate, reasonable position against a dogmatic or fanatical one. His incendiary attacks on enthusiasts in the *Essay*, on religious inquisitors in the *Letter*, and on absolutists in the *Two Treatises* – some of these attacks rising almost to the level of outright slander – are only the most famous examples of this pattern.[26] In the last third of the *Reasonableness*, in which this passage appears, Locke seems to see himself as defending a reasonable openness to faith – that is, an openness to the possibility that miracles really do occur – against what he considered the irrationally dogmatic skepticism of the deists toward miracles.

However, even if we take as mere hyperbole the claim that no one has ever denied Jesus's miracles, we are still left with the lack of an explicit argument in the *Reasonableness* for the historical accuracy of scripture. That this issue was not important for Locke is not too surprising; as we have already seen, the deists against whom Locke was arguing in the *Reasonableness* did not typically challenge the accuracy of scripture, but instead argued that the teachings of scripture were accessible through natural reason alone. And since the deists were the only significant potential audience of the *Reasonableness* who were not already theistic Christians, Locke was not faced with any potential adversaries who might have questioned the judgment that scripture is accurate. This was a point on which Locke simply didn't require a strong defense.

Despite this lack of explicitness, however, the text does give us some idea of why Locke was so confident in the accuracy of scripture. There is an implicit argument in Locke's repeated assertion in this passage that the miracles of Jesus and the apostles were performed "in all parts," "before all sorts of people," and "before so many witnesses of all sorts in broad daylight." Locke emphasizes the number and variety of witnesses, the open performance of miracles in public before crowds of people who were not already believers, and the variety of different nations in which the miracles were accepted. The implicit argument seems to be that phony miracles could not have gathered such a large and dedicated following so quickly, embracing people from so many different nations, religions, and social stations.[27] One could also infer from Locke's emphasis on the large number of witnesses an argument that if scripture had not conformed to the events as they happened, it would have been refuted early on by living eyewitnesses. The books of the New Testament were all written and circulated during the first century, when many of the original eyewitnesses to the events they describe would still have been around.

This is a line of argument for belief in the accuracy of scripture that Christians have long used to defend the rationality of their faith. Very recently this approach was defended in a major work by theologian N. T. Wright that has received a great deal of attention.[28] Locke did not need to provide the complete argument for the historical evidence in favor of scripture's accuracy, but there is no shortage of others who have made it for him.

LOCKE'S INTERPRETIVE METHOD: FOUNDATIONS

The most important single thing to understand about Locke's account of Christian theology is the interpretive method on which it is based. The reason Locke's method for reading the Bible is so important, and shapes everything in his theology, is that Locke turns to the text of the Bible to adjudicate all disputes over Christian doctrine. He states his reasons for this Bible-centered method most succinctly in an appendix to the *Letter* on the subject of heresy and schism, in which he condemns the division of Christians from one another on any grounds other than disagreements over the meaning of biblical text. The Bible is "acknowledged by all Christians to be of divine inspiration, and therefore fundamental" (L 84, 61). For this reason it ought to be "the only foundation of faith" (L 84, 60). A

disagreement over the meaning of the Bible is at some level a disagreement over the character of Christianity itself, since the Bible is the basic
teaching of Christianity, but any other kind of disagreement is not.

No doubt one reason Locke elevates the Bible so far above all other
Christian teachings and institutions, making it "the only foundation of
faith," is because he thinks it is our only remaining link to the miracle-
working (and thus credible) revealers of the apostolic era. However, the
universal recognition of the Bible's authority among Christians provides
another, much more practical reason for doing so. Arguments based
on any other source, whether from ancient books written by the great
thinkers in the history of Christianity or from the pronouncements of
one or another ecclesiastical institution, will not be universally recognized as authoritative for Christians. No doubt virtually all Christians will
agree that, say, Augustine was a wise man and a great thinker, but "because Augustine says so" is not a dispositive argument for all Christians;
many Christians believe they can legitimately respond with "Augustine is
wrong." The Bible, and only the Bible, is dispositive for all Christians. If
it is agreed that the Bible requires a certain belief or rule, Christians will
not reply with "the Bible is wrong." Because the Bible is unique in this way,
only a theology drawn exclusively from the Bible can build a Christian
case for moral consensus. The fundamental problem moral consensus
seeks to alleviate is the fragmentation of religious groups, so it would
not accomplish anything to build a case for it based on the teachings
of one or another group. Locke must make an argument to unite all
Christians by showing, with arguments that all Christians must recognize
as authoritative, that Christianity requires moral consensus.

Because Locke's theology is drawn exclusively from the Bible, his
method for interpreting texts is paramount. Locke follows a method of
interpreting scripture that does not rely upon existing exegetical traditions, because those traditions are divisive. To illustrate Locke's interpretive method, we will take an overview of the *Essay*, the *Reasonableness*, and
the *Two Treatises*. Each of these works contains some comment on the
problems of exegesis. As we will see, Locke followed the same approach
to interpreting scripture throughout these works.

In the previous two chapters we saw that the *Essay* pays much attention
to the problems of language. All of the linguistic problems he identified
apply not only to our own thought and speech but to ancient texts as well.
These problems are further compounded, Locke writes, by the problems
of history and translation. Words change meaning over time and meaning
is often garbled or lost in translating foreign languages – some words

are untranslatable, and many others carry connotations that are difficult for a nonnative speaker to know. In "different countries" and "remote ages . . . speakers and writers had very different notions, tempers, customs, ornaments, and figures of speech, etc.," but "to us now they are lost and unknown" (E III.9.22, 489).

When a text has no special claim to authority this is not an urgent problem. Locke writes that where the meaning of such texts is clear we can benefit from them, and "if they do not use their words with a due clearness and perspicuity, we may lay them aside," because "our good and evil" do not depend "on their decrees." But some texts may contain "truths we are required to believe or laws we are to obey," so the problems of interpretation cannot always be avoided (E III.9.10, 481). In fact, these problems will be especially acute in the complex matters of religion, law, and morality that authoritative texts are likely to concern.

Although Locke devotes a some attention to the problem of getting people to read texts more carefully, he ultimately holds that we cannot completely remove this problem simply by being careful in interpreting ancient texts.[29] Communication is difficult not just because people are careless but because language is inherently imperfect. Even among "men of the same language and country," and in the same time period, "the signification of words" depends "very much on the thoughts, notions, and ideas of him that uses them," so interpreting language must "unavoidably be of great uncertainty," at least where difficult subjects are concerned (E III.9.22, 489). Similarly, the problems of history and translation can be alleviated with great effort but are never completely overcome.

A sacred text, even if it is divinely inspired and therefore infallible, will not guide us infallibly because we ourselves are fallible. "Though everything said in the text be infallibly true, yet the reader may be, nay cannot chose but be very fallible in the understanding of it. Nor is it to be wondered, that the will of God, when clothed in words, should be liable to that doubt and uncertainty, which unavoidably attends that sort of conveyance" (E III.9.23, 489–90). Thus, as Locke writes in one of the *Essay*'s very few overt endorsements of a political position, "it would become us to be charitable one to another in our interpretations or misunderstandings of those ancient writings" (E III.9.22, 489).

Also, crucially, in matters where epistemological problems might have extreme consequences – such as when we use violence to force others to conform to a rule – we would be well advised to rely on beliefs that are backed up by reason rather than those that are derived from textual interpretation alone. God has "given all mankind so sufficient a light of reason" that moral law is not exclusively available through scripture; it is also "spread before all the world" in "his works and providence," that is, in nature. Moral principles that are confirmed by rational analysis of the natural world are subject to fewer epistemological difficulties than those that depend on scripture alone, because the latter are "liable to the common and natural obscurities and difficulties incident to words" (E III.9.23, 490). This is not to say that reason must give independent assent to every point of theology. As we have shown in the last chapter, the *Essay* requires us to believe anything delivered in revelation, whether reason can confirm it or not. "Revelation, where God has been pleased to give it, must carry it, against the probable conjectures of reason" (E IV.18.8, 694). But we should also be mindful that the truths we receive from revelation are subject to epistemological problems. Locke does not explicitly say what he's getting at here, but the point seems to be that moral laws received only through scripture don't make good candidates for politically enforceable laws.

LOCKE'S INTERPRETIVE METHOD: APPLICATION

Locke states the guiding principle of his interpretive method in the *First Treatise*: "God, I believe, speaks differently from men, because he speaks with more truth, more certainty: but . . . I do not think, he speaks differently from them, in crossing the rules of language in use amongst them." We must proceed on the assumption that God speaks according to "the ordinary rules of language," such that his meaning will be clear to any ordinary reader who knows the language and historical context of the text, and sets aside his personal biases and predispositions (T I.46, 34). Our goal should be to understand each passage in the way "which best agrees with the plain construction of the words, and arises from the obvious meaning of the place" (T I.32, 25).[30] The *Reasonableness* gives us a similar summary of Locke's exegetical method. The first paragraph of the *Reasonableness* demands that we stick to "the plain direct meaning of the words and phrases," accounting of course for the time, place, and context in which they were written or spoken, rather than attributing "learned, artificial and forced" meanings to the text (R 1, 2).

The underlying premise of this method is that God provided a clear and accessible message in revelation. If God spoke to humanity any other way, Locke writes in the *First Treatise*, he would "lose his design in speaking, what thus spoken, they could not understand" (T I.46, 34). If scripture's purpose is to communicate God's will to all Christians, for Locke this implies that – at least in the matters that are of great importance to all readers – it would not contain counterintuitive, obscure, or hidden teachings, but would lay out the truth in a manner that would be clear and easily understood for anyone with a sufficient grasp of the language and the historical context in which the scriptures were written. That is the only way scripture could fulfill its purpose. Locke was not the first Christian to take this approach to scripture. He was familiar with the work of the theologian Richard Simon, to whom he is significantly indebted for his scriptural method.[31] But Locke was almost certainly the most influential Christian to take this approach.

Locke rejects the idea that scripture is written such that only a select few have special access to its meaning. This would leave everyone else in a position of almost certain damnation, since they would not have access to salvation in the teachings of scripture. It is unthinkable to Locke that God would arbitrarily offer salvation only to the lucky few who could correctly read scripture. If salvation is available to more than just the well-educated elite, as scripture itself declares is the case, and salvation can only be had through understanding scripture's teachings, it follows that scripture must be written such that any sufficiently informed and unbiased reader can understand it. If it were true that scripture could only be understood by a select few, then only that select few would be genuine Christians; everyone else would be followers of the select few rather than followers of Jesus himself. As Locke puts it in the *Paraphrase*, "if I must believe for myself . . . I must understand for myself."[32]

Of course, just because God has not concealed or mystified the meaning of his revelation does not mean that there are no epistemological problems to be overcome in understanding it. The language barrier alone – scripture, after all, is written in ancient languages – is an enormous obstacle, as Locke himself shows on several occasions. There is also the persistent problem of bias in the interpretation of language; since most words do not have mathematically rigid meanings and must be interpreted, it is easy for a reader to unconsciously interpret language in whatever way fits his predispositions. Filmer says Genesis 9:1–3 "may best be understood" as a grant of power to Noah alone, despite its explicit inclusion of Noah's sons. This prompts the following reply from Locke: "That indeed is best, for our author to be understood, which best serves to his purpose, but that truly 'may best be understood' by anybody else, which best agrees with the plain construction of the words, and arises from the obvious meaning of the place" (T I.32, 25). But even beyond these difficulties, a certain level of indeterminacy is inherent in all language, so even an educated and unbiased reader must apply degrees of assent to his interpretations. Some passages entitle us to hold certain interpretations at a very high degree of assent, while other passages require us to acknowledge that our interpretations cannot be very certain. In the *First Treatise* Locke strikes down a number of Filmer's scriptural arguments simply by showing that the meaning of the passages in question is too "doubtful" or "obscure" to legitimately support the coercive enforcement of any one interpretation (T I.49, 36; I.112, 77–8; and I.118, 81).

These problems make interpreting the Bible according to "the ordinary rules of language" a complex task. And because he excludes scriptural traditions, Locke is left without the interpretive resources others typically rely on to make sense of scripture. He must replace those resources with interpretive guidance drawn from scripture itself, or from uncontroversial sources such as accepted historical evidence about ancient times and places. In the *Two Treatises* he finds a number of ways to do this.

Where the definition of a word or phrase is needed, Locke looks at how that word or phrase is used throughout scripture, particularly where the word or phrase in question appears repeatedly in the same book. For example, Locke writes that the donation of "every moving thing" to Adam at Genesis 1:28 cannot include human beings along with the animals, because the Hebrew words signifying "every moving thing" are used in other passages in ways that clearly include only animals. This includes Genesis 9:2–3, where God donates "every moving thing" to Noah and his sons for food (T I.25–7, 20–2). If "every moving thing" includes humans, Genesis 9:2–3 endorses cannibalism! "And if God made all mankind slaves to Adam and his heirs" at Genesis 1:28 by giving Adam dominion over every moving thing, "methinks Sir Robert should have carried his monarchical power one step higher, and satisfied the world, that princes might eat their subjects too," under authority from Genesis 9:2–3 (T I.27, 22).

For longer passages, Locke looks to the immediate scriptural context of the passage and our historical evidence (where we have any) about the time and place of the author. Locke argues that Genesis 27:29 could not imply that Jacob had rightful political dominion over Esau, because "in the story we find the quite contrary, for [at] Genesis 32, Jacob several times calls Esau lord and himself his servant, and [at] Genesis 33[:3], 'he bowed himself seven times to the ground to Esau.'" Indeed, Genesis 27:29 could not even be addressing the general subject of whether or not Jacob had political dominion over Esau, because Esau "lived apart in Mount Seir, where he founded a distinct people and government, and was himself prince over them, as much as Jacob was in his own family" (T I.117, 80).

Locke also clears up the meaning of unclear passages by looking at how other scriptural authors have treated the same subject. When arguing that the donation of the world at Genesis 1:28 was made to all humanity and not specifically to Adam, he shows that elsewhere in the Bible David and Paul both write about the donation in ways that imply this interpretation. David "might be supposed to understand the donation of God in this text, and the right of kings, too, as well as" Filmer, but at Psalms 8:6–8 David finds "no such charter of monarchical power" in the donation (T I.28, 22). Similarly, at I Timothy 6:17 Paul "seems to have as little notion of any such private dominion of Adam as I" (T I.40, 30).

Finally, where the meaning of a passage cannot be clarified in these ways, Locke seeks out the meaning that it would have been reasonable for the author to intend, given what we know about him and the subject he was addressing. His treatment of Judges 11:27 is an example of this method. Locke argues that when Jephtha says, "the Lord the judge be judge this day between the children of Israel, and the children of Ammon," he is justifying his violent resistance against the Ammonites by appealing to the rightness of his cause under God's law (see T II.21, 125). His argument, as we will see when we take up this example in detail in Chapter 7, is that this is what it would have been reasonable for Jephtha to have meant given the context provided in the story scripture tells about him.

THE NEED FOR SALVATION: REASON, LAW, AND SIN

Jesus's mission was necessary, Locke writes in the *Reasonableness*, in order to provide salvation for humanity. The *Reasonableness* begins by outlining the need for salvation, which Locke argues for from scripture, specifically from the book of Genesis and the teachings of Jesus and his disciples. People need salvation because they have sinned against God's law, and God, being just, must punish them. "It seems the unalterable purpose of the divine justice that no unrighteous person, no one that is guilty of any breach of the law, should be in paradise" (R 10, 8). What people need to be "saved" from is the just punishment of their sin.[33]

All people are sinners because they do not perfectly obey the "law of works," which is the law God has laid down for our behavior. Locke writes that "whatever God requires anywhere to be done . . . that is a part of the law of works." On this account, the first revelation of the law of works was God "forbidding Adam to eat of the tree of knowledge" (R 20, 12). The most important revelation of the law of works, however, was that given to Moses. Locke uses the law laid down by Moses – or at least "the moral part of the law of Moses" as opposed to "ceremonial" and "political" parts of that law – as a reference point for talking about the law of works (R 22, 13). There have been other revelations of the law of works, including through Jesus and his disciples. Indeed, since it contains everything God wants from our behavior, the law of works, by the strict definition of that term, is indefinitely large and no revelation can contain it all. For simplicity's sake, we will follow Locke's practice and treat "the law of works" as more or less synonymous with the moral part of Moses's law, since that is by far the most clear, complete, and generally applicable revelation of the law of works.

Locke argues from scripture that anything short of perfect obedience to the law of works leaves us in need of salvation. "Exclusion from paradise and a loss of immortality is the portion of sinners, of all those who have in any way broken that law and failed of a complete obedience to it" (R 11, 8–9). No one lives up to this standard of perfection; Locke quotes Paul to the effect that all human beings, "having sinned, come short of the glory of God." Thus, "it follows that no one could then have eternal life and bliss" without salvation (R 12, 9).[34]

To those who ask why God requires perfect obedience, such that no one has ever successfully obeyed, Locke replies that a standard of perfection is "required" by "the purity of God's nature" and "must be the law of such a creature as man, unless God would have made him a rational creature and not required him to have lived by the law of reason" (R 14, 9).[35] The law of works is "the law of reason," because reason both discerns it and discerns why we must obey it. For Locke, reason can find God's law both through revelation, as we saw in the last chapter, and through analysis of human nature, as we will see in Chapter 6. Since people have reason, Locke writes, they must be morally required to follow it completely. If we authorize them to depart from reason in any way, no matter how trivial, reason itself will be destroyed, since there can be no rational argument for obeying reason sometimes and not obeying it other times. "If you will admit" rational creatures "to forsake reason in one point, why not in another? Where will you stop?" God made reason and determined what reason would command, so disobedience to the law of works/reason in even the smallest particular is disobedience to God. "To disobey God in any part of his commands (and it is he that commands what reason does) is direct rebellion" (R 14, 9). Thus, people need salvation because they are imperfectly rational – that is, imperfectly obedient to the law of reason.

In this account of why we need salvation, obedience to reason and obedience to the moral law of revelation are completely unified. They are the same thing. Locke equates "the law of works" with "the law of reason." He even goes so far as to label it the law "of nature": "this law was the law of reason, or, as it is called, of nature" (R 14, 9). In this, Locke diverges from the medieval use of the label "law of nature." For the medievals, that label applied only to laws discernable through natural reason alone. This served to emphasize the distinction between the part of God's moral law discernable without revelation and the part discernable only in revelation. Locke's works, by contrast, emphasize a different distinction: that between moral laws that are clearly discernable and moral laws that are not clearly discernable. Exactly where they are discernable, in nature or in revelation, is not an important point. Locke refers to all of God's moral law, whether delivered in nature or in revelation, as "the law of nature."

This conceptual unification of revelatory moral law, rational moral law, and natural moral law, which is made explicit in this passage in the *Reasonableness* but runs consistently throughout Locke's works, is perhaps the most fundamental intellectual commitment of moral consensus. For Locke, it is rational to search for God's moral law wherever we can find well-attested accounts of it, in revelation and in nature. The moral law discernable in nature and the moral law of revelation are one and the same law, laid down by the same author and perfectly harmonious in content. This unity serves moral consensus by carrying Locke's unification of reason and faith into the realm of moral law. We need not choose between obedience to the law of reason and obedience to laws delivered in revelation, since these laws are the same. This allows for the unification of different religious groups, because the law discernable in nature is equally persuasive to members of all religions, as it relies on no specific revelation. And members of the political community cannot legitimately argue that the laws of their religions overrule the law discernable in nature, since the latter has the same divine moral authority as the former.

SALVATION AND THE "SINGLE PROPOSITION"

Having offended against the law of works, all are liable to punishment and are thus in need of salvation. Here we come to what Locke calls the "law of faith," as distinct from the law of works. Jesus communicated the law of faith and attested to its divine authority with the evidence of miracles. As we have seen, Locke takes John's remark, "these are written that you may believe that Jesus is the Messiah, the son of God, and that believing you may have life in his name," as a statement of the purpose of Jesus's life and the apostles's mission (R 162, 122).[36] The law of faith is what allows us to "have life in his name." Locke's account of what we must do to obtain salvation under the law of faith is a crucial component of his Christian argument for moral consensus. It demonstrates that most matters of Christian doctrine are ancillary to the salvation of souls. This prepares the way for mutual Christian toleration, because it vitiates what was once the primary argument for compulsory religious orthodoxy: that only those Christians who subscribe to the whole body of orthodox doctrine will be saved.

The law of faith lays down the terms of the covenant of grace, by which, as Locke puts it, God "justifies" those who have Christian faith "by counting their faith for righteousness, i.e. for complete performance of the law" (R 25, 16).[37] Obviously, determining what beliefs constitute the faith that is counted for righteousness is crucial to our understanding of the law of faith. Locke argues that "all that was necessary to be believed for justification was no more but this single proposition: that 'Jesus of Nazareth was the Christ, or the Messiah' " (R 50, 31). That is, the only belief necessary for salvation through the law of faith is that Jesus of Nazareth is the Messiah (Hebrew for "anointed one") appointed by God to bring salvation to sinners as foretold in the Old Testament. To accept Jesus as the Messiah requires us to receive him in two roles: as "the promised deliverer" or savior, and as "king and ruler" (R 178, 134).

Locke supports this position with an extensive review of the teachings of Jesus and the apostles, showing that Jesus taught that belief in his Messiahship was necessary for salvation, that he never taught this about any other belief, and that the preaching of the apostles was directed to the promulgation of this single proposition (see R 32–50, 20–31; 141–2, 99–101; 152, 109–10; 157–9, 117–18; and 161–3, 120–3). Furthermore, when Jesus took his final leave of his disciples before the crucifixion, having at long last explicitly affirmed his Messiahship, "here one may expect all the articles of faith should be laid down plainly, if anything else were required of them to believe but what he had taught them and they believed already" (R 152, 109). Yet he gave them no "articles" other than to believe in him, that is, to believe in his Messiahship. And "one of his last actions, even when he was upon the cross, was to confirm his doctrine by giving salvation to one of the thieves that was crucified with him, upon his declaration that he believed him to be the Messiah" (R 159, 118).

Locke emphasizes the simplicity of Christian faith on this account. "Had God intended that none but the learned scribe, the disputer, or wise of this world, should be Christians or be saved, thus religion should have been prepared for them, filled with speculations and niceties, obscure terms and abstract notions." But "if the poor had the gospel preached to them," which Jesus tells us was "a mark . . . of his mission . . . it was, without doubt, such a gospel as the poor could understand – plain and intelligible" (R 252, 195). He even suggests that Jesus chose the original apostles for their humble origins and lack of education – "a company of poor, ignorant, illiterate men" – so that they would preach the gospel "without being more particular than he had ordered" (R 141, 100). Apostles "of quicker parts" would not have been "so easily kept from meddling beyond just what was prescribed to them" to teach (R 142, 101).

He also suggests that the learned and scholarly Paul, in contrast to the original apostles, was "better fitted for an apostle after than during our savior's ministry, and therefore" was not called "until after Christ's resurrection" (R 142, 101). That way Paul could lay out a more detailed and sophisticated Christian doctrine, and it would be clear that this larger doctrine was not necessary to salvation, because Jesus and the other apostles had not taught it. Locke adds that Paul's epistles are explicitly addressed to those who are already Christians, and thus "could not be designed to teach them the fundamental points and articles necessary to salvation," since the recipients, as Christians, were already saved (R 247–8, 186–90). At first glance this may appear to be wrong, since Paul's epistles (especially chapters 1–8 of Romans) contain detailed explanations of how salvation occurs. But Locke is not denying that Paul explains the mechanics of salvation; rather, he is saying that an understanding of these mechanics is not itself necessary to salvation. One can be saved through faith in Christ without understanding just how or why it is that faith in Christ brings about a person's salvation. The churches to which Paul was writing already believed in Christ's Messiahship, which is all that was necessary to make them Christian churches.

To understand the significance of the *Reasonableness'* position that only belief in Jesus' Messiahship is necessary for salvation, we must acknowledge that the *Reasonableness* discounts other large points of Christian theology to a certain extent, insofar as it denies that those doctrines are necessary to salvation. Locke's emphasis on Jesus's mission to inform us of the covenant of grace strongly implies a serious departure from normal Christian soteriology (that is, the study of salvation) in two points: the satisfaction or atonement of Christ and the Trinity.

Traditionally, virtually all Christian denominations have held that people are not Christians, and thus are not saved, unless they believe that Jesus came not merely to *promulgate* the covenant of grace through his teachings but to *implement* it through his crucifixion. Scripture does clearly teach that Jesus did this (see, for example, the aforementioned Romans 1–8) and historically most Christians have held that one must believe in a particular understanding of this event to be saved. The particular form of this belief that was prominent in Locke's time was the doctrine of the "satisfaction" – that in dying, Jesus made satisfaction to God for the sins of all those who believe in him. Other versions of this doctrine, such as the doctrine of the "atonement," give different accounts of how the crucifixion accomplished the covenant of grace. In particular, there is a deep division between Protestants and Catholics over the fundamental conception of how Christ's crucifixion makes salvation possible. Nonetheless, the central metaphysical importance of the crucifixion is common to all the major Christian theologies.

The second point of implicit deviation from standard soteriology concerns the doctrine of the Trinity – that God is one substance but exists in three persons, that of the Father, the Son, and the Holy Spirit. This doctrine, which is very clearly affirmed throughout the Bible, holds that Jesus is not merely the promised Messiah but is actually divine, is not merely a messenger from God but is himself God. This doctrine is closely connected to that of the satisfaction, since it is impossible that a mere mortal would be capable of making full satisfaction for the sins of humanity. Only God himself could make satisfaction for (or atone for, or in some other sense remove the consequences of) humanity's sin against God's law. Historically, most Christians have held that a person who does not believe in Christ's divinity, and hence the Trinity, is not a Christian and is not saved.

The doctrine of the Trinity is entirely absent from the *Reasonableness*, as we have noted previously. Locke did believe in the satisfaction, and the *Reasonableness* alludes to it in passing a few times.[38] Locke describes Jesus as "a mediator between God and man" (R 233, 163) and affirms that Jesus's mission included "laying down his life for others" (R 176, 132). Locke was quick to point out these allusions when his more conventional religious critics claimed that the *Reasonableness* didn't mention the satisfaction.[39] But the *Reasonableness* does not provide a doctrine explaining how the satisfaction works. Locke writes that our knowledge of the spiritual world is too limited for us to have a complete understanding of "what transactions there were between God and our savior, in reference to his kingdom." That does not give us any excuse to reject a truth conveyed by scripture, because "we shall take too much upon us, if we shall call God's wisdom or providence to account, and pertly condemn for needless, all that our weak, and perhaps biased, understanding cannot account for" (R 235, 164). Which is to say, we must believe in the satisfaction because scripture teaches it. But because the metaphysics of the satisfaction are above our understanding, we cannot make any particular understanding of the satisfaction necessary to salvation.

It was largely due to these factors that the publication of the *Reasonableness* was met with considerable outrage.[40] Moreover, Locke's emphasis on Jesus's role as a messenger from God may tend to undercut belief in the Trinity and the satisfaction, insofar as it may be taken as providing an alternative way of understanding Jesus's life and mission.

However, Locke's departures from normal Christian soteriology are not nearly as radical as they may at first appear to be. Locke never denies the Trinity; he simply doesn't mention it. He affirms the satisfaction; he just doesn't explain it. His purpose is not to oppose these doctrines, but to argue that no particular belief regarding those topics is necessary to make a person a Christian. Scripture does not say that any particular belief regarding Christological questions such as the relationship between Jesus and God or the metaphysics of the covenant of grace is necessary to salvation. It certainly does discuss these topics at some length, and it provides a number of clear and unambiguous teachings about them. But at no point does it clearly say that knowledge of these topics is necessary to salvation.

In fact, the New Testament contains a number of stories in which people are saved despite having no apparent knowledge of Jesus's divinity, his satisfaction for sin, or any other point of theology beyond his Messiahship. The Samaritan woman who met Jesus while drawing water at a well does not appear to have known anything about Jesus other than that he was the Messiah, but when he told her this and she believed it, she was saved, as were the people of her village when she passed on the good news to them.[41] The thief crucified on the cross next to Jesus also does not appear to have had a Christology beyond the fact of Jesus's Messiahship, but he was saved as well.[42] Locke cites both these stories and a number of others to support his case. There is also the matter of the believers of the Old Testament, who (according to Paul in Romans 4) were saved simply by faith in God's promise that a Messiah would someday be sent (see R 229, 161).

There are also a number of statements in the New Testament proclaiming categorically that all who accept Jesus's Messiahship are saved. In addition to the statement we have already considered – "these are written that you may believe that Jesus is the Messiah, the son of God, and that believing you may have life in his name" – John also put the point even more succinctly in one of his epistles: "Whosoever believeth that Jesus is the Messiah is born of God" (R 29, 18).[43] Locke collects many other such statements for our consideration. If we agree with Locke that scripture ought not to be read through the lens of what he calls "learned, artificial, and forced" interpretations, then these simple and unconditional statements put Locke's soteriology on very solid ground.

It is worth noting that another figure, universally recognized as a titan of Christian thought, has also endorsed the position that no understanding of the metaphysics of the crucifixion is necessary for salvation. He writes:

The central Christian belief is that Christ's death has somehow put us right with God and given us a fresh start. Theories as to how it did this are another matter. A good many different theories have been held as to how it works; what all Christians are agreed on is that it does work. I will tell you what I think it is like. All sensible people know that if you are tired and hungry a meal will do you good. But the modern theory of nourishment – all about the vitamins and proteins – is a different thing. People ate their dinners and felt better long before the theory of vitamins was ever heard of: and if the theory of vitamins is some day abandoned they will go on eating their dinners just the same. Theories about Christ's death are not Christianity: they are explanations about how it works.[44]

So wrote C. S. Lewis in *Mere Christianity*.

It is also worth noting that, although Locke believes a person can lack belief in the *divinity* of Jesus and still be a Christian, he insists that one must believe in the *Messiahship* of Jesus to be a Christian. As we have already seen, for Locke the office of Messiah includes the roles of "king and deliverer" (R 229,161). So a person must accept Jesus both as his sovereign lord and as his savior in order to be a Christian. The present-day associations of the word "unitarian" might well interfere with our understanding of Locke's position here. Unlike the "unitarians" of our time, seventeenth-century unitarians were Bible-believing, sin-repenting, Jesus-trusting, God-of-Abraham-worshipping Christians. Locke's position that these people were saved, while it is certainly unusual, should not be understood as being deeply radical.

Locke's soteriology carries the epistemological project of the *Essay* forward into the realm of theology. His doctrine that Jesus's Messiahship is the only article of faith necessary for salvation is implicitly based upon a separation of very certain from less certain theological beliefs. This is not to say that very certain beliefs are necessary to salvation while less certain beliefs are not; rather, it is the connection between a given belief and salvation that must be very certain. If scripture does not clearly and unambiguously teach that a given belief is necessary to salvation, this in itself proves that the belief is not necessary to salvation, since God would never leave us in doubt about what is necessary for salvation. To critics who demanded that a particular understanding of the satisfaction must be necessary to salvation, Locke replied: "To urge such points of controversy as necessary articles of faith, when we see our savior and the apostles in their preaching urged them not as necessary to be believed, to make men Christians, is (by our own authority) to add prejudices to prejudices."[45] The necessity of believing that Jesus is the Messiah is clearly declared in scripture, and no other article of faith is clearly declared in scripture as being necessary to salvation. Points of doctrine must not be elevated to matters of necessary theology unless that elevation can be justified from scripture with a very high degree of assent.

Locke does not hold that doctrines other than Jesus's Messiahship are unimportant, and still less that they are in any sense optional. Locke distinguishes between what is necessary to be believed for salvation and what is required to be believed of those who are saved (see R 249–52, 190–2).[46] All Christians are required to believe everything delivered by inspired scripture. These teachings "are truths, whereof no one can be rejected" (R 251, 191). But none of those beliefs, other than belief in Jesus's Messiahship, is necessary for salvation. "Though all divine revelation requires the obedience of faith, yet every truth of inspired scriptures is not one of those that by the law of faith is required to be explicitly believed for justification" (R 252, 192). This point becomes even more clear and explicit in the *Second Vindication*, because John Edwards, the critic to whom Locke was primarily responding in that work, had missed it.[47] In the *Second Vindication*, Locke describes the distinction between "what is *necessary* to be believed by every man to make him a Christian and what is *required* to be believed by every Christian."[48]

So Locke does hold that there is a large and complex body of doctrine that God requires us to believe. But that body includes everything in revealed scripture, a body so large and complex that our failure to believe all of it with perfect accuracy, like our failure to obey the law of works, is inevitable. However, the law of faith says that we are still saved so long as we believe that Jesus is the Messiah, no matter what else we may believe. We must make "fair endeavors" to understand scripture, "with a docility and disposition prepared to embrace and assent to all truths coming from God," because the need for such endeavors is implicit in the belief that Jesus is the Messiah (R 252, 192). But fair endeavors, not perfect success, is all that is required.

Thus, Locke's theology of a simple faith does not actually eliminate doctrinal questions like the satisfaction and the Trinity, since we are required to believe whatever scripture says about those questions. Rather, Locke seeks to establish that false beliefs about those questions are forgivable, and that in all faithful Christians they are in fact forgiven. Locke does not think these doctrinal questions don't matter, he just thinks that they don't matter to our one most important concern, which is securing our salvation.

Among intellectual historians of the seventeenth century, the view that Christianity is a simple faith in which all who believe in Jesus's Messiahship will be saved is associated most often with Hobbes. Some of Locke's contemporary critics, though they saw no other similarities between Locke's works and Hobbes's, accused Locke of following Hobbes in this point.[49] There is a surface similarity between Locke and Hobbes insofar as they both hold, as Hobbes puts it, the "only article of faith, which the scripture makes simply necessary to salvation, is this, that Jesus is the Christ."[50] However, the theological consequences they draw from this position, particularly for politics, are very different. Hobbes seeks to establish the simplicity of Christian faith in order to refute Christian arguments for toleration. If people are saved by their inward belief that Jesus is the Messiah, they can obey the sovereign in all matters (even if the sovereign commands them not to outwardly profess or practice Christianity) without danger of losing their salvation. Locke seeks to establish the simplicity of Christianity precisely as the basis of toleration, in order to create a community of tolerance and goodwill among Christians who mutually forgive one another for any failures of doctrinal understanding.

There is no reason to believe Locke acquired his theology from Hobbes, and good reason to doubt it. We will not take up here the scholarly dispute over whether Locke ever read Hobbes's account of salvation in *Leviathan*. On this there is no hope of a solid conclusion.[51] But Hobbes was not the first person to give an account of Christianity in which adherence to a minimal set of beliefs was sufficient to save all Christians. Higgins-Biddle, who calls this the "way of fundamentals," does an excellent job of tracing its origins and influence among liberal Anglicans, who were eventually labeled "Latitudinarians" by their detractors because they believed that there was wide latitude for error among those who were saved.[52] Higgins-Biddle writes that even before the English Civil War these liberal Anglicans were arguing that "reducing doctrine to a few, clearly revealed fundamentals could serve both to counter Jesuit attacks on Protestant individualism and to provide a basis for a more comprehensive Church of England."[53] Latitudinarian theology also supported "limited government authority and religious toleration."[54] And in 1647, theologian Jeremy Taylor argued, as Higgins-Biddle summarizes it, "that the fundamental article of faith was that Jesus was the Christ, the Son of God, man's redeemer." This is, for all intents and purposes, identical with the foundation of Christian theology in both Hobbes and Locke, and preceded both of them. Furthermore, while we have no evidence on whether Locke ever read Hobbes's theology, we have solid evidence that Locke was aware of Taylor's argument, and may have read it as early as 1661.[55] Thus, Locke is best understood not as a successor to Hobbes but as a restorer of the Latitudinarian way of fundamentals that Hobbes had appropriated for his own purposes.

But Locke, as usual, is not out to simply vindicate the Latitudinarians over others. By arguing that the "single proposition" of Jesus's Messiahship is the only belief necessary for salvation, he lays down the terms of Christian moral consensus. He shows that there is room for disagreement within Christianity – that is, that people can openly disagree over doctrine, even on matters of great importance, and still all be Christians. Locke seeks to create a community of all Christians based on their mutual belief that Jesus is the Messiah. Other points of Christian doctrine could be debated within this community, and no one would lose membership in the community no matter what position he held in those doctrinal debates, so long as he continued to profess Jesus's Messiahship.[56] In Locke's theology a dissenter can never be a threat to the Christian community, even if we grant that his beliefs are wrong. The dissenter either does or does not believe that Jesus is the Messiah. If he does not believe it, he is not really a dissenter at all, he is outside the Christian community altogether and irrelevant to it. If he does believe Jesus is the Messiah, then his other beliefs, false though they may be, make him a sinner, just like every other Christian, and his sins of false belief are forgiven, just like those of every other Christian.[57] This vision of an intellectually forgiving Christian community reaches its fruition in the *Letter Concerning Toleration*, which we will examine later.

WORKS AND SALVATION: THE STANDARD OF SINCERITY

The "single proposition" necessary for salvation actually implies not one requirement, but two: to believe that Jesus is the Messiah and to repent one's sins. Belief in Jesus's Messiahship is "all that was to be believed" for salvation, but not "all that was to be done" for salvation, because repentance is also necessary (R 50, 31). The latter is required because it is implied by the former; Jesus himself said that repentance is necessary for salvation, and if we believe that Jesus is the Messiah we must also believe that what he says is required for salvation is in fact required.[58] "As John began his preaching with 'Repent, for the kingdom of heaven is at hand,' Matthew 3:2, so did our savior begin his, Matthew 4:17, 'From that time began Jesus to preach and to say Repent, for the kingdom of heaven is at hand'" (R 168, 125).

Just as Locke argued that Jesus taught only one belief that was necessary for salvation, namely that he was the Messiah, so Locke argues that he taught only one action that was necessary, namely repentance. Locke argues, giving examples from scripture, that the need for repentance follows so clearly and directly from belief in Jesus's Messiahship that "one of them alone is often put for both" in scripture – that is, sometimes only one of these requirements is mentioned, but in those cases the other is always implied (R 168, 126). Also, the "reasonableness" and "necessity" of the requirement that we repent sin before we can be saved is apparent, Locke argues, because sin is the reason we need salvation in the first place (R 172, 128; see also 172–8, 128–35).

Locke defines repentance as "not only a sorrow for sins past, but (what is a natural consequence of such sorrow, if it be real) a turning from them into a new and contrary life" (R 170, 127).[59] This emphasizes that repentance is an act, not a belief. "Sorrow for sins past" could potentially be understood as primarily a matter of understanding – we perceive that our actions have failed to live up to our goal of obeying God – but "turning from them into a new and contrary life" can only be understood as an act of the will.

Locke's account of repentance emphasizes a point that is crucial for moral consensus. He repeatedly stresses that the good works produced by repentance follow from the intentions and sincerity of the person performing them. Good works are "works of sincere obedience"; people are saved if they believe in Jesus and make "a sincere endeavor after righteousness, in obeying his law"; the covenant of faith does not require "perfect obedience," since a perfectly obedient person would not need salvation in the first place, but it does require "sincere obedience"; perfect obedience, though unachievable, is "still sincerely to be endeavored after"; and so on (R 179, 135; 181, 136; 182, 137; and 212, 149).[60] So although repentance is an act rather than a belief, it is an act that is wholly internal. Good works are sincere works, meaning works motivated by a sincere desire to obey God. By this account, although works as such are external, the goodness of good works is internal, since it lies in the sincerity of the person performing the works. This position reflects an emphasis on sincerity in the works of several prominent Anglican Latitudinarians in Locke's time.[61]

Locke's theory of internally good works does not imply that there are no objective standards by which we can evaluate behavior. The law of works contains many objective prohibitions on behavior, and we do not need to know the intentions of the actor to recognize behavior that violates the law. Locke is far from denying that a repentant person can still violate the law; a repentant sinner is still a sinner, after all. But the distinction between the internal and external status of works allows us to argue that what really counts when it comes to the salvation of souls is entirely internal – the person's sincere desire to obey God's law.

Armed with this distinction, moral philosophy can lay down rules for external behavior without any necessary implications for the salvation of souls. Murder is wrong, stealing is wrong, and so on, but we have no way of knowing which murderers or thieves have repented their sins and which have not. Moral consensus relies on this distinction between enforcing moral laws and saving souls because objective moral laws can be laid down without any necessary commitment to a single religion. The political community can punish crime, because crime is an external matter, but it cannot deal in matters of salvation because it cannot judge who has sincerely repented.

THE CHRISTIAN DUTY OF TOLERATION: THE *LETTER*

The *Letter* was originally written in Latin, indicating it was intended for a broad European audience, as was appropriate to the level of international interest in the revocation of the Edict of Nantes and the failure of the Monmouth Rebellion. After it was published, it was quickly translated into Dutch and French, and shortly thereafter into English. The *Letter* was read and discussed throughout Europe. It was a vision statement for the entire Christian religion – a vision far from universally shared, of course, but one that resonated with at least some Christians in every part of Christendom.

In the first sentence of the *Letter*, Locke signals that his argument is a specifically Christian one.[62] Addressing himself to "the mutual toleration of Christians in their different professions of religion," he writes: "I esteem that toleration to be the chief characteristic mark of the true church," that is, the true followers of Christ. The long opening paragraph elaborates at length on the theme that anyone who persecutes others in the name of Christianity is "short of being a true Christian himself." Such people "have not really embraced the Christian religion in their own hearts," and "it would, indeed, be very hard for one that appears careless about his own salvation to persuade me that he were extremely concerned for mine" (L 1, 13–14). The inconsistency of persecution with true Christianity explains why the persecutors tolerate "whoredom, fraud, malice, and suchlike enormities ... moral vices and wickednesses," and "adultery, fornication, uncleanliness, lasciviousness, idolatry, and suchlike things" in themselves and in others who subscribe to their orthodoxies (L 1–2, 14–15).[63]

The initial justification for this position is not philosophically complex. Coercive enforcement of orthodoxy requires that we "persecute, torment, destroy, and kill other men ... deprive them of their estates, maim them with corporal punishments, starve and torment them in noisome prisons, and in the end take away their very lives," subjecting them to "torments and exercise of all manner of cruelties" (L 1, 14). This is inconsistent with the Christian religion because that religion requires "charity, meekness, and goodwill in general toward all mankind." Locke writes that according to the Bible, "no man can be a Christian without charity, and without that faith which works, not by force, but by love" (L 1, 13–14). Jesus Christ is the "prince of peace, who sent out his soldiers to the subduing of nations, and gathering them into his church, not armed with the sword or other instruments of force, but prepared with the gospel of peace and with the exemplary holiness of their conversation" (L 3, 16). Christians, therefore, owe "peace and goodwill toward all men, as well toward the erroneous as the orthodox" (L 34, 28). Not only must we refrain from harming the erroneous, "we must not content ourselves with the narrow measures of bare justice; charity, bounty, and liberality must be added to it" (L 27, 24).

But Locke goes on to build a much more sophisticated case. What is ultimately at stake here is our understanding of salvation, because the argument to which Locke responds throughout the *Letter* is that coercive orthodoxy saves souls. Surely it would be worth a few "torments and exercise of all manner of cruelties," and perhaps more than a few, if we could thereby save the souls of our victims from the even worse fate of damnation and perdition. For all of Locke's suggestions that persecution is inherently inconsistent with good intentions toward the persecuted – "nobody, surely, will ever believe that such a carriage can proceed from charity, love, or goodwill" (L 3, 15) – the *Letter* is primarily devoted to showing that even if persecution were so motivated, it cannot accomplish the object of those good intentions. The argument of the *Letter*, in capsule form, is that coercion cannot save souls. The *Letter* is actually a theological work about salvation, disguised as a work of political theory.

Early in the *Letter*, after the opening broadside against the vice and uncharitableness of persecutors, Locke presents what he labels as his three main arguments for toleration. The first is that "the care of souls is not committed to the civil magistrate," because "it appears not that God has ever given any such authority to one man over another" (L 9, 18). The second is that "such is the nature of the understanding that it cannot be compelled to the belief of anything by outward force" (L 10, 18). The third is that, even if magistrates had both the authority and the ability to change beliefs coercively, that "would not . . . help at all to the salvation of souls," because of "the variety and contradiction of opinions in religion" among magistrates. There is "but one truth, one way to heaven," so at best "one country alone would be in the right, and all the rest of the world put under an obligation of following their princes in the ways that lead to destruction" (L 11, 19).

These arguments are interrelated, and to a certain degree even interpenetrative, so they are not always clearly distinguished from one another in every part of the *Letter*. In particular, the first two arguments, which are more philosophically complicated than the third and receive much more attention in the *Letter*, are both based on the same premise: a distinction between inward and outward concerns. To support the first argument, Locke argues that magistrates cannot have authority over the beliefs of their subjects even by the subjects's own consent, because "no man can, if he would, conform his faith to the dictates of another. All the life and power of true religion consist in the inward and full persuasion of the mind." If our "profession" and "outward worship" do not match our inward persuasion, we actually increase our danger of damnation by offending God, in that we "add unto the number of our other sins those also of hypocrisy and contempt for his divine majesty" (L 9, 18). Similarly, to support his second argument, Locke argues that "true and saving religion consists in the inward persuasion of the mind," and "confiscation of estate, imprisonment, torments, nothing of that nature can have any such efficacy as to make men change the inward judgment that they have framed of things" (L 10, 18).

This distinction between inward and outward concerns arises from theology, in that its purpose is to separate the concerns of salvation from other concerns. We have seen above that the *Reasonableness* lays out an understanding of salvation as being entirely inward – it depends only upon belief in Jesus's Messiahship and a sincere endeavor to obey God. The *Letter* builds on this understanding of salvation by showing that because salvation is entirely inward, coercion cannot save souls. Thus "civil government . . . is confined to the care of the things of this world, and hath nothing to do with the world to come" (L 13, 20). Anyone who would seek to advance the business of the church, salvation, through coercive institutions "jumbles heaven and earth together, the things most remove and opposite" (L 33, 27).

The boundary on legitimate government power is not identical with the boundary between inward and outward concerns, such that all outward concerns are under the magistrate's authority. Locke draws the distinction between inward and outward concerns in order to discuss the unique properties of each type of concern, but the boundary of government authority is drawn according to the distinction between that which concerns salvation and that which does not. Salvation is wholly inward, but it is closely connected to certain outward matters, and those matters are just as protected from coercive interference as salvation itself. "Outward worship," including "rites and ceremonies," is beyond government authority "because whatsoever is practiced in the worship of God is only so far justifiable as it is believed by those that practice it to be acceptable unto him" (L 44, 35). Anything necessary for salvation belongs to the individual, while "life, liberty, health . . . the possession of outward things," and "these things belonging to this life," are subject, within limits, to regulation by government (L 6–7, 17).

This makes it legitimate for Christians to live under laws that regulate only outward behavior that concerns earthly interests, since eternal interests are inward and hence beyond the power of civil law. As Locke's first argument shows, the sovereign cannot help people become more repentant even if people consent to his attempts to do so – except, of course, in the same way anyone can help another become repentant, by exhorting him to repent. "It is one thing to persuade, another to command," and repentance, if not produced by persuasion, will not be forthcoming upon command (L 11, 19). And as Locke's second argument shows, where people do not consent to the sovereign's help, coercion cannot change their minds. Even if people submit outwardly, they are not saved inwardly. "I may grow rich by an art that I take not delight in, I may be cured of some disease by remedies that I have not faith in; but I cannot be saved by a religion that I distrust and by a worship that I abhor" (L 40, 34).

Later in the *Letter*, Locke reformulates the argument in a way that even more directly reflects the theology of the *Reasonableness* and the epistemology of the *Essay*. This new version of the argument consists of two steps, each illustrated with the metaphor of a road or path to heaven. First, Locke argues that most of the theological points on which we disagree are ancillary to salvation; that is, they concern not the path we walk to heaven, but the way in which we walk it. There may be only one road "which, according to the sacred geography, leads straight to Jerusalem," Locke writes, but "why am I beaten and ill-used by others because, perhaps, I wear not my buskins; because my hair is not of the right cut," because I have not been "dipped in the right fashion," or I eat food "which agrees with my stomach," or "I avoid certain by-ways, which seem unto me to lead into briars or precipices," and so forth (L 36, 30). Persecutors, by and large, are punishing people who are already on the road to Jerusalem, not for the road they walk but for the way they walk it.

However, this does not reach the heart of the argument, because of course some persecution does concern the path itself. To make a complete argument, Locke must argue that even if the victims of persecution are not in fact saved, they should not be persecuted. In the second step of his "road to Jerusalem" metaphor, he completes the argument by appealing to epistemology. "There is only one of these which is the true way to eternal happiness: but in this great variety of ways that men follow, it is still doubted which is the right one." The point here is not empirical but philosophical. It is not that people are in fact uncertain of the way to heaven, which might imply that their uncertainty could be corrected. It is that the way to heaven is inherently subject to the problem of human uncertainty. And there is no reason to believe that rulers are better suited to overcome the problems of uncertainty than others are: "For if it were so, how could it come to pass that the lords of the earth should differ so vastly as they do in religious matters?" And even if magistrates did know the way to heaven better than their subjects, Locke reminds us of his former argument that we are only saved if we believe for ourselves; the magistrate's certainty does not relieve the subject's uncertainty (L 37, 31).

In this second formulation of the argument, Locke appeals to premises defended in the *Reasonableness* and the *Essay*. The argument that persecution mostly concerns matters ancillary to salvation is not plausible without something like the theology of simple faith laid out in the *Reasonableness*, and the argument for the inherent problem of uncertainty in figuring out which is the one way to heaven requires something like the epistemology of limits laid out in the *Essay*. No doubt this dependence on larger philosophic commitments is why Locke presented this version of the argument later in the *Letter*, putting forward his simpler, inward/outward version of the argument first. However, this version of the argument shows the deeper connection between the *Letter*, the *Essay*, and the *Reasonableness*; when these works are considered together, we see how Locke unifies epistemology, theology, and politics in a single theory of moral consensus.

LOCKE'S CHRISTIANITY AND MORAL CONSENSUS

Locke shows us how to approach Christianity rationally, and what the content of Christianity is when examined rationally. By grounding Christian faith on the evidentiary force of miracles, supporting this approach not only with the epistemological analysis of the *Essay* but also with the testimony of Christian scripture itself, Locke shows that people can be Christian believers without giving up on a fundamental commitment to rational examination of beliefs. By developing an interpretive method for reading the Bible that sets aside the accumulated teachings of the various denominations and builds a Christian theology that arises from the Bible alone, he distinguishes the authoritative teachings of Christianity, delivered by prophets whose miracles testify to their divine authenticity, from teachings that are products of human convention and therefore not obligatory. This removes the grounds for interdenominational warfare, as it shows that the particular teachings of each denomination are not obligatory. Finally, by showing that the Bible endorses a simple set of requirements for salvation, Locke demonstrates that all Christians are saved, and therefore no church has any claim to be the one true and saving church of Christ.

Religious disputes among different Christian denominations were by far the most difficult obstacle to moral consensus in Locke's time. By showing that Christianity is not inconsistent with rational inquiry, Locke allows for rational discussion of doctrinal disputes. His method for reading the Bible provides common argumentative ground on which Christians of different denominations can carry out such disputes – if a group cannot justify its doctrines in scripture, it should not be surprised if other groups refuse to adopt those doctrines. Furthermore, by arguing from scripture that all those who have faith in Christ are saved, Locke removes the underlying impetus for such disputes. If no more than the "single proposition" of Jesus's Messiahship, coupled with inward repentance, is necessary for salvation, we need not fight to the death over any other doctrinal matters. Such questions have no bearing on who does or does not go to heaven. In particular, since only scripture is authoritative, each denomination must refrain from demanding that all Christians subscribe to the doctrines that are particular to its tradition. Only Jesus and the apostles, who performed miracles to prove their divine commission, have the authority to lay down obligatory Christian teaching.

When the alleged theological grounds for social discord are thus dispelled by the light of reason, Christianity is seen to be a force for social unity. As Locke shows in the *Letter*, the true teachings of Christianity – at least, the ones that are in scripture and are therefore authoritative – are directly contrary to all religious violence and even to nonviolent forms of discord and malice among religions. It forbids cruel and harmful behavior toward others, and promises rewards in the afterlife for those who treat all others with love, charity, and goodwill. The law of Christ, insofar as it requires humility and good behavior toward all persons, compels Christians to support moral consensus.

5

"The Only True Touchstone of Moral Rectitude"

The Religious Foundations of Morality

Locke held that politics, although it should not be devoted to any particular religion, must ultimately appeal to God's moral authority. The *Letter Concerning Toleration* argues that the political community ought not to be devoted to a particular religion, so one might think that Locke favors the compartmentalization of religion and politics favored by most liberal theorists today. Indeed, some Locke scholars have endorsed this view.[1] But even the argument of the *Letter* itself tends against this conclusion, and the whole body of Locke's philosophy is grounded on the opposite premise: that the only kind of moral law worthy of the name is religious moral law. To be a moral law properly so called, a law need not be revelatory – it can be discerned in nature instead – but it must bear God's authority. This is why moral consensus is so difficult to build; it must appeal to moral law grounded in divine authority, but it cannot appeal to any moral laws that are exclusive to one or another particular religion. This chapter and the ones following it show how Locke faced this difficult challenge.

Compartmentalization is the most influential doctrine on religion and politics today, particularly among the intellectual class. Theoretical attacks on it have become somewhat more frequent recently, but these criticisms are often very modest, aspiring only to allow some accommodation of religion in politics rather than to refute compartmentalization outright.[2] Obviously religion and politics are not actually separated in our society – far from it – but the ideal of such separation is not only completely dominant among professional liberal theorists, it is widespread among the general population, even among many of those who seek to bring religion into the public sphere. For example, some politicians regularly invoke God in speeches and other public communications, but profess to make policy on the basis of secular reasoning alone, on the grounds that their personal religious beliefs should not affect public policy. This is not to imply that such politicians are hypocritical; it is only to point out that the ideal of excluding religious arguments from politics can be decisive even over the conduct of those leaders who have made religion visible in our political life. Religion is considered "personal" while policy is "public." This distinction has consequences.

Although Locke sought to separate the internal from the external – that is, matters purely pertaining to belief and conscience as opposed to matters of life, liberty, and property – he did not recognize any firm distinction between religious, moral, and political philosophy. In Locke's philosophy, though internal and external matters are regulated differently in accordance with their different natures, both are regulated by God's law. And since government has the responsibility of enforcing moral law over the world of external matters, this means government is ultimately founded upon moral, and therefore religious, authority.

That all matters would be regulated by God's law was the normal way of looking at things in Locke's time, and Locke saw it as philosophically inevitable. God is omniscient and omnipotent, so naturally his law must take precedence in all things. While Locke did not have our own situation in view, he did argue that the separation of religion from politics in any society is impossible. Commenting on pre-Christian societies, he observes that whenever religious faith and rational philosophy are understood as enemies rather than as interdependent, and the two must compete for political influence, it is religion, not philosophy, that inevitably triumphs in the political sphere. This triumph of religion at the expense of philosophy causes enormous damage to both, as religion becomes irrational and philosophy becomes impotent. In order to counteract this political problem, Locke made it one of his most urgent missions to demonstrate that religion and rational philosophy are complementary rather than contradictory, and must work together in the public sphere.

Locke did not address the question of what would result from a successful separation of religion from politics, as he considered this an impossible outcome. However, from his analysis of moral reasoning we can deduce what he might have thought of the prospect. He would probably have thought that it would eliminate both the moral authority of government and the possibility of making moral claims against government, both of which are essential to free and liberal politics.

POLITICAL COMMUNITY BEYOND CHRISTIANITY
IN THE *LETTER*: FOUNDATIONS

The argument for toleration and a religious community of all Christians in the *Letter* culminates in the position that coercive power, and hence government, cannot be used for any ecclesiastical purpose. It follows that not only should Christians tolerate one another within the political community, but the political community itself should not be specifically devoted to Christianity. The *Letter* does begin by announcing that its topic is "the mutual toleration of Christians in their different professions of religion," and is mainly a discussion of Christian salvation (L 1, 13). However, it reaches the conclusion that "there is absolutely no such thing under the gospel as a Christian commonwealth." Locke points out that while Moses received a specifically political commission and set of civil laws from God, Jesus "prescribed unto his followers no new and peculiar form of government, nor put he the sword into any magistrate's hand" (L 56, 43). This lack of a specific political commission from Jesus, combined with the arguments made throughout the *Letter* that the business of salvation lies beyond both the magistrate's competence and his authority, establishes that governments ought not to be specifically Christian.

The *Letter* provides our most specific indication from Locke as to how and why the political community ought to be extended beyond Christians. This is not a subject on which Locke dwelled at any length. There were few non-Christians in the predominantly Christian societies that constituted his audience, and since non-Christians had been marginalized by those societies their presence was of little political consequence. Recall that the immediate exigencies of the *Letter* were the revocation of toleration for French Protestants and the failure of a Protestant rebellion against England's Catholic king. The problem causing so much grief in Europe, and to which the *Letter* and the rest of Locke's works are primarily devoted, was violence between factions of Christianity. The extension of the political community beyond Christianity was not, in that time and place, an issue of great moment even for a philosopher arguing in its favor.

We can, however, lay out a clear picture of the principles on which Locke argued for this position, and trace their consequences. They are contained most importantly in the *Letter*'s discussion of the exceptions to toleration. These exceptions lay out the boundaries of toleration in Locke's theory, and thus the limits of membership in the political community. They also implicitly limit the scope of the government itself, since government is required to tolerate all opinions within these boundaries.

The guiding principle Locke provides for drawing the boundaries of toleration is that "no opinions contrary to human society, or to those moral rules which are necessary to the preservation of civil society, are to be tolerated by the magistrate" (L 68, 50). Within this boundary, if people hold "other practical opinions, though not absolutely free from all error... there can be no reason why they should not be tolerated" (L 71, 52). In this principle we can see that for Locke the limits on toleration arise from moral law. Locke's concern in placing some opinions beyond the pale of toleration is not to protect people's material interests. When threats to the civil order are forbidden, the protection of material interests is a desirable by-product, but the underlying purpose is to protect the "moral rules" on which civil order is based. Otherwise, why would it be a requirement, or even a good thing at all, that government protect material interests and civil order?

Locke's distinction here between "human society" and "civil society" is interesting. Locke says that opinions cannot be tolerated if they are contrary to human society or to the moral rules necessary for civil society. Locke does not define the terms, but if we apply what Locke says about the creation of political society in the _Letter_, combined with what we know about Locke's political theory in the _Two Treatises of Government_, we can reasonably surmise that "civil society" is the political order created by a social contract, while "human society" is the natural moral order that exists independent of civil society or any other human creation. On this interpretation, "human society" appears to be virtually synonymous with "those moral rules which are necessary to the preservation of civil society." The contract underlying civil society only functions if its terms are morally obligatory, so to uphold it we must uphold the moral laws inherent in human society.

This underlying moral purpose is so strong that Locke describes forbidding dangerous opinions not as merely a prudentially advisable option but as mandatory. He does not write that government can forbid opinions that are outside the limits of toleration if it wants to. He lays down a strict command: "no opinions" outside those limits "are to be tolerated." Everything within the limits of toleration must be tolerated, but everything outside those limits must be forbidden. No doubt there is room for the prudence and good judgment of the political community to decide such matters as which forbidden opinions it is most important for society to spend scarce resources prosecuting, and how severe the penalties should be. And certainly we can imagine some opinions that might be a threat to human society under some circumstances but not under others – to take one of Locke's own examples, the belief that cattle must be sacrificed in religious rituals is normally not a threat to society, but it becomes threatening if there is a food shortage severe enough that the cattle must be used for food to avert starvation (L 48, 39–40). However, at least in principle there is no gray area – opinions dangerous to human society must be forbidden, and all others must be tolerated.

Before we look at the details of the boundaries of toleration in Locke's theory, we ought to take note of an important fact: while any theory of toleration other than total anarchism must be limited in some way, Locke limits not only the scope of action that is tolerable but the scope of *opinion* that is tolerable. Mere speech is punishable if it implies denial of the fundamental moral rules of society. Locke's willingness to prohibit by law not simply actions dangerous to society's moral order but even opinions dangerous to it – indeed, his insistence that we must do so – does not sit well with many readers today. Locke entertains no romantic notions about freedom of thought and self-expression. As we saw in Chapter 2, Locke spent so much time and effort writing the *Essay Concerning Human Understanding* because he understood that actions arise from thoughts, so controlling people's actions is ultimately a losing battle unless we can influence their thoughts as well. In the *Letter* he endorses using the coercive instruments of government alongside the persuasive instruments of argument for this purpose.

Given Locke's larger critique of government attempts to control opinions, there is a clear problem with Locke's willingness to coercively suppress dangerous opinions. What will such suppression accomplish? Locke does not specify how coercion would be effective against dangerous opinions. In light of his sophisticated understanding of the distinction between inward and outward means, the gap is significant. As Locke argues so eloquently in the *Letter*, people cannot control what seems true to them, so they can't sincerely conform to political orthodoxy even if they want to. How, then, would coercive suppression of dangerous opinions reduce the number of people holding such opinions, or the dangerousness of the opinions? And if coercion can effectively counteract the spread of opinions dangerous to society, why can't it effectively do the same for opinions dangerous to salvation?

Locke could make a partial reply to this objection by appealing to epistemology. The way to heaven is subject to some uncertainty, but the wrongness of seeking to kill or dominate others is not. People can disagree about which is the true religion without necessarily being in the grip of some fanatical ideology or suffering from some mental defect, but all normal people must agree that murder is wrong.

However, while this might help convince the reader that government does not violate natural law by suppressing dangerous opinions, it does nothing to establish that such suppression can be effective. Locke's own arguments inflict devastating damage upon any claim that suppression of opinions works. No justification for the suppression of dangerous opinions is likely to be tenable if we adhere to Locke's main arguments on the inward/outward distinction in the *Letter*.

Two things should be said in Locke's defense on this topic. First, the set of opinions against which Locke would employ coercion is sharply limited. Not only is it confined to opinions that are clearly and unambiguously wrong, it is further confined to opinions that imply harm to others. The magistrate's authority extends only to protection from harm. "Covetousness, uncharitableness, idleness, and many other things are sins," Locke writes in arguing for toleration, "which yet no man ever said were to be punished by the magistrate. The reason is because they are not prejudicial to other men's rights, nor do they break the public peace of societies" (L 54, 42). Second, no one in Locke's time had any experience with freedom of speech as we now understand it. As it has turned out, free exchange of opinions within a tolerant society has greatly reduced the occurrence of the kinds of dangerous opinions Locke was most concerned about. Few people today seek to establish special legal privileges for one religious denomination, or subvert the government in favor of a foreign ruler who claims a divine right to political power. However, Locke had no way to know with certainty that liberal politics would produce such far-reaching benefits. Given his strong preference that political theory be empirically informed by knowledge of human history, it seems almost certain that he would have adjusted his opinion in light of our subsequent experiences.

POLITICAL COMMUNITY BEYOND CHRISTIANITY IN THE *LETTER*: APPLICATIONS

Locke gives four examples of opinions dangerous to human society, and in the reasoning he provides we can see with more precision both the reason why the limits on toleration are morally mandatory and the nature of the moral law those limits are designed to protect. His first example is the most straightforward: open preaching against human society, or against the moral rules on which civil society is based. The second is closely related to the first: the teaching of doctrines "covered over with a specious show of deceitful words, but in effect opposite to the civil right of the community." Examples of the first type tend to be rare. Groups rarely challenge the rules of human society "nakedly and plainly," because this would "draw on them the eye and hand of the magistrate, and awaken all the care of the commonwealth." However, those "who attribute unto the faithful, religious, and orthodox, that is, in plain terms, unto themselves, any peculiar privilege or power" also deny the rules of human society, but they do this in a way their followers don't recognize as being dangerous. For example, Locke writes that the first type of opinion would include "any sect that teaches, expressly and openly, that men are not obliged to keep their promise," while the second type includes those who teach the doctrine that "faith is not to be kept with heretics." The first position is obviously immoral, while to many the second may not seem to be so at first glance. But it is "the same thing in other words," because those who teach that faith is not to be kept with heretics also "declare all that are not of their communion to be heretics, or at least may declare them to be so whensoever they think fit" (L 69, 50–1).

Locke's argument against these two types of intolerable opinion is sometimes described as an argument against toleration for the intolerant. That is a sufficient description only if we define "intolerance" very broadly, because this rule has enormous social consequences. Locke argues here not only for the suppression of bigotry against religious minorities but for the suppression of any teaching that applies different moral rules or a different moral status to people based on whether they are or are not members of a given religion or denomination. If we may treat people as morally different on the basis of a morally insignificant distinction (group memebership), then moral law itself is void because it can be undermined by the introduction of morally insignificant criteria. Locke shows how "faith is not to be kept with heretics" is equivalent to "men are not obliged to keep their promise," that "kings excommunicated forfeit their crowns" is equivalent to "princes may be dethroned by those that differ from them in religion," and people who teach that "dominion is founded in grace" are actually teaching that "the dominion of all things belongs only to themselves" (L 69, 50–1).

The underlying premise here, supported by Locke's arguments on salvation, is that membership in one or another church is not a morally significant distinction. Mere membership in a church cannot convey salvation, so it cannot convey a superior moral status. Only sincere faith can save souls, so only sincere faith could potentially serve as a legitimate ground for morally relevant religious distinctions. But in practice even sincere faith cannot serve this purpose because it is internal, and therefore beyond the scope of government's competence to know or regulate. There are no available grounds for morally relevant distinctions between persons arising from religion.

The logic of Locke's argument for toleration requires not only that government refrain from killing and arresting people over religion, but that government not play favorites among religions in any fashion. Even a government of one faith that permits the existence of other faiths is not truly tolerant, because it implicitly favors one faith over others. If the political community makes any distinction at all between legally favored and disfavored religions – indeed, if it so much as tolerates those who favor such distinctions – moral law itself is undone.

Locke's third example of something outside the limits of toleration is a church "which is constituted upon such a bottom that all those who enter into it do thereby *ipso facto* deliver themselves up to the protection and service of another prince." His example is a Muslim whose religion requires him "to yield blind obedience to the Mufti of Constantinople, who himself is entirely obedient to the Ottoman Emperor," with whom the Christian nations of Europe had been at war for some time. There is, however, very little doubt that Locke also intends to indicate that Catholics need not be tolerated in England, where the Catholic Church had long struggled, often violently, to restore English obedience to the ecclesiastical authority of Rome. Locke says of his hypothetical Muslim: "this Mahometan living amongst Christians would yet more apparently renounce their government if he acknowledged the same person to be head of his church who is the supreme magistrate in the state" (L 70, 51–2). This is undoubtedly a reference to the Pope, who is a head of state as well as the head of a church.

Locke has long been a target of criticism for this alleged intolerance of Catholics, not to mention Muslims as well. However, it is not the religion of Catholicism or Islam that Locke finds intolerable, but the violent and subversive political use to which those religions were put. England had been at war with the Vatican and the Ottoman Empire for centuries, and there really was no meaningful distinction between the Catholic Church and the Vatican, or between obedience to the Mufti of Constantinople and obedience to the Emperor.[3] Locke's argument boils down to this: if a group seeks to violently overthrow the government, you cannot legitimately claim legal protection for it simply on grounds that the group also happens to be religious. As Locke says, no magistrate could reasonably be expected to "give way to the settling of a foreign jurisdiction in his own country, and suffer his own people to be listed, as it were, for soldiers against his own government" (L 70, 51).

Crucially, Locke indicates that Catholicism and Islam should only be banned in nations where they are used for dangerous political purposes. Locke asks at one point, in what would have been recognized as a reference to the revocation of toleration in France, "is it permitted to worship God in the Roman manner? Let it be permitted to do it in the Geneva form also" (L 76, 55). He goes on to declare that "neither pagan nor Mahometan nor Jew ought to be excluded from the civil rights of the commonwealth because of his religion" (L 77, 56). It is transparent that Locke desires a political community in which all religions are tolerated; he only requires that each religion give up its ambitions for political domination in order to earn the right to such toleration.

This point is important because if we chalk up Locke's treatment of Catholics and Muslims in this passage to mere bigotry on his part, we will miss Locke's real argument. And if we miss Locke's argument here we will also miss his enunciation of a crucial premise of his philosophy. Locke indicates here the reason why religion can potentially threaten the state, and the reason he gives speaks directly to the religious foundation of moral law.

Locke writes that the problem of churches seeking political domination arises particularly when a church recognizes a leader "who has not only power to persuade the members of his church to whatsoever he lists... but can also enjoin it them on pain of eternal fire." It is because of the prospect of God's eternal rewards and punishments that religion carries the potential to disrupt societies. As Locke writes, if his hypothetical Muslim believes that obedience to a foreign mufti and emperor is required for him on pain of eternal damnation, it would be "ridiculous" for him "to profess himself to be a Mahometan only in his religion, but in everything else a faithful subject to a Christian magistrate" (L 70, 51). God's authority overrules all other sources of moral authority, including government, because God can dispense potentially infinite rewards and punishments.

The importance of this point for moral law, and hence for politics, becomes clear in the next and final example of an intolerable opinion. His argument is brief, because the principle for which he was arguing was so widely accepted at the time that it must have come across as a truism. It is worth quoting in full:

Those are not at all to be tolerated who deny the being of a God. Promises, covenants, and oaths, which are the bonds of human society, can have no hold upon an atheist. The taking away of God, though but even in thought, dissolves all; besides also, those that by their atheism undermine and destroy all religion can have no pretense of religion whereupon to challenge the privilege of toleration (L 71, 52).

The first sentence of this passage employs the most emphatic language used in any of Locke's four examples of intolerable opinions: atheism is "not at all to be tolerated." This urgency arises despite the absence of any accusation here that atheists aspire to political domination, or have any particular desire to disrupt the political community. Atheists are just inherently untrustworthy; when it comes to moral law, atheism "dissolves all."

Locke does not give the reason why "promises, covenants, and oaths . . . can have no hold upon an atheist," but it was intimated in his explanation of the previous rule forbidding obedience to hostile foreign powers: God's rewards and punishments are the key to all moral thought, and hence to control of all behavior. Where the previous example showed why religion's extraordinary power over thought and behavior can be dangerous, this example shows why the government must nonetheless embrace that power: because it makes moral law possible. Law is not law without rewards and punishments to back it up. The rewards and punishments provided by human beings in this world are insufficient for a truly moral law, because humans are too flawed and limited to reliably reward good behavior and punish evil. As we will see, Locke made this claim explicit in the *Essay* and argued for it at length in *The Reasonableness of Christianity*.

In taking Locke's point that civil society depends crucially on upholding moral law, we need not share his conclusion in favor of persecuting atheists. Experience has shown us that tolerating atheists does not in fact threaten the destruction of society; it is sufficient to punish only those who actually do break their "promises, covenants, and oaths." Atheism is not a threat simply because it isn't appealing to more than a handful of people. Despite the increased visibility of atheists in our tolerant society, they remain a tiny segment of the population, and there is little to suggest that there are any more atheists today than there were at any other time. This is a particularly plausible hypothesis when we consider that there must have been a significant number of people who concealed their atheism during times when atheism was punishable by law. Since it has been demonstrated that the social costs of tolerating atheists are minor, the high social costs of persecuting atheists cannot be justified.

Another conclusion we need not reach here concerns polytheists. Locke's formulation of the argument against atheism suggests that monotheism is the only alternative to atheism – the phrases "the being of a God" and "the taking away of God" assume that "God" is a single, particular deity. This conclusion, however, is not warranted if we understand the basis of the argument. Atheism destroys moral law because it denies that there will be divine rewards for morally good behavior and punishments for evil behavior; polytheism requires no such denial. What is required is not specifically "God's" rewards and punishments but divine rewards and punishments. Locke formulates this argument the way he does simply because there were virtually no polytheists in seventeenth-century England. As we have seen, he is explicit elsewhere in the *Letter* that toleration extends to polytheists (see L 48, 39–40 and 77, 56).

From the four examples that define the boundaries of toleration in Locke's theory, we can see that Locke is equally committed to two principles that tend in opposite directions: government must not be devoted to any one religion, but it must be devoted to religion over atheism and be based on moral laws enforced by a divine power.

We have seen sufficiently, here and in the previous chapter, Locke's reasons for the first of these principles. Politically favoring one religion over another is unjustifiable because the political realm is irrelevant to the only thing that might justify such favoritism, which is the salvation of souls, and it undermines moral law by making moral distinctions based on morally irrelevant criteria. However, the *Letter* glosses briefly over the second principle, the need for a religious foundation of moral law. The key to this principle is the rewards and punishments dispensed in the afterlife. To see in detail why moral law must arise from divine power, we must return to the *Essay* and the *Reasonableness*.

LOCKE'S VOLUNTARISM: LAW AND AUTHORITY IN THE *ESSAY*

Locke believes that only a religious moral theory can be sufficient for political purposes. This is the main subject of the third and final section of the *Reasonableness*, in which Locke seeks to show why revelation was necessary to convey the covenant of grace. The widespread compartmentalization of religion and politics in our time makes this section the most important part of the *Reasonableness* for our purposes. But to understand it in context we must begin by returning to the *Essay*, in order to clear up a common misunderstanding of the relationship between the *Reasonableness* and the *Essay*.

Scholars have sometimes taken the accounts of moral reasoning in these two books as contradictory or at least in strong tension. The "optimism" about moral law discerned by reason in the *Essay* has been contrasted to the "pessimism" of the *Reasonableness* on that subject.[4] But the analyses of reason and moral law in the *Essay* and the *Reasonableness* are consistent, reflecting mostly a change in emphasis appropriate to the different purposes and subject matter of the two books.[5]

Recall that in the *Essay* Locke argues that because God is all-knowing and all-powerful humanity's most urgent need, by nature, is to seek out and follow God's will. It follows that "morality is the proper science, and business of mankind in general," just as the various professions are "the lot and private talent of particular men" (E IV.12.11, 646). God gives each person "discerning faculties" in order to "keep him out of mistake and error" in moral matters (E IV.17.24, 687–8). Morality is all of humanity's vocation, in the original sense of that word – the activity God has called us to pursue.

For Locke, moral reasoning must always begin with logical knowledge of an omniscient and omnipotent God, relative to whom we are radically weak and therefore dependent. As Locke says, people give many different kinds of reasons to justify their moral choices. To explain why one should not break a promise, "a Christian" will say "because God, who has the eternal power of life and death, requires it of us," while "an Hobbist" will say "because the public requires it, and the Leviathan will punish you, if you do not," and "the old heathen philosophers" would have said "because it was dishonest, below the dignity of a man, and opposite to virtue, the highest perfection of human nature, to do otherwise" (E I.3.5, 68). Locke argues that only the Christian's answer, appealing to God's infinite power, can be the foundation of morality. He writes that "the true ground of morality . . . can only be the will and law of a god, who sees men in the dark, has in his hand rewards and punishments, and power enough to call to account the proudest offender" (E I.3.6, 69).

The other two answers are not *moral* answers in the strict sense of that term because they lack the sanction of an infinite power. The "Hobbist" would have us be motivated by fear of death, while the "old heathen philosophers" would have us be motivated by aesthetics. These are certainly powerful motivations, but they are not infinitely powerful. One might argue that self-interest, or aesthetic superiority, or some other criterion made certain moral laws choiceworthy. But there are always some people with unusual preferences, who choose to pursue what others take to be foolish or ugly. "The mind has a different relish, as well as the palate; and you will as fruitlessly endeavor to delight all men with riches or glory . . . as you would to satisfy all men's hunger with cheese or lobsters." Different people have different tastes, and taste itself cannot be a reason to prefer one set of tastes over another. "Men may choose different things, and yet all choose right, supposing them only like a company of poor insects, whereof some are bees, delighted with flowers, and their sweetness; others, beetles, delighted with other kind of viands." What one person perceives to be the fulfillment of human nature might seem grossly unnatural to another. "Hence it was, I think, that the philosophers of old did in vain enquire, whether *summum bonum* consisted in riches, or bodily delights, or virtue, or contemplation: and they might have as reasonably disputed, whether the best relish were to be found in apples, plums, or nuts; and have divided themselves into sects upon it" (E II.21.55, 269–70).

Locke's point is that morality, properly understood, ought to be something against which no rational reason could ever be given. The question he seems to be putting to us here is: why are people *obliged* to put the public's interests ahead of their own, or to sacrifice pleasure for the sake of dignity, if they are not inclined to do so? And what right do we have to force such a person, against his will, to do so? Only the command of an omnipotent deity can give us a rationale to override all possible competing claims and interests, which is necessary to make a law obligatory rather than merely commendable.

What's really at stake here is the definition of the word "moral." Locke is implicitly arguing that what makes a law a "moral" law is not that it is commendable but that it is obligatory. Since rational people can disagree about what ends are commendable, commendableness cannot be a universally binding source of obligation. Only God's omnipotence can serve that purpose. That is why Locke writes that God's will is "the only true touchstone of moral rectitude" (E II.28.8, 352). This point, though Locke does not develop it further in the *Essay*, is clearly stated in quite a few places (see E I.3.5–6, 68–9; II.21.55, 270; II.21.70, 281; II.28.8, 352; II.28.12, 356–7; and IV.12.4, 642).

The view that morality rests on God's will, rather than on some independent criterion of goodness such as reason, places Locke within the theological tradition of voluntarism. As Francis Oakley documents, Locke's voluntarist arguments have deep roots in medieval theology.[6] Oakley writes that by the late Middle Ages, natural law theory had divided into two separate traditions, "one of them grounded in one or another form of ontological essentialism," and the other "grounded in the type of theological voluntarism characteristic of William of Ockham (d. 1349) and of his fourteenth- and fifteenth-century . . . successors." He writes that the tendency to identify medieval natural law theory exclusively with the essentialists distorts our understanding of Locke. It is "simply improper to speak of any *single* 'classical and Christian' or even 'medieval' natural-law tradition which could then be contrasted with a 'modern' notion of natural law."[7] Oakley's point here is not that Locke's natural law theory is not "modern"; he does not take up that question. His point is that if we take into account the voluntarist tradition of medieval natural law theory, Locke's theory appears as a relatively continuous evolution of that strand of medieval thought rather than as a radical break from all medieval thought.

Voluntarism such as Locke's confronts us with a moral paradox, because it seems to collapse morality into nothing more than fear of God's power. If the voluntarist view is correct, how is it that obedience to God is a moral duty rather than simply something we do to avoid punishment? As Nicholas Wolterstorff puts it, "God's right to command obedience of us cannot be understood as consisting in God's being permitted to do so by the laws of obligation, if the laws of obligation are just God's laws."[8] How can we simultaneously argue that God has the right to command and that right is defined by God's command? Revelation can tell us that God should rule because he is wise, just, benevolent, and so on, but consider the source: we have God's word that God is good.

To start with, it bears noting that Locke, as befits his epistemology of limits, is quite comfortable with insoluble paradoxes of this kind. In a 1693 letter, he declared that it was his long-held position that he did not know how it was possible that God is omniscient and omnipotent while human actions are freely chosen, but that because God's omniscient omnipotence and human freedom are both logically necessary he was willing to believe in both even if he could not reconcile them.[9] Locke does not think it is possible to answer every question about the universe, and he follows his own advice to "sit down in quiet ignorance" of the great mysteries (E I.1.4, 45). As we saw in Chapter 2, it is a crucial premise of Locke's theory of moral consensus that we not demand an answer for every question that can be formulated. We only need answers for those matters which "concern our conduct" (E I.1.6, 46).

It should also be said in Locke's defense that theological intellectualism or rationalism, the opposite of voluntarism, raises its own moral paradox. Where voluntarism emphasizes God to the potential exclusion of goodness, intellectualism emphasizes goodness to the potential exclusion of God. If goodness, understood as adherence to reason or some other criterion, is a standard independent of God's will, then God is nothing but a cosmic policeman. If so, why not simply cut out the middleman by ignoring God and striving for goodness in itself? If the answer is that we can only reliably know what is good because God tells us, then intellectualism is effectively the same thing as voluntarism – goodness is whatever God says it is. If the answer is that we can know goodness without God but we cannot achieve it, and therefore need forgiveness and salvation from God, the question becomes: on what authority does God presume to forgive our sins against goodness if he is not the source of goodness in the first place? As Oakley shows, the voluntarist line of medieval thought first arose because in the work of Thomas Aquinas these "tensions . . . had for some . . . been intensified to the breaking point."[10] All this is not to say that intellectualism is patently false or that it cannot grapple with these difficult questions; it is only to say that intellectualism raises just as many paradoxical problems as voluntarism, so voluntarism is not to be rejected simply because it raises paradoxes.

What voluntarism such as Locke's ultimately asks for is moral submission as well as behavioral submission – not just obedience to God in action but submission of the mind and will to God. The submission is justified by God's power, on the grounds that no sensible person who truly believes in an omnipotent God would seriously entertain the idea of resisting him.[11] If we really believe that we are helplessly under God's power, we are going to choose to obey him regardless of his moral status. It would take an almost unimaginable vanity for a human being to know of God's existence and not willingly submit to his authority. Even if one did wish to pass judgment on God's worthiness to command, it couldn't be done in any meaningful way, since the human mind is not able to discern any obligatory moral standard independent of God's will by which God could be judged. If, on the other hand, we are willing to submit completely to God, the result, as Locke put it in writings at the end of his life, is trust in God's goodness.[12] Obedience to God takes on the status of a moral duty if we are willing to make this leap. Given the lack of appealing alternatives, particularly in light of Locke's rejection of total skepticism as a possibility, it is a plausible leap to make.

The universal moral jurisdiction of God's will is of crucial importance to Locke's theory of moral consensus. Locke is trying to transcend the divisions between different ecclesiastical and cultural traditions, which he can only do by appealing to God's universal authority. Because God's will is the only basis of morality, Locke can address the question of what rules of action are universally obligatory without having to settle arguments over what rules of action are choiceworthy. The former is a relatively small subset of the latter, so this approach minimizes the amount of social agreement necessary to make Locke's system of moral reasoning cohere. To live together in a society under moral consensus, people need not agree on the very broad question of which rules are good, but only on the much narrower question of which good rules are universally obligatory.

But, as we have seen, voluntarism requires an ultimate submission of the will. Locke's voluntarism incorporates a heavy emphasis on submission to God into the foundation of his political philosophy. While this is an advantage insofar as we need not agree on the broad question of what is choiceworthy so long as we agree on the narrower proposition that we are all obliged to obey divine law, the other side of this coin is that agreement on our obligation to obey God becomes absolutely indispensable. Any doubt or irresolution of will regarding God's authority is deadly for Locke's political theory. It is, of course, legitimate to debate what specifically is or is not God's will, but not that God's will is authoritative in principle. Moral and political theory come to pieces if we are not fully committed to the authoritativeness of divine law.

REASON, FAITH, AND MORALITY: LAW AND AUTHORITY IN THE *REASONABLENESS*

As we have seen in the previous two chapters, for Locke the way to investigate God's will is to search for signs of it in the world around us. The *Essay* does not proceed to ask what actual moral beliefs can be justified by this method because that is not its purpose; its purpose is to describe the method itself. The *Essay* is a book of philosophy, laying out the limits of what it is possible for us to know and a system for determining what we can legitimately believe. The *Reasonableness*, on the other hand, is a sort of philosophic history book. Its purpose is to examine the historical record to determine what we actually do know and what we actually should believe. Locke's concern in the *Essay* is theoretical possibilities, and in the *Reasonableness* it is the realization of those possibilities. Thus, while the two books treat the same themes and share the same doctrine, it is natural that there should be differences in how each book treats a given subject.

Where the *Essay* made the case for a certain method for constructing reliable beliefs about God's will, the last section of the *Reasonableness* makes the case against attempts to base morality on anything other than God's will. John Yolton points out that this section of the *Reasonableness* specifically concerns the historical case of Jesus Christ and is not a general account of religion and politics as such. But Yolton is too cautious in rejecting, as he seems to do, any use of this section for the illumination of Locke's politics generally. Yolton writes that Locke's contrast between the "morality of Jesus Christ and pagan morality means to convey nothing more."[13] However, as we will see, Locke's comparison of Christian and pre-Christian morality is meant to promote not only an interpretation of a particular set of historical events, but also the general position that religious political theory is necessary in all times and places for legitimate political authority. This is the premise on which Locke seeks to refute the deists, who argued that no revelation was necessary to establish moral law. And even Locke's strictly historical arguments about Christianity are based on, and in turn elucidate, general propositions about human nature and the needs of politics. Locke seeks to persuade deists of the truth of Christianity not simply because deist views are incorrect, but because deism is socially and politically dangerous insofar as it tends to remove religion from politics.[14]

Locke unfortunately invites confusion in this section of the *Reasonableness* by writing about "reason" without always distinguishing between natural reason (that is, reason without the assistance of revelation) and reason generally (which would include rational belief in revelation). But it is clear from the context that Locke means natural reason when he writes in this section that "reason" cannot be the basis of morality. Locke's case against "reason" includes assertions that it is not capable of establishing monotheism, it lacks the authority to establish moral philosophy, it cannot reform corrupt forms of worship, it does not establish rewards and punishments in the afterlife, and it does not promise spiritual aid from a higher power. But if "reason" is defined to include rational faith, it can provide all of these things. In this section, Locke must be arguing against the viability of morality based on natural reason alone, not on reason including faith.[15] As Eldon Eisenach points out, Locke is describing the failures of reason before the coming of Christ: "Locke uses the past tense for all statements referring to the weakness of unaided reason."[16] For Locke, Christ's miracles made possible a wholly rational moral philosophy that includes faith and revelation; reason's incapacity to provide a full morality was a temporary historical condition remedied by the coming of Christ.

With this ambiguous use of the word "reason" in the last section of the *Reasonableness*, Locke breaks his own linguistic rules by slipping into the practice of depicting "reason" and "faith" as opposed to one another. As we have seen, this was a linguistic practice Locke abhorred. To a large extent this ambiguity in the *Reasonableness* is caused by Locke's view of religious history — he believes that before Christ reason and faith were indeed separate and opposed, not in theory but in practice, because all the religions before Christ (other than Judaism) were false and superstitious. Therefore, when he writes about pre-Christian societies he can use "reason" as shorthand for "natural reason," because in his view, pre-Christian societies (other than Jewish ones) had no other kind of reason but natural reason.

But there is some ambiguity in Locke's writing even when he writes about reason and faith without reference to pre-Christian history. In part this may have been accidental; because Locke was joining an argument about morality between deists and theists in which the words "reason" and "faith" were used to describe opposing belief systems, it would be a natural mistake to lapse into that prevailing terminology. However, it also seems highly likely that the ambiguity of this section was at least partly calculated. Locke's harsh appraisal of the meager capacities of "reason," as contrasted with faith, seems to be a deliberate, even heavy-handed attempt to differentiate his views from deism. The careful distinction drawn in the *Essay* and upheld in every other part of the *Reasonableness* between natural reason and a reason that includes faith might fail, in some quarters, to sufficiently distinguish his philosophy from deism. In this section, where Locke takes up the subject of deism explicitly, he may have abandoned such subtlety on purpose, in order to forcefully remove any doubts about his view of deism.

Locke makes his negative case against nonreligious morality on two levels: logic and historical analysis. The logical part of the case is a full development of the position, stated more briefly in the *Essay*, that it is logically necessary for moral theory to begin with God because only God can be an obliging moral authority. Even if the deists were right that God's law could be known by reason alone, Christ's coming would still have been necessary to make that law morally obligatory.

He writes: "Let it be granted (though not true) that all the moral precepts of the gospel were known by somebody or other amongst mankind before." Evocatively, Locke describes a hypothetical project of collecting wisdom from all the philosophers in human history up until the coming of Christ – "some from Solon and Bias in Greece, others from Tully in Italy, and to complete the work, let Confucius, as far as China, be consulted, and Anacharsis, the Scythian, contribute his share" (R 242, 172).[17] Suppose, he writes, one could construct an exact duplicate of Christian morality by drawing elements from all available nonreligious sources. A morality constructed this way would still come to nothing, he says, because it would lack authority. Locke is strikingly adamant:

What will all this do to give the world a complete morality that may be to mankind the unquestionable rule of life and manners? . . . What would this amount to toward being a steady rule, a certain transcript of the law that we are under? Did the saying of Aristippus or Confucius give it an authority? Was Zeno a lawgiver to mankind? If not, what he or any other philosopher delivered was but a saying of his. Mankind might hearken to it or reject it as they pleased, or as it suited their interest, passions, principles, or humors. They were under no obligation; the opinion of this or that philosopher was of no authority (R 243 172–3).

If a philosopher had authority, Locke goes on to point out, we would be obliged to adopt all his opinions, on all subjects, without modification. Since no one actually treats philosophers this way, philosophy is not a source of authority.

The pre-Christian philosophers, and many philosophers after Christ as well, built eudemonic moralities on the pursuit of happiness in this world. As we will see in detail in the next chapter, Locke's moral theory is also eudemonic, in that it is founded on the presumption that people will pursue their own happiness. The difference is that Locke insists on grounding morality in divine command. In Locke's morality, we seek happiness in the next world rather than in this one.

Only divine command can provide an eternal and unfailing source of rewards and punishments, ensuring that moral good is always rewarded and evil is always punished. This perfect enforcement provides the authority that is missing from nonreligious moral theories. A moral theory built on the worldly consequences of actions might argue that obeying certain rules of action is wise, in that it would probably contribute to our happiness. However, such a theory would not be persuasive to a person who found that its account of happiness and how to achieve it did not suit his "interest, passions, principles, or humors." On the other hand, no reasonable person would deny that the infinite rewards of an omnipotent God would please him, or that the infinite punishments of an omnipotent

God would displease him. "The view of heaven and hell will cast a slight upon the short pleasures and pains of this present state.... Upon this foundation, and upon this only, morality stands firm and will defy all competition" (R 245, 185). We can argue about just what the law of God is, of course, but no one would contest that the law of God, whatever it is, is obligatory.

Locke's point is that, for philosophical reasons, religious arguments trump other arguments. It is not fanaticism or zealotry to prefer obedience to God's law over adherence to some civil or secular philosophic system. Given God's infinite power, preferring obedience to God is the only rational course. What reward can a politician or a political theorist offer us that compares favorably with eternal bliss, or what punishment that we would fear more than damnation? If a moral or political theory is built on something other than God's will, a person who believes that it is inconsistent with God's will would be foolhardy to adhere to it. For a political theory to convey genuine authority, it must ultimately rest on some account of God's will.

Although this is what we have labeled Locke's "logical" argument against nonreligious morality, in that it provides philosophical reasons to elevate religion over other types of belief, it has a historical aspect as well. Locke writes that "before our Savior's time, the doctrine of a future state, though it was not wholly hid, yet it was not clearly known in the world.... no nation of the world publicly professed it and built upon it" (R 245, 183–4). Priests used the idea of ghosts to scare their followers into obedience, he argues, but the afterlife did not serve as a basis of morality until the rise of Christianity.

This passage unfortunately reflects Locke's ignorance, typical of his time and place, of many nonwestern religious traditions. Contrary to Locke's assertion, rewards and punishments after death are present in religions other than Christianity, and this largely undermines his historical point. However, we need not accept Locke's assertion that Christianity is unique in providing an account of rewards and punishments in the afterlife to take his larger point that such rewards and punishments, and the moral authority they provide, are the key factor differentiating religious from nonreligious moral and political theories.

The supremacy of God's authority, arising from his infinite power, means that political theory must be based on religious moral law. Any other kind of political theory will not be able to rely on the allegiance of religious believers, who must choose God over the political community wherever the two are seen to present conflicting requirements. In particular, a society facing serious religious divisions will not be united by any theory that cannot show that it bears the stamp of religious authority. No nonreligious theory can be adequate to persuade a religious believer to unite in a political community with others whose religions he finds abhorrent. Appeals to divine power, by contrast, convey an irresistible authority. If people can be persuaded that moral consensus is required by divine law, they will have no choice but to adhere to it despite their religious differences.

The moral importance of rewards and punishments presents a serious challenge for political community based on moral consensus. As Locke argues, natural reason cannot make out rewards and punishments in the afterlife. This means that one key element of moral consensus, the divine rewards and punishments that give moral law its authority, cannot be justified by natural reason. The political community requires that its members subscribe to a shared moral law that they all agree is of divine authority, but the reasons they believe that law to be of divine authority will not be shared, but will arise from their particular religions. Although, as we will see in the next two chapters, Locke makes out the content of moral law in a way all religious groups can agree on, he cannot do the same for rewards and punishments. Each particular faith will continue to have its own account of divine power.

This is not fatal to moral consensus, because the important thing is that all agree on the content of the moral law on which the political community will be built, and also that this moral law is of divine authority. So long as there is agreement on these points, a political community of moral consensus can be built without agreement on exactly how (that is, through what revelation) we know the moral law is of divine authority. Political union, unlike religious salvation, requires only conformity of action. So long as everyone takes the community's moral law to be of divine authority, all will conform to it, regardless of what revelation they learn about God's authority from.

THE HISTORY OF REASON AND RELIGION

Locke's logical case against the viability of nonreligious morality complements his historical case, made at greater length, that no nonreligious morality has ever served as the moral basis for political legitimacy in any actual society, and for reasons that are not likely to change. Among those who have not received genuine revelation, Locke writes, people must choose between unassisted natural reason and the superstitions of

priestcraft, and the record shows that their "sense and lust," "careless in-
advertency," and "fearful apprehensions" drive them inexorably into the
arms of the priests. "Nor could any help be had or hoped for from reason, which could not be heard, and was judged to have nothing to do in
the case, the priests everywhere, to secure their empire, having excluded
reason from having anything to do in religion" (R 238, 165).

In the societies that existed until Christ came, he writes, moral philosophy was "cultivated with some care" by the philosophers, but it "got little
footing among the people" for two reasons. First, the people were afraid of
"displeasing the gods." Second, "lustrations and processions were much
easier than a clean conscience and a steady course of virtue" (R 241, 169–
70). Thus, piety (fear of the gods) and vice (the desire for loose moral
standards) both favor choosing religious rituals, however empty and superstitious, over a life devoted to nonreligious moral reasoning. Force
people to choose between religion and nonreligious rational philosophy,
and history teaches that they will choose religion.

Here again, as in the *Essay*, we see Locke's abhorrence for the separation of reason from religion. When reason and religion are understood
as enemies, the philosophers and the priests inevitably see each other
as rivals, and both sides know that in any open conflict the priests win
every time. This is why, Locke writes, even in cases where "the rational
and thinking part of mankind" discovered, by reason, "the one supreme
invisible God," they "kept this truth locked up in their own breasts as a secret, nor ever dared venture it amongst the people, much less amongst the
priests" (R 238, 165). Locke cites the examples of Socrates and Plato, who
(Locke believes) discovered monotheism rationally. Socrates "opposed
and laughed at" Athenian polytheism, "and we see how they rewarded
him for it"; Plato, for fear of similar reprisals, avoided openly professing
monotheism or building his moral theory on it (R 238, 166; see also 243,
176–7; and E IV.12.4, 642).[18] For Locke, the behavior of the philosophers
themselves is proof that even they believe that nonrevelatory philosophy
cannot supplant priestcraft.

Whatever one thinks of Locke's monotheist interpretation of Socrates
and Plato, which, to say no more, suffers from some obvious problems,
he makes a larger and more important point with his example of philosophy in Athens. If the priests of superstition prevailed over unassisted reason in Athens, they can prevail anywhere. "There was no part
of mankind who had quicker parts or improved them more, that had
a greater light of reason or followed it farther in all sorts of speculations, than the Athenians," yet they were submerged in "darkness and

error" when it came to religion (R 238–9, 166–7). Locke quotes Paul at length on their idolatry: "Ye men of Athens, I perceive that in all things ye are too superstitious" (R 238, 166).[19] Locke's point is that Athens provided the optimal conditions for the triumph of natural (that is, nonrevelatory) reason over religious superstition, and religious superstition not only defeated natural reason, it utterly trounced it. Given this fact, Locke implicitly asks, what hope is there for unassisted reason anywhere else?

Obviously it is problematic for us that Locke treats polytheism and idolatry as mere superstitions. Locke is triumphal in his assessment of the history of Christianity, contrasting the meager record of natural reason with the success of Christian revelation in refuting what he saw as the superstition of polytheism. For Locke, it is a particularly important point that, whereas natural reason did not make so much as a dent in the superstitious polytheism of classical Greece and Rome, Christianity opposes superstition "with such evidence and energy that polytheism and idolatry have nowhere been able to withstand it" (R 239, 167). This is not a view that political theory in our time can be built upon. For one thing, not all incorrect beliefs are superstitious beliefs; to treat a belief as superstitious is to imply that only very irrational people would assent to it. It is one thing to hold that polytheism entails incorrect beliefs, and quite another to treat polytheism as a superstition on the level of avoiding black cats and broken mirrors. Today, having far more familiarity with the real content of polytheistic religion than was available through biased secondhand accounts in seventeenth-century England, most monotheists would hold that polytheism is wrong but not necessarily superstitious. And even if monotheists were not so inclined, the time is past when liberal theory could take for granted an exclusively monotheistic audience.

But we do not have to make any commitment to Locke's view that polytheistic religions are mere superstitions – nor to the implied view, in the passage quoted previously, that Christianity is on the march toward the inevitable defeat of polytheism everywhere – in order to take Locke's point about the social power of religious leaders. This power is so great that philosophers who can appeal only to unassisted natural reason cannot aspire to replace them, regardless of whether the religious leaders' teachings are reasonable or superstitious. The important point here is that priests generally, whether deserving (rational) or undeserving (superstitious), have always enjoyed absolute dominance over philosophers of natural reason in every society.

This imbalance of power between priests and philosophers has important consequences for the moral foundations of the political order. When reason and religion are understood as opponents, Locke writes, the priests do not teach morality. Instead, they offer rituals – "observations and ceremonies," "feasts and solemnities," and "tricks of religion" – in its place. The end result is a perfect separation of religion from moral philosophy, to the extreme political disadvantage of the latter: "No wonder, then, that religion was everywhere distinguished from and preferred to virtue; and that it was dangerous heresy and profaneness to think the contrary" (R 241, 169–70). Thus, if reason and religion are understood as separate and opposed to one another, people learn morality from neither the priests nor the philosophers. The priests do not teach morality because, having rejected reason, they rely on forms and rituals rather than on moral reasoning. The philosophers teach morality, but almost no one listens to them because they lack the legitimacy and authority that only the divine can convey.

Of course, this is not to say that people do not learn morality at all under such conditions. A certain level of virtuous behavior is required for the maintenance of civil order. Locke identifies one source of moral teachings in pre-Christian societies that simultaneously employed reason and had the sanction of priestly ritual: the political rulers. "So much virtue as was necessary to hold societies together and to contribute to the quiet of governments, the civil laws of commonwealths taught and forced upon men who lived under magistrates" (R 241, 170). If morality is not taught for moral reasons, but rather for the instrumental purpose of upholding civil order, naturally it will be taught by the ruling class.

But, as Locke writes, even in the best cases the morality promoted by pre-Christian rulers never went beyond what was "directly to conduce to the prosperity and temporal happiness of any people." This would be the case where the rulers at least take an interest in citizens' security and prosperity. More often, unscrupulous rulers "with no other aims but their own power" promoted a moral code designed merely to "tie men together in subjection" (R 241, 170). This is the historical analogue of Locke's logical case that worldly happiness is an insufficient foundation for morality; he argues that historically, moral systems built on worldly rewards and punishments have often been the tools of absolutism and tyranny.

It should be clear why Locke considers this separation of religion and philosophy an unacceptable state of affairs. Moral philosophy properly understood and religion properly understood are interchangeable for him; if moral philosophy and religion are separated, both fail to perform their duties adequately. Without the power of God, philosophy lacks the obligatory force of moral authority, and without the assistance of revelation it is left with only the meager powers of natural reason. Meanwhile, a religion that rejects philosophy lacks the guidance of reason to help it accurately make out God's will, and thus avoid collapsing into ignorance and superstition. Philosophy is reduced to the status of good advice, while religion is reduced to a set of empty rituals. And since neither of these is sufficient for legitimate politics, the rulers will enforce their own morality, based on their own interests.

RELIGIOUS MORALITY AND MORAL CONSENSUS

Locke's account of the boundaries of toleration in the *Letter* shows that because politics is based on moral rules, the relationship between religion and politics must remain complex. Both extremes – a political community devoted to one particular religion, and a political community with no role for religion in political theory at all – are equally untenable. Granting a special status to members of one religion undermines moral rules because it introduces a morally insignificant distinction into moral reasoning, but excluding religion from political philosophy altogether undermines moral rules by removing divine will, the only possible basis for authoritative moral claims.

Locke's voluntarist account of moral law in the *Essay* and the *Reasonableness* shows that theories purporting to be moral theories cannot be sustained unless they arise from divine will, because people will live in the way they think will make them happy, and human tastes are divergent. What fulfills one person may make another miserable. Only God's power provides an irrefutable reason why a person should choose to live in one way rather than another. The *Reasonableness* also shows how this is reflected in human history, as people have always chosen religion over philosophy wherever the two are seen to conflict.

A lot has changed since Locke wrote this critique of nonreligious morality. The partially realized ideal of compartmentalization of religion and politics in our time makes it tempting to conclude that Locke's historical judgment was wrong – that natural reason has in fact replaced religion as the basis of politics. But it is not at all clear that this has happened. In fact, the discourse of professional political theorists is so completely isolated from practical political life that it is impossible to say with any certainty what moral theory guides our politics. Our theorists have come up with nonreligious liberal theories that mimic, in secular form, the morality of the older, explicitly religious liberal theories that emerged from the Enlightenment. However, this does not justify the conclusion that these new theories have actually replaced in practice the older, religious theories.

Rather, the isolation of the theorists from real politics suggests the opposite: as professional theorists have become more and more detached from our political life, our political life has relied more and more on the leftover cultural inertia of older theories. This is why religious rhetoric persists in the public square even among those who insist on compartmentalization. Political leaders, as Locke observed, have to have some way to make morally authoritative claims. Religion remains the only effective means of doing so. The rise of compartmentalization as an ideal in our political theory might have been expected to bring the disappearance of religion from politics, but it has not done that, because no other source of moral authority has emerged. In practice, the push for compartmentalization has attenuated the link between religion and politics but has not succeeded in separating them.

Locke, of course, does not have the opportunity to tell us what he thinks of our historical situation, but he raises something akin to this line of reasoning in his discussion of deism. He writes that once morality is communicated to us by revelation, we flatter ourselves that we could have figured it all out on our own: "When truths are once known to us, though by tradition, we are apt to . . . ascribe to our own understandings the discovery of what, in reality, we borrowed from others — or, at least . . . we are forward to conclude it an obvious truth, which, if we had sought, we could not have missed" (R 243, 177). Locke does not mean to discount all nonreligious moral reasoning as mere imitation of religion. He had high praise for the moral reasoning of some pre-Christian secular moral philosophers. His criticism of nonreligious moral theorists is not that their doctrines are false but that their doctrines lack authority. The "truths" he says we mistakenly ascribe to unassisted reason are those that connect moral theory to divine authority. The argument here is that people find nonreligious moral theories authoritative because they have been predisposed to do so by the influence of religion. Even if the reasoning of nonreligious theories is right, in themselves these theories can have no moral authority; to the extent that such theories are treated as authoritative, it is because their moral teachings are coincident with the teachings of authoritative religion.

Today, the evidence is stronger than ever that human tastes, as Locke observed in the *Essay*, are divergent rather than convergent. Unprecedented technological advances have made possible an explosive increase in the variety of life arrangements available, and comparatively widespread distribution of material wealth now allows virtually everyone, rather than just the very wealthy, to control to a very great extent how his life will be lived. At this moment in history, all arguments that one way of life is inherently the most fulfilling, the most in accord with human nature, look more problematic than ever before. Even the argument that allowing everyone to live however he chooses is most in accord with human nature relies upon the presumption of a certain amount of natural convergence in human tastes, and is not vindicated in any obvious way by the choices people actually make.

Moral theory must have some way of establishing authoritative laws that society will enforce. As Locke shows us, only God can morally unify people's divergent tastes. If a theory does not arise from God, "mankind might hearken to it or reject it as they pleased, or as it suited their interest, passions, principles, or humors." In a world where technology and prosperity have exponentially increased the diversity of interests, passions, principles, and humors in human life, divine authority is probably the only hope for social and political solidarity.

6

" 'Tis Reasonable to Think the Cause Is Natural"

Locke's Religious Eudemonism

Locke faces a difficult challenge in constructing his political theory. He must build it on God's moral authority, because he believes that no other source of authority is both legitimate and sufficiently convincing for the needs of politics. As John Dunn puts it, for Locke the human race would "exist in a condition of total anomie" if not for God.[1] However, the abuse of God's authority is the very problem that drew him into political theory in the first place. Politics based on religious enthusiasm, arbitrary scriptural interpretation, the pretensions of medieval scholastics to exclusive insights into nature, and claims on all sides of denominational supremacy had been the cause of recurring violence over the previous two centuries. The underlying reason for religious disagreement is that most of the available ways of learning about God are rife with epistemological landmines. Most religious truth is not laid out for us in such an obvious way that everyone can easily agree upon it. To build a religious moral theory that will unite rather than divide society, Locke must find a way of knowing God's law that is epistemologically simple and therefore equally clear to all.

Locke develops and implements a method for rationally investigating God's law by analyzing human nature, which is God's handiwork. Locke thinks that God's will is manifest in his construction of human nature, and that rational examination of human nature produces an understanding of God's will that is perfectly harmonious with that gained from rational examination of scripture.[2] Locke develops the intellectual foundations of this method in Book Two of the *Essay Concerning Human Understanding*. He further justifies its validity with scriptural arguments in *The Reasonableness of Christianity*. And in the *Two Treatises of Government* he carries it to fruition, using it to build a case for his account of moral law.

This method cannot be the sole basis of moral reasoning for Locke, because only revelation can reliably establish the divine rewards and punishments that make the natural law obligatory. But because this method is not subject to the epistemological difficulties that apply to scriptural analysis, its conclusions are more clear and easily proven than those we obtain through scripture. Thus, natural laws confirmed by this method are more rationally reliable. Locke's hope is that, by showing with this method that some natural laws are extremely certain, he can persuade conflicting religious factions that political life should be built only on those laws, and not on beliefs that are not equally clear to all, and are hence divisive.

Locke's use of this method is perhaps the highest fulfillment of his theory of moral consensus. The moral law justified by this method is authoritative because it is derived from divine will, but it is demonstrated by a rational method that will be persuasive to members of all religions. Locke cannot justify all moral laws with this method, so there are many moral questions that people will still disagree upon; these questions must remain outside the ambit of politics because there is no way of settling them that will be accepted as authoritative by members of all groups. For example, human nature does not tell us whether animal sacrifice is or is not an acceptable way to worship God, so opinions and practices on both sides of the issue must be legally tolerated. On the other hand, there are a number of subjects on which the moral design of human nature does give clear answers, most importantly (as we will see) in the case of murder. In such cases, the political community can compel all people to comply with the clearly discerned moral law.

THE FUNDAMENTALS OF PSYCHOLOGY: PLEASURE AND PAIN

The foundation of Locke's method for analyzing human nature is his account of motivation in human psychology. Book Two of the *Essay* canvasses the powers of the human mind, and establishes that moral knowledge and belief are constrained by the limits of those powers. But there is another aspect of human behavior that is not subject to such epistemological limitations – the motivating power of pleasure and pain. Our knowledge of pleasure and pain is immediate and certain. The reality of these ideas is inside us, so we cannot fail to perceive it accurately; if

I subjectively perceive that I am in pain, the objective truth can only be that I am in fact in pain.

Pleasure and pain are two of the most important ideas in Locke's epistemology. They are simple ideas, immediately understood by the mind, and almost constantly clamoring for our attention. Locke presents the ideas of pleasure and pain early in Book Two and they recur through the rest of the *Essay*. Locke's larger accounts of agency, will, freedom, and law can all be traced back to the fundamentals of pleasure and pain.

It is important to note that by "pleasure" and "pain" Locke does not simply refer to physical sensations, but to any experience we find enjoyable or repellant (see E II.20.15, 232). A licentious person may find great pleasure in physical indulgences, while a more chaste person may find such indulgences disgusting; in Locke's meaning, the former takes "pleasure" in physical indulgences but the latter finds them "painful," although the physical sensations would be the same for each. Locke does not address the perplexing question of whether there is an essential similarity between basic physical pleasures and higher pleasures such as art, religion, and love. That question has primarily been raised by the emergence of utilitarian philosophy and by scientific investigation of brain chemistry. In 1689, it was still fairly easy to speak of "pleasure" in an inclusive sense, similar to the broad way in which we now use words like "happiness" and "well-being," without committing to any larger thesis about the physical nature of pleasure and pain.

Pleasure and pain, especially pain, are the only motives for action that Locke finds in the human mind. "The motive, for continuing in the same state or action, is only the present satisfaction in it; the motive to change, is always some uneasiness" (E II.21.29, 249; see also II.7.3–6, 129–31 and II.20.1–3, 229–30). That we have the power to respond to our surroundings by acting, or by refraining from action, is for Locke one of the most clear and prominent ideas in the human mind, and he thinks there is no motivation that is not ultimately a matter of the actor's pleasure and pain.

This has sometimes been mistaken for egoism, but it is not.[3] A person's pleasure and pain are his only motivations, but this is not necessarily selfish. Selfishness or unselfishness will result from what kinds of things people take pleasure and pain in, and that depends on our beliefs. A charitable person is unhappy when he sees the misfortunes of others, and is motivated by his unhappiness to provide help. If he were not unhappy when contemplating the misfortunes of others he would have no motive to help them. Pleasure and pain are the tools of human motivation, and like all tools they can be used for good or ill. Indeed, in Locke's book about education his primary goal is to make the child moral by teaching him to associate good behavior with pleasure.[4] This kind of eudemonism has a long history in Christianity. As W. M. Spellman writes, "some variety of hedonism," which is to say, eudemonism, "had always been a part of Christian thought." In particular, the Anglican Latitudinarians of Locke's day were "most insistent upon its overall validity."[5] This view was also prominent among Puritans of the time.[6] The eudemonist approach to ethics appealed to a wide variety of Christians because it "provided them with additional evidence of man's fallen nature while underscoring the personal quality of God's sovereignty."[7]

Leo Strauss interprets Locke's eudemonism as a sign that Locke follows Hobbes in substituting psychology for moral reasoning. Strauss declares that for Locke self-preservation is "a right antedating all duties" because it is our strongest desire.[8] This premise is crucial to much of Strauss's case for reading Locke's politics as essentially Hobbesian. But it is a nonsequitur; Strauss attributes to Locke the view that desires create rights, but Locke never endorses such reasoning. Strauss produces this quotation to back his interpretation: "men . . . must be allowed to pursue their happiness, nay, cannot be hindered."[9] But in its original context this is only a statement that obedience to moral law must be shown to bring us happiness if moral law is to be effective. That is far from saying, as Strauss would have us read it, that the desire for happiness gives each person a right to do anything he thinks will make him happy. Locke points out in the *Essay* that human desires would overturn all morality if pursued without the restraint of moral laws derived from a source other than human desire itself (see E I.3.13, 75). Locke always maintained a strict distinction between moral obligation as such and psychological motivation as such; he believed, as we will see in this chapter, that they were complimentary parts of a divine plan in the construction of the universe, but he never substituted one for the other.[10] The proper moral role of pleasure and pain is to motivate people to do what is right, but the motivation is not what supplies the rightness.[11]

Locke's eudemonic view of human motivation has large consequences for his political and religious thought. Once we acknowledge the infinite superiority of God, we realize that our long-term happiness can only be secured by serving him and doing good. "The rewards and punishments of another life, which the almighty has established, as the enforcements of his law, are of weight enough to determine the choice, against whatever pleasure or pain this life can show" (E II.21.70, 281;

see also II.28.8, 352; IV.11.13, 638; and IV.13.3, 651). Because of this, God's law is "the only true touchstone of moral rectitude" (E II.28.8, 352). This, more than anything else, is why Locke's view that pleasure and pain are the only motivations for human behavior is not egocentric. If we are happiness-seeking creatures it is only because God has made us that way, and he has made our world such that happiness seekers can find God and learn reverence. We know that God is all-powerful, so we know that our happiness depends on him and thus we seek out his will and follow it. Before long we discover that our eternal happiness depends on resisting the temptation to seek short-term happiness in this world, so the apparent hedonism of Locke's psychology produces precisely the opposite of what we would call "hedonistic" personalities.

GOD'S DESIGN OF HUMAN NATURE

The idea that God constructed us to be motivated by happiness is the foundation of Locke's method for discerning God's law by analyzing human nature. Locke believes that pleasure and pain were ordained and constructed by God. If we never felt pleasure or pain, "we should have no reason to prefer one thought or action, to another . . . and so we should neither stir our bodies, nor employ our minds." But it has "pleased our wise creator, to annex" pleasure and pain "to several objects . . . as well as to several of our thoughts," so that "those faculties which he had endowed us with, might not remain wholly idle, and unemployed by us" (E II.7.3, 129). The belief that pleasure and pain are divinely constructed recurs throughout Locke's major works.

According to Locke, God has ordered the universe, and particularly human nature, such that greater happiness will generally result from doing what God wants us to do and greater unhappiness will generally result from doing what God does not want us to do. For Locke, this belief that pleasures and pains are constructed in harmony with moral law seems to follow naturally from the idea that the universe was designed by an intelligence. If our world is ordered by a higher power, it stands to reason that that power would arrange pleasures and pains to reward or punish behaviors as it wanted to encourage or discourage them. There is "nothing, that so directly, and visibly secures, and advances the general good of mankind in this world, as obedience to the laws" that God "has set them, and nothing that breeds such mischiefs and confusion, as the neglect of them" (E II.28.11, 356). By looking at what actions bring happiness or unhappiness, then, we can see God's design in the construction of the universe.

This does not mean that each individual who performs good works will be happy and each individual who performs bad works will be unhappy, at least in this world (as opposed to the afterlife). Locke did not take a firm stand on whether virtuous people would be happier than vicious people in this world. He comments at one point in the *Essay* that "wicked men have not much the odds to brag of, even in their present possession; nay, all things rightly considered, [they] have, I think even the worse part here" (E II.21.70, 282). But he writes in the *Reasonableness* that when moral virtue was laid out by secular reason in the ancient world, to non-philosophers it "appeared . . . little to consist of their chief end, happiness, while they kept them from the enjoyments of this life, and they had little evidence and security of another" (R 245, 182).[12] Probably the key to understanding this apparent contradiction is in the way people measure worldly happiness. In observing that virtue "appeared" not to promote happiness, Locke writes that "the portion of the righteous has been in all ages taken notice of to be pretty scanty in this world. Virtue and prosperity do not often accompany one another" (R 245, 182). The terms "portion" and "prosperity" refer to material wealth. No doubt virtue does appear to be inconsistent with happiness in the eyes of crassly materialistic people who measure happiness by wealth. It seems likely that in the *Essay* Locke had in mind a less materialistic way of measuring happiness. But however we read these statements, the important point is that Locke does not firmly commit to any position on the question of whether virtuous people are always, or even usually, happier than vicious people in this world.

What Locke does commit to, and rely on for his method of discerning natural law, is that God has constructed the universe such that good actions tend to promote the happiness of society. That is, good actions by one person promote the happiness of most people. Individuals find worldly happiness in many different ways: "Though all men's desires tend to happiness, yet they are not moved by the same object. Men may choose different things, and yet all choose right" (E II.21.55, 270). However, there are discernable patterns and consistencies in the ways in which *societies* find worldly happiness – that is, in what things are considered beneficial to society. What is called "virtue" or "vice" does differ somewhat in different societies, but "as to the main, they for the most part [are] kept the same everywhere" (E II.28.11, 356). Rules like the prohibitions on murder, theft, and breaking promises are universally praised by societies.

This indicates to Locke the presence of a moral design. God has, "by an inseparable connection, joined virtue and public happiness together; and made the practice thereof, necessary to the preservation of society," so "it is no wonder, that every one should, not only allow, but recommend, and magnify those rules to others, from whose observance of them, he is sure to reap advantage to himself" (E I.3.6, 69).[13] This is why "even in the corruption of manners, the true boundaries of the law of nature, which ought to be the rule of virtue and vice, were pretty well preserved" (E II.28.11, 356).

The relevant question for determining God's will is not to ask what actions will bring the actor worldly happiness, but what actions will bring worldly happiness to people generally. The only absolute guarantee of happiness for individuals is the infinite rewards of the afterlife, secured through submission to God. Obeying God, in turn, leads us not to pursue our own worldly happiness but the happiness of others. Thus, Locke's moral psychology begins with self-interest but reasons through God's command to the general interest.[14]

The vision of political and social life that emerges is one in which societies organize to protect themselves out of collective self-interest, and in doing so end up approximately enforcing God's law. God has organized the incentives of human nature and social behavior to produce this result. Locke's political individualism is sometimes taken to reflect a view of humanity as selfish and appetitive, but this is only half right. At the individual level, a person's self-interested nature does often cause him to act selfishly, but his own self-interest also leads him to the discovery of God's law and his duty to others. At the social level, a person's self-interest also leads him to respect the sacred rights of others and support governments that keep the peace. When an individual harms others through wicked actions, people will organize to prevent and punish such actions, thus using civil law to approximately enforce the divine law by pursuing their own happiness. In Locke's account, this is how governments are created to punish wicked actions, and it is also how rebellions are created to punish wicked governments.

The *Essay* introduces Locke's method of analyzing human nature in its analysis of the law of opinion. He writes that actions praised or blamed by popular opinion are called "virtue" and "vice." These are often mistaken for actions "in their own nature right and wrong," but they are only so when the law of opinion happens to coincide with divine law (E II.28.10, 353). Fortunately, according to Locke, this is usually the case. For obvious reasons, society praises as "virtuous" actions that contribute to the happiness and stability of society, and blames as "vicious" behavior that is disruptive and harmful to society. And it just so happens, according to Locke, that morally good behavior is also socially beneficial behavior while morally bad behavior is also socially bad behavior. "Since nothing can be more natural, than to encourage with esteem and reputation that, wherein every one finds his advantage; and to blame and discountenance the contrary, 'tis no wonder, that esteem and discredit, virtue and vice, should in a great measure correspond with the unchangeable rule of right and wrong, which the law of God hath established." Thus, the laws of opinion tend to coincide with the laws of God. This is why "even the exhortations of inspired teachers have not feared to appeal to common repute," as at Philippians 4:8, where Paul tells us to do "whatsoever is of good report" (E II.28.11, 356).

Because of this general correlation between what society praises as virtuous and what is actually virtuous, the law of opinion serves a moral purpose. While laws of opinion do not have moral authority in and of themselves, they have a strong tendency to reflect the true moral law, and thus they serve to approximately enforce the divine law with earthly punishments. Opinion provides immediate rewards and punishments to supplement the much greater, but further distant, rewards and punishments of the afterlife – "the penalties that attend the breach of God's laws, some, nay, perhaps, most men seldom seriously reflect on," but there is not "one of ten thousand, who is stiff and insensible enough, to bear up under the constant dislike, and condemnation of his own club" (E II.28.12, 357). It is easy to resist sin when one is sitting alone in one's living room reading the Bible, but that is not sufficient to sustain a virtuous life. Obedience to God is a full-time job, and one's thoughts are not likely to be fixed on the eternal joys of heaven at the moment when temptation arises and resistance is needed. Our concern for the opinions of others provides a much more immediate reason to resist sin at the moment of temptation, one that can carry us through until the danger has passed.[15]

Locke also justifies this method of analyzing human nature in the *Reasonableness*. There he refers to God's moral law as both "the law of reason" and "of nature" (R 14, 9). Throughout his works, when Locke says "natural law" he means all the universal laws of God, as opposed to those that apply only to particular people.[16] God's law is the law of nature both because it is a law governing actions in the natural world and because our reason can discern parts of it in nature, particularly in human nature.

Locke takes about fifteen paragraphs in the *Reasonableness* to unpack what he means by calling God's moral law "the law of nature." He repeats the *Essay*'s argument that natural rewards and punishments for behavior are divinely arranged, only now with scriptural evidence. Locke reprints Romans 2:14–15 in its entirety, where Paul observes that the gentiles, who have not accepted any revelation of the law of God, nonetheless "do by nature the things contained in the law," and thus "show the work of the law written in their hearts, their consciences also bearing witness." Locke inserts an explanatory note of his own into the quotation, so it reads: "the gentiles, which have not the law, do (i.e., find it reasonable to do) by nature the things contained in the law" (R 19, 11–12).[17] When Paul says "do by nature," Locke takes that to mean "find it reasonable to do" – that is, find it rational to do. When Paul says of the gentiles that God's law is "written in their hearts," for Locke this means that their reason causes them to follow it when they naturally seek their own happiness. By rationally calculating what laws will promote the happiness of their societies, the gentiles unwittingly calculate the will of God, because God has constructed their nature to produce exactly this result.

This is an unusual reading of this passage.[18] The assertion that God's law is "written in" the "hearts" of human beings is usually taken as a reference to some sort of instinctive or intuitive moral sense. Of course Locke rejects the idea of a moral sense as such, because it would have to be considered a form of enthusiasm in his epistemological system. In his reading of Romans 2:14–15, reason takes the role of a moral sense. It is a way of connecting our natural impulses to a divine moral framework without ascribing to those impulses themselves any sort of divine status. The key difference between Locke's account of human nature and an account that believes in a moral sense as such is that the latter reads God's will directly into each person's instincts while the former deduces God's will from the instincts of human beings in general. Locke's approach avoids the inherent dangers of enthusiasm while still upholding the presence of a moral plan in the design of human nature.

Locke holds that we can learn the law of God through reason by figuring out how best to promote general happiness. Reason tells us that God would construct the universe so that the path to general happiness will also lead us to God's law. Thus, to a certain extent, natural reason can shed some light on the question of what God wants from us by examining human nature.

In the *Reasonableness* Locke argues that this is exactly what the pre-Christian classical philosophers did. He observes that the rules of their nonreligious ethical systems look very similar to the rules of Christian ethics – don't kill, don't steal, and so on. If God's moral rules could only be known through revelation, it would be a fantastic coincidence that nonreligious ethical systems tend to be so similar to revelatory ones. But Locke argues that this similarity is not surprising; since "the law of nature is the law of convenience too . . . it is no wonder" that philosophers "should, by meditation," make out the precepts of the natural law, "even from the observable convenience and beauty of it" (R 242, 173). That is, because the universe is constructed to reward the behavior God wants to encourage, such behavior is prudent and aesthetically pleasing as well as moral. It makes sense, then, that the classical philosophers endorsed that behavior, having perceived God's moral design in nature.

SCRIPTURE AND HUMAN NATURE AS COMPLIMENTARY METHODS

Investigating God's will through human nature in this manner stands as an alternative to investigating God's will through scripture. They are not, however, mutually exclusive alternatives. In fact, Locke always treats them as perfect compliments. Each method has particular advantages and disadvantages, so the best way to reason about God's law is to use each method where it is more appropriate. By using both methods, applying each one to the cases for which it is best suited, we can build a unified account of God's will.

Neither of the two methods is sufficient on its own for politics. Natural reason alone can provide the precepts of the moral law, but cannot back them up with divine authority. In the *Reasonableness*, right after Locke observes that the classical philosophers produced ethical systems similar to Christian ethics, he goes on to explain why such systems failed to attract more than a tiny number of adherents. The philosophers' fundamental problem was that they "made not much mention of the deity in their ethics" (R 243, 176–7). Natural reason can prove God's existence, but not divine rewards and punishments. If the only reason to obey an ethical rule is its inherent choiceworthiness, it will not be obeyed with sufficient regularity, and we have no moral grounds on which to force people to obey it. Divine sanctions are necessary to transform a praiseworthy rule into an authoritative law (see R 245, 185). Meanwhile, revelation alone is insufficient because it produces too much social division. People come to radically different conclusions about what we know about God through revelation because revelation is epistemologically problematic – it is not so obviously true that everyone who perceives it agrees upon its validity and content.

Because of the perfect partnership between reason and faith in Locke's system, each method can compensate for the defects of the other without requiring us to abandon it. If our faith is rational, as Locke insisted faith must always be, it will not contradict any of the conclusions of right reason, and in turn the conclusions of reason will not contradict any of the conclusions of rightly regulated faith. We can therefore rely on faith to supply the politically necessary beliefs that natural reason cannot establish, while continuing to rely on reason to supply a guide to God's law that is epistemologically straightforward and thus provides social agreement.

Locke does not express, and his philosophic writings do not reveal, any general preference between learning God's law through natural reason and learning it through revelation. However, each of the two methods has particular advantages and disadvantages which make it more suitable for some purposes than for others. There are specific reasons to prefer one or the other in specific circumstances.

When we learn God's law through natural reason, we can see it only after it has been filtered through the imperfect rationality and general unpredictability of human behavior. Locke's method implies two ways to discern what will promote general happiness: by calculating logically what would make people happy, and by observing (as Paul did in Romans 2:14–15) what laws nations tend to enact. But the list of laws that will clearly contribute to general happiness, and that are common to large majorities of human societies – such as prohibitions on murder, assault, theft, and so on – is short. Thus, the scope of what we can learn about God's law through natural reason is very limited.

The corresponding advantage, however, is the high degree of certainty we can achieve using this method. In many cases, the logical argument that a law would contribute to general happiness is extremely clear. Also, the number of societies available for observation is very large, so any commonalities that emerge among such a great number of societies can be relied on with a high degree of certainty. Murder very obviously detracts from general happiness, and it is prohibited by every society, so we can be very certain it is against God's law.

Scriptural revelation, on the other hand, can cover a much broader range of information. For many problems, revelation is the only rational avenue of investigation we have. But because accepting a revelation as genuine requires us to make a judgment about how well attested by miracles it is, people disagree about which revelations are genuine. What's more, interpretations of scripture are subject to mistakes and the influence of sophistry. So while the content of true revelation is unquestionably infallible, what we learn from revelation after it is filtered through these epistemological problems is less clear and uniformly accepted than what we learn through natural reason alone.

Thus reason is very certain but narrow in scope, while our understanding of scripture is in most cases less certain but broad in scope. This explains why Locke relies so heavily on natural reason rather than revelation for beliefs about God's law in cases where a high degree of assent is called for, such as in laying out the first principles of a political system.[19] But the precepts of natural reason alone are merely prudential or aesthetically pleasing rules, not genuinely moral laws, so faith plays an integral part in Locke's political philosophy as well.

Locke uses this partnership between reason and faith to build a political theory based on the potential for moral consensus. Locke, confronted by large and widening social divisions over matters of ultimate belief, cannot build a political theory primarily on faith, so he builds one on a partnership between natural reason and a limited amount of faith. People who disagree on matters of faith can still agree on matters of natural reason. Locke's method of analyzing human nature is designed to show that some moral rules can be known with such great certainty that they can serve as the foundation of a political system even among people who disagree on ultimate beliefs. But to show that these rules are in fact moral laws, Locke has to rely on some ultimate beliefs. The most important of these are belief in God, which we can know through natural reason, and belief in the afterlife, which can only come from faith. As it happens, these particular ultimate beliefs are shared by virtually all members of society, so they can facilitate a moral consensus among different religious groups.

What makes this approach particularly promising as a model for political reasoning in times of cultural disharmony is that it harnesses the moral authority of religion without requiring agreement on the revelatory medium through which we receive that authority. The political community is open to anyone who believes that the universe is divinely governed, such that good behavior will be rewarded and evil punished, and who adheres to the moral rules that are confirmed by rational analysis of human nature. Locke founds the political community on divine moral laws, but does so in a way that does not require commitment to any particular revelation, so long as we are committed to some revelation that acknowledges divine authority consistent with rationally confirmed moral law.

REFUTING MORAL AND POLITICAL PARTICULARISM

One obvious problem for Locke's method is the need to show that there are, in fact, large patterns across all times and places in the ordering of human societies. Objections to natural law theory on grounds that it fails to do this became more frequent and more forceful after Hume's critique appeared in the following century. But even in Locke's time such concerns were present, and the *Two Treatises* shows a keen awareness of them.

The people of Europe were still coming to grips with the discovery of the Americas and increased exploration in other parts of the globe. Europe could no longer think of itself as the center of the world, and worldwide trade and colonization were bringing into question the idea that there could be one standard of behavior for all cultures. Perhaps most important, however, was the discovery that very large portions of the world population knew nothing of the Christian religion; Christianity could no longer be seen as the universal faith.[20] Throughout his adult life, Locke was fascinated by the travel accounts produced by the explorers of that era, and references to these accounts occur frequently in both the *Essay* and the *Two Treatises*.[21] As some of Locke's own examples show, these accounts were not always conducive to the conclusion that human societies tend to be very much alike and to have similar views of good and evil. It was a time when the intellectual currents seemed to be running against the universalism that had flourished in the natural law thought of the middle ages, and toward an emphasis on the distinctiveness of particular cultures.

It is precisely this emphasis on cultural distinctiveness that Locke seeks to combat. Across Europe, and particularly within England, the political landscape had been shaped by two centuries of violent warfare between religious cultures, each claiming to represent the one true faith. In such an environment, political emphasis on cultural distinctiveness had exactly the result one might expect it to have: England, though nominally a single nation, was made up of cultural groups that distrusted and despised one another, each struggling for political domination over the others. Locke grew up during the bloodbath of the English Civil War, and as an adult he lived in a society where memories of that conflict were fresh, and political violence was an ever-present possibility.

His political theory seeks to subdue cultural conflict by appealing to universal natural law. Richard Ashcraft has persuasively argued that Locke's decision to publish the *Two Treatises* should be understood not simply as an attempt to justify the Glorious Revolution, the legitimacy of which was not in much dispute in 1689. His more important purpose was to defend the universalistic natural-law interpretation of the Glorious Revolution against the culturally particularistic interpretation of that event as a defense of traditional English liberties.[22] The particularistic interpretation would later come to be identified with Edmund Burke, but it was already becoming a settled consensus in 1689: the Glorious Revolution was fought to defend the ancient English constitution against the dangerous innovations of James II, not to vindicate universally valid natural laws or human rights. Locke's publication of the *Two Treatises* against this backdrop was an attempt to stem the tide of cultural particularism, lest the historic opportunity to dedicate the political community to universalistic principles be lost, and England return to internecine warfare.

To justify a universalistic natural law by analyzing human nature, Locke has to refute the empirical perception of radical cultural difference. This is already a formidable task in an environment that emphasizes cultural differences, but it is further complicated by Locke's own high epistemological standards. Before we can legitimately conclude that a moral principle is visible in the design of human nature, the evidence for it must be very strong.

In order to overcome this high burden of proof, Locke isolates one moral law and concentrates on making the case for its presence in human nature. In the *Two Treatises* Locke omits other moral laws, whose presence in human nature is less obvious, in order to remain faithful to his high epistemological standards. This is not to say that other moral laws are not present in human nature; it is only to say that they are not sufficiently clear to meet the high standard of evidence that is appropriate for laying political foundations. This is why Locke declares that "it would be besides my present purpose, to enter here into the particulars of the law of nature" (T II.12, 120). Rather than follow the medieval scholastics in providing a detailed account of every provision of the natural law, filling volume after volume with arguments whose clarity and certainty vary from great to negligible, Locke concentrates on proving the validity of one very certain moral law to serve as the foundation of politics.[23]

The moral law Locke seeks to vindicate in his analysis of human nature is, as every student of Locke knows, the divine command to preserve the lives of human beings. By showing that the imperative to preserve human life is discernable almost everywhere in the construction of human nature, Locke argues that this imperative is God's will, since God is the designer of human nature. Locke then appeals to God's moral authority to elevate this imperative to the status of a universal moral law, binding on all people and societies, and hence on all cultural groups within a society. This allows for – indeed, it makes necessary – the construction of a common political community based on this universal moral law, even among people who disagree on other moral matters.

The observation that all the groups in one particular society are de-voted to preserving human life would not, by itself, be sufficient to provide common moral ground among them; it would establish only a coinciden-tal overlap in their cultural beliefs. The key element is the observation that preserving human life is a universal imperative of human nature, which allows Locke to ascribe that imperative to God. The crucial shared be-lief that serves to build moral consensus among different cultural groups is not simply that human life must be preserved but that this law is di-vinely ordained and therefore morally obligatory. Locke can only build a common political authority on the law of preservation if he can satisfy all cultural groups that this law is morally obligatory, and his analysis of human nature is designed to demonstrate this in a way that people of different faiths can accept. Locke's empirical observation that preserving human life is conducive to human nature is important only because hu-man nature is in turn a manifestation of God's design in the creation of the universe.

COMMON PRACTICES VERSUS UNIVERSAL PRACTICES

Deriving moral law from the construction of human nature requires us to draw a careful distinction between behaviors that do and do not reflect the fundamental design of human nature, lest the mere existence of a behavior be taken to imply the rightness of that behavior. After all, the reason politics is necessary in the first place is that people do evil as well as good, so we must be cautious when taking human behavior as a sign of natural law. Not only do some individual people transgress the natural law, but even some individual societies transgress it by maintaining social customs that are evil. For this reason, the social customs of an individual society cannot be the measure of the natural law. Locke particularly takes Robert Filmer to task for arguing that because some societies have allowed parents to kill their children by exposure, parents therefore have a right to do so (see T I.56–9, 40–3). Only the general pattern of behavior across all of humanity throughout history is a reliable guide to God's design in constructing human nature.

In a particularly revealing passage, Locke writes that a right founded on "common practice" as such is only "a positive and not a natural right," but "where the practice is universal, 'tis reasonable to think the cause is natural" (T I.88, 63). Here, "common practice" refers to a practice that is merely common to members of one society. This is contrasted with "universal" practices, which are observable as patterns across all societies. A custom does not create a natural right, but a universal custom is a sign of God's will in the design of human nature, and that design in turn justifies a natural right. We might say Locke anticipates Tolstoy: the good social behaviors in human history are the ones that are always the same, while each society's evil behaviors are evil in their own way.

An example will serve to illustrate this method. Arguing in the *First Treatise* for a universal duty to nurture and protect children, Locke observes that God "has in all the parts of the creation taken a peculiar care to propagate and continue the several species of creatures" by giving all creatures the desire to have children and to nurture and protect them, "and [God] makes the individuals act so strongly to this end" that it often overrides even self-preservation and becomes "the strongest principle in them." Thus, we can observe that even in "the dens of lions and the nurseries of wolves . . . these savage inhabitants of the desert obey God and nature in being tender and careful of their offspring." From observing this behavior in humans as well, we can see that God "requires us to preserve" our children "by the dictates of nature and reason, as well as [by] his revealed command" (T I.56, 41). Virtually all parents strongly desire to nurture and protect their children, so it must be God's will that children be nurtured and protected, and thus all parents – not just virtually all parents, but literally all parents – have a duty to nurture and protect their children whether they individually wish to do so or not.[24] Even where whole societies have adopted practices against this moral law – Locke notes historical practices of exposing or mutilating infants, and reproduces verbatim a gruesome travel account of savages in Peru who allegedly have children for the purpose of fattening and eating them – such societies are rare exceptions to the general rule of human nature, and thus ought to be understood as deviant rather than as manifestations of God's design (see T I.56–9, 40–3).

The explanation for immoral deviance from the general construction of human nature, whether by individual people or individual societies, is irrationality. The human will is not naturally oriented toward moral good, and contains all sorts of desires, including many horrible ones. Only reason points us in the morally correct direction, which it does by discerning God's commands. Commenting on the story of Peruvian cannibals who eat their own children, Locke writes that "the busy mind of man" can "carry him to a brutality below the level of beasts, when he quits his reason, which places him almost equal to the angels," and that "the imagination is always restless and suggests variety of thoughts, and the will, reason being laid aside, is ready for every extravagant project." When people follow the guidance provided by reason, they do good; when they ignore it and follow their desires without guidance, they do evil. "Fancy and passion must needs run him into strange courses, if reason, which is his only star and compass, be not that he steers by" (T I.58, 42).[25]

Thus, for Locke, reason plays the psychological role that many Christian theorists in Locke's time ascribed to innate ideas or enthusiastic religious feelings: it is the part of our souls that is naturally oriented toward God and the good. Locke's account of human desires as inherently disorderly roughly follows the Calvinist account of human depravity, but Locke breaks firmly from the predominant view of the Calvinists of his day by holding that reason is necessary to tame our depraved desires.[26] As his critique of enthusiasm in the *Essay* makes clear, reason is the only epistemologically reliable conduit for a connection with God. Of course we must bear in mind here that Locke includes rationally regulated faith as part of what he means by "reason." When Locke says that reason is our star and compass for successfully navigating the stormy waters of depraved human desires, he intends "reason" to include rational faith in the Bible's moral teachings. However, faith though it may be, this faith must be rational if it is to provide reliable navigation, and hence reason (including rational faith) is our guide to God's will.

THE DATA: NATURAL CAPACITIES, SOCIAL CUSTOMS, AND HISTORICAL PATTERNS

In the *Two Treatises* Locke supports the moral law that human life is to be preserved with arguments drawn from three types of observations of human nature: observations of people's natural capacities, of cultural practices, and of historical patterns. These three data sets are portrayed at various points in the *Two Treatises* as supporting the conclusion that the law of human preservation is visible in the design of human nature. There are too many instances in the *Two Treatises* where Locke draws on such arguments for us to recount them all and analyze them separately. Instead, we will look here at a set of examples, chosen because they are the best-developed instances of the argument. These examples are representative of Locke's overall ambition to show the moral design of human nature.

The natural capacities of human beings is the most straightforward, and by far the most famous, of Locke's three sets of data about human nature. Locke observes that human beings have both reason and physical strength, which allow them to exercise dominion over things – that is, to use and destroy things. "God makes him 'in his own image after his own likeness', makes him an intellectual creature, and so capable of dominion. For whatsoever else the image of God consisted, the intellectual nature was certainly a part of it, and belonged to the whole species, and enabled them to have dominion over the inferior creatures" (T I.30, 24).[27] He also observes that these traits belong roughly equally to the whole species, such that virtually all individuals possess them in a sufficient degree to exercise some dominion and to resist having dominion exercised over them. We are all "furnished with like faculties, sharing all in one community of nature" (T II.6, 117).

From these observations, Locke produces a negative argument concerning God's will. Due to the rough natural equality of capacity for dominion, human nature contains no "manifest declaration" of God's intent to "set one above another" (T II.4, 116). If nature contains no such manifest declaration, and neither does revelation (as Locke establishes in the *First Treatise*), it follows that God wants people to be naturally free and equal. Absent an explicit message from God to the contrary, "creatures born of the same species and rank promiscuously born to the same advantages of nature, and the use of the same faculties, should also be equal one amongst another, without subordination or subjection" (T II.4, 116).

This argument is sufficient for Locke's basic political purposes, because it establishes natural freedom and equality, but it is not sufficient for Locke's larger moral purposes. Natural equality and freedom by themselves do not establish any duty on the part of one human being to help preserve the lives of other human beings. We see this illustrated very clearly in Hobbes's political theory, which endorses natural equality and freedom but does not contain any natural duty of charity or any other form of assistance to one's fellow human beings. Indeed, natural equality and freedom do not even establish a duty for human beings to preserve themselves, much less others.

Locke could have constructed essentially the same political theory, at least in terms of its broad outline, on natural freedom and equality without the larger moral duty of preservation. But he is very clear that he wishes to build upon a deeper moral foundation, in which the preservation of both oneself and others is a moral duty. "When his own preservation comes not in competition," every person "ought . . . as much as he can, to preserve the rest of mankind" (T II.6, 117).[28] This deeper moral foundation provides justification for Locke to morally forbid suicide and other self-harmful acts. "Everyone" is "bound to preserve himself, and not to quit his station willfully" (T II.6, 117). It also upholds a positive duty of charity to those in utmost need. "Charity gives every man a title to so much out of another's plenty, as will keep him from extreme want, where he has no means to subsist otherwise" (T I.42, 31).[29] To see Locke's arguments for the broader moral law of human preservation, as opposed to just for natural freedom and equality, we must look at Locke's two other data sets: cultural practices and historical patterns.

We have already seen one example of Locke's argument from cultural practices in his defense of a natural duty to protect and nurture one's children in the *First Treatise*. Later in the *First Treatise*, Locke lays out the exact nature of this argument more explicitly, in observing the universal practice of inheritance of property from parents to children. This comes in Locke's chapter on "Monarchy by Inheritance," and begins as no more than an argument for a natural right of children to inherit property from their parents. However, Locke carries the argument further than that, and uses it to justify a general law that parents must protect and nurture their children. This version of the argument is more complete than the one we recounted above, and deserves more detailed attention.

The first step of this argument is to justify drawing general conclusions about human nature from the observation that a certain practice is universal. Locke argues that "the common consent of mankind" is not the reason for drawing such conclusions, because "that hath never been asked, nor actually given," and even "common tacit consent" would only amount to "a positive and not a natural right." However, "where the practice is universal," that is, if it is practiced virtually everywhere at all times, " 'tis reasonable to think the cause is natural" (T I.88, 63). The premise here is that a universal custom can only be a sign of some desire planted in human beings by God.

To complete the argument, Locke must now show what it is in human nature that drives societies to establish inheritance – some sign of what

God's purpose might have been in designing human nature this way. Locke writes that in addition to the desire for self-preservation, "God planed in men a strong desire also of propagating their kind, and continuing themselves and their posterity, and this gives children a title, to share in the property of their parents" (T I.88, 63). Thus, the cultural practice of inheritance is seen as a specific instance of the general tendency of human nature toward the preservation of children. This, in turn, is a sign of God's will that the species, and each individual member of the species, be preserved. "For children being by the course of nature, born weak, and unable to provide for themselves, they have by the appointment of God himself, who hath thus ordered the course of nature, a right to be nourished and maintained by their parents" (T I.89, 63).

Finally, Locke finds evidence for the law of human preservation in certain consistent historical patterns. When we can observe that people in similar situations always tend to react in the same kind of way, this is a pattern that, for Locke, reflects the design of human nature. For example, in arguing for a right to rebellion, Locke responds to the objection that upholding such a right will encourage frequent rebellion. His first response is to observe that "when the people are made miserable, and find themselves exposed to the ill usage of arbitrary power," they will always rebel. You can "cry up their governors, as much as you will for sons of Jupiter, let them be sacred and divine, descended or authorized from heaven," and "the same will happen" regardless. "He must have lived but a little while in the world, who has not seen examples of this in his time; and he must have read very little, who cannot produce examples of it in all sorts of governments in the world" (T II.224, 229). His second response is to observe that "revolutions happen not upon every little mismanagement in public affairs." Only when "a long train of abuses, prevarications, and artifices, all tending the same way, make the design [of tyranny] visible to the people" do they rebel (T II.225, 229). His third response is that "this doctrine" of a right to rebellion, far from encouraging more frequent rebellion, "is the best fence against rebellion," because it will show "those who are in power . . . the danger and injustice" of abusing that power (T II.226, 229–30). The threat of rebellion can reasonably be expected to deter rulers from indulging the temptation to tyrannize.

These three arguments are all presented as no more than observations of what typically happens, and should reasonably be expected to happen, in societies. They do not, on their face, have any moral dimension. They are simply empirical refutations of the empirical argument that "the people being ignorant, and always discontented," the right to revolution "lays a ferment for frequent rebellion" (T II.223–4, 228–9).

But Locke's comments in the ensuing paragraphs indicate that he also has a moral purpose in making these observations. "If the innocent honest man must quietly quit all he has for peace's sake, to him who will lay violent hands upon it," he writes, "I desire it may be considered, what kind of peace there will be in the world, which consists only in violence and rapine; and which is to be maintained only for the benefit of robbers and oppressors" (T II.228, 231). He asks: "Are the people to be blamed, if they have the sense of rational creatures, and can think of things no otherwise than as they find and feel them?" (T II.230, 232). Locke clearly wants us to come away with the impression that the behaviors he has observed – people never rebel upon slight causes, but always rebel when sufficiently oppressed, and the prospect of such rebellion will deter oppression in rulers – reflect a moral design.

Although Locke does not make this explicit, his reasoning on the subject of historical patterns seems to be something like the following. Rational happiness seekers will compare how happy different life arrangements and courses of action will make them, and choose accordingly. Individually, this may or may not actually make them happy, and it may or may not make them moral. But on average, across large samples of human behavior, aggregate groups of people seeking to maximize their individual happiness end up approximately enforcing God's moral law at the social level. People know that rebellion and civil war bring extreme hardship, so they don't rebel on slight causes. However, people also know that absolute refusal to rebel, even against the worst tyranny, will ultimately cause them even greater hardship, so they do rebel if they conclude that their governors are fundamentally corrupt. Finally, if such a right is openly acknowledged, governors know that they risk rebellion if they violate the people's trust, and are thus deterred from tyrannizing. Thus, the self-interested behavior of individuals can be seen to give rise to social incentives that promote the preservation of human life. The conclusion Locke is pulling us toward is that these historical patterns regarding rebellion are signs of moral design in human nature, specifically a design to preserve human life.

These three types of arguments – from natural capacities, cultural practices, and historical patterns – recur throughout the *Two Treatises*. Taken together, they constitute Locke's argument from human nature for the fundamental moral law of his political system, that human life must be preserved. As we will see in the next chapter, his state of

nature theory does not establish this law; rather, it takes the validity
of this law as a premise. It is Locke's eudemonistic analysis of human
nature, not the state of nature theory, that justifies the law of human
preservation.

LOCKE'S EUDEMONISM AND MORAL CONSENSUS

In grounding his ethical thought in the design of human nature, Locke
builds upon the eudemonism of ancient philosophy. John Marshall has
documented the particular debt Locke owes to the ethics of Cicero.[30]
Despite his "disagreements with Cicero over such issues as the divine basis
of morality and the reasons that motivated men to its practice," according
to Marshall, Locke's account of the content of moral law closely resembles
Cicero's, and Locke continually recommended Cicero to others, from
his early days teaching moral philosophy at Oxford until his last writings
on morality and education.[31] Like the ancient eudemonists, particularly
Cicero, Locke gives an account of human nature that shows its orientation
toward certain moral laws. Locke's moral theory is recognizably similar to
that of the ancient eudemonists in two of its key assumptions: that people
always seek the happiest life, and that it is the job of moral theory to show
that the moral life is the happiest life.

However, Locke's ethical theory reshapes the eudemonism of the ancients to suit the modern world. Marshall emphasizes Locke's modern
view of psychology in this regard, and not without justification. As we
have seen, Locke's version of eudemonism treats happiness, rather than
a broader concept of the flourishing of human capacities such as one
finds in Aristotle, as the motivation of human behavior. This is why, in
the *Essay*, Locke writes that the ancient quest to find the *summum bonum*,
the life that makes people most happy, was hopeless; for Locke the point
is happiness itself, and different people find it in a variety of different
life arrangements (see E II.21.55, 269). This rejection of the possibility
of a *summum bonum* paves the way for a political community that does
not privilege one way of life over all others – God has not constructed
human nature in such a way that one life plan stands out as the happiest.
The purpose of politics is negative instead of positive: not to promote the
happiest life, since that is different for each person, but to punish those
whose ways of life directly contradict the clear imperatives of human
nature.

But we also saw in the last chapter that for Locke the most important difference between Christian and pre-Christian political theory was

not psychology, but the role played in the political community by divine authority. This is also reflected in Locke's modernization of ancient eudemonism. For Locke, the moral life is the happiest life not because it is necessarily an inherently happy or fulfilling life, but because it is rewarded by God. In the *Reasonableness,* Locke writes that ancient eudemonism fails because it does not provide moral authority to back up its political arrangements – happiness as such is desirable to all people but is not a moral imperative (see R 242–3, 172–81). "The philosophers" of the ancient world "indeed showed the beauty of virtue; they set her off so, as drew men's eyes and approbation to her," but they left her "unendowed" (R 245, 184).

Locke's eudemonism is designed to establish moral authority for its ethical rules rather than simply show that they are most conducive to human nature. If a person is happy living a life of vice, fraud, and violence, how do you convince him that he would be happier with a life of piety and virtue, particularly when such a life will not bring him the material advantages and pleasures he craves? For Locke, the ancient eudemonists' appeal to the consolations of philosophy and other such abstract sources of happiness are deeply insufficient for politics. It is at least possible that some people stand to gain more worldly happiness for themselves if they are unjust, and even the mere possibility of this leaves us without a sufficiently clear moral mandate for justice. On the other hand, the worldly enticements of vice pale utterly in comparison with the wrath of a vengeful God. This, for Locke, is why God's law commands moral authority. God's infinite power makes it unthinkable that we could ever find greater happiness in disobedience to him than in obedience, so no rational person would favor disobedience. Locke breaks with the ancients in that for him, human nature is ethically significant only because it was designed by God.

Locke's eudemonistic theory unites the rationality of ancient eudemonism with the moral authority of medieval Christian ethical thought. The content of the moral law is made out by rational analysis of human nature, just as in ancient eudemonist theory. It is therefore not subject to the epistemological problems associated with faith and scriptural interpretation. However, for Locke this moral law is moral because it is legislated by a divine power. The political community that enforces it can thus draw upon the moral authority of the divine.

This unification of rational method and religious moral authority is the fulfillment of Locke's theory of moral consensus – it delivers a moral law that is both highly certain and morally authoritative. This moral law is narrow in scope, of course, and leaves most areas of moral theory untouched. Where the preservation of human life is not at stake, political communities must remain neutral and allow members of the community to follow their consciences. However, wherever human preservation is at stake, the political community has a governing mandate that is simultaneously very clear to reason and backed up by divine moral authority.

7

"The Servants of One Sovereign Master"

Authority and Moral Consensus

The all-important problem for politics is authority. Who has legitimate authority to rule, and on what terms? This problem arises most acutely where the political community is fragmented. If a community shares a common culture, religion, and worldview, the question of authority is not likely to be urgent, as there will probably be broad agreement on the identity of the authoritative ruler and the terms of his authority. But a society characterized by deep tensions between members of different cultural groups does not begin with a shared account of authority. If it is to survive as a unified political community, it must provide a persuasive argument in favor of its rulers' authority to rule, and the terms on which they rule. Otherwise members of one or another group may cease to view the political community as legitimate.

Building an argument that will simultaneously appeal to members of different religions and cultures is a difficult task. For Locke, shared political authority among different cultural groups is possible because, and only because, human beings are "all the servants of one sovereign master, sent into the world by his order and about his business" (T II.6, 117). Since all human beings are under God's authority, a government built upon God's law can serve as a binding authority on all people. Despite the conflict religion frequently causes within society, it is precisely through our submission to the divine that Locke builds a common political community. His *Two Treatises of Government* does this using his rational approach to scriptural interpretation and his rational method of analyzing human nature. These two lines of argument – scriptural and natural – work together to justify the moral law that human life must be preserved. This provides a foundation for politics that is both highly certain (because it is made out with the natural argument) and morally authoritative (because it is delivered in scripture). By building moral consensus around a set of shared beliefs about God that are very certain, Locke makes religion a source of political solidarity rather than a source of division.

What's more, the universal scope of God's authority serves not only to unite the political community but also as a check upon abuses of government power. A government built on God's authority is always bound by God's law, and its authority is a limited trust granted under that law for a specific purpose. God is the only truly "sovereign master"; all others with any form of authority, whether they are rulers, parents, heads of households, masters of servants, or lords of slaves, have their authority in trust from God, and lose their authority if they violate that trust.

The *Two Treatises'* argument as a whole consists of two large steps. The first is to show that no particular person has a manifest authorization from God to rule others. Locke shows that the Bible provides no such authorization, and that human nature reflects God's desire for natural equality among human beings. The second step is to show how legitimate authority can, and must, be created despite the absence of a direct grant of authority from God to any particular person. Locke shows that if people had no common political authority (a situation he calls "the state of nature"), the moral law of human preservation would require them to create a consensual government.

This is the reason government by consent of the governed is morally mandatory. No one has a naturally occurring or supernaturally revealed grant of authority over others, as was shown in the first step of the argument. But Locke's state of nature theory shows that we must have an authoritative government of some kind. The only way to form an authoritative government in the absence of a natural or supernatural grant of such authority is by mutual consent, so consensual government is the only legitimate option.

While reviewing Locke's account of how we can create a mutually binding authority by consent, we will take notice of his doctrines on a number of political issues – for example, family and parenting, property rights, warfare, and political resistance. Locke is more or less the founder of political liberalism, and naturally his arguments in each of these areas will carry important consequences for any political theory that takes his philosophy as its starting point. However, our concern here is for the way in which Locke builds a shared political authority based on moral consensus among conflicting groups, not for the details of specific political issues. The precise content of property and family law must unfortunately receive only cursory attention here. We are concerned not with the policy arguments that occur within the liberal polity, but with the ultimate foundations of that polity as laid by Locke's philosophy of moral consensus. Rather than get sidetracked by the details of Locke's positions on various political issues, which are more than adequately discussed in other Locke scholarship, we will concentrate our attention on the aspects of Locke's theory that serve to unite conflicting religious and cultural groups.

THE USE OF WORDS IN THE *TWO TREATISES*

Before going any further in our analysis of the *Two Treatises*, it is worth pausing to appreciate a startling feature of that work's political argument: the way in which it uses words. Locke's audience was accustomed to seeing words such as "reason" and "power" employed in political theories with rigid uniformity, such that they became a sort of jargon. Each political theory relied on highly specialized rules of language use. This was the method of political theorists from at least the medieval Scholastics to Hobbes, and later it continued to flourish in sources as diverse as Bentham and Kant. The same kind of rigid jargon is a dominant feature of liberal political theory today. But Locke deviates from this prevailing practice in interesting ways, using words in a more fluid and flexible manner. Some of the most important terms in the *Two Treatises* are not always used with precisely the same meaning, but shift between two or more subtly different meanings.

A method of strict language use is not very problematic in times of relative cultural uniformity. It didn't much matter that Aquinas used Catholic jargon to build his political theory, because in thirteenth-century Europe everyone who counted was Catholic. But after the Reformation and the rise of distinct national cultures, each religious group, philosophic school, or cultural tradition developed its own separate political and theological jargon, and the discourse of each group became isolated from those of the others. As Locke shows in his critique of language in Book Three of the *Essay Concerning Human Understanding*, this isolation not only prevented any meaningful philosophic exchange between groups, it allowed each group to maintain a protective shell of unexamined assumptions buried within the structure of its language (see E III.1–11, esp. 10–11).[1] He writes that "the several sects of philosophy and religion . . . to support some strange opinions, or cover some weakness of their hypothesis, seldom fail to coin new words" in order to protect themselves from clear rational scrutiny of their arguments (E III.10.2, 491).

"Artificial ignorance, and learned gibberish" were tools for exercising power over others, used by "those, who have found no easier way to that pitch of authority and dominion they have attained" (III.10.9, 495). Each group could dismiss as nonsense any discourse that failed to follow its particular language rules, preventing any outsider from effectively challenging the premises on which those rules were based.

Locke renders these language barriers irrelevant by refusing to develop a political jargon.[2] He uses key terms with different meanings in different places. Perhaps the most striking example is his use of the word "power" in the *Second Treatise*. The word "power" appears countless times in that text, but is used with two meanings. Sometimes it is used to mean "force" or "violence," as in: "he who would get me into his power without my consent, would use me as he pleased. . . . To be free from such force is the only security of my preservation" (T II.17, 123). Other times it is used to mean "right" or "authority," as in: "Political power then I take to be a right of making laws with penalties of death," and, "the legislative can have no power to transfer their authority of making laws, and place it in other hands" (T II.3, 116 and II.141, 188). Both uses of "power" appear throughout the *Second Treatise*, sometimes cheek by jowl with one another. Other words are also used in this manner; "reason," for example, sometimes refers to the mental faculty of reason and sometimes to the set of propositions confirmed by that faculty (for example, II.6, 117 and II.63, 145). Furthermore, there are key terms that are used with the same meaning throughout the text but are not explicitly given formal definitions, such as "authority." Locke does not even appear to maintain the limited epistemological jargon he developed in the *Essay*. In fact, it is hazardous to assume that the detailed and precise definitions of certain words in the *Essay*, such as "person," also apply to the *Two Treatises*.[3]

This fluid rather than rigid use of language almost never causes Locke's texts to become confused. Each word is used with no more than a handful of different meanings, and in each instance the immediate context makes clear what meaning a word is intended to carry. In the sentence, "the legislative can have no power to transfer their authority of making laws, and place it in other hands," no one would take the word "power" to mean "force" or "violence"; clearly the intended meaning is "right" or "authority." There are some exceptions, of course. In the chapter "Of Tyranny," when Locke says that tyrants are those who substitute their will for "the law," who prevent subjects from appealing to "the law," and whose actions violate "the law," it is unclear whether he means the natural law or the laws laid down by a legitimate legislature (T II.199–210, 216–22).

No doubt this particular ambiguity serves Locke's immediate tactical purposes well, as those who favor natural law theory will read it one way,
while traditionalists who favor "ancient constitution" theory will read it
another, and Locke can simultaneously draw on both parties' contempt
for tyranny. However, these instances of genuine ambiguity are rare, and
it would be unfair to accuse Locke of deception or confusion in his overall
theory because of his fluid use of language.

On the contrary, scholarly disputes over such narrow issues as the
boundaries of property rights in Locke's theory have often distracted us
from noticing that most of Locke's argument is relatively clear and unambiguous. To see this, one need only compare the scholarly disputes over
Lockean property theory with analogous disputes over, say, Plato's Ideas,
or Rousseau's general will, or just about anything in Nietzsche. While
Locke leaves us arguing over boundary issues like whether he would allow the artisan class to vote, most philosophers of Locke's caliber leave
us arguing over the basic meaning of their most fundamental political
concepts. As Hans Aarsleff was bold enough to write thirty years ago, "the
perplexities that have evolved" in Locke scholarship, "often almost to the
point of dogmatic assertions of fact, have no basis in Locke's thought, but
are the products of misunderstanding, misreading, or inadequate attention to Locke's writings."[4] In the time since Aarsleff wrote those words, as
scholars have corrected one another's mistakes and retreated from their
more extravagant claims, scholarly readings of Locke's politics that once
diverged radically from one another have given way to a rough consensus
not achieved in scholarship on most other great political thinkers.[5]

It is natural to ask, however, what Locke hopes to gain by using words
in this fluid way. Aarsleff, taking notice of this method, argues that Locke
uses it to avoid developing any dependence on particular terms, and to
subvert the use of certain terms that were fashionable in his time but that
he considered to be empty of any real meaning.[6] This may be true as far
as it goes, but it doesn't show the larger significance of the method. By
avoiding strict language use, Locke avoids raising philosophic conflicts
with the jargon-based belief systems of the different groups he hopes to
persuade. This allows him to put forward arguments for positions that
members of these groups can agree on without requiring them to give
up their other, more controversial beliefs.

For example, we know from the *Essay* that Locke is firmly against
innatism – the view, widespread in his time, that there are innate ideas
in the human mind, including innate moral ideas. However, in the *Two
Treatises* he puts forward an account of natural law that both innatists

and noninnatists can agree with. Contrary to the claims of some scholars, the *Two Treatises* is not innatist – it never endorses innatism and it does not require innatist beliefs to complete its argument.[7] However, because Locke does not define the term "reason" in the *Two Treatises*, he need not directly contradict the innatist understanding of reason. It is a central component of his argument in the *Second Treatise*, indispensable to all that follows, that "reason . . . teaches all mankind, who will but consult it, that being all equal and independent, no one ought to harm another" (T II.6, 117). Locke supports this with a rational argument that does not appeal to innate ideas, but he also says nothing that would directly contradict the existence of innate ideas. An innatist who read the *Second Treatise* could easily agree with its argument, and indeed would not even be aware that Locke was opposed to innatism unless he had also read the *Essay* and knew that the two were written by the same author.[8] Of course, an innatist also has other reasons besides the ones given by Locke to believe that all rational people will know that "no one ought to harm another," because he believes that this idea was planted in the human mind by God. Locke disagrees with this, but he leaves that disagreement unacknowledged in order to build moral consensus among innatists and noninnatists.

For Locke the important point, at least where politics is concerned, is not to settle all epistemological questions but to set out the fundamental beliefs around which the political community will be organized and to provide a justification with maximum appeal. Beliefs like "reason tells us God's moral law" and "murder is against God's moral law" must be agreed upon. The truth or falsehood of other beliefs held by groups within the political community, such as "innate ideas tell us God's moral law," need not be addressed in the community's shared political philosophy, so long as everyone in the political community agrees on the community's foundational beliefs.

Thus, interestingly, the political aspect of moral consensus requires that the epistemological aspect of moral consensus be held at arm's length. As we saw in Chapter 2, innatism blocks open philosophic inquiry, and thus must be refuted so we can use reason to persuade people that their controversial views are inherently uncertain. However, Locke keeps this program separate from his political program of building solidarity among different groups. Opposition to innatism is not to be carried out in the coercive realm of political institutions. Innatists hold views that are antithetical to open examination of beliefs, but they can still be members in good standing of civil society. Locke's purpose in the *Two Treatises* is to build a political community of all people who are willing to abide by the basic rules of civil society, including innatists. His fluid use of language allows him to do this without raising the epistemological controversies he pursues in the *Essay*.

Locke's fluid use of language contains an important lesson for political theorists in any time of cultural disharmony, including our own. Cultural controversies can be buried in the definitions we give to words, so adopting a rigid set of definitions can often be a way of shutting off discourse between groups who disagree. To take an example, at the outset of *A Theory of Justice*, John Rawls defines "principles of social justice" as principles "for choosing among the various social arrangements which determine [the] division of advantages and for underwriting an agreement on the proper distributive shares."[9] This definition shapes the entire project of seeking out principles of justice that follows in the remainder of the book. But many people simply reject the idea that who ends up with which advantages and shares has anything to do with justice, or that society can be meaningfully said to "distribute" these things.[10] No matter; Rawls proceeds to lay down 583 pages of political theory for people who happen to agree with the definition of "social justice" chosen on page 4. What Rawls presents as nothing more than a definition of one of his terms is actually a way of foreclosing large areas of philosophic argument. Rawls need not concern himself with showing that advantages and shares ought to be treated as things distributed by society. He has defined that problem out of existence.

This particular problem with *A Theory of Justice* was noticed almost immediately upon its publication, and has been more than adequately discussed in the mountain of scholarship on that book. It is not our intention to imply here that *A Theory of Justice* fails on this one problem. Rather, the point is that Rawls, in creating his theory, did not confront the beliefs buried in his definition of "social justice," and therefore omitted a fundamental portion of his argument at the outset. In the decades that followed, a school of "Rawlsian" political theory developed, with an internal discourse that adopted Rawls' rigid definitions of "justice as fairness," "primary goods," "secondary goods," and the like. As a result, a very large segment of professional political theory became isolated in a distinct world of discourse separate from the political community, a world defined by a set of rigid language rules that rendered its theories incomprehensible to anyone who was not initiated into the meaning of Rawlsian jargon. By maintaining a separate world of discourse with a unique set of rules for language use, Rawlsians keep themselves isolated from the discourse of non-Rawlsian political theorists.

In a society characterized by deep cultural disagreements, a theory cultivated in an isolated world of discourse cannot be successful in the world of practical politics. By walling themselves off in a separate discourse world, Rawlsians have facilitated the cultivation of an intricately detailed and minutely articulated Rawlsian political theory, but by the same token they have all but eliminated any chance that this theory will be persuasive to anyone outside the group of initiates who understand the arcane discourse in which it is articulated. To his great credit, Rawls himself seems to have realized this, in that he later abandoned the approach of *A Theory of Justice* in favor of a new approach designed to seek broad social consensus on political questions without resorting to a rigidly defined, highly specialized discourse.[11] It is a lesson other political theorists of all ideological stripes would do well to learn.

THE FOUNDATIONAL PROBLEM: AUTHORITY

For Locke, authority is the central political concern. The problem of authority runs throughout the *Two Treatises*, shaping his approach to almost every political topic. From the beginning of his refutation of Filmer's biblical absolutism, he frames the issue in terms of Adam's alleged "royal authority," writing that "the question is not here about Adam's actual exercise of government, but actually having a title to be governor" (T I.11–13, 11–13 and I.18, 16). And in the *Second Treatise* Locke once again begins with the problem of authority, writing that Filmer's failure to show "the least shadow of authority" from Adam leaves the reader in danger of thinking "that all government in the world is the product of only force and violence"; hence the need for another account of authority, which the *Second Treatise* provides (T II.1, 115). This conceptual opposition between force and authority, between violence and right, dominates the *Two Treatises*. Societies are held together either by brute force or by legitimate authority, because authority is the only thing that can induce subjects to submit to government voluntarily.

The first word of the *Two Treatises* is "slavery": "Slavery is so vile and miserable an estate of man, and so directly opposite to the generous temper and courage of our nation; that 'tis hardly to be conceived, that an Englishman, much less a gentleman, should plead for it" (T I.1, 5). Thus, Locke begins his case by making clear exactly what is at stake in arguments about political authority. If authority is absolute and unlimited, if there is no right to resist an unjust ruler, then the human race is a slave race. Human beings are born and bred for the service of others, created by

God for the purpose of serving their masters as chattel.[12] Filmer does not actually portray absolutism as a form of enslavement, of course, but Locke's point is valid – if there is no right to resist, then rulers who use their subjects as chattel are morally entitled to obedience, and any argument that rulers ought to refrain from doing so, and instead rule in the public interest, is rendered ineffectual, and argued in vain.

Locke does not give a formal definition of "authority," but it is easy enough to see what he means by it from his use of the word. The meaning of the word "authority" is consistent throughout the *Two Treatises*. It is not surprising that Locke does not use this particular term fluidly, as he does so many others, because authority is something about which the community must be in full agreement. There can be no dodging of controversial beliefs when it comes to settling what "authority" means.

The concept of authority is central to the definitions of both the state of nature and civil society. The state of nature is where people are "without a common superior on earth, with authority to judge between them." In civil society violent conflicts are quickly brought to an end, but in the state of nature they are not, "for want of positive laws, and judges with authority to appeal to." And disputes are very likely to turn violent in the state of nature, "where there is no authority to decide between the contenders" (T II.19–20, 124–5). A person joins civil society when "he authorizes the society . . . to make laws for him . . . to the execution whereof, his own assistance (as to his own decrees) is due." When people do this, they are "setting up a judge on earth, with authority to determine all the controversies, and redress all the injuries, that may happen to any member of the commonwealth." This judge is "a known authority, to which everyone of that society may appeal . . . and which everyone of the society ought to obey" (T II.89–90, 159).

To possess authority, then, is to be a person with a moral right to judge the disputes of others, and to whose judgment others should voluntarily defer. A person with authority must therefore be someone who inspires voluntary obedience in others. As Locke says in the foregoing passage, when a person "authorizes" society to make laws for him, he agrees to treat those laws as if they were "his own decrees." If people do not obey when the authority figure commands, that figure has no hope of serving as a binding judge of disputes; whomever he rules against will simply disobey him. For a ruler's authority to be meaningful, people must obey him even when they disagree with his judgment in particular cases. Locke writes that a compact to create civil society "would signify nothing, and be no compact," if each party were "left free, and under no other ties, than he was in before . . . if he were no further tied by any degrees of the society, than he himself thought fit." Parties to the compact agree, in all future disputes, to "submit to the determination" of the political authority thus created, "and to be concluded by it" (T II.97, 164).

The only thing that will inspire such voluntary obedience is moral right. For Locke, the phrase "moral authority" would be redundant, because there is no other kind of authority. A would-be authority figure must show that he has a right to exercise power before he can actually do so authoritatively. "Nobody in conscience can be obliged to obedience till it be resolved" who specifically is entitled to this obedience, but when such obligation has been shown, people will obey (T I.105, 73; see also I.124–5, 85–6 and II.163–6, 199–201). If it were not so, the whole exercise of political theory would be useless, as political power would simply go to whomever could seize it and keep it. "There would be no distinction between pirates and lawful princes . . . and crowns and scepters would become the inheritance only of violence and rapine" (T I.81, 60).[13] And if people perceive that a ruler, by his wicked actions, has forfeited his moral claim to obedience, they will no longer have any good reason to defer to his judgment – in fact, they will have good reasons not to do so. "The use of force without authority, always puts him that uses it into a state of war, as the aggressor, and renders him liable to be treated accordingly" (T II.155, 194).

Because authority is inherently moral, all authority must ultimately come from God.[14] This is reflected in the *Two Treatises*, which always justifies moral laws as expressions of God's command. Although he mostly takes this voluntarist view of morality for granted in the *Two Treatises*, Locke does allude to his reasons for accepting it: anyone who uses violence "must be sure he has right on his side . . . as he will answer at a tribunal, that cannot be deceived, and will be sure to retribute to everyone according to the mischiefs he hath created" (T II.176, 206). Locke refers here to the Last Judgment, at which the infinite rewards and punishments of the afterlife will be meted out. This bridges the gap between individual and social motivations – individuals do what is best for society because an all-powerful God commands them to do so.[15]

Government, in turn, is authoritative if it enforces God's law. The rewards and punishments of government are more immediate, and hence in some circumstances more effective, than those of the afterlife. "The magistrate's sword" is "for a 'terror to evildoers,'" Locke writes, quoting Romans 13:3, "and by that terror to enforce men to observe the positive laws of society, made conformable to the laws of nature," that is, to God's law (T I.92, 65–6). Government serves as a local enforcer of God's eternal moral law. This is why it is possible for a government to bear legitimate authority from God even though God has not specifically appointed one or another person to rule; God's law gives it authority.

As God is the foundation of authority, authority must in turn be the foundation of the political community. This is why Locke declares that Filmer's doctrine "cuts up all government by the roots" when it places "the obedience of mankind" in a source of authority (inheritance from Adam) that "nobody can claim" (T I.126, 87). Authority is the "roots" of politics. It must be so because only authority can resolve disputes and prevent violent conflict. Potentially violent disputes arise inevitably, despite the accessibility of the natural law to all rational people, because the natural law is unwritten and therefore hard to apply to the details of complex circumstances, and also because people are biased in their judgment when they judge their own cases (see T II.124–5, 178–9).[16] The only alternative to settling disputes by appeal to an earthly authority is to settle them with violence, so the political community must either fall back on authority or resolve all its disputes with violence, in which case it would quickly cease to exist.

The great problem of authority is determining who has the right to exercise it. Although it can only be conveyed by moral right, authority is possessed by people, not by moral theory as such. Subjects "cannot obey anything, that cannot command, and ideas of government in the fancy, though never so perfect, though never so right, cannot give laws, nor prescribe rules to the actions of men." Only human beings can perform these functions, so an abstract theory of political power "would be of no behoof for the settling of order, and establishment of government in its exercise and use amongst men, unless there were a way also taught how to know the person, to whom it belonged to have this power" (T I.81, 59). To establish an authority to govern a political community, then, we must show not only the moral theory by which disputes ought to be resolved within it, but which specific person has the right to resolve such disputes. And therein lies the problem. "The great question which in all ages has disturbed mankind, and brought on them the greatest part of those mischiefs which have ruined cities, depopulated countries, and disordered the peace of the world, has been, not whether there be power in the world, nor whence it came, but who should have it" (T I.106, 73).

This is essentially an epistemological problem – the ruler must justify with sufficient clarity his claim that he, in particular, is entitled to rule. Political theory is therefore fundamentally concerned with epistemology.

People obey only when they perceive the ruler's right to rule, and "that cannot be the reason of my obedience, which I know not to be so; much less can that be a reason of my obedience, which nobody at all can know to be so" (T I.124, 85).

It is not enough to dodge this epistemological problem by showing that it is necessary for someone, anyone, to rule. Without further qualifications, this argument would justify all existing governments indiscriminately, and thus encourage ambitious people to violently seize power wherever they can because such seizures would be self-legitimizing. "A man can never be obliged in conscience to submit to any power, unless he can be satisfied who is the person, who has a right to exercise that power"; otherwise, "he that has force is without more ado to be obeyed, and crowns and scepters would become the inheritance only of violence and rapine" (T I.81, 59–60). The concentration of power in the hands of a particular individual must be justified by some argument independent of the mere fact that such concentration has already been accomplished by that person, or that it must necessarily be accomplished by someone.

This epistemological analysis of the problem of authority, found in the *First Treatise*, is usually read (when it is read at all) only as part of Locke's specific case against biblical absolutism. It is true that this argument is one of Locke's most devastating rejoinders to Filmer. Locke annihilates the doctrine of sovereignty from Adam with a question consisting of two monosyllabic words: "Who Heir?" But Locke does not raise the epistemological problem of authority simply to wield it against Filmer. This problem is one of the fundamental topics of the *Two Treatises* as a whole. The *Second Treatise* is as much devoted to it as the *First Treatise*. After all, the immediate exigency of the *Two Treatises* is the question of Charles II's (and later James II's) right to rule. The *Second Treatise*'s detailed discussion of how to know when a ruler has forfeited his right to rule addresses the same epistemological problem of authority laid down in the *First Treatise*. Whether we are talking about authority from a scriptural claim or authority from popular consent, the basic problem is always the same: who has the right to rule, and on what terms?

From this account of authority, we can draw two criteria that Locke demands from any justification of government authority. First, Locke defines "authority" in the context of politics as the power to resolve disputes, so a justification of authority must specifically convey the power to resolve disputes if the authority is to be a specifically political authority. Grants of authority over property or children are not identical with grants of authority over political communities. Authorization to guide a child's upbringing or to dispose of property does not convey the broader power of dispute resolution that is necessary for political authority. Second, a justification of authority must specify the particular individual or individuals who are to wield this authority. Otherwise, anyone might legitimately lay claim to the authority thus justified, and violence and chaos will result. Only a grant of specifically political authority to a specific person or group can successfully establish an authoritative judge of social conflicts.

THE NONAUTHORITARIAN EXEGESIS OF THE *TWO TREATISES*

Because authority is not truly authority unless it is ultimately backed up by a divine mandate, the job of political theory is to find a divine grant of political authority to some particular person. The natural place to begin looking for such a grant is in divine revelation, because that is where God speaks to us directly. A sufficiently clear grant of political authority in revealed scripture would trump any other claim, at least among those who accept that scripture as genuinely revelatory, because of the miraculous authority of scripture's authors. Locke takes for granted that the Bible is genuinely revelatory, an assumption to which he is entitled given his historical situation and his audience. This premise compels him to search the Bible for a grant of political authority before seeking such authority in any other source.

Thus Locke's argument in the *First Treatise* that there is no scriptural basis for political authority is an indispensable premise of his argument for limited and consensual government in the *Second Treatise*. To justify his political theory, Locke must refute not only biblical absolutism but the less extreme doctrine of biblical authoritarianism. That is, he must not only show that scripture contains no grant of unlimited political authority, he must show that scripture contains no grant of political authority whatsoever, at least not in the sense of authorizing any one specific person to rule. So although Locke presents the *First Treatise* as a response to the biblical absolutism of Robert Filmer, and his most important targets are the court sycophants who were using Filmer's theory in seeking to persuade the king that his power was absolute, his true purpose is to refute all those who claim any right to rule derived from scripture.[17]

Unfortunately, there is no space to examine all of the many scriptural arguments Locke employs in the *First Treatise*. Our treatment will have to be broad and leave out the details of numerous scriptural disputes. We will not, however, follow the well-established scholarly tradition of skipping the *First Treatise* entirely.[18] Our purpose here is not to adjudicate between Locke and Filmer – the outcome of that dispute is not in much doubt. But Locke had a larger and more important question to answer: can the Bible serve as a political foundation? Locke understood the enduring importance of this question, because he understood that religion cannot be effectively compartmentalized from politics. If a person believes that an all-powerful God has issued commands that are inconsistent with liberal politics, it would be simply irrational for that person to be a political liberal on the grounds that religion and politics are separate concerns. Locke put the *First Treatise* first because its arguments are first in importance; without the case made in the *First Treatise*, nothing in the *Second Treatise* can be sustained.

This is why the structure of the *First Treatise* does not follow the structure of Filmer's works, but rather the structure of the Bible itself. Locke's main purpose is not to reply to Filmer's biblical exegesis but to provide an exegesis of his own that will stand against biblical authoritarianism generally.[19] To understand what is at stake here, we need only recall that in Locke's time the overwhelming majority of people in Europe understood the Bible to be the supreme guide to human life, such that nonbiblical reasoning was only admissible where the Bible was silent or its message unclear. For such people, if there is a grant of political authority in the Bible then that grant must serve as the foundation of politics and no other can be acceptable. To make way for a politics of moral consensus that will unite members of different religions, Locke must not only refute Filmer's specific arguments for a basis of authority in the Bible, he must show that no such basis could ever be justified.

As we have seen, Locke develops a scriptural method built on "the plain construction of the words" of scripture, and "the ordinary rules of language" (T I.32, 25 and I.46, 34). In the *Two Treatises*, Locke uses this interpretive method to build a biblical exegesis of enormous epistemological power. Locke argues, against the accumulated weight of a millennium and a half of Christian exegetical tradition, that the Bible contains no grant of authority to existing political institutions, no specifically patriarchal grant of authority to fathers over children, and, most radically, no general grant of authority to husbands over wives. This goes far beyond simply refuting Filmer, providing a new scriptural exegesis that not only denies biblical absolutism but removes most aspects of political authority from the Bible's ambit. Yet Locke's exegesis is so solidly and straightforwardly built on the "plain construction" of biblical text,

according to the "ordinary rules of language," that it hardly seems radical. Indeed, the scriptural arguments of the *First Treatise* are so strong
that today they are often considered so obviously right as hardly to be
worth the reading.[20] Most Christians today are so thoroughly persuaded
of the nonauthoritarian understanding of the Bible that they have difficulty understanding why the argument against biblical authoritarianism
was ever controversial or important. The diminishment of this huge political question in our time is in large part a testament to the rational
force of Locke's arguments.

Early in the *First Treatise*, Locke establishes that the key criterion on
which he will critique Filmer's exegesis is epistemological. He demands
that political authority be supported with "arguments clear and evident,
suitable to the weightiness of the cause" (T I.10, 11). The greater the grant
of power, the greater the epistemological certainty with which the grant
must be justified, because people will only submit voluntarily to great
exercises of power where the arguments for it are clear. A political theory must be "proved and established with all that evidence of arguments,
that such a fundamental tenet" requires, and must be accompanied by
"reasons sufficient to justify the confidence with which" it is asserted
(T I.11, 11). If the arguments for authority are insufficiently certain and
people do not submit voluntarily, then the whole exercise of justifying
government is futile to begin with. The question of who should wield
power is of such moment that "a reformer of politics, one would think,
should lay this sure, and be very clear in it.... Matters of such consequence as this is, should be in plain words, as little liable as might be to
doubt or equivocation" (T I.106–8, 73–4). Absolute power, if it were to be
granted, ought to be granted only where there are "undeniable proofs"
(T I.10, 11).

Having set the epistemological bar high, Locke dissects Filmer's biblical exegesis to show that Filmer can't justify his arguments with sufficient
certainty. Locke is able to directly falsify some of Filmer's arguments from
biblical text – for example, Locke analyzes the original Hebrew of Genesis
1:28, where God donates the world for human use, showing that the use of
the plural pronoun to indicate the recipient of the donation proves that
God was donating the world to humanity as a whole rather than to Adam
in particular (see T I.21–30, 18–24). However, most of Locke's arguments
are not so much direct refutations of Filmer as they are demonstrations
that Filmer's assertions are insufficiently supported by scripture. Locke
often makes such arguments by providing an alternative exegesis of biblical passages and arguing that his exegesis is more likely to be right than

Filmer's. The existence of a more-plausible alternative is sufficient to render Filmer's exegesis unacceptable on epistemological grounds; Locke's alternative need not be decisively shown to be right, since the high epistemological standard required to justify a claim of authority places the burden of proof on Filmer, not Locke.

An example will serve to show how Locke does this. In Genesis 3:16, God says to Eve that "thy husband... shall rule over thee," but "shall rule" is not the same as "ought to rule," and therefore, according to Locke, "God, in this text, gives not... any authority to Adam over Eve, or to men over their wives, but only foretells what should be the woman's lot" (T I.47, 35). Locke points out that in this passage God is telling Adam and Eve why life outside Eden will be painful and miserable for them, so there are no grounds for reading it as an endorsement of the things it describes as being good or legitimate. This overthrows the patriarchal reading of Genesis 3:16 that had been dominant since the early church, but once the argument is made there seems to be no way of denying it. "Shall" is not "ought to," no matter how many years it was read otherwise, or by how many people. Let the exegetical tradition supporting the patriarchal reading be as ancient and as majestic as one might wish it to be, and still "shall" remains "shall," and cannot be transformed into "ought to." And if the patriarchal reading is favored by persons who claim to have a special authority to interpret scripture that others do not possess, so much the worse for their claim, since they would use that authority to read "shall" as if it meant "ought to" when there is no textual basis for doing so.[21]

Recall that the first of the two requirements we found in Locke's treatment of authority was that government can only be justified by a specifically political grant of authority. To determine whether Adam received any specifically political authority from God, Locke breaks down Adam's situation into four aspects or constitutive parts – creation, donation, marriage, and fatherhood – representing Adam's relationships with God, the physical world, Eve, and his children, respectively. Locke devotes a chapter to each of these relationships, showing in each case that none of them is specifically political in character.

The main point of this analysis is to focus our attention very clearly on the question of exactly what political authority is, as distinct from other types of authority. Locke uses his scriptural method to show that Filmer attributes to the Bible things that the Bible does not actually say, but the deeper problem with Filmer's reading – and, by extension, any reading that ascribes political authority to the Bible – is that it is too cavalier about what constitutes a grant of political authority as opposed to other types of authority. Locke repeatedly points out that if political and parental authority are not distinguished from one another, every parent will have a claim to be king, and likewise for other nonpolitical types of authority. "Princes certainly will have great reason to thank him [Filmer] for these new politics, which set up as many absolute kings in every country as there are fathers of children" (T I.71, 51). It is not enough to show that some kind of authority is present in the Bible; one must show that a specifically political authority is present.

The second requirement for a grant of authority was that it must specifically distinguish the particular person who could claim it. In his discussion of the Bible, Locke makes a subtle distinction between what we might call an abstract basis for authority and a specific grant of authority. Locke does not deny that the Bible clearly endorses the existence and exercise of political authority. He even makes reference to Paul's description of government as a "terror to evildoers" (T I.92, 65).[22] As he puts it early in the *Second Treatise,* "God hath certainly appointed government to restrain the partiality and violence of men" (T II.13, 121). However, the Bible does not say which specific persons should have this authority. It therefore does not contain a specific grant of authority, in that it does not support any one person's particular claim to be the rightful political ruler. Locke is particularly concerned with this point in several chapters devoted to the question of what would have happened to Adam's alleged political authority after his death. Either Adam's authority passes only to each eldest son in line after him, in which case "one only can have it" and that person's identity is unknowable, or Adam's sons all shared the inheritance of his power, in which case "everyone is his heir, and so everyone has regal power," because every person has an equally just claim to be one of Adam's heirs (T I.105, 72–3).

For these reasons, biblical authoritarianism – including not only Filmer's biblical absolutism but any claim to political authority from the Bible – can be seen to fail on both the criteria Locke sets down for a grant of authority. Adam's relationships arising from creation, donation, marriage, and fatherhood cannot convey any specifically political authority, that is, the authority to resolve disputes. And even if they did, such a grant of authority would fail on the second criterion, because all are equally descended from Adam and thus no one can claim an exclusive entitlement to political authority from him. Since the arguments for political authority from the Bible fail, members of the political community will not voluntarily submit to them.

A BRIEF DIGRESSION: THE *TWO TREATISES*
AND THE NEW TESTAMENT

The *First Treatise* devotes the bulk of its time and attention to the book of Genesis, and particularly to Adam and Eve. As Joshua Mitchell has pointed out, for Locke the defining moment for humanity as a unified race is not the life of Jesus but the life of Adam.[23] Since the political community must encompass all human beings, he looks to Adam for any sign of a scriptural grant of authority that would be universally binding. Because of this focus on Adam, the New Testament receives much less attention than the Old Testament in the *Two Treatises*. For Locke Jesus is a wholly apolitical figure, the purpose of whose life was to provide salvation.[24] Nonetheless, for Locke's political theory in the *Two Treatises* to be persuasive to Christian readers, it must be shown to be fully consistent with the moral teachings of the New Testament. This is, as we will see, a question on which some Locke scholars have challenged Locke's theory. We will therefore digress briefly from our account of the *Two Treatises'* argument in order to examine its compatibility with the New Testament.

There are good reasons for Locke's selection of Adam as the focus of his political exegesis of the Bible. Political authority has been necessary since God expelled Adam and Eve from Eden. Contrary to widespread belief, Locke does not deny that human beings are naturally social; he writes that human beings are naturally constructed in such a way that they are "quickly driven into society" (T II.127, 179). The force that drives them into society, as we will see in detail below, is the need to alleviate the potential for violent conflict, which in turn is primarily caused by differences in moral judgment. Differences in moral judgment originated when Adam and Eve ate from the Tree of Knowledge of Good and Evil, bringing sin into the world. So if God were going to grant political authority by revelation (other than to the Israelites, who are a special case) one would expect him to give it in the opening chapters of Genesis.

The *First Treatise* moves on from the expulsion of Adam and Eve, going forward through the book of Genesis, but stops abruptly after a hurried discussion of early political authority among the Israelites. Locke informs us in a note that a large portion of text that had originally stood between the first and second treatises was lost (see T Preface, 3). We can only speculate, but from the abruptness of the *First Treatise's* ending it seems likely that what was lost was a continuation of his exegesis through the rest of the Bible.

The abrupt ending of the *First Treatise*, and the suggestion that more scriptural interpretation was lost from the original text, is worth noting because of an important gap in Locke's exegesis. Locke's neglect of the remainder of the Old Testament, though noticeable, is excusable. Any reader satisfied with Locke's reading of Genesis would probably have been equally satisfied with his reading of the rest of the Old Testament. In any event, the Old Testament is mostly about the Israelites, who – as Locke frequently makes a point of observing – are a special case in terms of political authority, "where God himself immediately interposed" (T II.101, 165). However, the truncated *First Treatise* does not confront the possibility of a grant of political authority in the New Testament. Such a grant would refute Locke's Adamic argument for political universalism, as it would imply a special political command or authority given to Christians but not to the rest of humanity.

The most important passage that might be brought against Locke here is Romans 13:1–5, where Paul, discussing governments, declares (in the translation used in Locke's time) not only, "let every soul be subject to the higher powers," but even, "the powers that be, are ordained of God. Whosoever therefore resisteth the power, resisteth the ordinance of God: and they that resist, shall receive to themselves damnation." Locke's failure to confront this passage in the *Two Treatises* can only be considered a glaring omission. If Romans 13:1–5 constitutes a grant of political authority to existing governments, and forbids revolution under all circumstances, then Locke's political theory is inconsistent with the Bible.

In particular, if this passage specifically endorses existing governments rather than merely endorsing the existence of some government, then it passes both of Locke's requirements for a grant of political authority: that the grant be specifically political in character, and that it specify which individuals are entitled to it. True, Locke argues in the *First Treatise* that a political theory that endorses all existing governments must be wrong, because under such a theory "there would be no distinction between pirates and lawful princes, he that has force is without any more ado to be obeyed, and crowns and scepters would become the inheritance only of violence and rapine" (T I.81, 60). However, if Romans 13:1–5 endorses all existing governments, the weight of Paul's miraculous authority overrules Locke's argument.

But the challenge this passage represents for Locke's political theory is not insurmountable. Although Locke provides no exegesis of Romans 13:1–5 in the *Two Treatises*, the foundations of a Lockean exegesis are present in that work. As we have already noted, in the *First Treatise* Locke alludes to this passage by appropriating Paul's description of government as "a terror to evildoers." This phrase implies that Paul only endorses government that does, in fact, serve as a terror to evildoers, rather than being itself an evildoer. Locke eventually made just this argument in his *Paraphrase and Notes on the Epistles of St. Paul.* There, Locke draws our attention to verses 3–4:

> For rulers are not a terror to good works, but to the evil. Wilt thou then not be afraid of the power? Do that which is good, and thou shalt have praise of the same: for he is the minister of God to thee for good. But if thou do that which is evil, be afraid; for he beareth not the sword in vain: for he is the minister of God, a revenger to execute wrath upon him that doth evil.

As Locke points out, "by what is said [at] verse 3 it seems that St. Paul meant here magistrates having and exercising a lawful power."[25] Locke could also have drawn our attention to Paul's comment at verse 4 that rulers are to be obeyed because they "execute wrath upon him that doth evil." If a ruler executes his wrath upon the innocent, would Paul have us obey him? Paul does not say, but his emphasis in verses 3–4 on the goodness of government, and the use of its power "for good" to terrify "the evil," suggests not.

If this is the case, then Paul has not actually specified which governments must be obeyed. Locke argues that Paul enjoins Christians to obey lawful authority, but does not meddle in the question of which authorities are lawful, because it is not the place of religious prophets to answer that question. "St. Paul in this direction to the Romans does not so much describe the magistrates that then were in Rome, as tell whence they and all magistrates everywhere have their authority; and for what end they have it, and should use it."[26]

This ultimately amounts to an argument that when governments do evil, they cease to be governments in the proper understanding of the term. If a government consistently does evil and attacks the innocent, then it does not conform to Paul's description of what a government is and does. Hence, it is not actually a government at all, but simply a band of outlaws with the outward trappings of a government.

This, in a coincidence far too convenient to be merely accidental, is exactly what Locke argues in the climactic chapter of the *Two Treatises.* In this chapter, entitled "Of the Dissolution of Government," Locke goes to great lengths to argue that the events leading up to the Glorious Revolution, in which Charles II undermined and ultimately abolished Parliament, constituted not just a wrongful seizure of power by the executive but a complete dissolution of government in the proper understanding of that term. Since the legislature expresses the will of the community, it is "in the legislative, that the members of a commonwealth are united," so if the legislature to which the community has consented is dissolved, the government created by the community can properly be said to have dissolved (T II.212, 223). Locke even carries the argument to a much more general level, declaring that government is dissolved "when the legislative, or the prince, either of them act contrary to their trust" by attacking or exploiting subjects (T II.221, 226).

A reader of the *Two Treatises* not familiar with Romans 13:1–5, and with Christian political theory in general, might wonder why it is such an important point for Locke that an evil government forfeits not only its moral right to rule but also its ontological status as a government. The forfeiture of a government's political authority is sufficient to justify rebellion on the terms laid out explicitly in the *Two Treatises*; it would not be necessary on those terms to show that such a government also ceases to be a government at all. But once we consider Paul's comments at Romans 13:1–5, the importance of the point immediately becomes clear. If an evil government is still a government, Paul's injunction not to rebel against government forbids all rebellion. But if an evil government ceases to be a government, Paul's comments do not bar rebellion against such governments. No doubt Locke left the connection to Romans 13: 1–5 unstated as a tactical maneuver, in hopes of making his theory appear to be less of a radical break from existing biblical exegesis than it actually was. Had Locke been perfectly honest, he would have made this connection more explicit.

The alleged inconsistency of Locke's political theory with the moral teachings of the New Testament is one of the major arguments of Leo Strauss's interpretation of Locke. Strauss declares that Locke's political teachings in the *Two Treatises* are "unbiblical" and "alien to the Bible," and digress from "the biblical point of view."[27] He gives a series of examples of topics on which he believes Locke is "unbiblical," including divorce, the accumulation of wealth, and the right to revolution. This assertion of inconsistency with the Bible lends greater plausibility to Strauss's other arguments about Locke, which would be less persuasive if they were not supported by the underlying premise that the *Two Treatises* undermines biblical teachings.

But Locke is "unbiblical" on these points only if we believe that the Bible provides – clearly and explicitly, with no room for reasonable disagreement over interpretation – the political doctrine Strauss ascribes to it. Strauss's use of the definite article in the phrase "the biblical point of view" is particularly revealing. It seems that for Strauss there is one and only one "biblical" point of view on a given topic. Any digression from the singular "biblical" point of view is "unbiblical" and grounds for suspicion that the author is insincere when he professes to believe in Christianity.

Locke's careful attention to the nature of scriptural interpretation, which we examined in some detail in Chapters 3 and 4, stands in stark contrast to Strauss's approach to the Bible. For Locke, the traditional understanding of the meaning of a Bible passage carries no authority. An exegesis must be carefully justified in the text of scripture itself. Romans 13:1–5, one of Strauss's major examples of an alleged divergence between Locke and the Bible, is a case in point. Strauss considers only the traditional understanding of the passage as forbidding all revolution; he does not raise the possibility that Romans 13:1–5 could legitimately be read in another way. Locke's endorsement of a right to revolution is "unbiblical" only if there are no reasonable grounds for understanding Romans 13:1–5 in the way Locke argues we ought to understand it. Similar reasoning applies for Locke's other alleged deviations from the Bible. It is true that the Bible clearly teaches that divorce and greed, for example, are wrong, but the Bible does not clearly teach that these things must therefore be made illegal. There is even some support in the biblical text for not making them illegal. There is nothing in Locke's politics that violates the clear teachings of the Bible, and where the Bible is not sufficiently clear Locke leaves subjects free to follow their consciences.

APPLYING MORAL LAW: THE STATE OF NATURE

Having shown that there is no basis in revelation for a specific grant of political authority, Locke must now show how political authority can be established in a manner that is open to members of different religions but is nonetheless grounded in a divine mandate. As we saw in the previous chapter, Locke analyzes human nature to justify his premise that the preservation of human life is a divine law. This law serves as the basis of his political arguments.

Locke illustrates the consequences of the law of human preservation with a method of empirically informed theoretical reconstruction – his famous theory of the state of nature. This theory seeks to show what people in such a state are obliged to do, or refrain from doing, in enforcing the moral law of human preservation.[28] This serves to effectively distinguish practices that are rooted in eternal moral obligations from practices that are merely human conventions. By making this distinction Locke separates moral claims that are genuinely obligatory on all persons from those that are ultimately no more than appeals to the particular traditions of this or that cultural group. Moral consensus requires that the former but not the latter be coercively enforced, so accurately making out the difference between these two types of claims is essential.[29]

It is imperative for readers of the *Second Treatise* to understand that Locke does not use the state of nature to justify the moral law of preservation, but rather to illustrate the implications of that law. Locke's state of nature theory takes the moral law of human preservation as a given premise, and uses the state of nature to illustrate its practical consequences in a variety of situations, most importantly its consequences for the creation of an authoritative state. Locke's state of nature serves the same function as Kant's categorical imperative: it does not justify the content of morality; instead, it demonstrates the application of moral rules to particular situations. In Locke's politics, we learn God's law through the observation of actual historical human behavior, not through abstract theorizing.

In this, Locke is very much the opposite of Hobbes. Locke is indebted to Hobbes for the concept of a state of nature, but he uses that concept for a different purpose. Hobbes uses the state of nature to demonstrate the necessity of peace and therefore the validity of his natural law theory, which takes peace to be the all-important moral imperative. Dunn sums up the contrast succinctly: "Hobbes's problem is the construction of political society from an ethical vacuum. Locke never faced this problem in the *Two Treatises* because his central premise is precisely the absence of any such vacuum."[30] The all-important fact in Hobbes's state of nature is the absence of any enforceable moral law, which makes that state unbearable, and hence justifies ending it by creating civil society. The all-important fact in Locke's state of nature is the very opposite, the existence of a known and enforceable moral law, the enforcement of which is best carried out by the creation of civil society. Thus, while Hobbes creates civil society in order to reverse humanity's natural moral situation, Locke creates civil society in order to bring our natural moral situation to a more complete fulfillment.[31]

This illustrates the radical difference between the foundations of politics in Hobbes and Locke. Hobbes's reason for ending the state of nature is, ultimately, not a truly moral reason but simply a psychological one.[32] We must have peace simply because we must have it; we cannot bear the alternative. Locke was remarkably perceptive when, in a draft of the *Essay*, he included "a Hobbist" among his examples of people who cannot justify their moral theories and seek to cover this up by attributing morality to innate ideas allegedly placed in the mind by God.[33] In Hobbes's case, the innate idea is self-preservation. Hobbes provides no moral justification for self-preservation, neither from divine command nor from any account of the objective desirability of preserving human life. The assertion that the natural law of self-preservation arises from God's command is made repeatedly throughout *Leviathan* but remains unsubstantiated.[34] Locke, by contrast, lays out a moral justification for his account of natural law – an argument from divine command, as derived from observations of human nature. This is why Locke demands that all people must seek to preserve all human life, where Hobbes proceeds from the assumption that each person will seek to preserve only himself.

Here we are again responding to the interpretation of Strauss. Strauss asserts that the fundamental fact of Locke's state of nature, as for Hobbes's, is the desire for self-preservation and the absence of any prior moral law constraining it. Strauss writes that the pursuit of self-preservation and happiness is "a right antedating all duties" for Locke, "for the same reason that, according to Hobbes, establishes as the fundamental moral fact the right to self-preservation: man must be allowed to defend his life against violent death because he is driven to do so by some natural necessity which is not less than that by which a stone is carried downward."[35] Thus, Strauss claims that Locke's moral law is justified not by God, but by a natural psychological force (the desire for self-preservation) that is not itself morally justifiable. Locke's state of nature appears to rest on a moral vacuum, just as Hobbes's does.

Of course Locke acknowledges the strength of our natural desire for self-preservation, but what he says about that desire is quite different from the view that Strauss attributes to him. Locke argues that the desire for self-preservation is a sign that it is God's will that all human life be preserved, and thus that all have a moral duty to preserve others as well as themselves.[36] Locke is explicit about this moral duty in several places. "When his own preservation comes not in competition," every person "ought . . . as much as he can, to preserve the rest of mankind" (T II.6, 117; see also I.42, 31). For Locke the pursuit of self-preservation, even in the state of nature, is firmly constrained by the law that all human life, not just one's own, must be preserved.

Strauss provides a snippet from Locke to show that Locke thinks that in the state of nature "any man may do what he thinks fit."[37] Had Strauss provided the full quotation, however, it would have been clear that Locke is speaking in this passage only of freedom from the constraints of civil law, not of freedom from the constraints of natural law: "No man in civil society can be exempted from the laws of it. For if any man may do, what he thinks fit, and there be no appeal on earth, for redress or security against any harm he shall do; I ask, whether he be not perfectly still in the state of nature" (T II.94, 162–3). A person in the state of nature is not constrained by civil law from doing what he thinks fit, but there is no suggestion in this passage, or any other, that such a person is also free from natural law. Locke was in fact quite explicit that in the state of nature each person has the liberty "to do whatsoever he thinks fit for the preservation of himself and others within the permission of the law of nature" (T II.128, 179).

We have described Locke's state of nature theory as an "empirically informed theoretical reconstruction." This requires some unpacking. To call a theory "empirically informed" is simply to say that it takes certain empirical observations as premises, rather than pretending that we have no information at all about the way things actually are. Specifically, Locke's state of nature theory is premised on his empirical observations of human nature, and on his derivation of the moral law of preservation from these observations.

The meaning of "theoretical reconstruction" is trickier. The state of nature itself is not a hypothetical concept, any more than the concepts of a "state of drunkenness" or a "state of preparedness" are hypothetical. The state of nature has real existence. Every person is in a state of nature until such time as he explicitly consents to join a political community. "All men are naturally in that state, and remain so, till by their own consents they make themselves members of some politic society" (T II.15, 122). Those who have given only tacit consent to political society are still in a state of nature. "Submitting to the laws of any country, living quietly, and enjoying the privileges and protection under them, makes not a man a member of that society" (T II.122, 177; see also II.119–22, 176–7). Such people, having tacitly consented to the laws of that society, must continue to obey its laws as long as they remain within its territory, but they are not members of that society and are thus still in a state of nature. Furthermore, subjects of different nations are always in a state of nature relative to one another. "Though in a commonwealth the members of it are distinct persons still in reference to one another . . . yet in reference to the rest of mankind, they make one body, which is, as every member of it before was, still in the state of nature with the rest of mankind" (T II.145, 189).

But while the concept of a state of nature is not hypothetical, Locke uses it to provide a theory of how persons in such a state might behave in certain hypothetical situations. This is less convoluted than it sounds. We might use the concept of a "state of drunkenness" to speak about how a drunken person might be expected to behave in a given situation; the state of drunkenness is a real state that real people are often observed to be in, but we can use that concept to make hypothetical statements as well. Locke does something similar with the state of nature. In particular, Locke is interested in a hypothetical situation in which everyone is simultaneously in a state of nature.[38] Locke's state of nature theory reconstructs, based on the empirical data we have about human behavior, a theoretical account of how people would behave if they were all in a state of nature. Thus the state of nature itself is real, but the larger theory we refer to as "Locke's state of nature theory" is a theoretical reconstruction.

The state of nature represents the fundamental relationship between human beings and God – the "natural" person is the person as he proceeds from God's creation, when there are no other strings yet attached to him.[39] In the state of nature, people are in "a state of perfect freedom to order their actions, and dispose of their possessions, and persons as they see fit, within the bounds of the law of nature, without asking leave, or depending upon the will of any other man" (T II.4, 116). The distinguishing characteristic of a person in the state of nature is that he is under no authority other than God's, and thus is beholden to obey God and no other.

For such a state to exist, of course, it would have to be the case that human beings are not naturally subject to any authority other than God. In other words, there is no naturally occurring authority other than God's authority over humanity. As with the law of preservation, this is a premise of Locke's state of nature theory rather than a conclusion justified by it. When introducing the state of nature, Locke justifies this premise by arguing that natural freedom and equality (the opposite of natural authority) are a necessary consequence of the law of preservation. "There cannot be supposed any such subordination among us, that may authorize us to destroy one another, as if we were made for one another's uses, as the inferior ranks of creatures are for ours." The right to destroy implies "use" and "subordination." Because there can be no natural right of one human being to destroy another under the law of preservation, there can also be no natural right to use and subordination. Thus, the natural law is that "being all equal and independent, no one ought to harm another in his life, health, liberty, or possessions" (T II.6, 117).

Although Locke's account of natural law requires that no one destroy another for his own use, Locke rejects the possibility that no one may ever destroy another for any purpose. That would leave God's law unenforced and powerless. "The law of nature would, as all other laws that concern men in this world, be in vain, if there were nobody that in the state of nature, had a power to execute that law" (T II.7, 118). God's law demands the preservation of human life, and if God's law is going to mean anything then there must be an executive power attached to it.

To determine who wields this executive power, Locke takes the premises he has laid down and makes a bold deduction. If the executive power of God's law is definitely possessed by somebody, but due to natural equality it is not exclusively possessed by any particular people, the only possibility is that it is possessed by everybody. "For in that state of perfect equality, where naturally there is no superiority or jurisdiction of one, over another, what any may do in prosecution of that law, everyone must needs have a right to do" (T II.7, 118). Locke argues that although this idea of a universally held executive power "will seem a very strange doctrine," it is not really strange at all; not only is it logically necessary in the absence of a particular divine grant of authority, it is implied by actual legal practices, such as the punishment of foreigners (T II.9, 119).[40] When reformulated to include this executive power, the supreme natural law becomes: "force is to be opposed to nothing, but to unjust and unlawful force" (T II.204, 218).

In Chapters 2–6 and the beginning of Chapter 7 of the *Second Treatise*, Locke uses the state of nature to establish a series of moral rules, all derived from the divine law of human preservation, governing various activities – primarily violence, property, parenthood, and marriage. For example, when approached by an armed thief who demands his money, a person in the state of nature may kill that thief, because he knows that the thief might decide to kill him. The thief, merely by threatening violence, has endangered lives, and thus violated the law of nature. Even though he tells his victim he will not kill if he is given what he wants, we know that thieves often do kill their victims anyway. "Because using force, where he has no right, to get me into his power, let his pretense be what it will, I have no reason to suppose, that he, who would take away my liberty, would not when he had me in his power, take away everything else." The thief's very thievery establishes that he is a person who disregards the natural law, and thus a continuing threat to the lives of all other people. "And therefore it is lawful for me to treat him, as one who has put himself into a state of war with me, i.e. kill him if I can" (T II.18, 123). By killing the thief, our hypothetical person ensures the preservation of his own life, plus the lives of all those the thief might have gone on to kill, and also the lives of those who would have been killed by other thieves who are instead deterred from thievery by the example made of this particular thief (see T II.11, 120 and II.8, 118).

Locke frames most of these political doctrines concerning violence, property, parenthood, and marriage in terms of individual rights. By differentiating obligations rooted in God's moral law from obligations that are merely human conventions, Locke provides grounds on which individuals can make overriding moral claims. However, the only reason individuals have rights, and the only reason those rights are inviolable, is that God's law creates such rights. Individual rights are not good in themselves; they are instrumental to the moral law of human preservation.[41] Rights claims are thoroughly religious for Locke, because they are generated only by appeal to God's law that human life is to be preserved.[42] For this reason, they can be exercised only in accordance with, and for the purpose of fulfilling, that law. As Ashcraft puts it in discussing Locke's theory of property, rights are "totally enshrouded in a network of obligations."[43] Although there is no space to examine how this is manifested in each of the separate political topics Locke takes up, we can observe as a general matter that because rights are justified as instrumental to the preservation of all human life, they are limited by the requirements of such preservation. No individual can claim a right to do anything that is inconsistent with the general preservation of human life.[44]

By separating God's law from human convention in matters of violence, property, parenthood, and marriage, Locke's state of nature theory provides a crucial step in building authority on moral consensus. Cultural traditions cannot, by definition, be universally obligatory. In a society characterized by social conflict between multiple traditions, moral claims based on tradition will divide rather than unite society. God's moral law, by contrast, is obligatory for all members of society. By using state of nature theory to show the validity of certain universal moral obligations, Locke builds a moral theory that is binding on members of any culture or tradition. This provides a basis for political community on God's law as such rather than on particular human tradition.

THE FOUNDATIONS OF POLITICAL COMMUNITY:
MORAL LAW AND CONSENT

Under the natural law of human preservation, each person is born free, an authority unto himself. However, there are problems for enforcing the law of human preservation in the state of nature that require the creation of a common political authority. As we have seen, political authority can only serve its function of settling disputes if it is something that people obey voluntarily. For this reason we need a moral argument demonstrating that some specific person deserves obedience. No sufficiently clear grant of authority can be shown in scripture, so only the consent of the people provides a basis for authority that the people will recognize as legitimate. As Eldon Eisenach points out, this theory of morally authoritative government by consent of the people fuses the most attractive qualities of medieval divine right and modern natural right theories; all authority comes ultimately from God, but the political constitution and the appointment of government officers is accomplished by human consent.[45]

Despite the existence of a natural executive power of the law of nature, the state of nature is morally insufficient. The enforcement of God's law in that state is subject to too much uncertainty. Locke argues that although all rational people acknowledge the natural law of human preservation, applying that law to particular circumstances is very difficult. Even when people are well intentioned, they still come into conflict whenever two people disagree about what is right in a given situation. They both agree that justice should be done, but each one honestly believes that he is in the right and the other is in the wrong.

Locke's optimism about universal access to the natural law through reason is tempered by a healthy appreciation of the equally universal human tendency to discover and latch onto lame excuses for doing things that we know, or ought to know, are wrong. The two reasons Locke presents for why moral disagreements occur in the state of nature both reflect this. First, an unwritten law cannot address the wide variety of practical questions that inevitably arise in the application of that law to specific circumstances, so people will often convince themselves that the natural law doesn't forbid their actions when in fact it does. In the state of nature "there wants an established, settled, and known law. . . . For though the law of nature be plain and intelligible to all rational creatures; yet men . . . are not apt to allow of it as a law binding to them in the application of it to their particular cases" (T II.124, 178). The second reason is closely related to the first: people are almost always "biased by their interest" when they must judge their own cases, and thus "men being partial to themselves, passion and revenge is very apt to carry them too far, and with too much heat, in their own cases" (T II.124–5, 178–9). Given these two problems, it is not only possible that people will honestly think they are right when they are in fact wrong, it is likely to happen quite often.

Locke also gives a third reason why the state of nature is morally insufficient: because of the relative weakness of individuals, in the state of nature "there often wants power to back and support the sentence when right, and to give it due execution," such that enforcing the natural law is "many times . . . dangerous, and frequently destructive, to those who attempt it" (T II.126, 179). But he does not elaborate much further, and does not develop the point later. Here we see another interesting contrast with Hobbes: while Hobbes and Locke each acknowledge both the problem of humanity's natural weakness and the problem of humanity's natural hypocrisy, Hobbes is fascinated by the former while not giving much attention to the latter, and Locke is fascinated by the latter while not giving much attention to the former. For Hobbes the fundamental problem is power; for Locke the fundamental problem is moral judgment.

So far we have spoken of how moral conflict can arise even when people are well intentioned, but obviously it is not always the case that the parties to conflict are in fact well intentioned. But while Locke acknowledges that some people do wrong deliberately, he does not seem to think this is the reason government is necessary. Conflict among well-intentioned but misguided people is what Locke treats as the truly important and problematic type of case. Presumably some people would still do wrong even if the differences between right and wrong were always perfectly clear even in practical application. But in such a case everyone would agree that the actions in question were wrong, and people would presumably be able to cooperate in exercising their executive power of the natural law. The logic of Locke's case suggests that it is the far more pervasive problem of moral disagreement arising from flawed moral judgment that makes government necessary.

We can also see how differences in moral judgment are at the heart of violent conflict by looking at another line of argument in the *Second Treatise*, its appeal to the biblical example of Jephtha. In Judges 11:27, Jephtha, the leader of the Israelites, declares in a message to the Ammonites, who are about to invade Israel, "the Lord the judge be judge this day between the children of Israel, and the children of Ammon." Locke quotes this passage very early in the *Second Treatise*, in Chapter 3, where he defines the state of war (see T II.21, 125). He uses it to argue that whenever a person uses violence in a sincere attempt to uphold justice, he is appealing to God's judgment, and is analogous to Jephtha in doing so. Throughout the *Second Treatise*, Locke calls this the "appeal to heaven" (for example, T II.21, 125; II.168, 201; II.176, 206; and II.241–2, 240). Most of Jephtha's message consists of a lengthy rehashing of the history of conflict between the Israelites and the Ammonites. The Ammonites believe that the Israelites have stolen their land, and Jephtha's message attempts, unsuccessfully, to persuade them that it was not so. Both sides believe they are in the right, and violence occurs because they have no common judge on earth to settle the conflict peacefully.

Violence, on Locke's reading, is an appeal for God to settle a certain moral issue at the Last Judgment, because it cannot be morally settled in this world. A person's violent actions are justified if, and only if, his cause is just under God's law. In using violence, a person is rejecting the moral judgment of the other side, which he believes has done him wrong. Instead, he appeals to God's judgment by taking matters into his own hands. "Where there is no judge on earth, the appeal lies to God in heaven" (T II.21, 125). Here on earth the question being fought over will be settled by force; the moral resolution of the question will have to wait for God's judgment in the next world.

The institution of a government, which can exercise the executive power of the natural law on behalf of the community, alleviates the problems individuals face when they enforce the natural law.[46] It does this by acting as a common moral authority. The purpose of this authority is to maximize the accuracy of our enforcement of divine moral law. Government spells out a detailed and particular written law to make clear the application of the unwritten natural law, it is a neutral judge to determine who is in the right when disputes arise, and it marshals the collective power of the community against offenders who might be too strong for any individual to punish. Government authority exists to preserve "the common good . . . by providing against those three defects above mentioned" (T II.131, 180). Thus, the purpose of government is moral: it does justice more reliably than do individuals in the state of nature, because its written law and its neutral position allow it to judge right and wrong more accurately in particular cases, and its strength carries those judgments into effect more efficiently.

That the purpose of government is to improve enforcement of the moral law is clear from Chapter 8 of the *Second Treatise*, its first full chapter on the constitution of government. Recent Locke scholarship has neglected Chapter 8 of the *Second Treatise*, much to its own disadvantage.[47] This chapter makes clear where the real heart of Locke's political theory lies: not in the constitutional mechanisms of elections, separation of powers, and the like, but in the moral law those mechanisms are designed to serve.

In this chapter, Locke is not concerned yet with government in advanced societies. Instead, he begins his account of government with an anthropology of politics – he shows why, on his account of politics, it makes perfect sense that people in primitive societies should give their consent to be ruled by a tribal patriarch and to create no institutional limits on his exercise of power. Tribal patriarchy was the government "which, by experience they had found both easy and safe," and "they had neither felt the oppression of tyrannical dominion, nor did the fashion of the age, nor their possessions, or way of living . . . give them any reason to apprehend or provide against it" (T II.107, 168–9). The purpose of this argument is to demonstrate that consent theory can adequately explain the existence of undemocratic, illiberal governments, thus refuting a common objection to consent theory, namely its alleged inconsistency with the empirical facts of human history. That early governments, back to the furthest reaches of history, were tribal patriarchies "destroys not that, which I affirm," though it has "given occasion to men to mistake, and think, that by nature government was monarchical" (T II.106, 168).[48]

This should serve to remove any impression that Locke's account of liberal, democratic constitutional arrangements is intended to be written in stone. God's moral law of human preservation is the only universally applicable rule of politics; all else is flexible. Under the conditions that prevail in primitive society, that law is best served by tribal patriarchy, so for primitive societies Locke endorses tribal patriarchy. He gives no sign that he sees anything inconsistent or problematic in this. He declares that it is "natural," "no wonder," and "not at all strange" if primitive societies adopted the "frame of government" that was "best suited to their present state and condition; which stood more in need of defense against foreign invasions and injuries, than of multiplicity of laws" (T II.107, 168–9).

If all people are naturally free and independent, under no authority but God's, the only possible basis on which human authority might be built is consent. Since authority must be something to which people submit voluntarily, only consent will create authority. "Men being . . . by nature, all free, equal and independent, no one can be put out of this estate . . . without his own consent. The only way whereby anyone . . . puts on the bonds of civil society is by agreeing with other men to join and

unite into a community" (T II.95, 163). Consent satisfies the two requirements for a basis of authority that we have identified: it conveys a specifically political authority, and it conveys that authority to clearly identified
individuals.

To emphasize that only consent can create legitimate political authority, Locke pointedly draws a stark contrast between "civil society,"
which is created by consent, and "absolute monarchy." Because absolute
monarchy is not held together by consent, it can only be held together
by brute force. "The subject, or rather slave of an absolute prince" is "exposed to all the misery and inconveniences that a man can fear from one"
who is "unrestrained" by a neutral third party judge in his relationship
with his subjects. He is, in short, still in the state of nature, but in the
worst possible way, because of the presence of a person "corrupted with
flattery, and armed with power" (T II.91, 160).

There is not, as some have suggested, a tension, balance, or equilibrium between the concerns of moral law and consent in the *Two Treatises*.[49]
They are in perfect harmony, because consensual government is the best
possible way to enforce the moral law. In the state of nature "there are
many things wanting" for the enforcement of the moral law of preservation (T II.124, 178). This is why "notwithstanding all the privileges of the
state of nature," people are "quickly driven into society" (T II.127, 179).
Authoritative government is necessary to enforce moral law as well as
possible, and consent is the only possible basis of legitimate government
authority. Consensual government is therefore morally necessary.

There are, of course, numerous issues arising from Locke's theory
of consent that we do not have space to treat adequately. Of greatest
interest is Locke's account of "tacit consent," which holds that people
who choose to enter, or remain within, the territory of a government
tacitly consent to obey it while they are there. "The government has a
direct jurisdiction . . . over the land" (T II.121, 177). This is because the
land is "annexed to, and under the government of that commonwealth"
by the consent of the landowners living under that government. For this
reason, "every man, that hath any possession, or enjoyment" of the land
in a government's territory, whether he has inherited a large estate or is
simply passing through on the road, "doth thereby give his tacit consent"
to obey that government (T II.120, 176–7).

Though we cannot take up this question in the detail it deserves, we
can at least suggest that the idea of tacit consent is much more plausible
in the context of a theory where the moral order of society is divinely
ordained. It is morally necessary that disputes be settled by a neutral

third party judge. This implies a moral obligation on the part of each individual to either submit to the existing government (provided that government is not tyrannical) or put himself out of that government's territory so that disputes will not arise between its subjects and himself.

Locke's account of consent provides a way to build political authority on moral consensus. Moral consensus is necessary because people recognize that a neutral judge and a written legal code are required for the accurate enforcement of the moral law, and moral consensus is possible because people can voluntarily submit themselves to just such an authority. Governments created by consent need not appeal to any tradition or custom as authoritative in itself; the consent of the governed conveys sufficient moral authority without such potentially divisive appeals.

AUTHORITY AS A TRUST

Because Lockean government exists to enforce God's law, and (due to natural freedom) cannot be justified for any other purpose, its just power is limited to the performance of that function. For Locke, all proper authority – whether of a parent, the head of a household, or a government – is given in trust for the performance of a specific task according to God's law, and can never be exercised for any other purpose. Locke's theory of limited government arises from this portrayal of political power as a trust given under God's law. Just as parents and heads of households do not properly have political power (the power to destroy), government does not have the authority of a parent (to educate) or the head of a household (to dispose of property), except insofar as a limited amount of such power is necessary for government to carry out its primary function. Government's commission from the community is to prevent the destruction of innocent human life, so it does not have authority to suppress false opinions or discourage the accumulation of property, neither of which causes destruction of human life under ordinary circumstances.[50] And if a government directly violates its trust by destroying innocent lives rather than preserving them, it forfeits its trust and may be resisted under the same moral law that dictated its creation.

In the second paragraph of the *Second Treatise*, Locke begins that treatise's treatment of political authority by differentiating it from four other types of authority. "The power of a magistrate over a subject, may be distinguished from that of a father over his children, a master over his servant, a husband over his wife, and a lord over his slave" (T II.2, 115). Each type of authority is defined by the role that the authority figure is authorized to play – ruler, parent, employer, head of household, or lord, respectively.

These roles are authorized because they are functions that must be performed in order to fulfill God's law of human preservation. We have already seen how political authority is necessary for the accurate enforcement of the natural law. Parental authority is also necessary to preserve life, because a child would not survive if his parents were to "turn him loose to an unrestrained liberty, before he has reason to guide him. . . . This is that which puts the authority into the parents' hands to govern the minority of children" (T II.63, 145). Similarly, "the end of conjunction between male and female, being not barely procreation, but the continuation of the species," families and households are necessary to raise children (T II.79, 154). When husband and wife disagree over how their common goods are to be used, someone must have the authority to make "the last determination"; Locke says this role "naturally falls to the man's share, as the abler and stronger" (T II.82, 155). We need not follow him to this conclusion, of course, and some scholars argue that there is even reason to believe Locke himself had reservations about it.[51] The important point is that for Locke political, parental, and conjugal authority are legitimate only because they are necessary to preserve life. The other two forms are established by similar reasoning, though at less length because Locke is less interested in them.

Because these roles exist for the fulfillment of God's law, they represent limited trusts placed in particular persons under God's authority. There are two major limits inherent in such trusts. We will consider the first one here and take up the second later. The first limit is that all authority is properly confined to the power and function for which it was appointed under God's law. Each form of authority has a specific, defined power attached to it, in order that the purpose of the role may be carried out. The power attached to political authority is "a right of making laws with penalties of death, and consequently all less penalties, for the regulating and preserving of property," which includes the lives, liberties, and possessions of subjects (T II.3, 116). Because children cannot understand the law of preservation, parental authority entails the power "to supply the defects of this imperfect state, till the improvement of growth and age hath removed them" (T II.56, 142). And "the power that every husband hath" is "to order the things of private concernment in his family, as proprietor of the goods and land there," and to have the final say in all things of "common concernment" to the household (T I.48, 35). These powers are all limited by the purpose of the original grant of authority.

The ruler can punish with death, but only for distinctly political purposes, as opposed to purposes that are parental or conjugal in nature, and still less for selfish purposes. The parent governs the child, but only in the child's own interest, and only during the child's minority. The husband governs only the business that is necessary to the maintenance of the household, and beyond that has no power over his wife. Similar limits also apply to masters of servants, and even to lords of slaves.[52]

The limit on political power implied in the division between parental and political authority is essential for the maintenance of moral consensus. Government is excluded from playing any more than a minimal role in the education of the human beings under its authority. This allows for members of each cultural group to sustain their own beliefs without being excluded from full membership in society. This is a case Locke makes more explicitly in the *Letter Concerning Toleration*, but it also follows from the *Two Treatises'* differentiation in types of authority. If the commission to educate is given by God to parents, and government's only role is to ensure that parents do not endanger the preservation of their children or of others, this implies that government must allow parents to educate their children within the religious and cultural tradition of their choice, excluding only practices that are dangerous to human preservation. This separation of political and educative authority allows for the political unification of disparate cultural and religious groups. So long as all acknowledge the binding law of human preservation, all are free to privately maintain their separate traditions.

To map out the particular limits of political authority, the *Second Treatise* lays out the boundaries of permissible government action and the institutional mechanisms that best promote and enforce the natural law under the conditions of modern society. Locke does not provide a detailed instruction manual for designing governments, because the specific constitution of government must vary considerably in different times and places.[53] Much is left to the practical judgment of particular political communities. Rather than dictate exactly what institutions are necessary, Locke describes what *kind* of institutions are necessary, given what we know about the nature of government business, the way people behave, and particularly, the way government officials respond to incentives.

The authority of government institutions is derived, in all cases, from the moral law of human preservation. Political authority "is a power, that hath no other end but preservation" (T II.135, 183–4). Political institutions are therefore dependent upon that law for their legitimacy – so much so, in fact, that Locke says laws and institutions ought to be carefully and judiciously suspended wherever human preservation clearly requires it. Locke observes that "many accidents may happen, wherein a strict and rigid observation of the laws may do harm...and a man may come sometimes within the reach of the law...by an action, that may deserve reward and pardon." For this reason, "'tis fit that the laws themselves should in some cases give way to the executive power, or rather to this fundamental law of nature and government, *viz.* that as much as may be, all the members of the society are to be preserved" (T II.159, 197–8). The executive branch's power to mitigate or suspend the law in such cases is called "prerogative power." As Locke indicates, when the executive exercises prerogative power, it is not properly the will of the executive to which the law gives way, but the natural law of human preservation.

As is the case with all powers, legitimate use of the prerogative power is limited. Obviously, a power to suspend formal regulations cannot itself be formally regulated, but it can be informally regulated. Locke provides a subtle explanation of how political communities tend to allow more exercise of prerogative to "a good prince, who is mindful of the trust put into his hands, and careful of the good of his people," but tend to resist the exercise of prerogative by "a weak and ill prince, who would claim that power...as a prerogative belonging to him by right of his office, which he may exercise at his pleasure" and for his own selfish ends (T II.164, 200). The ultimate form of popular resistance to abuse of the prerogative is in the threat of revolution (see T II.168, 201–2).

The important achievement of the *Two Treatises* in laying out the form of government is not in constitutional mechanisms, which are only provided in general outline and can, by executive prerogative, be suspended when necessary. It is in Locke's method of building a constitutional government on a single moral law. Rather than provide a lengthy list of moral laws derived from various sources to govern politics, Locke shows that a single moral law, combined with keen insight into human behavior, can be used to design an entire political system. This approach makes it possible to build moral consensus among groups with different accounts of morality, because they all agree on the moral law of human preservation, which is the sole basis of political authority.

After laying out the limits of government power, Locke returns to a subject first broached at the very beginning of the *Second Treatise*: what people should do when others break the moral law and no common authority exists to judge and punish the offender. But where the early chapters of the *Second Treatise* were concerned with hypothetical violations among people who are all in a state of nature, the last chapters are concerned with the very real cases in which violations are committed by governments. Because a government is a common political authority over its subjects, by definition one government cannot share a common political authority with other governments or with its own subjects. So we have come full circle, and are back to the limiting case with which we began: what are we authorized to do under God's law where there is no common political authority, as is the case between a tyrant and his subjects?

Here we come to the second limit that applies to all forms of authority, which is that any person who uses his power to subvert the divine law directly violates his trust, and therefore forfeits his authority. Locke demonstrates this with a nonpolitical example that most people will agree with: abusive or neglectful parents forfeit their parental authority. Parental power is "inseparably annexed" to proper "nourishment and education" of children. The "bare act of begetting . . . if all his care ends there" conveys no power to the parent, and parental power "belongs as much to the foster-father of an exposed child, as to the natural father of another" (T II.65, 146). By exposing his child, leaving him to die rather than caring for him as God's law commands, the biological parent forfeits his parental authority. A foster parent who rescues the child and cares for him thereby acquires parental authority indistinguishable from that of an ordinary biological parent. Political authority is forfeited in a similar manner when it is exercised against God's law.

After outlining permissible conduct in waging a just war, thus disposing of cases in which governments come into conflict with one another, Locke takes up cases of conflict between governments and their own subjects. "Using force upon the people without authority, and contrary to the trust put in him, that does so, is a state of war with the people," and "in all states and conditions the true remedy of force without authority, is to oppose force to it" (T II.155, 194). The crux of Locke's case for a right to revolution is that political authority is a trust that can be forfeited. For Locke it seems to follow, without significant problems, that if government receives its power under divine law it can be resisted under the same divine law. "For where there is no judicature on earth, to decide controversies amongst men, God in heaven is judge" (T II.241, 239–40). Where there is no judge but God, we may, as we saw in the account of Jephtha, "appeal to heaven." Locke repeatedly reminds us of his account of Jephtha by describing rebellion as an "appeal to heaven." This emphasizes that just rebellions are claims made under God's moral law, which cannot be nullified by any political compact. Those who are oppressed "may appeal, as Jephtha did, to heaven, and repeat their appeal" until they restore "such a legislative over them, as the majority should approve, and freely acquiesce in" (T II.176, 206).

The main problem Locke wrestles with is not the argument for a right to revolution in the abstract, but mapping out the practical boundaries of this right. Here, the question of the moral law's content, last taken up in the early chapters of the *Second Treatise*, returns to the surface, only this time as a matter of applied epistemology rather than abstract theory. Locke is concerned with how one can know when a particular type of offense against the moral law – government abuse of power – has occurred. Locke is going to conclude the *Two Treatises* with an argument for a right of revolution against unjust governments, so how one judges which governments are truly unjust is a matter of paramount importance. If people resist government "as often as anyone shall find himself aggrieved," it would "unhinge and overturn all politics, and instead of government and order, leave nothing but anarchy and confusion" (T II.203, 218). The most serious objection Locke acknowledges to the right to revolution is that it "lays a ferment for frequent rebellion" (T II.224, 229). To rebut this charge he must show that people will be able to tell when rebellion is genuinely justified and when it isn't.

This matter is particularly delicate for Locke because, as we have seen, the purpose of government on his account is to act as an authoritative moral judge. In deciding when rebellion is justified we are passing moral judgment over the entity that was created specifically to perform the function of passing moral judgment for us. This tension cannot be completely resolved. The people must ultimately retain the right to judge government's performance, and yet these moral judgments are made without neutral arbitration and thus remain subject to the same difficulties that led to government's creation in the first place.

A clear and persuasive set of rules for determining when governments have become rebellious can significantly alleviate the seriousness of this problem. In chapters entitled "Of Usurpation" and "Of Tyranny," Locke provides a number of epistemological signposts by which we can determine whether a government is truly corrupt or has merely made some mistakes in implementing its laws. For example, usurpation occurs when someone "gets into the exercise of . . . power, by other ways, than what the laws of the community have prescribed" (T II.198, 216). One type of case in which tyranny occurs is that in which an executive officer "exceeds the power given him by the law" (T II.202, 218).[54]

However, a complete and specific list of acts that justify resistance would be impossible, and ultimately Locke simply appeals to an empirical observation: people do not, in fact, rebel lightly. "Great mistakes in the ruling part, many wrong and inconvenient laws, and all the slips of human frailty" do not incite rebellion. People only rebel "if a long train of abuses, prevarications, and artifices, all tending the same way, make the design visible to the people," proving to them that government is deliberately abusing its trust (T II.225, 229). Thus, the empirical evidence suggests that the danger arising from this problem is less serious than the partisans of absolute government claim.

Locke's continuing concern for the problems of moral judgment shows that we have, at the end of the argument, come back to the same issue that brought us to the origin of government. Although we create government to enforce the moral law more accurately than we can do as individuals, we can never finally abdicate our individual responsibility to exercise moral judgment on some level, if only in the extreme last resort. No one – not even we ourselves – can ultimately remove the burden of moral judgment from our shoulders. "No man, or society of men" has "a power to deliver up their preservation . . . to the absolute will and arbitrary dominion of another" (T II.149, 191).

This is so because we are always under God's law of preservation, and thus always responsible to God for our own preservation. "God and nature" never allow "a man so to abandon himself, as to neglect his own preservation" (T II.168, 202). And since we always retain this ultimate right and responsibility of judgment, the only truly ultimate authority for resolving disputes is God, who will settle everything in the Last Judgment. As we have already noted, Locke writes: "He that appeals to heaven, must be sure he has right on his side; and a right too that is worth the trouble and cost of the appeal, as he will answer at a tribunal, that cannot be deceived, and will be sure to retribute to everyone according to the mischiefs he hath created" (T II.176, 206).

POLITICAL AUTHORITY AND MORAL CONSENSUS

That the people retain the ultimate right of moral judgment over government is a constant reminder, lurking in the background throughout the *Two Treatises*, that Locke's political theory, however ingenious, is still just a best-case scenario for coping with, rather than finally solving, the recurring problems of the human situation. The problems of private moral judgment are never fully alleviated; in extreme circumstances every person must still judge for himself. However, while acknowledging this lack of finality in Locke's political theory, we should not underestimate the importance of his achievement. Locke has not ultimately removed the prospect for violence from the community, but he has removed it from the arena of religious and cultural conflict, where it had long run rampant and done so much damage. He has built a political community that is simultaneously morally authoritative and open to members of all religions. Having come upon a scene in which religious groups were engaged in what they all saw as a death struggle for control of society, he leaves for us a scene in which all these groups agree to live under a common moral authority that is not particularly beholden to any of them.

A society that does not share a common religion will never be able to reach a broad and stable consensus on moral theory generally. Since the realm of the divine is both the foundation of moral thought and its most perfect manifestation, people who disagree about religion are inevitably going to disagree about morality. To provide a moral theory that can unite such people into a political community with a shared moral vision of society is nothing short of a monumental achievement. Despite its lack of an ultimate resolution of the potential for conflict, and for all the questions of constitutional design that it leaves unanswered, the *Two Treatises* is nonetheless an intellectual achievement equal to any other in the history of political theory. It shows us that political solidarity built upon moral rather than merely prudential reasoning is possible even in modern societies that are multireligious and culturally heterogeneous.

8

"The Opinion of This or That Philosopher Was of No Authority"

Locke and Us

Throughout this book, while examining how Locke built his epistemological, theological, and political theories in reaction to the cultural fragmentation of his day, we have sought to hold contemporary political concerns at a critical distance in order not to distort our reading of Locke. But our ultimate purpose has obviously been political. At the beginning of the twenty-first century, we stand in need of an epistemology that will steer us between the violent Scylla of fanaticism and the all-consuming Charybdis of relativism. We stand in need of a theology that can reconcile belief in divine revelation with rational regulation of our beliefs and behavior. And we stand in need of a political theory that will unite members of different religious and cultural traditions into a single political community. In short, we stand in need of a philosophy of moral consensus, a philosophy like the one left to us by John Locke.

By far the most likely objection we might expect to hear made against Locke is that public moral theory with a religious foundation, even an ecumenical one such as Locke envisions, cannot be sustained today. It is thought by many that in the modern world religion cannot play more than a peripheral supporting role in public philosophy. The driving concern behind this objection seems to be that religion is too primordial, too closely associated with fanaticism, too potentially dangerous to serve as the foundation of public philosophy.

But Locke speaks especially to the problems of our time, not in spite of his religious beliefs but precisely because of them. The profession of political theory has been neglecting religious political philosophy at just the moment when such philosophy is most urgently needed, and

Locke is well qualified to help fill that need because he shares our fear of the primordial fanaticism that religion can unleash. The choice between fanatical theocracy and morally emasculated neutralism is a false choice. If we can overcome our predisposition to see everything in terms of this false choice, we can learn from Locke the existence of a third possibility: an ecumenical religious philosophy of liberalism.

POLITICAL THEORY AND MORAL PRINCIPLES

One of the problems that political wisdom formed in the context of religious belief can address is the potential decay of the moral principles that define our politics – primarily equality and freedom. Professional theorists of liberalism are no longer effectively promoting the moral principles on which liberalism is based. As liberal political theory has become increasingly hostile toward incorporating any acknowledgement of order or higher meaning in the universe, it has been reduced to working out the consequences of preexisting moral beliefs whose truth and widespread acceptance are taken for granted. Our liberal theorists have published hundreds of books debating which political arrangements will best serve the principles of equality and freedom, but they seem unable to produce a convincing argument that equality and freedom are normative obligations. They recognize the need to justify these principles, of course, but they tend either to work around the problem by appealing to an observed consensus – people already support equality and freedom, therefore theorists need not justify them – or smother it in a dense fog of misappropriated pseudo-Kantian jargon.[1]

Whatever merit these theories my have by their own standards of discourse, they appear to have little merit by the standard of society at large, which is ultimately the standard that counts in politics. Outside of professional theorists and their ambassadors in the legal profession, how many people believe anything remotely like the theories of John Rawls or Robert Dworkin? Parents do not teach their children to treat others as equals because that is what they would do if they were in the original position behind a veil of ignorance, nor do they teach anything resembling that formula, or any other formula of our liberal theorists. Whatever its efforts to justify its moral principles to itself, current liberal theory does not serve as a source of moral principles in the general population. And if lawyers and judges sometimes find it convenient to borrow these theories for their own purposes, so much the worse – to the extent that they do so, our legal system incorporates a philosophy that is fundamentally alien to the way in which the general public learns about and thinks about morality.

Social principles must be constantly renewed if they are to endure. A society could not exist if it did not demand that its members make sacrifices – often enormous or ultimate sacrifices – for its shared principles. Persuading people that the principles of their society are worthy of such sacrifices requires continuing effort, as each rising generation must be persuaded anew. If a society loses the intellectual sources of its principles, eventually its members will no longer find those principles persuasive, and one way or another those principles will be replaced with new ones. This process is not immediate, of course; when the intellectual sources of principles fade away, the principles themselves do not disappear as quickly because of the tremendous power of cultural inertia. But unsupported principles must eventually recede.[2]

No one is more acutely aware of this fact than liberalism's potential competitors. Communitarians, neo-Aristotelians, Burkean conservatives, and postmodernists do not agree on much, but they all seem to agree that liberalism's major weakness is its inability to maintain public cohesion around moral principles. All of these movements, in their most distinctive forms, aspire to replace liberalism as the dominant source of our political principles. That is why theorists belonging to these movements, unlike so many of their liberal counterparts, pay close attention to the sources of moral principles in politics, seeking moral authority in communities, human nature, cultural traditions, or radical autonomy.

For the most part, these movements retain the central political principles of equality and freedom, but changing the source of moral authority for those principles necessarily changes our understanding of the principles themselves, sometimes quite radically. These changed understandings of our principles are what distinguish these movements from liberalism. For example, if freedom is valued because our community or our cultural tradition values freedom, then our idea of freedom will generally not include the freedom to do things disapproved of by those entities, and it cannot possibly include the freedom to do things that actively undermine those entities. Of course, liberalism also limits freedom and equality in the same way; the point is that there is a great deal of difference between liberal "freedom," communitarian "freedom," and postmodernist "freedom."

To a large extent, these illiberal movements exist because of the vacuum of moral authority that occurred when liberalism abandoned God in favor of moral neutralism. Without God, liberalism had no persuasive case for why its principles, rather than some other set of principles, should be adopted by society, upheld through painful sacrifice, and enforced through the justice system. In their various ways, all of liberalism's intellectual competitors are struggling to take advantage of this moral vacuum by finding something to replace God in political theory.

The difficulty facing all of these movements in one way or another is that they require us to abandon, or at least seriously discount, the individualism and rationalism of the Enlightenment. For any of these movements to become dominant, the heroic individualism of the Enlightenment would have to give way to a more communal understanding of human existence, in which each individual understands himself not as an independent moral agent but as an appendage of the social structure into which he was born. The relevant social structure could be his local community, his political system, his cultural heritage, his ethnic or language group, or some combination thereof, but the radical departure from Enlightenment individualism is the same in every case. And if individualism goes, rationalism goes with it – since identity would be understood as a social construct and individuals would no longer be understood as independent moral agents, morals would be inculcated primarily by upbringing and habit rather than by rational persuasion. Rationalism seeks a moral and political order supported by argument rather than just by the existence of certain social practices.

With the loss of Enlightenment individualism and rationalism, we would also lose government by consent of the governed. The Enlightenment ideal is a society whose members are persuaded by argument to acknowledge its authority. Should the Enlightenment's rationalism and individualism fail, our ideal would be well-reared citizens who obey society's rules because they recognize society as the source of their identity, not because they were persuaded as such to do so. They might be said to consent to their government in a weak meaning of "consent," in that they would accept their governors as legitimate, but this would be consent given on the basis of habit and social practice rather than rational argument.

If liberalism is truly as moribund as its critics claim, then a radical revision of the Enlightenment, or at least of some of its major aspects, may well be necessary. But as a general rule such a radical break from the existing philosophic framework should be avoided whenever possible. Ambitious new public philosophies seeking to replace Enlightenment liberalism have left behind a mixed track record at best over the past two centuries. Revising the rationalism and individualism of the Enlightenment would be tampering with the moral foundations of society, which are much easier to tear down than they are to rebuild. Should liberalism fail, one of its competitors might replace it in promoting equality and freedom, but it is also possible that those principles would simply die off, and with them the moral order of our society. If we can find a way to revive our moral principles within the framework of Enlightenment liberalism, we ought to do so rather than seek a new source of moral principles.

This is especially true of the United States, which is still what Lincoln called it: "a nation dedicated to a proposition." That proposition, contained in the Declaration of Independence, is uncompromisingly rationalist ("We hold these truths to be self-evident") and individualist ("that all men are created equal, that they are endowed by their creator with certain unalienable rights," and so on). It would be extremely difficult for an intellectual movement to make a case that the Declaration is consistent with communal and/or nonrationalist philosophy, and any movement that is perceived as incompatible with the Declaration is going to have a long uphill struggle to political viability in America. Such a movement would require the world's only superpower to discount the principles of its foundational and universally acknowledged source of civic moral authority. One need not be a reactionary to view this as dangerous – indeed, as potentially disastrous. The Declaration is a unifying and authoritative moral force over American society, and it is not clear that anything else could take its place.

However, if we are going to retain our Enlightenment individualism and rationalism, liberal political theory must once again become a source of renewal for liberal moral principles in the general population. To do this, it must revive a language of moral justification for liberalism and make a moral case that the population at large will find persuasive.

Liberalism's deepest historical roots lie in the European religious reforms of the sixteenth and seventeenth centuries. These eventually culminated in the moral doctrine that people should be treated politically as free and equal because all human beings are equally precious creations of God and reflections of his image. Of course, Christianity had always taught that humans were equal in the eyes of God. What changed was the application of this idea to the moral questions of politics. It was no longer enough to say that God would treat us all equally; liberals demanded that political authorities follow God's example in this regard.

In the past four centuries, many other moral arguments for equality have been presented, from Hobbes's equality of mortality to Kant's equality of autonomy to Mill's equality of utility and everything in between.

However, none of these has had anything close to the same breadth, depth, and endurance of popular acceptance as the idea that we are all equally precious as God's creations. To the extent that the moral imagination of the West can be said to reflect any dominant influence, it is still dominated, especially in the general population outside the universities, by this simultaneously religious and liberal idea. Rediscovering this religious vocabulary of liberalism could go a long way toward promoting the principles necessary to support the liberal social order.

UPHOLDING NECESSARY POLITICAL LIMITS

Religion can also play a useful political role in preventing the Enlightenment ideas that shape our society from running to extremes. Individualism and rationalism, like all political ideals, become dangerous if too much is claimed for them. In their proper form, individualism and rationalism lead not to government that is neutral among sets of moral commitments – such neutrality is impossible, as it is impossible to act (or refrain from acting) without doing so according to some moral scheme – but to government from voluntary social solidarity. Independent moral agents become citizens by voluntarily submitting to the authority of society's principles. But the idea that each person is an independent moral agent can give rise to the extreme conclusion that morality is purely subjective and there are no morally necessary limits on individual behavior. Similarly, the goal of justifying government authority by rational argument can give rise to the extreme conclusion that every social question ought to be resolved by argument – that is, that an action or choice must be allowed if any argument can be made for it.

Extreme forms of individualism and rationalism are dangerous because government action must have a basis in shared moral principles if it is to be accepted as legitimate. This is what gives governments the moral authority they need to effectively carry out their mission. If politics were not based on shared moral principles – if we were to accept the familiar argument that "you can't legislate morality" – anyone could claim a right to do anything he wanted. This would undermine the social cooperation on which legitimate government always depends. A society not governed by moral authority would have to be governed by brute force.

But just as every political ideal can run to extremes, every political ideal can be prevented from doing so. What's needed is a philosophic counterbalance, something that is not inconsistent with individualism and rationalism but will limit the kind of claims that can be made on their behalf. A political philosophy that incorporates religious belief can provide this. It is one thing to say that individuals are independent moral agents, and quite another to say that individuals are independent moral agents who will answer to God in the next life for their sins in this one. This formulation rules out the possibility that morality is simply subjective; God is undeniably an objective moral authority. Likewise, belief in God can put rationalism in a proper perspective. While religious belief makes reasoned argument all the more important for discovering the part of God's will that reason is able to discover, it also reminds us how much of God's will is not rationally discoverable. Religious belief provides limits on the individual autonomy granted by Enlightenment liberalism. If people are free and equal because God made them so, then freedom and equality are conditioned on God's law.

The idea that political principles are conditioned on God's law is not inherently illiberal; it is liberal or illiberal only insofar as our understanding of God's law, and of human authority to enforce that law, is liberal or illiberal. If the purpose of political power is to transform individuals and save their souls, and authorities are given a broad mandate to enforce their particular interpretation of God's law, then the political system will be illiberal. But if the purpose of political power is to protect the God-given freedom and equality of individuals, and authorities are required to allow expansive latitude for differing interpretations of God's law wherever possible, then the political system will be liberal. A religious political philosophy can be as tolerant as any other political philosophy. Moreover, a religious theory of toleration has an advantage that secular theories of toleration cannot match: it makes available the argument that toleration is commanded by God, and that intolerance and persecution are sins against the almighty.

Obviously the toleration of different religious interpretations cannot be infinite, or there will be no basis for drawing the boundaries that are necessary to uphold a liberal order. Some people think that God's law requires them to kill heretics, and a liberal political system must punish those who act on such beliefs. Such limits must apply to any theory of toleration, whether or not that theory is based on religious belief. But, once again, religious theories of toleration have an advantage over secular theories. Because a religious theory of toleration is not beholden to the idea that public philosophy must be perfectly neutral with regard to religious belief, it can place the necessary limits on toleration without contradicting its own principles. The necessary limits on toleration, like toleration itself, can be justified by appeal to God's law.

FORMAL AND INFORMAL PUBLIC ROLES FOR RELIGION

Religion can justify liberalism and uphold necessary limits on individual behavior in both formal and informal capacities. Formally, it can justify – that is, provide moral authority for – government action. If asked why government should force people to respect each others' rights, and why enforce one particular understanding of rights rather than another, we must give some kind of morally satisfactory answer. "Because it is God's law, and in particular it is a part of God's law that government is authorized to enforce" is one such answer, alongside "because it is most fitting for human nature," "because it is what our society has always done," "because it is what we would choose in an original position behind a veil of ignorance," and many others.

All such justifications are to some extent impositions of moral belief. If we are to have any formal justification for government action, we must enforce some kind of moral view in doing so – that is the only way to give government moral authority. Formally enforcing a particular understanding of religion is no more arbitrary or capricious than formally enforcing a particular understanding of human nature, cultural tradition, original neutrality, or anything else. All political philosophies ultimately rest on some claim of moral authority; the question is not whether a given political philosophy will enforce a moral order, but whether it will enforce a moral order that the general population will voluntarily accept and that will cope sufficiently well with the political problems of the society on which it is imposed.

Informally, religion can promote virtuous behavior, thus reducing the need for the formal exercise of political power. If people generally behave themselves of their own accord, there will be less need for political authority to keep them in line. This is not merely a convenience; it is crucial to the liberal character of the political community. Since the use of political power tends to increase the twin dangers of corruption in the rulers and dependence in the ruled, to remain free a society must exercise political power as little as possible. That is why it was a commonplace from ancient times up through (and including) the Enlightenment that political freedom depends upon a virtuous population. The understanding of "virtue" and how to promote it changes dramatically from Aristotle to Adam Smith, but the fundamental wisdom is the same. Political power exists to restrain individuals where they fail to properly restrain themselves; if people rarely restrain themselves, government must become more and more powerful and intrusive to restrain them; and no political community can remain free if its government becomes too powerful and intrusive.

Political observers have often taken note of these informal social benefits of religion, frequently with the hope that religion could promote virtue in the private sphere even if it is not an integral part of a nation's shared public philosophy. But there are good reasons for pessimism about maintaining the informal benefits of religion under a cultural regime of public/private separation. The problem is not simply that if religion is strictly confined to the "private" sphere it cannot provide the formal moral authority that all government must have to govern legitimately, although that alone would be a sufficient reason to reject the confinement of religion to "private" life. The deeper problem lies in understanding the distinction between religion's two potential roles as "public" and "private," rather than as "formal" and "informal," as we have been labeling them.

Religion's informal capacity to promote virtue is not a matter of strictly "private" concern. If the population must be virtuous for the government to retain its liberal character, then promoting virtue among the population must be understood as public business. More to the point, where religion is understood as strictly private it tends to lose its effectiveness in promoting virtue. As Tocqueville understood so well, religion cannot simply be left alone to fend for itself on the social stage. Understood as strictly private, religion tends to degenerate into a sort of feel-good "spirituality" with no moral content. This occurs because when people think of their beliefs as private they have no obvious motive to regulate their own beliefs properly, and they inevitably end up believing in things that do not impose upon themselves any burdensome moral rules or requirements. And, to draw a page from Locke, on the opposite extreme there is the problem of religious enthusiasm – left entirely to their own devices, people often do not properly regulate their religious beliefs and become dangerously irrational, and illiberal.

Tocqueville understood this as a problem of guidance – leave people to choose their religion with no external guidance from society, and you have no complaint coming when they end up rejecting traditional religion in favor of a self-serving pseudo-spirituality that confirms them in their worst, most dissolute behaviors. Locke understood the problem of public religion more as a problem of teaching people to properly regulate their own beliefs, as opposed to Tocqueville's approach of directly providing them with the content of their beliefs through an authoritative church institution. However, the basic concern is very similar for both

Locke and Tocqueville: if religion is understood as strictly private, society will have no recognizable grounds on which to encourage people to hold reasonable, well-examined beliefs rather than enthusiastic or self-serving ones.

Religion must be public if it is to have the elevated social status that it needs to be effective in promoting virtue. The proper liberal role in which religion can promote virtue should be understood as "informal" but not as strictly "private." This does not mean that government as such must subsidize churches as such. The public role of religion need not be institutionalized in such a manner – although it bears noting that most western nations do provide large-scale institutional subsidies for religion, and are not generally considered illiberal or intolerant because of this. Rather, the important point is this: religion will not promote virtue unless people understand that they have a public responsibility to take it seriously and to properly regulate their beliefs.

This should not be understood as calling for an imposition of one particular set of religious beliefs, which would be illiberal. Awareness of one's responsibility to take religion seriously and regulate one's beliefs rationally cannot be conveyed through any kind of legal enforcement, because government could not coerce people into changing their beliefs even if it wished to do so. This is, as we have seen, a point Locke was at great pains to make. Similarly, to seek out guidance in religion need not mean that any person should ever believe something that doesn't appear to him to be true simply because someone else teaches it. Again, Locke invested great effort in arguing that people should be faithful to their own well-considered beliefs. But careful examination of religious beliefs, which for most people will include receiving guidance from others whose lives are devoted to such examination, is essential if religion is to remain a virtuous social influence rather than an inchoate blob of pseudo-spirituality or a dangerous source of extremism.

A GOD-SHAPED HOLE IN POLITICAL THEORY

Political theory cannot simply ignore people's ultimate beliefs. We might say, with apologies to Pascal, that there is a God-shaped hole in political theory that nothing else can fill. All political theories must engage in the formal business of morally justifying government action and the informal business of promoting virtue. In particular, liberal political theory has a special interest in the latter; since it seeks to limit the power and influence of government over individuals, it must find an alternate way of restraining individual behavior. Both these problems – moral authority for government and virtue for citizens – require political theorists to take account of, and even help refine and redirect, ultimate beliefs.

Political philosophers are not just – indeed, are not even primarily – political architects, designing elaborate structures to be built upon ground whose existence and stability are taken for granted. Political philosophers are first and foremost political geologists, surveying the ground upon which the political community must build its institutions, judging which sites are stable enough for construction, and figuring out how to make the less stable sites more stable. As Locke puts it, if its foundations are unconvincing then a philosophy is no more than "a castle in the air," and to show that it is internally consistent is only to show that "it shall be all of a piece, and hang together" (E I.4.25, 103).[3] Political theories that do not confront the deep and perplexing problems of ultimate belief are engaged in just this sort of airborne architecture – their castles are all of a piece and hang together, but there is no ground upon which to build them.

Locke writes of the nonreligious political philosophy of the ancient world: "Mankind might hearken to it or reject it as they pleased, or as it suited their interest, passions, principles, or humors. They were under no obligation; the opinion of this or that philosopher was of no authority" (R 242, 173). This sounds remarkably like a description of our own situation. Theorists following John Rawls' *A Theory of Justice* may refine that theory until it is articulated in such minute detail that they can tell us how many primary goods can dance on the head of a pin, but it will do nothing to provide moral authority for the theory of the original position. The same goes for Robert Dworkin's theory of social insurance, Robert Nozick's theory of absolute individual rights, Bruce Ackerman's theory of dialogic neutrality, Michael Walzer's theory of spheres of justice, and so on. We can hearken to these theories or reject them as we please, or as they suit our interests, passions, principles, or humors. We are under no obligation – the opinion of this or that professor of political theory is of no authority.

As Locke shows so forcefully, only the infinite rewards and punishments of God "will cast a slight upon the short pleasures and pains of this present state ... Upon this foundation, and upon this only, morality stands firm and will defy all competition" (R 245, 185). Locke makes this point to demonstrate not only that morality grounded on God's law will defy all competition from immorality, but also – and, for his purposes and ours, more importantly – that any theory grounded on God's law will always defy all competition from any theories not so grounded. God's power casts a slight on whatever benefit is to be had in this present state from adherence to any political theory. No professor of political theory can show us a good reason for disobeying almighty God.

What arises from this observation is that political theory must give some account of the divine if it is to operate among people who believe in the divine, which has included the overwhelming majority of the human race in all times and places. Given that people do indeed have religious beliefs, and diverse and conflicting ones at that, a social order that did not incorporate religion would fall apart every time a religious leader roused his followers to disobey its rules for some reason – perhaps because those rules offend their beliefs in some way, or perhaps because they seek to convert the members of other religions to their own faith. Whatever the reason, if obedience to God and obedience to the political community are seen to conflict, any rational person would choose obedience to God. This is why every really great political philosopher in the history of political philosophy has given an account of the divine in his works.

Furthermore, in a society where people believe different and contradictory things about the divine, a political theory must give an account of the divine that will be acceptable to members of all the groups it is to govern. This is why all the great political philosophers in the modern era have wrestled with the difficult questions of religious epistemology. Hobbes concluded that because religious disputes can become serious enough to threaten the civil order, ultimately there is no alternative to uniformity, imposed by force if necessary. Rousseau sought uniformity through different means, by rounding out the corners and smoothing down the hard edges of religion, moving disparate faiths together toward a Romantic civil religion arising from conscience. Kant argued for a set of religious beliefs discerned through natural reason alone. Burke thought that we should participate in the evolving religious beliefs of our cultural tradition, as any longstanding tradition would necessarily contain more wisdom than the thoughts of an individual. Adam Smith and John Stuart Mill argued that allowing competition and free exchange of ideas among different religious groups would tend, in the long run, to promote true religious beliefs over false ones. Marx, of course, sought to refute the existence of the divine by explaining religious belief as a manifestation of the dominance of the ruling class, and Nietzsche aspired to replace existing religions with new myths that would liberate the creative energies of great individuals.

Not until the nineteenth century did the idea of building political theory with no reference to the divine whatsoever get serious consideration from prominent figures, and only in the twentieth century did the divine disappear from political theory almost entirely. With a handful of exceptions, the most important figures in twentieth-century political thought have all refrained from giving any account of the divine. This is all the more remarkable when we consider that in the twentieth century the nations of the free world fought life-and-death struggles against two ideologically driven superpowers whose official systems of thought denied theistic religion. In public political discourse, religion played a crucial role in rallying the free peoples of the world against the evil empires of the Nazis and the Soviets. The profession of political theory chose this moment to fall silent on the subject of the divine.

It is interesting, to say no more, that as political theory has ceased to concern itself with accounts of the divine, it has simultaneously experienced a precipitous decline in intellectual greatness. The twentieth century saw some of the most momentous political events in the history of the human race. These events were fraught with implications for political thought, arising as they did from the clash of great ideologies. And yet the twentieth century produced not a single political thinker whose name elicits the same level of intellectual admiration as the names of many thinkers from the immediately preceding centuries: Hobbes, Locke, Rousseau, Kant, Burke, Smith, Mill, Marx, and Nietzsche, just for a start. Perhaps it is too early for such historical judgments, but even so, it is difficult to imagine future generations casually placing any name from the twentieth century next to these names. Correlation is not causation, so we will not jump to any conclusions. However, the hypothesis that the intellectual diminishment of political theory was caused by its retreat from the divine is one worthy of exploration by some future historian bold enough for the task.

RECONNECTING WITH THE DIVINE

Political theory is inherently moral. It imposes rules, justifies systems of authority, and provides the normative commitments that guide political action. To accomplish this, it must promote a moral vision of the political community that the population at large will accept. Liberal political theory today is not successfully promoting its moral vision because it refuses to craft that vision in the context of belief in the divine. For most people, morality starts with belief in the divine, and where the demands of the divine conflict with other demands the divine takes precedence. Liberalism is effectively living on borrowed legitimacy; it is coasting on cultural inertia arising from previous generations of liberal theorists whose moral visions were persuasive in the population at large. No political ideology can last long this way. If liberalism is to survive in the long term, it must provide a moral vision of society that people will find persuasive. In short, it must return to the divine.

Locke is only one of the thinkers to whom we might turn in order to reconnect liberal political theory with an account of the divine. No doubt any serious revival of religious liberalism would seek to draw upon the wisdom of a variety of thinkers. What such a revival would look like in whole is therefore far beyond the scope of this book. Our purpose here has been to show, with Locke's help, that there is, in fact, a middle way we can take between fanaticism and relativistic neutralism; that there is, in fact, a way we can reconcile religious belief and full-fledged commitment to reason; that there is, in fact, a way for us to build political community among people of different religions that is based on moral law rather than merely on coincidental overlap in their preferences. In other words, our purpose has been to show what moral consensus is, and how it can address the necessary moral concerns of political theory in a way that is not illiberal or exclusionary.

Locke faced a breakdown of moral and cultural unity far more severe than the one we are experiencing now, and a prospect of religiously motivated violence that was at least as immediate, coming as it did from within the political community rather than from abroad. His political theory was fundamental in shaping the modern world, perhaps more so than any other. To a very great extent we are living in the world Locke envisioned for us. The only large exception to this is in the aspiration among our intellectuals and other elites to compartmentalize religion and politics. If we are willing to give up on this attempted compartmentalization and reconnect our political foundations with the divine, Locke is the natural figure to whom we would turn first for help. His theory of moral consensus in epistemology, theology, and politics points the way to an effective method of reconciling, in our own time, religious and cultural diversity with the need for social and political solidarity built on a moral foundation. If we can learn from Locke that building such a society is possible, and see in his works how we might go about it, it would be the first great step in restoring to liberalism a vibrant moral life.

Notes

1: "Reason Teaches All Mankind, Who Will But Consult It"

1. Eldon Eisenach. *Two Worlds of Liberalism.* Chicago: University of Chicago Press, 1992, p. 53. See also John Dunn. *The Political Thought of John Locke.* New York: Cambridge University Press, 1969; James Tully. *A Discourse on Property.* Cambridge: Cambridge University Press, 1980; John Colman. *John Locke's Moral Philosophy.* Edinburgh: Edinburgh University Press, 1983; John Dunn. *Locke.* New York: Oxford University Press, 1984; Ruth W. Grant. *John Locke's Liberalism.* Chicago: University of Chicago Press, 1987; W. M. Spellman. *John Locke and the Problem of Depravity.* Oxford: Clarendon Press, 1988; Richard Ashcraft. "Introduction." In *John Locke: Critical Assessments,* ed. Richard Ashcraft. New York: Routledge, 1991, vol. 1; John Marshall. *John Locke: Resistance, Religion and Responsibility.* New York: Cambridge University Press, 1994; Richard Ashcraft. "Anticlericalism and Authority in Lockean Political Thought." In *Margins of Orthodoxy,* ed. Roger Lund. Cambridge: Cambridge University Press, 1995; Nicholas Wolterstorff. *John Locke and the Ethics of Belief.* Cambridge: Cambridge University Press, 1996; W. M. Spellman. *John Locke.* New York: St. Martin's Press, 1997; Peter Myers. *Our Only Star and Compass: Locke and the Struggle for Political Rationality.* New York: Rowman & Littlefield, 1998; Nicholas Jolley. *Locke: His Philosophical Thought.* New York: Oxford University Press, 1999; and Jeremy Waldron. *God, Locke, and Equality.* Cambridge: Cambridge University Press, 2002.
2. See Marshall, *Resistance, Religion and Responsibility,* p. xix.
3. The most famous example of a theorist applying Locke's political theory outside the context of his religion is Robert Nozick's *Anarchy, State, and Utopia* (United States: Basic Books, 1974). Nozick himself acknowledges the absence of a justifying foundation for his version of Locke's theory and observes a similar lack of foundation in the *Second Treatise* (see p. 9). Part of the purpose of this book is to show how Locke's religious thought provides that foundation, making Locke's classical liberalism fundamentally different from Nozick's libertarianism. A more recent attempt at extracting Locke's politics from his

religion is Alex Tuckness' *Locke and the Legislative Point of View* (Princeton, NJ: Princeton University Press, 2002). Tuckness is much more sensitive to the original religious context of Locke's thought; consequently, the political theory he extracts from it retains little of its really important and interesting content. The most famous example of a theorist concluding that Locke's religiosity disqualifies him from serious consideration as a guide to contemporary problems is Dunn, *Political Thought*; see also Dunn, *Locke*; John Dunn. "What Is Living and What Is Dead in the Political Theory of John Locke?" In *Interpreting Political Responsibility: Essays 1981–1989*, John Dunn. Princeton, NJ: Princeton University Press, 1990; and the discussion below.

4. For a discussion of liberal neutralism, see Myers, *Our Only Star*, chapter 1.

5. This method has been followed by Locke scholars before, most recently by Myers (see Myers, *Our Only Star*; see also Peter Myers. "Locke on Reasonable Christianity and Reasonable Politics." In *Piety and Humanity*, ed. Douglas Kries. New York: Rowman & Littlefield, 1997).

6. Raymond Polin. "John Locke's Conception of Freedom." In *John Locke: Problems and Perspectives*, ed. John W. Yolton. Cambridge: Cambridge University Press, 1969, p. 1.

7. See esp. W. von Leyden. "Introduction." In *Essays on the Law of Nature*, John Locke. New York: Oxford University Press, 1954; Hans Aarsleff, "The State of Nature and the Nature of Man in Locke." In *Problems and Perspectives*, ed. Yolton; Dunn, *Political Thought*, p. 19–40; Ashcraft, *Revolutionary Politics*, p. 75–127; Ashcraft, *Locke's Two Treatises*, p. 35–59; Michael Zuckert. *Natural Rights and the New Republicanism*. Princeton, NJ: Princeton University Press, 1994, p. 187–215; and Marshall, *Resistance, Religion and Responsibility*, p. 157–204.

8. See Tully, *Discourse*; Tully, *An Approach*; Ashcraft, *Revolutionary Politics*; and Marshall, *Resistance, Religion and Responsibility*.

9. See Dunn, *Political Theory*; Dunn, *Locke*; Grant, *Locke's Liberalism*; Colman, *Locke's Moral Philosophy*; and A. John Simmons. *The Lockean Theory of Rights*. Princeton, NJ: Princeton University Press, 1992.

10. Ashcraft proved the value of using one approach to inform the other by publishing a historical analysis of the *Two Treatises* followed immediately by a theoretical analysis of the same text that drew upon his historical work (see Ashcraft, *Revolutionary Politics*; and Ashcraft, *Locke's Two Treatises*); other good works on Locke combining historical and theoretical insight include Spellman, *Problem of Depravity*; Spellman, *John Locke*; and Jolley, *Philosophical Thought*.

11. See Dunn, *Political Thought*, p. 79–83, 94–5, and 187–90.

12. See Dunn, *Political Thought*, p. 80 and 187; and Dunn, *Locke*, p. 66–8, 84–5, and 88.

13. See Dunn, *Political Thought*, p. 245–61.

14. See Francis Oakley. "Locke, Natural Law, and God – Again." *History of Political Thought* 18 (1997): 624–51; see also Steven Forde. "Natural Law, Theology, and Morality in Locke." *American Journal of Political Science* 45 (2001): 396–409, p. 398.

15. Tully, *Discourse*, p. 3–12, esp. p. 4.

16. See Tully, *Discourse*, p. 86.
17. Tully, *Discourse*, p. 42.
18. Tully, *Discourse*, p. 8–9.
19. See E II.11.2, 156 and E IV.17.4, 676; see also Walter Ott. "Locke and the Scholastics on Theological Discourse." *The Locke Newsletter* 28 (1997): 51–66; Vivienne Brown. "On Theological Discourse in Locke's *Essay*." *The Locke Newsletter* 29 (1998): 39–57; and Walter Ott. "Locke and the Idea of God: A Reply to Vivienne Brown." *The Locke Newsletter* 30 (1999): 67–71. See also Richard Ashcraft. "Faith and Knowledge in Locke's Philosophy." In *Problems and Perspectives*, ed. Yolton, p. 207.
20. See Richard Ashcraft. *Revolutionary Politics and Locke's Two Treatises of Government*. Princeton, NJ: Princeton University Press, 1986, esp p. 228–85; Richard Ashcraft. *Locke's Two Treatises of Government*. London: Allen & Unwin, 1987, p. 176–80 and 262–4; David Wootton. "John Locke and Richard Ashcraft's *Revolutionary Politics*." *Political Studies* 40 (1992): 79–98; Richard Ashcraft. "Simple Objections and Complex Reality: Theorizing Political Radicalism in Seventeenth-Century England." *Political Studies* 40 (1992): 99–115; and Marshall, *Resistance, Religion and Responsibility*, p. 264–5, 275–7, and 282–3.
21. See Ashcraft, *Locke's Two Treatises*, p. 151.
22. See Ashcraft, *Locke's Two Treatises*, p. 115, 118–20, 185–6, 206–16.
23. Ashcraft, *Locke's Two Treatises*, p. 100–1.
24. Ashcraft, *Locke's Two Treatises*, p. 100; see also T II.12, 120.
25. See Ashcraft, *Revolutionary Politics*, p. 252–69, 281–3, 501, 546–51, 572, and 577–83; and Ashcraft, *Locke's Two Treatises*, p. 93–4, 176–80, 255, and 262–4.
26. See Marshall, *Resistance, Religion and Responsibility*, p. 271 and 276–7. Marshall also points out that Locke was deeply unsympathetic to most dissenters (p. xix) and argues persuasively against Ashcraft's view that there is an "ideology of dissent" in Locke's works (p. 76–7, 225–6, 245, 265, 274–5, and 282–3).
27. See Myers, *Our Only Star*, p. 210.
28. Dunn, *Political Thought*, p. x.
29. Dunn, "What Is Living," p. 9.
30. See Dunn, "What Is Living," p. 13–14 and 20–5.
31. Dunn, "What Is Living," p. 12–13.
32. Dunn, "What Is Living," p. 14–15.
33. Dunn, "What Is Living," p. 15.
34. Dunn, "What Is Living," p. 21.
35. Dunn, "What Is Living," p. 15 and 19–20.
36. Dunn, "What Is Living," p. 18.
37. For a good treatment of Lockean property as a broad mandate under divine command, see David C. Snyder. "Locke on Natural Law and Property Rights." *Canadian Journal of Philosophy* 16 (1986): 723–50.
38. Some commentators, most notably Dunn and Ashcraft, have given great interpretive weight to the religious and political affiliation of Locke's family during the Civil War (see Dunn, *Political Thought*, p. 11–18; and Ashcraft, *Revolutionary Politics*, p. 77–8). However, Locke himself never endorsed the

parliamentary cause for which his father fought, or even expressed sympathy for it. He disparaged Cromwell and, despite his support for toleration, generally distrusted religious dissenters. See Marshall, *Resistance, Religion and Responsibility*, p. xix.

39. See Ashcraft, *Revolutionary Politics*, p. 17–20 and 115–16.
40. See Marshall, *Resistance, Religion and Responsibility*, p. 357.
41. See "Chronology of His Times." In *Two Treatises of Government*, ed. Mark Goldie. London: Everyman, 1993, p. xi.
42. See J. R. Milton. "Locke's Life and Times." In *The Cambridge Companion to Locke*, ed. Vere Chappell. Cambridge: Cambridge University Press, 1994, p. 14.
43. See Ashcraft, *Revolutionary Politics*, p. 3.
44. See John C. Higgins-Biddle. "Introduction." In *The Reasonableness of Christianity as Delivered in the Scriptures*. Oxford: Clarendon Press, 1999, p. lxxxv; see also Milton, "Locke's Life," p. 8.
45. See John Rawls. *Political Liberalism*. New York: Columbia University Press, 1993.
46. See Aarsleff, "State of Nature," and Forde, "Natural Law."
47. Forde, "Natural Law," p. 403; see also p. 402 and 408. Forde believes that Locke's desire for "minimum controversy" leaves his argument with "important gaps," in particular, an account of why reason makes human beings morally significant. However, Locke is clear and straightforward on this point: reason makes us moral agents because it allows us to know and live by the moral law God has laid down for human beings, under which life is sacred; those without reason live by the moral law of animals, which does not require reason, and under which life is not sacred (see T II.6–8, 117–18; and II.11, 120).
48. As Resnick points out, critiques of the excessive "rationality" of current liberal theory would not apply to Locke's version of "rationality" (see David Resnick. "Rationality and the *Two Treatises*." In *John Locke's Two Treatises of Government: New Interpretations*, ed. Edward J. Harpham. Lawrence: University Press of Kansas, 1992, p. 82–3). Resnick goes on to comment that, while it is a good thing to correct former impressions of Locke as a simplistic, unhistorical, abstract, atomistic-individualist rationalist, we must recover some appreciation of the fact that he is, after all, a rationalist (see p. 86).
49. Ashcraft says that Locke should not be understood as "modern" because his philosophy relies so heavily on belief in God (Ashcraft, "Faith and Knowledge," p. 206–7). But, as the example of Locke helps to show, the important difference between the medievals and the moderns is not belief in God as such but attitude toward the authority of tradition. See Wolterstorff, *Ethics of Belief*, p. 227–46.
50. Aarsleff, "State of Nature," p. 134.
51. See, for example, Dunn, *Locke*, p. 88.
52. Richard Ashcraft. "The Politics of Locke's *Two Treatises of Government*." In *New Interpretations*, ed. Harpham, p. 16. For a brief history of Locke scholarship up to 1987, see Ashcraft, *Locke's Two Treatises*, p. 298–305.

53. See Leo Strauss. *Natural Right and History.* Chicago: University of Chicago Press, 1953, p. 202–51; and C. B. Macpherson. *The Political Theory of Possessive Individualism.* London: Oxford University Press, 1962, p. 194–262.

54. See Dunn, *Political Thought*; see also Dunn, *Locke.*

55. See Eisenach, *Two Worlds*, p. 60–1; and Marshall, *Resistance, Religion and Responsibility*, p. 329–83, esp. 367–70.

56. See Dunn, *Political Thought*, p. 262–7; Ashcraft, *Locke's Two Treatises*, p. 35–59; Eldon Eisenach. "Religion and Locke's *Two Treatises*." In *New Interpretations*, ed. Harpham, p. 50–81; and Marshall, *Resistance, Religion and Responsibility*, p. 205–91.

57. Dunn, *Political Thought*, p. 265.

58. Dunn, *Political Thought*, p. 98; see also p. 95, note 1.

59. For previous responses to the Straussian reading of Locke, see John Yolton. "Locke on the Law of Nature." In *Critical Assesments*, ed. Ashcraft; Francis Oakley and Elliot W. Urdang. "Locke, Natural Law, and God." *Natural Law Forum* 11 (1966): 92–109; John Dunn. "Justice and the Interpretation of Locke's Political Theory." *Political Studies* 16 (1968): 68–87; Dunn, *Political Thought*; Hans Aarsleff, "Some Observations on Recent Locke Scholarship." In *Problems and Perspectives*, ed. Yolton; Henning Reventlow. *The Authority of the Bible and the Rise of the Modern World.* U.K.: Fortress Press, 1985; Grant, *Locke's Liberalism*; and Oakley, "Again." For a more extensive list of citations on the controversy, see Oakley, "Again," p. 635, note 5.

60. Grant, *Locke's Liberalism*, p. 9.

2: "Sit Down in Quiet Ignorance"

1. See especially Peter Laslett. "Introduction." In *Two Treatises of Government*, John Locke. Cambridge: Cambridge University Press, 1960.

2. See esp. John Dunn. *The Political Thought of John Locke.* New York: Cambridge University Press, 1969; John Dunn. *Locke.* New York: Oxford University Press, 1984; John W. Yolton. *Locke: An Introduction.* Oxford: Basil Blackwell, Ltd., 1985; Ruth W. Grant. *John Locke's Liberalism.* Chicago: University of Chicago Press, 1987; and David Wootton. "John Locke: Socinian or Natural Law Theorist?" In *Religion, Secularization and Political Thought: Thomas Hobbes to J. S. Mill*, ed. James Crimmins. London: Routledge, 1989.

3. See Richard Ashcraft. "Faith and Knowledge in Locke's Philosophy." In *John Locke: Problems and Perspectives*, ed. John W. Yolton. Cambridge: Cambridge University Press, 1969; Yolton, *Locke*, p. 74–91; G. A. J. Rogers. "John Locke: Conservative Radical." In *Margins of Orthodoxy*, ed. Roger Lund, Cambridge: Cambridge University Press, 1995.

4. See John C. Higgins-Biddle. "Introduction." In *The Reasonableness of Christianity as Delivered in the Scriptures*, John Locke. Oxford: Clarendon Press, 1999, p. xxxvi.

5. See James Tully. *A Discourse on Property.* Cambridge: Cambridge University Press, 1980, p. 3–34. For a more radical interpretation of Locke on these lines, see Peter Myers. *Our Only Star and Compass: Locke and the Struggle for Political Rationality.* New York: Rowman & Littlefield, 1998, p. 67–135.

6. See Hans Aarsleff. "The State of Nature and the Nature of Man in Locke." In *Problems and Perspectives*, ed. Yolton; Raymond Polin. "John Locke's Conception of Freedom." In *Problems and Perspectives*, ed. Yolton; Tully, *Discourse*, p. 35–50; Yolton, *Locke*, p. 17–33; and Myers, *Our Only Star*, p. 137–77.

7. See Richard Ashcraft. "Anticlericalism and Authority in Lockean Political Thought." In *Margins of Orthodoxy*, ed. Roger Lund, Cambridge: Cambridge University Press, 1995; and Higgins-Biddle, "Introduction," p. xix.

8. See Nicholas Wolterstorff. *John Locke and the Ethics of Belief*. Cambridge: Cambridge University Press, 1996, esp. Preface and Introduction (p. ix–12).

9. For citations to this discussion, see David Owen's review of Wolterstorff's book in *The Locke Newsletter* 30 (1999): 103–27.

10. Two recent studies of the *Essay* clarifying this point are Nicholas Jolley. *Locke: His Philosophical Thought*. New York: Oxford University Press, 1999; and Wolterstorff, *Ethics of Belief*.

11. See Wolterstorff, *Ethics of Belief*, p. xvii–xix and 180–226, and Rogers, "Conservative Radical," p. 103–8.

12. See Leo Strauss. *Natural Right and History*. Chicago: University of Chicago Press, 1953, p. 212–14; see also Thomas Pangle. *The Spirit of Modern Republicanism*. Chicago: University of Chicago Press, 1988, p. 203 and 207; Michael Zuckert. "Locke and the Problem of Civil Religion." In *The American Founding: Essays on the Formation of the Constitution*, ed. J. Jackson Barlow, Leonard W. Levy, and Ken Masugi. United States: Greenwood Press, 1988, p. 113; Michael Rabieh. "The Reasonableness of Locke, or the Questionableness of Christianity." *The Journal of Politics* 53 (Nov. 1991): 933–57, p. 952 and Myers, *Our Only Star*, p. 44–5 and 47. Rahe writes that for Locke religion was not knowledge, and concludes from this that for Locke religion was "mere unsubstantiated belief" (Paul A. Rahe. *Republics Ancient and Modern: Classical Republicanism and the American Revolution*. Chapel Hill: University of North Carolina Press, 1992, p. 310). For other views, see Wolterstorff, *Ethics of Belief*; Ashcraft, "Faith and Knowledge"; and Stephen Williams. *Revelation and Reconciliation: A Window on Modernity*. New York: Cambridge University Press, 1995, p. 24–55.

13. Strauss, *Natural Right*, p. 212; see also E IV.18.4, 691.

14. Strauss, *Natural Right*, p. 212.

15. See J. R. Milton. "Locke's Life and Times." In *The Cambridge Companion to Locke*, ed. Vere Chappell. Cambridge: Cambridge University Press, 1994, p. 6.

16. See Milton, "Locke's Life," p. 10–11.

17. See *Revolutionary Politics and Locke's Two Treatises of Government*. Richard Ashcraft. Princeton, NJ: Princeton University Press, 1986, p. 109–10; and Nicholas Wolterstorff. "Locke's Philosophy of Religion." In *Cambridge Companion*, ed. Chappell, p. 174.

18. See Ashcraft, *Revolutionary Politics*, p. 94–5.

19. See Ashcraft, *Revolutionary Politics*, p. 105–6.

20. See also E IV.12.4 and IV.12.11, where Locke explains that "morality is the proper science, and business of mankind in general"; and Ashcraft, "Faith and Knowledge," p. 197. Locke is so emphatic about his moral purposes in the *Essay* that one can only wonder on what basis Rahe claims that

the *Essay* presents itself as having no moral agenda (see Rahe, *Republics*, p. 306–7).

21. See John Marshall. *John Locke: Resistance, Religion and Responsibility.* New York: Cambridge University Press, 1994, p. 355.

22. Cox and Zuckert portray this distinction as a sign of Locke's duplicity, arguing that "civil" discourse is for the ignorant masses who can't handle the truth (see Richard Cox. *Locke on War and Peace.* Oxford: Clarendon Press, 1960, p. 30; Michael Zuckert. "Of Wary Physicians and Weary Readers: The Debates on Locke's Way of Writing." *The Independent Journal of Philosophy* 2 (1978): 55–66, p. 58). However, the distinction arises from subject matter, not audience; one uses "philosophical" discourse in cases where linguistic precision is required, and "civil" discourse where it is not, regardless of whether one is speaking to a philosopher or a peasant.

23. See Wolterstorff, *Ethics of Belief,* p. 3, 232, and 244.

24. See W. M. Spellman. *John Locke.* New York: St. Martin's Press, 1997, p. 2.

25. See Wolterstorff, *Ethics of Belief,* p. 8.

26. See Wolterstorff, *Ethics of Belief,* p. 3, 221–4.

27. Locke maintained a formal distinction between "innate ideas" and "innate principles," but the distinction is not important for our present purposes so it is not strictly maintained here.

28. Yolton, *Locke,* p. 150.

29. See J. B. Schneewind. "Locke's Moral Philosophy." In *Cambridge Companion,* ed. Chappell, p. 221; and Roger Woolhouse. "Locke's Theory of Knowledge." In *Cambridge Companion,* ed. Chappell, p. 150.

30. See John W. Yolton. *John Locke and the Way of Ideas.* London: Oxford University Press, 1956, p. 26–71; and Marshall, *Resistance, Religion and Responsibility,* p. 292.

31. Rahe argues that this statement implies there is no duty to believe in any moral or religious proposition, and portrays it as an effort to sow doubt and mistrust about religion (see Rahe, *Republics,* p. 309). But it is only an insistence that beliefs not be held blindly. Locke's critique of total skepticism implies that we do have a duty to believe wherever good reasons can be shown for belief; this statement only emphasizes that good reasons must actually be shown before that duty applies. Rahe even asserts that this statement favors atheism over faith, but one can just as easily demand reasons to believe in atheism as to believe in religion.

32. Rahe and Myers take this as an argument against the evidentiary force of scripture (see Rahe, *Republics,* p. 311; and Myers, *Our Only Star,* p. 43). But many of the authors of scripture were personal eyewitnesses to the events they describe, so by Locke's rule their testimony is "a good proof." Locke was primarily attacking oral traditions, in particular Catholic claims regarding early church history (on Locke and oral traditions see Higgins-Biddle, "Introduction," p. xxii–xxiii).

33. See Jolley, *Philosophical Thought,* p. 37.

34. See Yolton, *Way of Ideas,* p. 86–98; and Vere Chappell. "Introduction." In *Cambridge Companion,* ed. Chappell, p. 26.

35. See Chappell, "Introduction," p. 28.

36. See Jolley, *Philosophical Thought*, p. 80–99.
37. See Plato. *Phaedo*. In *Euthyprho, Apology, Crito, Phaedo*, trans. Benjamin Jowett. New York: Prometheus Books, 1988.
38. On the importance of the afterlife in Locke's concept of moral law, see Aarsleff, "The State of Nature"; W. M. Spellman. *John Locke and the Problem of Depravity*. Oxford: Clarendon Press, 1988; Rabieh, "Reasonableness"; Marshall, *Resistance, Religion and Responsibility*; Spellman, *John Locke;* and Jolley, *Philosophical Thought*.
39. The reference is to I Corinthians 15:32.
40. Wootton includes "the immortality of the soul" in a list of subjects that "Locke passes over in silence" in the *Reasonableness* (Wootton, "Socinian," p. 47). In this assertion Wootton relies on the extremely fine distinction between immortality of the soul as such and eternal life more generally; Locke says nothing about the former in the *Reasonableness* but makes absolutely crucial arguments about the latter. Given the importance of the subject for Locke's system, one wishes Wootton had been more clear about this.
41. See Rogers, "Conservative Radical," p. 111 and 113.
42. Woolhouse, "Theory of Knowledge," p. 162.
43. Edwin McCann. "Locke's Philosophy of Body." In *Cambridge Companion*, ed. Chappell, p. 57.
44. McCann, "Philosophy of Body," p. 59.
45. See Polin, "Conception of Freedom"; and Jolley, *Philosophical Thought*, p. 123–42.
46. Jolley, *Philosophical Thought*, p. 125; see also p. 127.
47. See Jolley, *Philosophical Thought*, p. 143 and 155.
48. Jolley, *Philosophical Thought*, p. 144.
49. Francis Oakley. "Locke, Natural Law, and God – Again." *History of Political Thought* 18 (1997): 624–51, p. 636; see also p. 628.
50. The difference between "real essences" and "nominal essences" is important because Locke uses it to distinguish his idea of essences from the scholastic idea of essences, which defines the essence of an object in terms of its genus and species (see Jolley, *Philosophical Thought*, p. 155). While the scholastics thought they were talking about real essences, Locke believed the scholastic approach did not deal with the actual physical essences of objects but was just a series of debates over the definitions of words. He labels this kind of essence as a "nominal essence," distinguishing it from a "real essence." A nominal essence is just the essence of a word, which is its definition, whereas a real essence is the essence of the object itself rather than the essence of the word that describes it.

3: "The Candle of the Lord"

1. This image recurs regularly in many of Locke's works. It refers to Proverbs 20:27. On the use of this image in the *Essay* see S. P. Clark. "'The Whole Internal World His Own': Locke and Metaphor Reconsidered." *Journal of the History of Ideas* 59 (1998): 241–65, p. 259–63.

2. The most important contemporary criticisms of Locke's works are Edward Stillingfleet. *The Bishop of Worcester's Answer to Mr. Locke's Letter*. London: Printed by J. H. for Henry Mortlock, 1697; Edward Stillingfleet. *The Bishop of Worcester's Answer to Mr. Locke's Second Letter*. London: Printed by J. H. for Henry Mortlock, 1698; John Edwards. *Socinianism Unmask'd*. London: Printed for J. Robinson and J. Wyat, 1696; and John Edwards. *The Socinian Creed*. London: Printed for J. Robinson and J. Wyat, 1697. For more contemporary responses to the *Reasonableness*, see Victor Nuovo. *John Locke and Christianity: Contemporary Responses to* The Reasonableness of Christianity. Dulles, VA: Theommes Press, 1997. For details on Locke's exchanges with his critics, see W. M. Spellman. *John Locke and the Problem of Depravity*. Oxford: Clarendon Press, 1988; John Marshall. *John Locke: Resistance, Religion and Responsibility*. New York: Cambridge University Press, 1994; and John C. Higgins-Biddle. "Introduction." In *The Reasonableness of Christianity as Delivered in the Scriptures*, John Locke. Oxford: Clarendon Press, 1999.

3. On the deists' use of the *Essay* and Locke's other works, see Henning Reventlow. *The Authority of the Bible and the Rise of the Modern World*. U.K.: Fortress Press, 1985, p. 243–85; Spellman, *Problem of Depravity*, p. 211–12; Stephen Williams. *Revelation and Reconciliation: A Window on Modernity*. New York: Cambridge University Press, 1995, p. 44–53; and Higgins-Biddle, "Introduction," p. xv–xlii. For a brief history of deistic readings of the *Reasonableness*, see Higgins-Biddle, "Introduction," p. xxvii–xxxvii.

4. See E I.1.5, 45; I.4.12, 90; II.15.1, 196; II.18.7, 225; II.20.18, 233; II.21.56, 271; II.21.66, 278; II.23.13, 304; II.28.4, 351; III.5.14, 437; III.9.10, 481; III.9.22, 489; III.10.5, 493; III.10.12–13, 496–7; IV.2.14, 537; IV.10.1, 619; IV.11.3, 631; IV.11.8, 635; IV.12.11, 646; IV.20.3, 708; IV.20.6, 710; and IV.20.16, 717.

5. Some Straussians have read Locke as a relativist. See Leo Strauss. *Natural Right and History*. Chicago: University of Chicago Press, 1953, p. 229–30; Paul A. Rahe. *Republics Ancient and Modern: Classical Republicanism and the American Revolution*. Chapel Hill: University of North Carolina Press, 1992, p. 498; Michael Zuckert. "Of Wary Physicians and Weary Readers: The Debates on Locke's Way of Writing." *The Independent Journal of Philosophy* 2 (1978): 55–66, p. 84; Thomas Pangle. *The Spirit of Modern Republicanism*. Chicago: University of Chicago Press, 1988, p. 176–9 and 181; and Michael Zuckert. "An Introduction to Locke's First Treatise." *Interpretation* 8 (1979): 58–74, p. 71. All of these authors miss the distinction between moral ideas themselves and the relationships between moral ideas. The meanings of moral terms are set by human beings, but the relationships between those terms once they are defined are eternal truths made by God. These relationships, not the terms in which they are expressed, are the basis of moral law.

6. The draft chapter, "Of Ethics in General," examines the ethical implications of the psychological theory laid out in Book Two, a subject we will take up in Chapter 6. See Hans Aarsleff. "The State of Nature and the Nature of Man in Locke." In *John Locke: Problems and Perspectives*, ed. John W. Yolton. Cambridge: Cambridge University Press, 1969, p. 119–22; see also James Tully. *A Discourse on Property*. Cambridge: Cambridge University Press, 1980;

and Richard Ashcraft. *Locke's Two Treatises of Government.* London: Allen & Unwin, 1987.

7. Locke to Molyneux, Sept. 20, 1692 (vol. 4, no. 1538) and April 5, 1696 (vol. 5, no. 2059). In *The Correspondence of John Locke,* ed. E. S. De Beer. Oxford: Clarendon Press, 1978; see Spellman, *Problem of Depravity,* p. 127–8.

8. See Peter Laslett. "Introduction." In *Two Treatises of Government,* John Locke. Cambridge: Cambridge University Press, 1960, p. 79–92.

9. See Zuckert, "Wary Physicians," p. 64; Rahe, *Republics,* p. 296; Pangle, *Modern Republicanism,* p. 198; and Peter Myers. *Our Only Star and Compass: Locke and the Struggle for Political Rationality.* New York: Rowman & Littlefield, 1998, p. 25.

10. See John Dunn. *The Political Thought of John Locke.* New York: Cambridge University Press, 1969, p. 79–83, 94–5, and 187–90; and John Dunn. *Locke.* New York: Oxford University Press, 1984, p. 66–8, 84–5, and 88; see also Ruth W. Grant. *John Locke's Liberalism.* Chicago: University of Chicago Press, 1987, p. 21–6 and 198–9; and Steven Forde. "Natural Law, Theology, and Morality in Locke." *American Journal of Political Science* 45 (2001): 396–409, p. 400. Forde acknowledges that Locke's moral reasoning is more probabilistic than the demonstrative-morality reading would suggest.

11. See David Wootton. "John Locke: Socinian or Natural Law Theorist?" In *Religion, Secularization and Political Thought: Thomas Hobbes to J. S. Mill,* ed. James Crimmins. London: Routledge, 1989, p. 39, 50, and 54.

12. See Tully, *Discourse,* p. 8. Tully misapplies a quote from Yolton, mistakenly thinking that Yolton agrees with his reading of Locke's idea of demonstration (see John W. Yolton. *Locke and the Compass of Human Understanding.* Cambridge: Cambridge University Press, 1970, p. 92).

13. See John W. Yolton. *Locke: An Introduction.* Oxford: Basil Blackwell, Ltd., 1985, p. 41–3.

14. See Nicholas Wolterstorff. *John Locke and the Ethics of Belief.* Cambridge: Cambridge University Press, 1996.

15. Locke scholars unimpressed with Locke's proof of God include Wolterstorff and Dunn (see Nicholas Wolterstorff. "Locke's Philosophy of Religion." In *The Cambridge Companion to Locke,* ed. Vere Chappell. Cambridge: Cambridge University Press, 1994, p. 189; and Dunn, *Political Thought,* p. 21). However, neither of them actually argues that the cosmological proof is wrong; Wolterstorff only says that Locke's version of the proof is overly simple, while Dunn faults it not for any logical problems but for being coldly logical and passionless. See also Nicholas Jolley. *Locke: His Philosophical Thought.* New York: Oxford University Press, 1999, p. 97.

16. Locke's unfortunate lack of explicitness here leads Zuckert to assert that Locke's proof of God violates his own statement, made elsewhere, that we should not argue against the possible existence of a thing simply because we cannot conceive of that thing (see Zuckert, "An Introduction," p. 70). Locke does dramatically proclaim that something coming into existence out of nothing is inconceivable, but this is a literary flourish rather than a necessary component of his argument. Of more importance is Locke's claim that this axiom is an "intuitive certainty"; Book Four of the *Essay* provides a

detailed discussion of intuitive certainties that supports the reading outlined here over Zuckert's reading, as we will show.

17. See J. B. Schneewind. "Locke's Moral Philosophy." In *Cambridge Companion*, ed. Chappell. Dunn asserts that Locke simply assumed that once he had proven the existence of a God, he had proven the existence of the Christian God (see Dunn, *Political Thought*, p. 194; see also Dunn, *Locke*, p. 84). But Locke makes no such assumption; although the *Essay* does not take up this subject because it is outside the work's intended scope, for Locke it is the revelations of Jesus that establish that the God he has proven is in fact the Christian God. That is why he argues in the *Reasonableness* that the coming of Jesus was necessary to provide assurance of rewards and punishments in the afterlife (see R 245,182–5).

18. Francis Oakley. "Locke, Natural Law, and God – Again." *History of Political Thought* 18 (1997): 624–51, p. 631.

19. See Wootton, "Socinian," p. 42; see also Schneewind, "Moral Philosophy," p. 206–7.

20. See Oakley, "Again," esp. p. 633–51.

21. See also Richard Ashcraft. "Faith and Knowledge in Locke's Philosophy." In *Problems and Perspectives*, ed. Yolton, p. 214.

22. See Marshall, *Resistance, Religion and Responsibility*, p. 146.

23. Richard Ashcraft. "The Politics of Locke's *Two Treatises of Government*." In *John Locke's* Two Treatises of Government: *New Interpretations*, ed. Edward J. Harpham. Lawrence, KS: University Press of Kansas, 1992, p. 19; see also Ashcraft, *Locke's Two Treatises*, p. 36–7.

24. Marshall claims that on this point Locke's epistemology presumes that God is good to man, in that it presumes that God must have provided us with a way to find out what we need to know (see Marshall, *Resistance, Religion and Responsibility*, p. 146). Locke does presume that God would have a will for us to follow and would communicate it to us, and while he does sometimes remark that God has been good to us in communicating his will to us, God's goodness need not be the basis of the presumption that he has communicated his will. This presumption is highly plausible even if we do not assume God is good to us, provided we are certain that God exists and created us. God must have some kind of will for us or he wouldn't have created us in the first place, and that creation would be in vain if God didn't communicate his will.

25. Jolley, *Philosophical Thought*, p. 21.

26. Wolterstorff, *Ethics of Belief*, p. 167.

27. Wolterstorff, *Ethics of Belief*, p. 172.

28. Wolterstorff, *Ethics of Belief*, p. 246.

29. Wolterstorff, *Ethics of Belief*, p. 82.

30. One possible implication of this doctrine, reflected in some of Locke's other works and privately expressed opinions, is that some parts of scripture may not be divinely inspired, depending on just how far the scope of authority conferred by miracles extends. Locke expressed concern that any distinction between scripture that is or is not inspired must be drawn with great scholarly care and in a spirit of deep humility before God. Nonetheless, while he always firmly upheld the stories of the lives of Jesus and the apostles in the

gospel accounts and the book of Acts as God's divine word, he entertained the possibility that the apostolic epistles were not of divine authority (see Marshall, *Resistance, Religion and Responsibility*, p. 340). This produces a problem for moral consensus insofar as it opens the door to undermining all of scripture, and hence removing the religious belief necessary to sustain moral consensus. If the power to perform miracles does not convey God's endorsement on all the teachings delivered by the miracle worker, it is hard to see on what grounds some can be rejected and others accepted. But Christians who adopt an epistemology based on miraclulous evidence need not follow Locke to this conclusion. The overwhelming majority of Christian thinkers in history have concluded that this argument is mistaken even on its own premises – the parts of the Bible that Locke accepts as God's word endorse the conclusion that all of the Bible is God's word.

31. Wolterstorff, *Ethics of Belief*, p. 132–3.

32. Rabieh takes Locke's lack of precision in specifying how to distinguish true miracles as evidence of insincerity, but in Locke's system this is a matter of judgment and simply cannot be systematized in the way Rabieh demands (see Michael Rabieh. "The Reasonableness of Locke, or the Questionableness of Christianity." *The Journal of Politics* 53 (Nov. 1991): 933–57, p. 937).

33. Rabieh says that acceptance of miracles in Locke's system is "provisional," and that reason cannot "rely on" miracles (see Rabieh, "Reasonableness," p. 951). It should be clear from the foregoing analysis that this is a serious misrepresentation of Locke's epistemology.

34. John Locke. *A Discourse of Miracles*. In *The Reasonableness of Christianity*, with *A Discourse of Miracles* and part of *A Third Letter Concerning Toleration*. ed. I. T. Ramsey. Stanford, CA: Stanford University Press, 1958, p. 80.

35. Zuckert and Rabieh argue that Locke mentions this incident to show why his outward epistemology of miracles cannot work (see Rabieh, "Reasonableness," p. 950; and Michael Zuckert. "Locke and the Problem of Civil Religion." In *The American Founding: Essays on the Formation of the Constitution*, ed. J. Jackson Barlow, Leonard W. Levy, and Ken Masugi. United States: Greenwood Press, 1988, p. 111). Zuckert also makes a similar argument for Locke's mentioning Emperor Julian, who rejected Christianity. But since accepting a miracle as genuine is a matter of judgment, it is inevitable that some will judge incorrectly; this does not disprove the epistemological efficacy of miracles. Furthermore, this weakness could be observed in any theologian who relies on miracles, of whom there have been quite a few whose religious sincerity is not questioned. There is also an alternative explanation for Locke's having mentioned Julian in the *Reasonableness*: as Higgins-Biddle points out, in Locke's time Julian's apostasy from Christianity was being used as an example of why governments should not have authority over religious matters (see Higgins-Biddle, "Introduction," p. 146, note 4). Although the subject of toleration is not taken up in the *Reasonableness*, Locke surely approved of that argument and may have been alluding to it.

36. Locke, *A Discourse of Miracles*, p. 82.

37. Reventlow draws a line between "rational" and "authoritative" arguments in Locke's works, identifying scriptural arguments with the latter and arguing

that Locke's appeal to scripture represents the failure of his "rational" arguments (see Reventlow, *Authority of the Bible*, p. 259 and 268). But Locke sees nothing irrational about relying upon God's authority; to do so is the height of rationality. Rabieh writes that Locke must be incoherent if he is serious about reconciling rationalism and faith; this simply rules out Locke's whole argument by unjustified fiat (see Rabieh, "Reasonableness," p. 938). Wootton does much the same thing (see Wootton, "Socinian," p. 62).

38. Forde cheats by quoting only half of this statement ("reason is natural revelation") without mentioning the other half, which makes Locke appear to endorse a natural theology over revelation when he in fact does not (see Forde, "Natural Law," p. 399).

39. See Strauss, *Natural Right*, p. 205; see also Richard Cox. *Locke on War and Peace*. Oxford: Clarendon Press, 1960, p. 42–3 and 45; and David Foster. "The Bible and Natural Freedom in John Locke's Political Thought." In *Piety and Humanity*, ed. Douglas Kries. United States: Rowman & Littlefield, 1997, p. 195 and 201.

40. Strauss, *Natural Right*, p. 212.

41. See Strauss, *Natural Right*, p. 214.

42. See Strauss, *Natural Right*, p. 202. The root of Strauss's mistake here is his incorrect assertion that for Locke a law is not a "natural law" unless it is discernable without revelation. He justifies this by referring to a line in the *Essay* in which Locke affirms the existence of "a law, knowable by the light of nature; i.e. without the help of positive revelation" (E I.3.13, 75). Strauss, in the course of jumbling together phrases drawn from over a dozen different places in Locke's writings, incorrectly uses this passage to assert that Locke wrote that the natural law is "knowable by the light of nature, i.e. without the help of positive revelation." He later appeals to this when showing that Locke does not make out the natural law independent of revelation because only revelation can provide an account of rewards and punishments in the afterlife (see Strauss, *Natural Right*, p. 212). But in the original passage, Locke says only that there is "a law" known to natural reason, not that the natural law is known to natural reason, and still less that the natural law includes *only* laws known to natural reason. In a different part of the passage Locke also affirms that there is "a law of nature," and the tone of the passage does suggest that there is some relationship between the law of nature and the aforementioned law that is discernable by natural reason alone, but nowhere does Locke suggest that "a law of nature" and "a law, knowable by the light of nature" are two different ways of saying exactly the same thing, such that a law is not a natural law unless it is known exclusively through natural reason. Since Strauss's method requires us to pay close attention to exact word choices, it forbids using this passage the way Strauss uses it. For Locke "natural law," or "law of nature," simply means the eternal moral law of God, whether known through natural reason or through revelation (see for example R 14, 9).

43. See Dale Kuehne. "Reinventing Paul: John Locke, the Geneva Bible, and Paul's *Epistle to the Romans*." In *Piety and Humanity*, ed. Kries, p. 226.

44. On this point see Higgins-Biddle, "Introduction," p. xxxiii–xxxv.

45. Clark reads this passage and others like it as celebrations of, rather than heavily sarcastic criticisms of, enthusiasm (see Clark, "Internal World," p. 264). This reading not only ignores the heavy sarcasm of Locke's prose, it also has the effect of pulling down the entire epistemological edifice of the *Essay*.

4: "The Only Foundation of Faith"

1. Peter H. Nidditch. "Introduction." In *An Essay Concerning Human Understanding.* John Locke. Oxford: Clarendon Press, 1975, p. xvi.
2. John Locke. *The Works of John Locke,* third edition. London: A. Bettesworth, E. Parker, J. Pemberton, and E. Symon, 1727, vol. 2, p. 558.
3. See Dewey D. Wallace, Jr. "Socinianism, Justification by Faith, and the Sources of John Locke's *The Reasonableness of Christianity.*" In *John Locke: Critical Assessments,* ed. Richard Ashcraft, vol. 2, New York: Routledge, 1991, p. 166 and 169–74.
4. John C. Higgins-Biddle. "Introduction." In *The Reasonableness of Christianity as Delivered in the Scriptures,* John Locke. Oxford: Clarendon Press, 1999, p. xvii.
5. Samuel C. Pearson. "The Religion of John Locke and the Character of His Thought." In *Critical Assessments,* ed. Ashcraft, vol. 2, p. 142.
6. Locke, *Works,* 1727 edition, vol. 2, p. 559.
7. John Toland. *Christianity Not Mysterious.* London, 1696; Matthew Tindal. *Christianity as Old as the Creation: Or, the Gospel, a Republication of the Religion of Nature.* London, 1731.
8. On the deists and the *Reasonableness* see Higgins-Biddle, "Introduction," p. xv–xlii. Higgins-Biddle recounts how Locke later admitted that his argument could not stand if the accuracy of scripture was denied (see p. xxxvi).
9. See John Marshall. *John Locke: Resistance, Religion and Responsibility.* New York: Cambridge University Press, 1994, p. 389.
10. Higgins-Biddle, "Introduction," p. lxviii.
11. Marshall argues that Locke was probably a unitarian, in particular because of a unitarian manuscript that may have been written by Locke (see Marshall, *Resistance, Religion and Responsibility,* p. 384–451, esp. 418–24). Higgins-Biddle objects to this conclusion (see Higgins-Biddle, "Introduction," p. xii–xxiv, esp. xviii–xix). He points out that after William's 1696 order, even some people who affirmed the Trinity were persecuted for explaining it in the wrong way, and thus Locke may have believed in the Trinity but avoided commenting on the subject in public for political reasons (see p. lxviii). Obviously to side with Higgins-Biddle here we must believe that the unitarian manuscript described by Marshall was not Locke's, although the evidence for Locke's authorship seems strong. At the very least, Locke was intensely interested in unitarianism; he acquired and read many books on the subject (both trinitarian and unitarian), and he conversed and corresponded with numerous unitarians. It is also possible that Locke avoided professing an opinion on the Trinity because he was in a state of uncertainty about it, and held whatever opinion he held about it at a low degree of assent. Certainly his lifelong intellectual emphasis on respecting the limits of human

knowledge could have made him reluctant to hold firmly to any opinion on a matter so far above the powers of human understanding. On another note, if Marshall is right and Locke was indeed a closet unitarian, or if he was at least doubtful about the Trinity, a desire not to be persecuted may not have been his only motive for concealing his beliefs. In some unpublished statements, Locke declares that there is no moral duty to promulgate one's opinions if they are radical and could have dangerous social consequences, particularly if those opinions are uncertain (see G. A. J. Rogers. "John Locke: Conservative Radical." In *Margins of Orthodoxy*, ed. Roger Lund, Cambridge: Cambridge University Press, 1995, p. 110 and 112). Zuckert takes these as hints of insincerity in Locke's endorsement of Christianity (see Michael Zuckert. "Of Wary Physicians and Weary Readers: The Debates on Locke's Way of Writing." *The Independent Journal of Philosophy* 2 (1978): 55–66, p. 56), but closet unitarianism or doubts about the Trinity are a much more obvious explanation.

12. See Marshall, *Resistance, Religion and Responsibility*, p. 347.
13. See W. M. Spellman. *John Locke and the Problem of Depravity*. Oxford: Clarendon Press, 1988, p. 84 and Higgins-Biddle, "Introduction," p. lxx–lxxiv. Wootton appeals to the consensus view that Locke was Socinian in order to attribute to Locke certain Socinian intellectual positions that Locke did not in fact hold (see David Wootton. "John Locke: Socinian or Natural Law Theorist?" In *Religion, Secularization and Political Thought: Thomas Hobbes to J. S. Mill*, ed. James Crimmins. London: Routledge, 1989).
14. Locke, *Works*, 1727 edition, vol. 2, p. 558.
15. John Locke. *The Correspondence of John Locke*, ed. E. S. De Beer. Oxford: Clarendon Press, 1978, vol. V, letter 1901.
16. See R 58, 35-6; 62, 39–40; 76–8, 50–51; 82, 52–3; 95, 60; 101, 63; 111, 73; 115–16, 76–7; 143–5, 101–4; 162, 122; 237, 164–5; and 240, 168–9.
17. See also John 2:11 and 2:23.
18. See also Luke 7:19–23.
19. See also John 10:25.
20. See also John 20:31.
21. Rabieh argues that here Locke violates his own stated rule that scripture must be read by the meaning that each word would have had in its original time and place – by this rule, argues Rabieh, Jesus' claim to be "the Messiah" must be read as a claim to be a temporal liberator, since that is what the Jews meant by that term, so Locke is secretly showing us that the Christian interpretation of "Messiah" is really an attempt to cope with Jesus' failure to serve as a temporal liberator (see Michael Rabieh. "The Reasonableness of Locke, or the Questionableness of Christianity." *The Journal of Politics* 53 (Nov. 1991): 933–57, p. 950, note 14). This is a misapplication of Locke's rule for reading scripture. Locke's touchstone for the meaning of words in scripture is not the definition used by the majority – in this case the Jews – in the original time and place, but the intended meaning of the speaker – in this case Jesus – understood in the context of the original time and place (see R 1, 2). Since Jesus clearly communicated that the Jews were mistaken in their understanding of the term "Messiah," Locke's rule not only allows

us to read Jesus' claim to be the Messiah in the way Locke does, it positively requires this reading.

22. Strauss and some of his followers have tried to portray Locke's story of Jesus' "concealment" and "reservedness" as a hint from Locke that Locke is carrying on an elaborate charade of his own (see Leo Strauss. *Natural Right and History*. Chicago: University of Chicago Press, 1953, p. 208; Richard Cox. *Locke on War and Peace*. Oxford: Clarendon Press, 1960, p. 30; Paul A. Rahe. *Republics Ancient and Modern: Classical Republicanism and the American Revolution*. Chapel Hill: University of North Carolina Press, 1992, p. 301; for a brief opposing view see Henning Reventlow. *The Authority of the Bible and the Rise of the Modern World*. U.K.: Fortress Press, 1985, p. 263–4). But this gets it backwards: in Locke's story, the sole purpose of Jesus' concealment was to sustain his complete and unmistakable innocence, so that his death would be a perfect martyrdom. He did not want to actually deceive anyone; on the contrary, as Locke shows, he went out of his way to make it quite obvious to everyone that he was the Messiah (Locke's choice of the word "concealment" unfortunately tends to obscure this element of his account). The Straussian view of Locke is the reverse of this – that Locke practiced concealment not to keep himself innocent but to commit a great historic crime, namely the destruction of traditional religion, and that Locke wanted to deceive all but a privileged few about his true intentions. If anything, Locke's account of Jesus' mission of innocence and truth stands in stark contrast to Strauss's account of Locke's alleged mission of subversion and deception.

23. See also Luke 4:41 and Mark 3:11–12.

24. See also Mark 8:27–30.

25. Due to the importance of the point and the brevity and hyperbole of Locke's statements, this passage has become something of a touchstone for Straussian critics seeking to show that Locke's embrace of Christianity is insincere (see Strauss, *Natural Right*, p. 210–12; Rabieh, "Reasonableness," p. 949–51; Michael Zuckert. "Locke and the Problem of Civil Religion." In *The American Founding: Essays on the Formation of the Constitution*, ed. J. Jackson Barlow, Leonard W. Levy, and Ken Masugi. United States: Greenwood Press, 1988, p. 111; Peter Myers. *Our Only Star and Compass: Locke and the Struggle for Political Rationality*. New York: Rowman & Littlefield, 1998, p. 44; and Steven Forde. "Natural Law, Theology, and Morality in Locke." *American Journal of Political Science* 45 (2001): 396–409, p. 406). However – in addition to the argument made here for a sincere interpretation – the Straussian reading is inconsistent with the brazen and obvious inaccuracy of Locke's statements, to which the Straussians themselves appeal. If, as the Straussians argue, it is (and was for Locke's audience) flagrantly wrong to say that no one has ever denied Jesus' miracles, then such a statement cannot be a key to a special, concealed understanding that only a few careful and attentive readers would notice. No doubt an esoteric writer must leave clues that are not too subtle, lest even attentive readers should miss them, but he must also refrain from leaving clues that are too obvious if he wants to keep his esoteric writing esoteric. It strains credibility to argue that Locke carefully concealed his real teaching in all his published works, covering perhaps thousands of pages of

delicately constructed esoteric writing, leaving only subtle, indirect clues of his real intentions for attentive readers to find, and then left a clue so flamboyantly obvious that even the most careless, inattentive reader couldn't help but stop and take notice of it. What, then, was the point of all that painstaking deception?

26. Particularly awful is Locke's deployment in the *Letter* of what were, in his time, crude stereotypes of Catholics (see Richard Ashcraft. *Revolutionary Politics and Locke's* Two Treatises of Government. Princeton, NJ: Princeton University Press, 1986, p. 498).

27. On the historical accuracy of these events, considered separately from the authenticity of the miracles, it is worth noting that in the *Essay* Locke used historical facts as an example of beliefs that can be so certain that they effectively pass for knowledge, proving that the distinction is not always important. He points out, for example, that no one doubts that there was once a man named Julius Ceasar, despite our lack of any evidence for his existence other than the word of historians (see E IV.16.8, 662; see also Higgins-Biddle, "Introduction," p. cxiii, note 1).

28. See N. T. Wright. *The Resurrection of the Son of God.* U.K.: Fortress Press, 2003.

29. On Locke's account in the *Essay* of the duty to read ancient texts carefully, and the problems of language Locke says a careful reader must be conscious of, see Marshall, *Resistance, Religion and Responsibility*, p. 353–5.

30. Harris, without supporting argument, accuses Locke of choosing this literalistic method of interpretation because it best serves his political agenda of refuting absolutism (see Ian Harris. "The Politics of Christianity." In *Locke's Philosophy: Content and Contexts*, ed. G. A. J. Rogers. New York: Oxford University Press, 1994, p. 202). Harris does not address the possibility that Locke's political agenda might have arisen from his religious beliefs, including his reading of scripture, rather than vice versa. Certainly the epistemology laid out at such length in the *Essay* provides ample support for Locke's interpretive method independent of its political ramifications.

31. See Spellman, *Problem of Depravity*, p. 136 (note 28).

32. John Locke. *Paraphrase and Notes on the Epistles of St. Paul*, ed. Arthur W. Wainwright. Oxford: Clarendon Press, 1987, p. 115. In the preface to the *Paraphrase* Locke lays out his system of scriptural exegesis in more detail than he does in the *Reasonableness*, but it is recognizably the same system. Straussians have portrayed Locke's comments on exegesis in the *Paraphrase* as a description of how to look for hidden, ironic meanings in texts (see Cox, *War and Peace*, p. 29, and Zuckert, "Wary Physicians," p. 57). But Locke's argument is that the meaning of scripture, at least on the most important subjects, is clear and accessible to all, requiring only a sufficient grasp of the language and history. He does discuss the need to read carefully and pay attention to word choices, but his rationale is that this is necessary to prevent our many prejudices and predispositions from blinding us to the otherwise open and unconcealed meaning of the text.

33. In this section of the *Reasonableness* Locke critiques the traditional Christian doctrine of imputed guilt, which holds that all human beings are not only guilty of their own sin but are also guilty (in a different way) of Adam's sin,

since Adam was the federal representative of humanity before God under the covenant of works. We need not review this critique at length here, but two things ought to be said about it. First, it is not integral to Locke's epistemology, theology, or politics in any way, so we need not adopt it as part of his theory of moral consensus. Second, and more importantly, scholars have seriously distorted Locke's critique of imputed guilt in ways that make it look much more radical than it actually is. Locke affirms that there was a fall of humanity as described in Genesis, and that all people are sinners who need salvation. The first sentence of the *Reasonableness* is: "It is obvious to anyone who reads the New Testament that the doctrine of redemption, and consequently the gospel, is founded upon the supposition of Adam's fall" (R 1,1). He affirms that all human beings, "having sinned, come short of the glory of God" (Romans 3:23; R 12, 9). As we will see in detail in Chapter 6, his account of the human will in the *Two Treatises* reflects a strong account of human depravity. Locke denies *imputed* guilt, not guilt itself. Foster portrays Locke's skepticism toward the traditional doctrine of original sin as a sign of his denial of Christianity, but this stretches it well beyond what Locke actually claims. Particularly puzzling is Foster's strange assertion that Locke doesn't believe in the fall because he believes that Adam and Eve ate food in the garden of Eden (see David Foster. "The Bible and Natural Freedom in John Locke's Political Thought." In *Piety and Humanity*, ed. Douglas Kries. United States: Rowman & Littlefield, 1997, p. 201–2). At Genesis 2:16, God explicitly gives Adam permission to eat from any tree in the garden other than the tree of knowledge. On Locke and original sin see Spellman, *Problem of Depravity*, p. 2–3, 56–7, 104–5, and 203, and Marshall, *Resistance, Religion and Responsibility*, p. 134–5, 145, and 433.

34. See also Romans 3:23.

35. Pangle asserts that Locke says people have a right to immortality and bliss, but the logic of Locke's case implies that only a perfectly just person would have such a right, and no such person has ever existed (see Thomas Pangle. *The Spirit of Modern Republicanism*. Chicago: University of Chicago Press, 1988, p. 146–7). Rabieh avoids this confusion in his treatment of the subject, but makes a different mistake; Locke, contrary to Rabieh's assertions, says that perfect justice entitles a person to eternal life but not that it entitles him to eternal life on earth, as opposed to in heaven (see Rabieh, "Reasonableness," p. 948, note 12). Rabieh also implausibly asserts that because no one would go to heaven without salvation, Locke's account of salvation makes God and Jesus appear as mercenary, self-interested actors who offer salvation only because that is the only way they can have any souls to rule over in heaven (see p. 953–5). If so, all Christianity is equally guilty of this mercenary worldview, since it was Christ himself who taught that no one goes to heaven without salvation.

36. See also John 20:31.

37. Describing justification through the covenant of grace in these terms diverges in some ways from the views that were dominant among Protestants in Locke's time, but is solidly within the ambit of Anglican Latitudinarianism, and in some ways less radical than what other Latitudinarians were saying at that

time (see Wallace, "Socinianism," p. 169 and 174). It is consistent with the Calvinist understanding of justification as well.

38. Locke is clearer on this point in his private manuscripts, where he affirms that Christ's death was a "payment" for human sin, that it "satisfied" God's justice, and that it was "a full and satisfactory ransom for our sins" (see Higgins-Biddle, "Introduction," p. lxxii).

39. See Higgins-Biddle, "Introduction," p. li and lxxi.

40. On reaction to the *Reasonableness*, see Nuovo, *Locke and Christianity*; Spellman, *Problem of Depravity*; and Higgins-Biddle, "Introduction"; see also Marshall, *Resistance, Religion and Responsibility*, p. 384–451.

41. See John 4:1–26 and 4:39–42.

42. See Luke 23:39–43.

43. See John 20:31 and 1 John 5:1.

44. C. S. Lewis. *Mere Christianity*. San Francisco: HarperCollins, 1952, p. 54.

45. See Higgins-Biddle, "Introduction," p. li.

46. Pangle asserts that Locke denies the presence of a rich, complex theory in the Bible (see Pangle, *Modern Republicanism*, p. 153); however, Locke only separates the simple, necessary theory from the complex, required-but-not-necessary theory.

47. See Higgins-Biddle, "Introduction," xliv–xlvi. Once the point was laid out so explicitly in the *Second Vindication*, even Edwards, who was willfully blind to much of the nuance and subtlety of the *Reasonableness*, was forced to acknowledge it.

48. *The Works of John Locke*, London, 1823, reissued Aalen: Scientia, 1963; vol. 7, p. 352.

49. See Higgins-Biddle, "Introduction," p. lxxiv–lxxviii. In a curious lacuna, Strauss and his followers have paid almost no attention to this similarity between Locke and Hobbes, even while building arguments on other points of similarity between their theologies that are both less clear cut and less philosophically important.

50. Thomas Hobbes. *Leviathan*. Cambridge: Cambridge University Press, 1991, chapter 43, paragraph 11, p. 407.

51. See Higgins-Biddle, "Introduction," p. lxxv–lxxvii. Strauss implies that any competent political and theological commentator in the late seventeenth century must have read both Hobbes and Spinoza (see Strauss, *Natural Right*, p. 211). This imposes an anachronistic standard of competence. Hobbes and Spinoza may be permanent landmarks of seventeenth century thought to us, their greatness having become obvious, but given the overwhelming disrepute in which those thinkers stood in the seventeenth century itself there is no reason to assume that every competent commentator of that era would have read them.

52. See Higgins-Biddle, "Introduction," p. lxi–lxv, lxxviii, and lxxx.

53. Higgins-Biddle, "Introduction," p. lxii.

54. Higgins-Biddle, "Introduction," p. lxxviii.

55. Higgins-Biddle, "Introduction," p. lxiii; see also Jeremy Taylor. *A Discourse on the Liberty of Prophesying*. London, 1647. Even after having been accused of following Hobbes's theology, Locke declared that not only had he never read

Hobbes's argument on that point before, he had no intention of looking it up even after having been accused of following it, such was his disdain for that author. The detractor who had accused Locke of following Hobbes accepted Locke's word on this point, and asked his readers to accept it as well (see Higgins-Biddle, "Introduction," p. lxxvi).

56. Thus, Locke refutes the view that Christianity is an inherently violent religion, which Rahe attempts to attribute to him (see Rahe, *Republics*, p. 300).

57. On Locke's forgiving view of "error" see Marshall, *Resistance, Religion and Responsibility*, p. 443–4.

58. Rahe misunderstands this point when he writes that Locke puts works ahead of faith (see Rahe, *Republics*, p. 304). Repentance is entailed by faith, since we cannot claim to have faith in Jesus if we don't repent as he commanded us to.

59. Pangle argues that repentance does not entail guilt for Locke (see Pangle, *Modern Republicanism*, p. 155); one wonders how Pangle can read the phrase "sorrow for sins past" as not entailing guilt.

60. See also "sincere obedience" at R 213, 149; and Marshall, *Resistance, Religion and Responsibility*, p. 454–5.

61. See Wallace, "Socinianism," p. 171–5.

62. On the specifically Christian nature of the duty of toleration, see Marshall, *Resistance, Religion and Responsibility*, p. 367–70.

63. These would have been recognizable to Locke's audience as stereotypes of the Catholic Church (see Ashcraft, *Revolutionary Politics*, p. 498). No doubt one of Locke's less respectable rhetorical purposes here was to associate persecution with Catholicism, which was widely despised in England. However, Locke does not explicitly link these qualities to the Catholic Church, and we have no reason to believe that Locke's disdain did not extend equally to all intolerant churches – in attacking such churches he includes those who brag about "the reformation of their discipline," a clear reference to Calvinists, as well as those who brag about "the antiquity of places and names, or of the pomp of their outward worship" (see L 1, 13).

5: "The Only True Touchstone of Moral Rectitude"

1. Eisenach portrays Locke as a supporter of compartmentalization (see Eldon Eisenach. *Two Worlds of Liberalism*. Chicago: University of Chicago Press, 1992, p. 2, 74, 77, 82–3, 88, 92, 96, and 110–11). Eisenach associates religion exclusively with inward beliefs. Locke does hold that inward beliefs are beyond the scope of government's competence, but for him religion has a role to play beyond inward beliefs; moral laws governing external behavior are necessary to politics and must be derived from religious reasoning, so for Locke religion can never be separated from politics.

2. See Stephen L. Carter. *The Culture of Disbelief: How American Law and Politics Trivialize Religious Devotion*. New York: Basic Books, 1993; Stephen L. Carter. *God's Name in Vain: The Wrongs and Rights of Religion in Politics*. New York: Basic Books, 2000; and E. J. Dionne and John J. DiIulio. *What's God Got to Do with the American Experiment?: Essays on Religion and Politics*. Washington, DC: Brookings Institution Press, 2000. For outright repudiations of

compartmentalization, see Robert Bork. *Slouching Towards Gomorrah.* New York: Regan Books, 1996; and Robert P. George. *In Defense of Natural Law.* Oxford: Clarendon Press, 1999.

3. See Richard Ashcraft. *Revolutionary Politics and Locke's* Two Treatises of Government. Princeton, NJ: Princeton University Press, 1986, p. 503; and John Marshall. *John Locke: Resistance, Religion and Responsibility.* New York: Cambridge University Press, 1994, p. 110–11.

4. See, for example, Henning Reventlow. *The Authority of the Bible and the Rise of the Modern World.* U.K.: Fortress Press, 1985, p. 277; and W. M. Spellman. *John Locke and the Problem of Depravity.* Oxford: Clarendon Press, 1988, p. 129.

5. On the essential unity of the *Essay*, the *Reasonableness*, and the *Discourse of Miracles*, see Samuel C. Pearson. "The Religion of John Locke and the Character of His Thought." In *John Locke: Critical Assessments*, ed. Richard Ashcraft. New York: Routledge, 1991, p. 142.

6. See Francis Oakley. "Locke, Natural Law, and God – Again." *History of Political Thought* 18 (1997): 624–51, p. 628–33, 635–6, 640, and 642–4. James Tully describes Locke's position as a "compromise" between voluntarism and intellectualism because he says that we know God's law through reason but it is obligatory because it is God's will (James Tully. *A Discourse on Property.* Cambridge: Cambridge University Press, 1980, p. 41). This is an accurate summary of Locke's view, but, as Oakley argues, the "voluntarist" label applies to any thinker who holds the latter position. Locke might best be described as a voluntarist with an unusually high opinion of reason.

7. Oakley, "Again," p. 628.

8. Nicholas Wolterstorff. *John Locke and the Ethics of Belief.* Cambridge: Cambridge University Press, 1996, p. 138. Wolterstorff calls this a "deep fissure" in Locke's moral philosophy; for his part, Locke is more sanguine about paradoxes than Wolterstorff seems to be.

9. See John Locke. *The Correspondence of John Locke*, ed. E. S. De Beer. Oxford: Clarendon Press, 1978, vol. IV, letter 1592; see also Marshall, *Resistance, Religion and Responsibility*, p. 131 and E IV.17.10 (p. 682).

10. Oakley, "Again," p. 635.

11. See Richard Ashcraft. *Locke's Two Treatises of Government.* London: Allen & Unwin, 1987, p. 39–41.

12. See Marshall, *Resistance, Religion and Responsibility*, p. 454.

13. John W. Yolton. "Locke on the Law of Nature." In *Critical Assesments*, ed. Ashcraft, p. 22.

14. See John C. Biddle. "Locke's Critique of Innate Principles and Toland's Deism." *Journal of the History of Ideas* 37 (1976): 418–21; see also John C. Higgins-Biddle. "Introduction." In *The Reasonableness of Christianity as Delivered in the Scriptures.* Oxford: Clarendon Press, 1999, p. xv–xllii.

15. Locke also writes in this section that the morality revealed by the Christian faith is perfectly rational, in that once it is revealed reason can see its reasonableness, although reason was too weak to work out the same morality on its own (see, for example, R 241, 171). This implicitly reaffirms that faith for Locke must be rational faith; otherwise there would be no reason to hold our interpretations of revelation to a standard of reasonableness.

16. Eisenach, *Two Worlds*, p. 86.

17. It is interesting that Locke omits Plato and Aristotle from this list. No doubt he left out Plato because of his belief that Plato had rationally deduced the existence of a single supreme God and had sought morality in that God (see, for example, E IV.12.4, 642), although he thought that ultimately Plato failed to ground his moral theory in God's will (see, for example, R 238, 166; and 243, 176–7). Plato would therefore be a problem case here; no doubt Locke wanted to stick with more clear-cut examples of philosophers who did not have any place for God in their moral theory. The case of Aristotle is less clear. In the *Essay* Locke praises Aristotle but condemns at length the scholastic philosophy pursued in Aristotle's name (see, for example, E IV.17.4, 671). Perhaps Locke just wanted to avoid the distraction of opening up that particular can of worms yet again in the *Reasonableness*.

18. Strauss, Zuckert, and Rahe portray this reading of Plato as yet another hint from Locke that he is concealing his true doctrine about God (see Leo Strauss. *Natural Right and History*. Chicago: University of Chicago Press, 1953, p. 208; Michael Zuckert. "Locke and the Problem of Civil Religion." In *The American Founding: Essays on the Formation of the Constitution*, ed. J. Jackson Barlow, Leonard W. Levy, and Ken Masugi. United States: Greenwood Press, 1988, p. 107–8; and Paul A. Rahe, *Republics Ancient and Modern: Classical Republicanism and the American Revolution*. Chapel Hill: University of North Carolina Press, 1992, p. 301). But, as with Locke's account of Jesus' concealment, Locke does not depict Plato as actually deceiving anyone or constructing a false doctrine, as Strauss and Rahe depict Locke doing. Rather, Locke depicts Plato judiciously holding back his beliefs on a certain topic as opposed to actually professing beliefs he does not hold. This is much the same thing Locke may have done with any doubts he had regarding the Trinity. He never lied about these doubts, if he had them; he just didn't publicize them. And in the case of Plato there is this additional fact: Locke does not give us the impression that he approves of Plato's concealment!

19. See also Acts 17:22. Some translators do not attribute to Paul a pejorative attitude toward the Athenians in the speech Locke quotes, and interpret Paul's words simply as an observation that the Athenians, although ignorant of the true religion of Christianity, devote much attention to divine matters (one translation gives us "in all things you are very religious"). But Locke, who was a formidable scholar of biblical languages, endorses the pejorative interpretation that prevailed in his day, and furthermore he clearly agrees with what he takes to be Paul's low opinion of the ancient Athenians.

6: "'Tis Reasonable to Think the Cause Is Natural"

1. John Dunn. *The Political Thought of John Locke*. New York: Cambridge University Press, 1969, p. 24.
2. See Hans Aarsleff. "The State of Nature and the Nature of Man in Locke." In *John Locke: Problems and Perspectives*, ed. John W. Yolton. Cambridge: Cambridge University Press, 1969, p. 105.

3. Rabieh invests a great deal in the idea that Locke's psychology is "mercenary" (see Michael Rabieh. "The Reasonableness of Locke, or the Questionableness of Christianity." *The Journal of Politics* 53 (Nov. 1991): 933–57, p. 948).
4. See John Locke. "Some Thoughts Concerning Education." In *Some Thoughts Concerning Education* and *Of the Conduct of the Understanding,* ed. Grant and Tarcov; see also W. M. Spellman. *John Locke.* New York: St. Martin's Press, 1997, p. 79–97.
5. W. M. Spellman. *John Locke and the Problem of Depravity.* Oxford: Clarendon Press, 1988, p. 119–20.
6. Spellman, *The Problem of Depravity,* p. 193.
7. Spellman, *The Problem of Depravity,* p. 120.
8. Leo Strauss. *Natural Right and History.* Chicago: University of Chicago Press, 1953, p. 227 and 250; see also Richard Cox. *Locke on War and Peace.* Oxford: Clarendon Press, 1960, p. 83, 86, and 88; Thomas Pangle. *The Spirit of Modern Republicanism.* Chicago: University of Chicago Press, 1988, p. 186–7 and 214; and Paul A. Rahe. *Republics Ancient and Modern: Classical Republicanism and the American Revolution.* Chapel Hill: University of North Carolina Press, 1992, p. 285.
9. See Strauss, *Natural Right,* p. 226; for the quote in its original context see R 245, 182).
10. See Francis Oakley. "Locke, Natural Law, and God – Again." *History of Political Thought* 18 (1997): 624–51, p. 626–7 and 645.
11. See John Marshall. *John Locke: Resistance, Religion and Responsibility.* New York: Cambridge University Press, 1994, p. 188–9; and Steven Forde. "Natural Law, Theology, and Morality in Locke." *American Journal of Political Science* 45 (2001): 396–409, p. 399.
12. Rabieh and Forde rely heavily on reading this comment in the *Reasonableness* as a statement that Christian virtue doesn't actually lead to happiness in this life (see Rabieh, "Reasonableness," p. 945; and Forde, "Natural Law," p. 407). But this reading is inconsistent with Locke's use of the word "appeared"; Locke does not say that virtue laid out by secular reason was inconsistent with happiness, only that it "appeared" to be so. Furthermore, with the words "portion" and "prosperity" Locke indicates that it appears so because virtue is not conducive to the accumulation of material wealth. Locke's point seems to be that crassly materialistic people will not always be persuaded by secular arguments that virtue is conducive to worldly happiness, since they measure happiness by wealth. The infinite rewards and punishments of the afterlife are therefore necessary to show those people that God's law is authoritative. In addition, neither Rabieh nor Forde mentions the passage in the *Essay* where Locke says that he thinks true virtue probably *does* lead to greater happiness even in this life. Myers, by contrast, reads this comment in the *Essay* and a few other passages as signs that Locke surreptitiously draws our attention exclusively to the happiness of the virtuous in this life (see Peter Myers. *Our Only Star and Compass: Locke and the Struggle for Political Rationality.* New York: Rowman & Littlefield, 1998, p. 148–9). However, as Marshall points out, Locke always maintained the distinction between self-interest as such and morality as such, even though he often used the former as a method

for discerning the latter (see Marshall, *Resistance, Religion and Responsibility*, p. 188–9).

13. See also John C. Higgins-Biddle. "Introduction." In *The Reasonableness of Christianity as Delivered in the Scriptures.* Oxford: Clarendon Press, 1999, p. cvii.

14. See Forde, "Natural Law," p. 400.

15. Strauss, and quite a few scholars following him, have argued that Locke forges this connection between opinion and morality in order to effectively replace God's law with the law of opinion as the ultimate moral authority (see Strauss, *Natural Law*, p. 212–14 and 229–30; Cox, *War and Peace*, p. 24; Pangle, *Modern Republicanism*, p. 202–3 and 207; Michael Zuckert. "Locke and the Problem of Civil Religion." In *The American Founding: Essays on the Formation of the Constitution*, ed. J. Jackson Barlow, Leonard W. Levy, and Ken Masugi. United States: Greenwood Press, 1988, p. 113; David Wootton. "John Locke: Socinian or Natural Law Theorist?" In *Religion, Secularization and Political Thought: Thomas Hobbes to J. S. Mill*, ed. James Crimmins. London: Routledge, 1989, p. 43, 45, and 47; Rabieh, "Reasonableness," p. 946–52; Rahe, *Republics*, p. 292–3; Myers, *Our Only Star*, p. 47; and Forde, "Natural Right," p. 400 and 407). This argument draws almost all of its plausibility from the premise that Locke casts doubt on belief in rewards and punishments in the afterlife; public opinion allegedly supplies the rewards and punishments necessary for political theory in the absence of divine power. The premise that Locke casts doubt on religion has been refuted at length in previous chapters. Here we need only add that Locke takes great pains, particularly in the long note he attached at E II.28.11, 354–5 but also in the main body of his treatment of the law of opinion, to point out that he is not arguing that existing laws of opinion are right, but only that those laws are evidence of a universal design of human nature (see Aarsleff, "State of Nature"; and Myers, p. 58–60).

16. See Forde, "Natural Law," p. 397.

17. See also John Locke. *Paraphrase and Notes on the Epistles of St. Paul.* ed. Arthur W. Wainwright. Oxford: Clarendon Press, 1987, p. 499; and Dale Kuehne. "Reinventing Paul: John Locke, the Geneva Bible, and Paul's *Epistle to the Romans.*" In *Piety and Humanity*, ed. Douglas Kries. United States: Rowman & Littlefield, 1997, p. 221.

18. The standard interpretation of this passage from Romans is so ingrained as to be unreflectively taken by some as its only possible meaning; Schneewind cites it as exemplary of the traditional Christian natural law doctrine he takes Locke to be rejecting (see J. B. Schneewind. "Locke's Moral Philosophy." In *The Cambridge Companion to Locke*, ed. Vere Chappell. Cambridge: Cambridge University Press, 1994, p. 201). Schneewind does not mention, and does not seem to be aware of, Locke's interpretation of this passage in the *Reasonableness*.

19. As was discussed in the previous chapter, Strauss, Cox, and Foster argue that it is a sign of Locke's insincerity that he says the natural law is God's law but does not primarily draw his account of it in the *Two Treatises* from scripture (see Strauss, *Natural Right*, p. 205 and 214–19; Cox, *War and Peace*, p. 42–3 and 45; and David Foster. "The Bible and Natural Freedom in John Locke's

Political Thought." In *Piety and Humanity*, ed. Douglas Kries. United States: Rowman & Littlefield, 1997, p. 195 and 201).

20. See Spellman, *John Locke*, p. 3.
21. On Locke's interest in travel accounts, see Richard Ashcraft. "Locke's Political Philosophy." In *Cambridge Companion*, ed. Chappell, p. 238. Cox argues that Locke manipulates historical and anthropological sources of this kind, asserting that they actually support the opposite conclusions from the ones Locke draws (see Cox, *War and Peace*, p. 42–3, 96–7, 100–1). However, even Cox's own account of these alleged manipulations makes clear that Locke does not in fact abuse his sources. For example, in the case of Vega's story of two men on a desert island, the important point for Locke's purposes is that the two men recognized that they were morally obliged to keep their word to one another despite the absence of an enforcing authority; the trouble between them was caused by the lack of an unbiased judge to resolve disputes in which each one honestly thought he was right and the other was wrong. In the case of Acosta's account of the Indians, Locke is primarily interested in Acosta's report that some Indians lived without government, which would have proved that it was possible to have society without government; Acosta's comments on Indian origin myths, which Cox treats as the pivotal issue, are actually irrelevant to Locke's concerns. On another note, Pangle asserts that Locke plays up anthropological accounts of horrible cultural practices in order to show us that morality is merely conventional (see Pangle, *Modern Republicanism*, p. 175). But Locke is at pains to make the opposite point – that the deviation of one or another society from a given moral law does not disprove the validity of the law itself.
22. Locke originally wrote the *Two Treatises* in the early 1680s to urge rebellion against the king, but in 1689 that rebellion had already been achieved. The very revolution that made Locke's return to England and his publication of the *Two Treatises* possible simultaneously rendered that publication unnecessary – unless Locke had some other purpose for publishing it (see Richard Ashcraft. *Revolutionary Politics and Locke's* Two Treatises of Government. Princeton, NJ: Princeton University Press, 1986, p. 550–1 and 591).
23. Pangle argues that Locke presents the preservation of human life as God's only purpose, which would be at odds with the clear teachings of the Bible (Pangle, *Modern Republicanism*, p. 160). However, Locke never writes that preservation is God's only purpose; rather, preservation is the only moral law that is so clearly laid out in human nature that we can safely found political systems upon it. Other moral laws are subject to epistemological difficulties that prevent them from being coercively enforced.
24. Pangle's assertion that Locke recognizes no parental duty to protect children, only a strong natural desire to do so, is false (see Pangle, *Modern Republicanism*, p. 233). Locke explicitly describes this natural desire as a manifestation of God's will in the design of human nature, which in turn supports the conclusion that parental protection is a moral duty.
25. Strauss and scholars following him assert that for Locke reason is weaker than, or dependent upon, the passions (see Strauss, *Natural Right*, p. 227,

240–3, and 250; Cox, *War and Peace,* p. 83, 86, and 88; Pangle, *Modern Republicanism,* p. 160, 179–80, 185–7, and 214; and Rahe, *Republics,* p. 295, 457, and 498–9). It is true that for Locke, as the *Essay* argues, we are motivated by pleasure and pain, and reason helps us figure out what will bring us pleasure and remove pain. But, as we saw in the last chapter, any rational person will see that the infinite rewards and punishments of God overwhelm any other source of pleasure and pain, so for any rational person obedience to God's law will be the supreme goal. Given that we can only learn God's law through reason, as we saw in Chapter 3, this makes reason by far the most important faculty of the soul. Indeed, there is a sense in which the desires depend on reason for Locke; all rational people desire above all else to please God, and reason is our only hope of discerning what we must do to please God. Disobedience to God is inherently irrational. In particular, Pangle thinks that Locke's "star and compass" metaphor shows the dependence of reason on the passions, but the point of the metaphor is that every "ship" is trying to reach the same destination – heaven – and reason is the only hope of safe navigation there.

26. Myers is right in pointing out that to describe affections as dangerous to justice is not necessarily to imply that affections are evil (see Myers, *Our Only Star,* p. 124). But as Locke's "star and compass" metaphor makes clear, Locke believes that human desires are not naturally oriented toward good, except insofar as they are controlled by reason, and that is tantamount to saying they are depraved.

27. Zuckert asserts that Locke omits "the biblical reason" not to murder, which is that humanity is made in God's image (see Michael Zuckert. "Of Wary Physicians and Weary Readers: The Debates on Locke's Way of Writing." *The Independent Journal of Philosophy* 2 (1978): 55–66, p. 61–2). As we can see from this passage, Locke does not omit God's image from the *Two Treatises;* for Locke, reason is the clearest sign of God's image in humanity, and in turn it is reason that allows us to live under God's moral law (see T II.8, 118). Thus, when Locke builds all morality and political authority upon reason, he builds it upon the image of God in humanity.

28. This larger moral purpose of preserving all human life, not just one's own, stands against Pangle's assertion that on Locke's reasoning we cannot justify self-sacrifice and risk in the name of helping others (see Pangle, *Modern Republicanism,* p. 270–1).

29. Pangle writes that Locke's formulation of charity as a right possessed by the person in need rather than as a duty in the person who has more than he needs is objectionable, but does not specify why it is so (see Pangle, *Modern Republicanism,* p. 144). Formulating charity as a right rather than a duty gives the poor person a stronger moral claim to receive it. According to Locke, a starving person need not wait for others to rise to the occasion and give him food; he has "title" under God's law to take what he needs. And, as Tully points out, Locke's system of moral reasoning assumes that a right in one person creates a correlative duty in all others, so there is in fact a duty of charity for Locke (see James Tully. *A Discourse on Property.* Cambridge: Cambridge University Press, 1980, p. 132). Forde overlooks the

presence of charity in the *Two Treatises* entirely (see Forde, "Natural Right," p. 401).

30. See Marshall, *Resistance, Religion and Responsibility*, p. 299–326.
31. Marshall, *Resistance, Religion and Responsibility*, p. 315.

7: "The Servants of One Sovereign Master"

1. See also John Locke. "Of the Conduct of the Understanding." In *Some Thoughts Concerning Education* and *Of the Conduct of the Understanding*. John Locke. Indianapolis, IN: Hackett Publishing Company, 1996, p. 205.
2. As Myers observes, this linguistic method is an example of what Locke called "civil discourse" in the *Essay* – discourse in which great precision is either impossible or not required (see Peter Myers. *Our Only Star and Compass: Locke and the Struggle for Political Rationality*. New York: Rowman & Littlefield, 1998, p. 38–9).
3. Locke scholars of various interpretive schools have attempted to use Locke's discussion of "persons" in the *Essay* to explain the centrally important concept of "persons" in the *Second Treatise* (see John W. Yolton. *Locke: An Introduction*. Oxford: Basil Blackwell, Ltd., 1985, p. 17–33; and Michael Zuckert. *Natural Rights and the New Republicanism*. Princeton, NJ: Princeton University Press, 1994, p. 278–83), but there is no evidence that Locke means the same thing by this word in both places. His concern in the *Essay* is to explain why we do not need a metaphysical explanation of the soul as a basis for believing in eternal life; his concern in the *Second Treatise* is the connection between human beings, their labor, and their property. Pangle, Zuckert, and Foster argue that Locke's account of people owning their own persons substitutes self-ownership for God's ownership of human beings (see Thomas Pangle. *The Spirit of Modern Republicanism*. Chicago: University of Chicago Press, 1988, p. 160; Zuckert, *Natural Rights*, p. 220–1, 239, 276, and 278–83; and David Foster. "The Bible and Natural Freedom in John Locke's Political Thought." In *Piety and Humanity*, ed. Douglas Kries. United States: Rowman & Littlefield, 1997, p. 183 and 200). However, a careful reading reveals that Locke says nothing about "self-ownership." As Zuckert points out, Locke uses precisely the same formulation every time he states his position on this issue (Zuckert, *Natural Rights*, p. 278). His position is that God owns human beings, and human beings own their persons. Contrary to Zuckert's characterization, human beings owning *their persons* is not the same as human beings owning *themselves*, or "self-ownership," particularly if we do not take it for granted, as Zuckert does, that Locke means the same thing by "person" in the *Two Treatises* as he meant in the *Essay*.
4. Hans Aarsleff. "The State of Nature and the Nature of Man in Locke." In *John Locke: Problems and Perspectives*. ed. John W. Yolton. Cambridge: Cambridge University Press, 1969, p. 99.
5. This characterization of the state of Locke scholarship will no doubt strike many as strange, if not downright inexplicable, given that Locke scholars are famous for the complexity and intransigence of their disputes. "One cannot but be wary before trespassing on the bitter and protracted debate

on Locke's theory of property" (S. P. Clark. "'The Whole Internal World His Own': Locke and Metaphor Reconsidered." *Journal of the History of Ideas* 59 (1998): 241–65, p. 256). But to the extent that these debates are actually as complex and rancorous as they are notorious for being, which is not most of the time, it is largely because they boil down to niceties and semantics. Once Macpherson's more overextended arguments in favor of a Marxist reading of Locke were pulled back to more defensible positions, the debate over his theories mostly came down to how broadly we ought to define such terms as "bourgeois" and "capitalist," and how closely Locke had to be linked to certain historical trends before we could legitimately pin these labels on him. Similarly, arguments over the readings of Tully and Ashcraft have mostly come down to definitions and boundary problems. For some time now there has been a surprisingly broad consensus on the basic content of Locke's political theory – adherents of the Straussian interpretation being the perennial exception. See C. B. Macpherson. *The Political Theory of Possessive Individualism.* London: Oxford University Press, 1962; John Dunn. "Justice and the Interpretation of Locke's Political Theory." *Political Studies* 16 (1968): 68–87; John Dunn. *The Political Thought of John Locke.* New York: Cambridge University Press, 1969; James Tully. *A Discourse on Property.* Cambridge: Cambridge University Press, 1980; James Tully. *An Approach to Political Philosophy: Locke in Contexts.* New York: Cambridge University Press, 1984; Neal Wood. *The Politics of Locke's Philosophy.* Berkeley: University of California Press, 1983; Richard Ashcraft. *Revolutionary Politics and Locke's* Two Treatises of Government. Princeton, NJ: Princeton University Press, 1986; David C. Snyder. "Locke on Natural Law and Property Rights." *Canadian Journal of Philosophy* 16 (1986): 723–50; Richard Ashcraft. *Locke's Two Treatises of Government.* London: Allen & Unwin, 1987; David Wootton. "John Locke and Richard Ashcraft's *Revolutionary Politics.*" *Political Studies* 40 (1992): 79–98; Richard Ashcraft. "Simple Objections and Complex Reality: Theorizing Political Radicalism in Seventeenth-Century England." *Political Studies* 40 (1992): 99–115.

6. See Aarsleff, "State of Nature," p. 129.
7. See Myers, *Our Only Star*, p. 39–41; and Aarsleff, "State of Nature," p. 129–31.
8. Since the *Two Treatises* were published anonymously, not everyone in Locke's audience would have been aware that it was written by the author of the *Essay*, although a few did know and many more suspected it.
9. John Rawls. *A Theory of Justice.* Cambridge, MA: Harvard University Press, 1971, p. 4.
10. See Robert Nozick. *Anarchy, State, and Utopia.* United States: Basic Books, 1974; and Friedrich Hayek. *The Mirage of Social Justice.* Chicago: University of Chicago Press, 1976.
11. See John Rawls. *Political Liberalism.* New York: Columbia University Press, 1993.
12. On Locke's rhetorical use of the concept of slavery, see James Farr's outstanding article on the role of slavery in Locke's life and political thought (James Farr. "'So Vile and Miserable an Estate': The Problem of Slavery in Locke's Political Thought." *Political Theory* 14 (1986): 263–89).

13. See also Ashcraft, *Locke's Two Treatises*, p. 78.
14. See Dunn, *Political Thought*, p. 93 and 127; and John Dunn. *Locke*. New York: Oxford University Press, 1984, p. 53. Forde correctly points out, against Strauss's reading of the *Two Treatises*, that if Locke did not sincerely believe that laws had to be legislated by God to be properly considered moral, he need not have taken that position. He could have saved himself a lot of trouble by following Grotius rather than Pufendorf on that point, arguing that moral laws were good in themselves rather than good because willed by God (see Steven Forde. "Natural Law, Theology, and Morality in Locke." *American Journal of Political Science* 45 (2001): 396–409, p. 398). This would have been perfectly acceptable to Locke's audience, and would have made it much easier for Locke to construct the esoteric political theory Strauss attributes to him.
15. See Forde, "Natural Law," p. 400.
16. Cox asserts that Locke contradicts himself on the question of whether knowing the natural law is easy or hard (see Richard Cox. *Locke on War and Peace.* Oxford: Clarendon Press, 1960, p. 70–1, 80–1, and 93). However, Locke's position is that knowing the abstract law of nature – that human life is to be preserved, and force is to be opposed to nothing but to unjust force – is easy, but applying that rule to specific circumstances is hard, because of the problems of moral judgment.
17. On Locke's purpose of attacking court sycophants, see Charles Tarlton's indispensable article on the *First Treatise* (Charles D. Tarlton. "A Rope of Sand: Interpreting Locke's *First Treatise of Government*." In *John Locke: Critical Assessments.* ed. Richard Ashcraft. New York: Routledge, 1991, vol. 2). As Tully points out, the argument that kings had absolute power was not rooted in medieval political theory, but was relatively new (see Tully, *Discourse*, p. 157). Scholars following Strauss have pointed out that Locke frequently suggests Filmer works to disguise his argument, interpreting this as a hint from Locke that Locke is doing the same (see Cox, *War and Peace*, p. 34–5; Michael Zuckert. "Of Wary Physicians and Weary Readers: The Debates on Locke's Way of Writing." *The Independent Journal of Philosophy* 2 (1978): 55–66, p. 58; Pangle, *Modern Republicanism*, p. 137; and Paul A. Rahe. *Republics Ancient and Modern: Classical Republicanism and the American Revolution.* Chapel Hill: University of North Carolina Press, 1992, p. 493.). However, Locke only accuses Filmer of presenting his argument in a way that will mitigate its extreme political consequences and thus make it seem more palatable, not of actually deceiving his audience as to the content of his doctrine.
18. For an unsparing (and entirely deserved) roasting of this tradition in Locke scholarship, see Tarlton, "Rope of Sand," p. 87–91.
19. Scholars following Strauss have correctly observed that Locke uses Filmer as a convenient way to take up the subject of the Bible, but this does not justify their assertion that he attacks Filmer in order to attack the Bible (see Cox, *War and Peace*, p. 4–6; Michael Zuckert. "An Introduction to Locke's First Treatise." *Interpretation* 8 (1979): 58–74, p. 64–6; Pangle, *Modern Republicanism*, p. 134–45; and Foster, "Natural Freedom," p. 184–8). Throughout the

First Treatise Locke differentiates Filmer's account of the Bible from what the Bible actually says. Zuckert and Foster assert that Locke treats himself and Filmer as the only possible political alternatives, such that Locke need only refute Filmer to establish his consent doctrine. However, Locke provides an independent argument in the *Second Treatise* to establish his consent doctrine, based on his analysis of human nature. That argument relies crucially on the premise that scripture contains no specific grant of political authority, so the argument against Filmer in the *First Treatise* is a necessary prelude to the more general argument in the *Second Treatise*.

20. See Tarlton, "Rope of Sand"; and Zuckert, "Locke's First Treatise."

21. Locke does not discuss the passages in the New Testament that appear to grant husbands authority over wives. We will not take up here the longstanding arguments among biblical scholars over the meanings of those passages, but we will note that there are reasonable people on both sides of those arguments, and that they are not particularly relevant to Locke's analysis since any New Testament grant of authority to husbands cannot be legally enforced in any way for two reasons. First, the New Testament passages describe only a spiritual form of leadership for the husband rather than a specifically political leadership that might have legal implications; second, if these passages do constitute a grant of authority this grant is still only a specific rule for Christians rather than a general rule for all humanity (as a grant to Adam would have been), and thus under a Lockean understanding of the gospel it could not be enforced by law.

22. See also Romans 13:3.

23. See Joshua Mitchell. *Not by Reason Alone: Religion, History and Identity in Early Modern Thought*. Chicago: University of Chicago Press, 1993, p. 75 and 80.

24. As Mitchell points out, for Locke human beings are sacred because of what they are (rational agents under God's law) not because of what they do (e.g., worship Jesus). See Mitchell, *Not by Reason Alone*, p. 96–7.

25. John Locke. *Paraphrase and Notes on the Epistles of St. Paul*, ed. Arthur W. Wainwright. Oxford: Clarendon Press, 1987, Paraphrase of Romans 13:1, second footnote, section b (p. 588). Locke suggests that the main reason Paul took up the subject of obedience was to remove any thought that Christians might be entitled to disobey non-Christian rulers (see *Paraphrase*, Content of Romans 13:1–7, section d, p. 586; and Paraphrase of Romans 13:1, first footnote, p. 588). Interestingly, in Locke's paraphrase, Paul's statement that government is instituted "for good" becomes "for thy good," meaning the good of citizens (*Paraphrase*, Paraphrase of Romans 13:4, p. 587). On Locke's reading of Romans 13:1–5 in the *Paraphrase* see Dale Kuehne. "Reinventing Paul: John Locke, the Geneva Bible, and Paul's *Epistle to the Romans*." In *Piety and Humanity*, ed. Kries, p. 225–6.

26. *Paraphrase*, Content of Romans 13:1–7, section e (p. 586–7); see also Content of Romans 13:1–7, sections e–j (p. 586–7); and Paraphrase of Romans 13:1, second footnote, sections c–d (p. 588).

27. Leo Strauss. *Natural Right and History*. Chicago: University of Chicago Press, 1953, p. 214–18. In addition to portraying Locke's political positions as "unbiblical," Strauss and scholars following his method have identified a host

of specific instances in Locke's works in which they claim Locke distorts or violates the obvious meaning of the scriptural passages he quotes (see Strauss, *Natural Right*, p. 218 and 224; Cox, *War and Peace*, p. 39–41 and 54–7; Zuckert, "Wary Physicians," p. 59–61; Pangle, *Modern Republicanism*, p. 135, 139, 142–6, 154, 156–8, and 165; Rahe, *Republics*, p. 490–2; Foster, "Natural Freedom," p. 192–4, 198, and 202–3; and Forde, "Natural Law," p. 399). It is unfortunate that there is no space to provide a full discussion of every individual scriptural passage that is thus disputed, because Locke's interpretive method, understood in the larger context of his epistemological concerns as laid out in the *Essay*, provides strong arguments in favor of his scriptural interpretations in each of these cases. As with Romans 13:1–5, Locke shows time and again that the Bible does not actually say what many people think it does.

28. See Dunn, *Political Thought*, p. 106.

29. In justifying some of the premises of his method for distinguishing universal moral laws from particular cultural traditions, Locke often quotes the writings of Richard Hooker. Strauss and some scholars following him suggest that the reason Locke frequently cites Hooker is because Locke wishes to give the false impression that his argument is fully consistent with Hooker's (see Strauss, *Natural Right*, p. 165 and 207; Cox, *War and Peace*, p. 59–61; Zuckert, "Wary Physicians," p. 59–60; and Pangle, *Modern Republicanism*, p. 133). Locke clearly does seek to use Hooker to provide legitimacy for his argument, but not in the way Strauss argues. Locke never suggests that his argument and Hooker's are fully consistent. Rather, Locke seeks to show that certain premises endorsed by Hooker, such as the natural equality of human beings, imply the political doctrines endorsed in the *Two Treatises*. Where Locke diverges from Hooker, he wants us to conclude that Hooker has failed to follow his own premises to the correct conclusions. Obviously it would have been more forthright of Locke to state clearly where he disagrees with Hooker, rather than only quoting Hooker on points of agreement, but since Locke's conclusions are clearly different from Hooker's it would have been idiotic for Locke to think he could dupe us into missing the differences altogether.

30. Dunn, *Political Thought*, p. 79. See also Forde, "Natural Law," p. 402.

31. See Aarsleff, "State of Nature," p. 100.

32. This would not be true in Hobbes's jargon. In Hobbes's use of the term "moral," both the study of God's law and the study of psychological motivation would be classified as "moral philosophy" (see Thomas Hobbes. *Leviathan*. Cambridge: Cambridge University Press, 1991, chapter 15, paragraph 40, p. 110–11). Here we use "moral" in its current sense.

33. See John C. Higgins-Biddle. "Introduction." In *The Reasonableness of Christianity as Delivered in the Scriptures*. Oxford: Clarendon Press, 1999, p. xciii.

34. See Greg Forster. "Divine Law and Human Law in Hobbes's *Leviathan*." In *History of Political Thought* 24 (2003): 189–217.

35. Strauss, *Natural Right*, p. 227; see also p. 227–31.

36. See Tully, *Discourse*, p. 46–7 and 63.

37. See Strauss, *Natural Right*, p. 228.

38. Locke believed that this situation had actually occurred in human history, and that if Acosta's travel reports were to be believed it was still the case among the Indians in America (see T II.102, 166).
39. See Richard Ashcraft. "The Politics of Locke's *Two Treatises of Government*." In *John Locke's* Two Treatises of Government: *New Interpretations*, ed. Edward J. Harpham. Lawrence: University Press of Kansas, 1992, p. 238. Foster asserts that if people are "free" in the state of nature, they must have no duties to God, but he provides no supporting argument for this reading (see Foster, "Natural Freedom," p. 189–90). Locke never uses the word "free" in this way; he is quite clear that people in the state of nature are "free" in that they are free from human authority, as distinct from God's authority. They are politically free, free relative to one another.
40. Pangle reads Locke's comments on his "strange doctrine" as an admission that his doctrine is alien to previous moral theory (see Pangle, *Modern Republicanism*, p. 132). However, a careful reading of the passage shows that Locke does not actually say his doctrine is strange, only that it "will seem" so.
41. See John Marshall. *John Locke: Resistance, Religion and Responsibility*. New York: Cambridge University Press, 1994, p. 219.
42. See Richard Ashcraft. "Anticlericalism and Authority in Lockean Political Thought." In *Margins of Orthodoxy*, ed. Roger Lund, Cambridge: Cambridge University Press, 1995, p. 81 and 89.
43. Ashcraft, *Revolutionary Politics*, p. 262.
44. For an excellent account of the moral obligations that define Locke's account of marriage and parenting, see Myers, *Our Only Star*, p. 197–206. On the moral dimension of Locke's theory of labor and property, see Dunn, *Political Thought*, p. 222–8 and 245–9; Tully, *Discourse*, p. 110; Ashcraft, *Revolutionary Politics*, p. 264–5 and 277–8; Marshall, *Resistance, Religion and Responsibility*, p. 177; and Myers, *Our Only Star*, p. 193–4. The alleged amorality of Locke's theory of property is one of the most common arguments for Strauss's interpretation of Locke. Strauss argues that Locke "emancipates acquisitiveness" (Strauss, *Natural Right*, p. 240–2; see also Pangle, *Modern Republicanism*, p. 162), that in Locke's account people labor for selfish reasons (see Strauss, *Natural Right*, p. 243; see also Pangle, *Modern Republicanism*, p. 248; and Rahe, *Republics*, p. 294), and that such labor is necessary because God has been, on Locke's account, decidedly stingy and unloving toward humanity in the "penury" of the natural resources he has provided (Strauss, *Natural Right*, p. 224–5; see also Cox, *War and Peace*, p. 91, Zuckert, "Locke's First Treatise," p. 73, Pangle, *Modern Republicanism*, p. 143 and 166; Michael Zuckert. "Locke and the Problem of Civil Religion." In *The American Founding: Essays on the Formation of the Constitution*, ed. J. Jackson Barlow, Leonard W. Levy, and Ken Masugi. United States: Greenwood Press, 1988, p. 114; and Foster, "Natural Freedom," p. 197). It is true that Locke denies the existence of an upper limit on the total amount of goods a person can legitimately acquire, but so do countless other natural law theorists whose religious sincerity is not questioned. The important point is whether it is Locke's purpose to remove upper limits on acquisition, or if this is just a side effect of his pursuit of other purposes. The view one takes on this point will

depend on whether one finds Strauss's general reading of Locke's state of nature theory persuasive. The argument that people labor for selfish reasons depends on what one means by selfishness. Locke is a Christian eudemonist standing in a long line of Christian eudemonist thinkers, and he describes a divinely designed framework of rewards and punishments that encourage labor. The argument from natural penury, one of the most common arguments for Strauss's reading, depends upon the premise that it would be cruel for God to put humanity in a naturally penurious state. This is difficult to sustain in light of Genesis 3:17–19, where God makes it abundantly clear just who is really to blame for the penury of humanity's natural condition. If anybody's argument deserves to be called unbiblical on this point, it is Rousseau's argument that humanity's natural conditions are materially sufficient and comfortable. Furthermore, as Myers points out, natural penury serves the purpose of stimulating human faculties, as we must work and think in order to sustain ourselves in a harsh natural world (see Myers, *Our Only Star*, p. 120). As Paul says in a quote that Locke is fond of, God truly has "given us all things richly to enjoy," but we must work to earn those things before we can enjoy them.

45. See Eldon Eisenach. *Two Worlds of Liberalism*. Chicago: University of Chicago Press, 1992, p. 104.

46. As Eisenach puts it, the transition from the state of nature to civil society is a process of rule learning through natural consequences (see Eisenach, *Two Worlds*, p. 95).

47. Ashcraft is a notable exception; see Ashcraft, *Locke's Two Treatises*, p. 158–9 and 163; and Ashcraft, "Politics of Locke's *Two Treatises*," p. 41. It is unfortunate that Ashcraft's inclusion of Chapter 8 in his analysis of Locke does not cause him to realize that Locke is not primarily interested in the complexities of constitutional theory.

48. Locke makes similar comments on why Adam and Noah were unlimited monarchs, due to the close family relationship that was shared by all existing people at that time (see T II.36–7, II.132–4; II.94, 162; II.110–11, 171–2). Pangle reads these comments on the "innocence" of those small, tightly-knit political communities as reflecting a view that humanity did not fall into sin after leaving Eden, but in light of Locke's comments in Chapter 8 of the *Second Treatise* they are much more easily explained as descriptions of the simple community of family ties in which Adam and Noah lived; people back then were "innocent" in the sense that they had not yet experienced the dangers and oppressions of rule by one person that were to develop in later societies (see Pangle, *Modern Republicanism*, p. 165).

49. See Peter Josephson. *The Great Art of Government*. Lawrence: University Press of Kansas, 2002; and Patrick Riley. "On Finding an Equilibrium Between Consent and Natural Law in Locke's Political Philosophy." *Political Studies* 22 (1974): 432–52.

50. In the *Letter*, Locke discusses some cases in which evil opinions or private uses of property do cause destruction of others; these include religions that preach intolerance of others (see L 69, 52) and using cattle for purposes other than food during a famine (L 50, 39–40).

51. As we have already seen, in the *First Treatise* Locke presents a deft and, for its time, deeply radical argument that the Bible contains no general grant of conjugal authority. At the conclusion of this argument, he writes: "there is, I grant, a foundation in nature" for male superiority (see T I.47, 35). Such an inadequate conclusion to such a powerful and radical argument that tends entirely in the other direction, and phrased in such a palpably hesitant manner, suggests insincerity on this point. The concession in the *Second Treatise* that there is a natural basis for male superiority is similarly delivered in a single sentence, and in the middle of an argument that tends strongly in the other direction. It is possible that Locke felt arguing for women's equality would be simply too radical for his audience, and not of sufficient importance for his main point to warrant the trouble it would cause him. On this argument see Melissa Butler. "Early Liberal Roots of Feminism: John Locke and the Attack on Patriarchy." *American Political Science Review* 72 (1978): 135–50; and Myers, *Our Only Star*, p. 202. For an overview of other interpretations of Locke's view of conjugal authority, see Ruth Sample. "Locke on Political Authority and Conjugal Authority." *The Locke Newsletter* 31 (2000): 115–46.

52. For example, a just victor can keep those who unjustly resisted him as slaves, but he cannot keep their land and possessions, nor can he enslave their families, nor any children they subsequently bear (T II.179–82, 207–9).

53. This is the answer to Ashcraft's frustrated demand that Locke provide more details and more unambiguous positions on such questions as who should have the right to vote and how strict the separation between the legislature and the executive must be (see Ashcraft, *Locke's Two Treatises*, p. 115–19, 151, and 185–6).

54. Ashcraft observes that Locke employs two concepts of tyranny in the *Second Treatise*, one classical and one modern: power exercised against community interests, or power exercised beyond established legal right. Ultimately, tyranny must be judged relative to context; what is acceptable in a primitive society might be tyrannical in an advanced one (see Ashcraft, "The Politics of Locke's *Two Treatises*," p. 228–9, 231, and 249).

8: "The Opinion of This or That Philosopher Was of No Authority"

1. Perhaps the most famous examples of these two ways of avoiding the problem were produced by the same person, John Rawls. His *A Theory of Justice* (Cambridge, MA: Harvard University Press, 1971) attempts to wrestle Kant into endorsing his political theory, while his later *Political Liberalism* (New York: Columbia University Press, 1993) appeals to existing liberal consensus. A somewhat different attempt to take advantage of existing consensus is Michael Walzer's *Spheres of Justice* (United States: Basic Books, 1983). The book's subtitle advertises it as "a defense of pluralism and equality," but its argument explicitly rests on existing habit and custom. A defense of pluralism and equality is precisely what Walzer does not provide.

2. For an excellent and much more complete statement of this argument against liberal neutralism, see Peter Myers. *Our Only Star and Compass: Locke*

and the Struggle for Political Rationality. New York: Rowman & Littlefield, 1998, p. ix–x, 1–22. See also Steven Forde. "Natural Law, Theology, and Morality in Locke." *American Journal of Political Science* 45 (2001): 396–409, p. 396.

3. Locke modestly admits the possibility that his own philosophy may be just such a castle in the air, but it is clear from the passage that he thinks otherwise.

Bibliography

Aarsleff, Hans. "The State of Nature and the Nature of Man in Locke." In *John Locke: Problems and Perspectives*, ed. John Yolton, Cambridge: Cambridge University Press, 1969.

Aarsleff, Hans. "Some Observations on Recent Locke Scholarship." In *John Locke: Problems and Perspectives*, ed. John Yolton, Cambridge: Cambridge University Press, 1969.

Aarsleff, Hans. "Locke's Influence." In *The Cambridge Companion to Locke*, ed. Vere Chappell, Cambridge: Cambridge University Press, 1994.

Ashcraft, Richard. "Faith and Knowledge in Locke's Philosophy." In *John Locke: Problems and Perspectives*, ed. John Yolton, Cambridge: Cambridge University Press, 1969.

Ashcraft, Richard. *Revolutionary Politics and Locke's* Two Treatises of Government. Princeton, NJ: Princeton University Press, 1986.

Ashcraft, Richard. *Locke's Two Treatises of Government*. London: Allen & Unwin, 1987.

Ashcraft, Richard, ed. *John Locke: Critical Assessments*. 4 vols. New York: Routledge, 1991.

Ashcraft, Richard. "The Politics of Locke's *Two Treatises of Government*." In *John Locke's* Two Treatises of Government: *New Interpretations*, ed. Edward Harpham, Lawrence: University Press of Kansas, 1992.

Ashcraft, Richard. "Simple Objections and Complex Reality: Theorizing Political Radicalism in Seventeenth-Century England." *Political Studies* 40 (1992): 99–115.

Ashcraft, Richard. "Anticlericalism and Authority in Lockean Political Thought." In *Margins of Orthodoxy*, ed. Roger Lund. Cambridge: Cambridge University Press, 1995.

Biddle, John C. "Locke's Critique of Innate Principles and Toland's Deism." *Journal of the History of Ideas* 37 (1976): 418–21.

Bork, Robert. *Slouching Towards Gomorrah: Modern Liberalism and American Decline*. New York: Regan Books, 1996.

Brown, Vivienne. "On Theological Discourse in Locke's *Essay.*" *The Locke Newsletter* 29 (1998): 39–57.

Butler, Melissa. "Early Liberal Roots of Feminism: John Locke and the Attack on Patriarchy." *American Political Science Review* 72 (1978): 135–50.

Carter, Stephen L. *The Culture of Disbelief: How American Law and Politics Trivialize Religious Devotion.* New York: Basic Books, 1993.

Carter, Stephen L. *God's Name in Vain: The Wrongs and Rights of Religion in Politics.* New York: Basic Books, 2000.

Chappell, Vere, ed. *The Cambridge Companion to Locke.* Cambridge: Cambridge University Press, 1994.

Clark, S. P. "'The Whole Internal World His Own': Locke and Metaphor Reconsidered." *Journal of the History of Ideas* 59 (1998): 241–65.

Colman, John. *John Locke's Moral Philosophy.* Edinburgh: Edinburgh University Press, 1983.

Cox, Richard. *Locke on War and Peace.* Oxford: Clarendon Press, 1960.

Dionne, E. J. and John J. DiIulio. *What's God Got to Do With the American Experiment?: Essays on Religion and Politics.* Washington, DC: Brookings Institution Press, 2000.

Dunn, John. "Justice and the Interpretation of Locke's Political Theory." *Political Studies* 16 (1968): 68–7.

Dunn, John. *The Political Thought of John Locke.* New York: Cambridge University Press, 1969.

Dunn, John. *Locke.* New York: Oxford University Press, 1984.

Dunn, John. "What Is Living and What Is Dead in the Political Theory of John Locke?" In *Interpreting Political Responsibility: Essays 1981–1989,* John Dunn. Princeton, NJ: Princeton University Press, 1990.

Eisenach, Eldon. *Two Worlds of Liberalism.* Chicago: University of Chicago Press, 1992.

Eisenach, Eldon. "Religion and Locke's *Two Treatises.*" In *John Locke's Two Treatises of Government: New Interpretations,* ed. Edward Harpham, Lawrence: University Press of Kansas, 1992.

Edwards, John. *Socinianism Unmask'd.* London: Printed for J. Robinson and J. Wyat, 1696.

Edwards, John. *The Socinian Creed.* London : Printed for J. Robinson and J. Wyat, 1697.

Farr, James. "'So Vile and Miserable an Estate': The Problem of Slavery In Locke's Political Thought." *Political Theory* 14 (1986): 263–89.

Forde, Steven. "Natural Law, Theology, and Morality in Locke." *American Journal of Political Science* 45 (2001): 396–409.

Forster, Greg. "Divine Law and Human Law in Hobbes's *Leviathan.*" *History of Political Thought* 24 (2003): 189–217.

Foster, David. "The Bible and Natural Freedom in John Locke's Political Thought." In *Piety and Humanity,* ed. Douglas Kries. United States: Rowman & Littlefield, 1997.

George, Robert P. *In Defense of Natural Law.* Oxford: Clarendon Press, 1999.

Grant, Ruth W. *John Locke's Liberalism.* Chicago: University of Chicago Press, 1987.

Harpham, Edward J., ed. *John Locke's* Two Treatises of Government: *New Interpretations.* Lawrence: University Press of Kansas, 1992.

Harris, Ian. "The Politics of Christianity." In *Locke's Philosophy: Content and Contexts,* ed. G. A. J. Rogers, New York: Oxford University Press, 1994.

Hayek, Friedrich. *The Mirage of Social Justice.* Chicago: University of Chicago Press, 1976.

Higgins-Biddle, John C. "Introduction." In John Locke *The Reasonableness of Christianity as Delivered in the Scriptures.* Oxford: Clarendon Press, 1999.

Hobbes, Thomas. *Leviathan.* Cambridge: Cambridge University Press, 1991.

Jolley, Nicholas. *Locke: His Philosophical Thought.* New York: Oxford University Press, 1999.

Josephson, Peter. *The Great Art of Government.* Lawrence: University Press of Kansas, 2002.

Kuehne, Dale. "Reinventing Paul: John Locke, the Geneva Bible, and Paul's *Epistle to the Romans.*" In *Piety and Humanity,* ed. Douglas Kries. United States: Rowman & Littlefield, 1997.

Laslett, Peter. "Introduction." In *Two Treatises of Government,* John Locke. Cambridge: Cambridge University Press, 1960.

Lewis, C. S. *Mere Christianity.* San Francisco: HarperCollins, 1952.

Locke, John. *The Works of John Locke,* third edition. London: A. Bettesworth, E. Parker, J. Pemberton, and E. Symon, 1727.

Locke, John. *A Letter Concerning Toleration,* ed. Patrick Romanell. Englewood Cliffs, NJ: Prentice-Hall, 1950.

Locke, John. "A Discourse of Miracles." In *The Reasonableness of Christianity,* with *A Discourse of Miracles* and part of *A Third Letter Concerning Toleration,* ed. I. T. Ramsey. Stanford, CA: Stanford University Press, 1958.

Locke, John. *The Works of John Locke.* London, 1823, reissued Aalen: Scientia, 1963.

Locke, John. *The Reasonableness of Christianity as Delivered in the Scriptures,* ed. George W. Ewing. Washington, DC: Regnery, 1965.

Locke, John. *The Correspondence of John Locke,* ed. E. S. De Beer. Oxford: Clarendon Press, 1978.

Locke, John. *An Essay Concerning Human Understanding,* ed. by Peter H. Nidditch. New York: Oxford Press, 1979.

Locke, John. *Paraphrase and Notes on the Epistles of St. Paul,* ed. Arthur W. Wainwright. Oxford: Clarendon Press, 1987.

Locke, John. *Two Treatises of Government,* ed. Mark Goldie. London: Everyman, 1993.

Locke, John. *Political Writings of John Locke,* ed. David Wootton. New York: Penguin, 1993.

Locke, John. *Some Thoughts Concerning Education* and *Of the Conduct of the Understanding,* ed. Ruth W. Grant and Nathan Tarcov. Indianapolis, IN: Hackett Publishing Company, 1996.

Locke, John. *Political Essays,* ed. Mark Goldie. Cambridge: Cambridge University Press, 1997.

Macpherson, C. B. *The Political Theory of Possessive Individualism.* London: Oxford University Press, 1962.

Marshall, John. *John Locke: Resistance, Religion and Responsibility.* New York: Cambridge University Press, 1994.

McCann, Edwin. "Locke's Philosophy of Body." In *The Cambridge Companion to Locke,* ed. Vere Chappell, Cambridge: Cambridge University Press, 1994.

Milton, J. R. "Locke's Life and Times." In *The Cambridge Companion to Locke,* ed. Vere Chappell, Cambridge: Cambridge University Press, 1994.

Mitchell, Joshua. *Not by Reason Alone: Religion, History and Identity in Early Modern Thought.* Chicago: University of Chicago Press, 1993.

Myers, Peter. "Locke on Reasonable Christianity and Reasonable Politics." In *Piety and Humanity,* ed. Douglas Kries. New York: Rowman & Littlefield, 1997.

Myers, Peter. *Our Only Star and Compass: Locke and the Struggle for Political Rationality.* New York: Rowman & Littlefield, 1998.

Nidditch, Peter H. "Introduction." In *An Essay Concerning Human Understanding,* John Locke, New York: Oxford Press, 1979.

Nozick, Robert. *Anarchy, State, and Utopia.* United States: Basic Books, 1974.

Nuovo, Victor. *John Locke and Christianity: Contemporary Responses to* The Reasonableness of Christianity. Dulles, VA: Theommes Press, 1997.

Oakley, Francis and Elliot W. Urdang. "Locke, Natural Law, and God." *Natural Law Forum* 11 (1966): 92–109.

Oakley, Francis. "Locke, Natural Law, and God – Again." *History of Political Thought* 18 (1997): 624–51.

Ott, Walter. "Locke and the Scholastics on Theological Discourse." *The Locke Newsletter* 28 (1997): 51–66.

Ott, Walter. "Locke and the Idea of God: A Reply to Vivienne Brown." *The Locke Newsletter* 30 (1999): 67–71.

Owen, David. Review of *John Locke and the Ethics of Belief* by Nicholas Wolterstorff. *The Locke Newsletter* 30 (1999): 103–27.

Pangle, Thomas. *The Spirit of Modern Republicanism.* Chicago: University of Chicago Press, 1988.

Pearson, Samuel C. "The Religion of John Locke and the Character of His Thought." In *John Locke: Critical Assessments,* ed. Richard Ashcraft, New York: Routledge, 1991.

Plato. *Euthyprho, Apology, Crito, Phaedo,* trans. Benjamin Jowett. New York: Prometheus Books, 1988.

Polin, Raymond. "John Locke's Conception of Freedom." In *John Locke: Problems and Perspectives,* ed. John Yolton, Cambridge: Cambridge University Press, 1969.

Rabieh, Michael. "The Reasonableness of Locke, or the Questionableness of Christianity." *The Journal of Politics* 53 (Nov. 1991): 933–57.

Rahe, Paul A., *Republics Ancient and Modern: Classical Republicanism and the American Revolution.* Chapel Hill: University of North Carolina Press, 1992.

Rawls John. *A Theory of Justice.* Cambridge, MA: Harvard University Press, 1971.

Rawls, John. *Political Liberalism.* New York: Columbia University Press, 1993.

Resnick, David. "Rationality and the *Two Treatises.*" In *John Locke's* Two Treatises of Government: *New Interpretations,* ed. Edward Harpham, Lawrence: University Press of Kansas, 1992.

Reventlow, Henning. *The Authority of the Bible and the Rise of the Modern World.* U.K.: Fortress Press, 1985.

Riley, Patrick. "On Finding an Equilibrium Between Consent and Natural Law in Locke's Political Philosophy." *Political Studies* 22 (1974): 432–52.

Rogers, G. A. J., ed. *Locke's Philosophy: Content and Contexts.* New York: Oxford University Press, 1994.

Rogers, G. A. J. "John Locke: Conservative Radical." In *Margins of Orthodoxy,* ed. Roger Lund. Cambridge: Cambridge University Press, 1995.

Sample, Ruth. "Locke on Political Authority and Conjugal Authority." *The Locke Newsletter* 31 (2000): 115–46.

Schneewind, J. B. "Locke's Moral Philosophy." In *The Cambridge Companion to Locke,* ed. Vere Chappell, Cambridge: Cambridge University Press, 1994.

Simmons, A. John. *The Lockean Theory of Rights.* Princeton, NJ: Princeton University Press, 1992.

Snyder, David C. "Locke on Natural Law and Property Rights." *Canadian Journal of Philosophy* 16 (1986): 723–50.

Spellman, W. M. *John Locke and the Problem of Depravity.* Oxford: Clarendon Press, 1988.

Spellman, W. M. *John Locke.* New York: St. Martin's Press, 1997.

Stillingfleet, Edward. *The Bishop of Worcester's Answer to Mr. Locke's Letter.* London: Printed by J. H. for Henry Mortlock, 1697.

Stillingfleet, Edward. *The Bishop of Worcester's Answer to Mr. Locke's Second Letter.* London: Printed by J. H. for Henry Mortlock, 1698.

Strauss, Leo. *Natural Right and History.* Chicago: University of Chicago Press, 1953.

Tarlton, Charles D. "A Rope of Sand: Interpreting Locke's *First Treatise of Government.*" In *John Lockes: Critical Assessments,* ed. Richard Ashcraft, New York: Routledge, 1991.

Taylor, Jeremy. *A Discourse on the Liberty of Prophesying.* London, 1647.

Tindal, Matthew. *Christianity as Old as the Creation: Or, the Gospel, a Republication of the Religion of Nature.* London, 1731.

Toland, John. *Christianity Not Mysterious.* London, 1696

Tuckness, Alex. *Locke and the Legislative Point of View: Toleration, Contested Principles, and the Law.* Princeton, NJ: Princeton University Press, 2002.

Tully, James. *A Discourse on Property.* Cambridge: Cambridge University Press, 1980.

Tully, James. *An Approach to Political Philosophy: Locke in Contexts.* New York: Cambridge University Press, 1984.

von Leyden, W. "Introduction." In *Essays on the Law of Nature,* John Locke. New York: Oxford University Press, 1954.

Waldron, Jeremy. *God, Locke, and Equality: Christian Foundations in Locke's Political Thought.* Cambridge: Cambridge University Press, 2002.

Wallace, Jr., Dewey D. "Socinianism, Justification by Faith, and the Sources of John Locke's *The Reasonableness of Christianity.*" In *John Locke: Critical Assessments,* ed. Richard Ashcraft, New York: Routledge, 1991.

Walzer, Michael. *Spheres of Justice.* United States: Basic Books, 1983.

Williams, Stephen. *Revelation and Reconciliation: A Window on Modernity.* New York: Cambridge University Press, 1995.

Wolterstorff, Nicholas. "Locke's Philosophy of Religion." In *The Cambridge Companion to Locke,* ed. Vere Chappell, Cambridge: Cambridge University Press, 1994.

Wolterstorff, Nicholas. *John Locke and the Ethics of Belief.* Cambridge: Cambridge University Press, 1996.

Wood, Neal. *The Politics of Locke's Philosophy.* Berkeley: University of California Press, 1983.

Woolhouse, Roger. "Locke's Theory of Knowledge." In *The Cambridge Companion to Locke,* ed. Vere Chappell, Cambridge: Cambridge University Press, 1194.

Wootton, David. "John Locke: Socinian or Natural Law Theorist?" In *Religion, Secularization and Political Thought: Thomas Hobbes to J. S. Mill,* ed. James Crimmins. London: Routledge, 1989.

Wootton, David. "John Locke and Richard Ashcraft's *Revolutionary Politics.*" *Political Studies* 40 (1992): 79–98.

N. T. Wright. *The Resurrection of the Son of God.* U.K.: Fortress Press, 2003.

Yolton, John W. *John Locke and the Way of Ideas.* London: Oxford University Press, 1956.

Yolton, John W., ed. *John Locke: Problems and Perspectives.* Cambridge: Cambridge University Press, 1969.

Yolton, John W. *Locke and the Compass of Human Understanding.* Cambridge: Cambridge University Press, 1970.

Yolton, John W. *Locke: An Introduction.* Oxford: Basil Blackwell, Ltd., 1985.

Yolton, John W. "Locke on the Law of Nature." In *John Locke: Critical Assesments,* ed. Richard Ashcraft, New York: Routledge, 1991.

Zuckert, Michael. "Of Wary Physicians and Weary Readers: The Debates on Locke's Way of Writing." *The Independent Journal of Philosophy* 2 (1978): 55–66.

Zuckert, Michael. "An Introduction to Locke's First Treatise." *Interpretation* 8 (1979): 58–74.

Zuckert, Michael. "Locke and the Problem of Civil Religion." In *The American Founding: Essays on the Formation of the Constitution,* ed. J. Jackson Barlow, Leonard W. Levy, and Ken Masugi. United States: Greenwood Press, 1988.

Zuckert, Michael. *Natural Rights and the New Republicanism.* Princeton, NJ: Princeton University Press, 1994.

Zuckert, Michael. *Launching Liberalism: On Lockean Political Philosophy.* Lawrence: University Press of Kansas, 2002.

Index